after
the
apostles

after the apostles

CHRISTIANITY IN THE SECOND CENTURY

Walter H. Wagner

FORTRESS PRESS   Minneapolis

AFTER THE APOSTLES

Cover design: Jim Gerhard
Cover art: A wall painting in the catacombs of Callixtus, Rome, second century C.E.

Library of Congress Cataloging-in-Publication Data
Wagner, Walter H., 1935-
    After the apostles : Christianity in the second century / Walter H. Wagner.
      p.   cm.
    Includes bibliographical references and index.
    ISBN 0-8006-2567-6 (alk. paper) :
    1. Church history—Primitive and early church, ca. 30-600.
    I. Title.
    BR166.W33   1994   93-11517
    270.1—dc20   CIP

Manufactured in the U.S.A.   AF 1-2567

98   97   96   95   94   2   3   4   5   6   7   8   9   10

Contents

Preface

Confidence, frustration, and opportunity generated this book. I am sure that the events, movements, and persons of the first two centuries of the Common Era are uncommonly important for people and developments in subsequent times. The first century's significance for Christians and Jews is obvious. Those were the years of Jesus' ministry and the start of the Christian movement. For good and ill, the world has been and will continue to be deeply influenced by the church and the results of its commitment to Jesus. Among Jews, the first century was more than just another century of repression by a foreign power. Many Jews lived in the Diaspora, that is, outside of Palestine. They adapted their language, sacred writings, and institutions to the cultures around them. Widespread resentment against Rome, especially in the Holy Land, led to insurrections. The uprising of 66–73 C.E. resulted in the destruction of Jerusalem and its Temple (70 C.E.) and the self-immolation of the rebel-patriots at Masada (73 C.E.). Judaism and Jews are still marked by those tragedies. Pagans, too, were shaped by the first century. The ideals and structures of the Roman Empire were taking form through noble visions and in spite of blatant tyrants. The Empire provided the cultural and political context in which Christians moved and interacted with other persons, ideas, and institutions.

The second century, too, was tumultuous. Military men decided who would rule the Empire, for how long, and at what price. Philosophers, orators, and preachers clamored for attention and loyalty to their respective versions of the truth. Traditional Greco-Roman assumptions and institutions were challenged by different movements and perspectives. Sometimes political stability barely masked confusion beneath society's surface. Christianity was perceived by many Roman officials as a movement that contributed to the unrest, a movement of which to be wary.

As the century opened, it was clear that Christianity and Judaism had separated from each other, and Christian statements about Jews contained ominous undertones. Christians were also divided among themselves over central issues of belief and practice. A more or less official theology and a more rather than less official organizational pattern were emerging. Both Christians and Jews were sorting out which pieces of literature each would consider to be Scripture, and each faith community sought to devise methods to interpret their holy books. The second was a century in which traditions and expectations were becoming unhinged, but new combinations had not yet gained wide or even authoritative acceptance.

Frankly, it was a messy century. I think that its very messiness is particularly helpful to us for several reasons. First, the churning and instability allow us to see behind the later formulations and apparent certainties of what came to be called Christian orthodoxy and its relationships to political-social institutions. The options and the persons who struggled with them may be seen and understood more clearly as we are able to feel their passionate concerns more fully. Second, by examining the interrelationships of culture, a community's issues, and the engagements of key leaders and teachers, we may comprehend the unhinging and recombining of assumptions and expectations in our own time. Finally, by considering the second century's wealth of ideas, leaders, and initiatives, we may discern ways to join creativity with tradition as we prepare to move into another century.

My own involvement with the period and its people entered a new phase when I moved from a denominational position to teaching and parish ministry. The need to rethink basic cultural and theological issues gave me the opportunity to introduce some persistent concerns and ancient colleagues to college, seminary, and graduate students. In the process of engaging students in the present with people in the past, I realized that rabbinic and ministerial colleagues as well as the elusive "interested general reader" would be interested in the discussions.

As I engaged in the second century's events, I realized that five particular challenges to Christians, and the ways in which Christians responded, were critical for later Christian belief, practice, and influence. The challenges were: Who created the world and what value does the world have? What is the nature and destiny of humans? Who was Jesus? What roles does the church have? How are Christians and culture related? Christians had no single answer for any of these questions. For that matter, Jews and pagans also differed significantly among themselves when they responded to questions about creation, humanity, divinity, and culture.

I discerned five important, sometimes disturbing leaders who responded to the challenges. Their responses covered a wide range of choices accepted and rejected by Christians then and now. The five are Ignatius of Antioch, Justin Martyr, Clement of Alexandria, Tertullian, and Irenaeus of Lyons. Later generations have not known how to deal with these persons. Ignatius is regarded either as a hero or as a deranged person. Justin and Clement, criticized and praised for using pagan philosophy, would not be considered orthodox by today's standards, although their ideas helped to establish that orthodoxy. Tertullian provided Latin Christianity with its basic theological vocabulary, but he left the church of the majority, disgusted with what he considered to be compromises with sinful behavior by the bishop of Rome. Irenaeus, on the other hand, provided later generations with a sweeping view of history in order to defend Christianity from some of its own members, and he insisted on Rome's unique place in determining divine truth. I am confident that people today will find the challenges and the leaders who responded to them valuable—and interesting—in understanding the past and the present.

There are, however, no books or studies that tell the story of the second century's challenges and leaders in ways that bring events, ideas, and persons together in a readily comprehensible manner. Some fine studies deal with separate concerns, movements, and thinkers, but most monographs assume a high degree of familiarity with the history and ideas of the era. A number of surveys sweep across the opening centuries of the Common Era, yet the surveys are prone to make overly concise summaries of persons and movements, thereby losing the dynamics of persons who struggled with vital issues. Several excellent translations are available, but the actors, scenes, and story lines of the original source materials tend to baffle the unprepared reader. No available work, then, met my need to introduce the issues and persons to students today, and none put the factors together in ways that might stimulate discussion among those who were already or wanted to become conversant with the period. While I appreciate and build on the research and ideas of predecessors, I stake out some new positions. If those already familiar with the field take issue with particular interpretations, then dialogue about the century will be enlivened.

The first of the study's parts, "Kingdom and Empire," deals with Jewish, Christian, and pagan relationships and problems. Part II, "Challenges for Christians," takes up the five issues, while the responses of the five leaders to each challenge constitute Part III. "Assessments" concludes the work. A table of Roman rulers from Julius Caesar to Severus Alexander and a map of the Empire around 200 C.E. are provided at the beginning. Endnotes for the whole precede a glossary of terms. Biblical quotations, unless otherwise noted, are from the New Revised Standard Version.

Some comments about terminology and language are in order. I used the readily understandable "Before the Common Era" (B.C.E.) and Common Era

(C.E.) in place of the theologically loaded "Before Christ" (B.C.) and "In the Year of the Lord" (A.D.). References to "Old Testament" and "New Testament" are not so easily resolved. Second-century Christians and Diaspora Jews used a wider canon than do Jews and Christians today. Indeed, Christians today still do not agree upon the extent of the "Old Testament." Further, early Christians and the Diaspora Jews under consideration used Greek translations of the works related to Judaism known generally as the Septuagint (abbreviated LXX). Wherever possible, I use gender-inclusive language. The fact that each of the five leaders was male is noteworthy in itself. More to the point is what they wrote about females. One set up an antithetical pattern with Eve as the disobedient and Mary as the obedient virgin. Another went further, calling women the devil's gateway to human damnation and insisting that women be ashamed of their gender throughout this life. A third argued that women were admitted to salvation to the same degree that men were, and even considered God to have a female as well as a male dimension. So more than generic pronouns are at stake.

No introduction is complete without acknowledging the assistance of others. I am indebted to Laura Caiaccia, Nathan Wagner, and Kristen Wicks, who, while at Muhlenberg College, helped with comments about the work's clarity and usefulness for undergraduate and nascent graduate students. As the work is directed also toward scholars and those elusive "interested general readers," I solicited and received generous help from Albert Gendebien (professor emeritus, Lafayette College, Easton, Pennsylvania) and Robert Moser (member, Morgenland Lutheran Church, Orefield, Pennsylvania). My colleague, Dr. Darrell Jodock (Muhlenberg College), made careful, probing comments about the work while it was in progress. His encouragement is deeply appreciated. J. Michael West, together with other editorial staff members of Fortress Press, Charles Puskas, Julie Odland, and James D. Ernest, gave skilled guidance that brought the work to you. Naturally, the final result is my responsibility. The book is dedicated in love and with appreciation to my wife, Deborah, and my son, Nathan.

—Walter H. Wagner

after the apostles

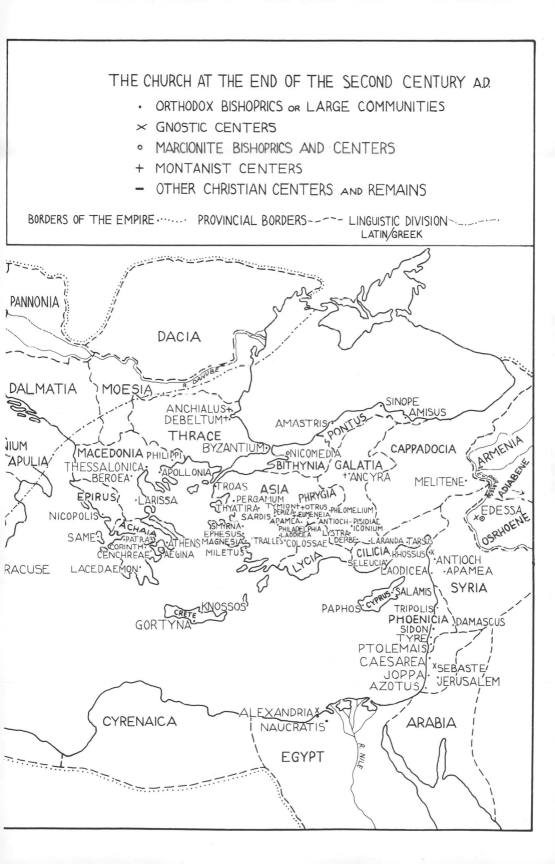

THE CHURCH AT THE END OF THE SECOND CENTURY A.D.

- • ORTHODOX BISHOPRICS or LARGE COMMUNITIES
- × GNOSTIC CENTERS
- ∘ MARCIONITE BISHOPRICS AND CENTERS
- + MONTANIST CENTERS
- — OTHER CHRISTIAN CENTERS AND REMAINS

BORDERS OF THE EMPIRE········ PROVINCIAL BORDERS------ LINGUISTIC DIVISION-··-··-
LATIN/GREEK

Rome's Rulers
31 B.C.E.–235 C.E.

THE JULIO-CLAUDIAN DYNASTY: 31 B.C.E.–68 C.E.

Augustus (Octavian)	31 B.C.E.–14 C.E.
Tiberius	14–37
Gaius (Caligula)*	37–41
Claudius	41–54
Nero*	54–68

THE LONG YEAR: 68–69

Galba*	68–69
Otho*	69–
Vitellius*	69–

THE FLAVIAN DYNASTY: 69–96

Vespasian	69–79
Titus	79–81
Domitian*	81–96

ADOPTIVE AND ANTONINE EMPERORS: 96–192

Nerva	96–98
Trajan	98–117
Hadrian	117–138
Antoninus Pius	138–161
Marcus Aurelius	161–180
Lucius Verus	161–169
Commodus*	180–192

VIOLENT INTERLUDE: 193

THE SEVERAN DECADES: 193–235

*Died by assassination, suicide, or in battle

Part I

Kingdom and Empire

Ask, and it will be given you;
Search and you will find;
Knock, and the door will be opened for you.
For everyone who asks receives,
And everyone who searches finds,
And for everyone who knocks, the door will be opened.
Matthew 7:7-8

Humans ask, seek, and knock in their quest to discover who they are, where they have come from, why they are here, and toward what destiny, if any, they are heading. These are concerns with which religious people grapple. Through myths, rituals, narratives, teachings, symbols, writings, and institutions, men and women attempt to express what they are convinced divine powers have disclosed to them and what their experiences confirm. Whatever else believers may say about the origin of their faith, religions partake of and are influenced by human history, culture, and language. Christianity is no exception. The Christian message emphasizes both that Jesus is of eternal importance and that he is of a particular time, place, and people. The message claims that no matter in what culture or age a woman or man may live, Jesus offers everlasting peace with God, fellowship with other persons, and guidance through life. During the second century, Christians faced hard situations. Some of these were caused or exacerbated by some believers' accentuating Christianity's historical-cultural specificity while others gave priority to its eternal and universal scope. The second century was a time of sharp disappointments, gradual adjustments, bitter controversies, and grave hazards for Christian communities. There was an urgency to their asking, seeking, and knocking, for they were responding to internal and external demands to state who they were, where they came from, why they existed, and where they were going.

Thus the five challenges and the five leaders who responded to them are understood most clearly when examined in their historical and cultural contexts. Part I, "Kingdom and Empire," deals with four contexts. The initial chapter presents some basic Jewish and Christian expectations about the kingdom of God and Christian frustrations about its nonoccurrence. Chapter 2 sketches early relationships between Jews and Christians. The third and fourth chapters focus on the historical framework of the second-century Roman Empire and dilemmas faced by pagan Greco-Romans.

Asking, knocking, and searching entailed risks for individuals, their communities, and the wider societies. The backgrounds, expectations, motives, and goals of the inquirers were vital concerns for the seekers themselves and for those who engaged them.

> For nothing is hidden that will not be disclosed,
> nor is anything secret that will not become known and come to light.
> Then pay attention to how you listen;
> for to those who have, more will be given;
> and from those who do not have, even what they seem to have will be taken
> away.
>
> Luke 8:17-18

1

Christian Expectations and Frustrations

Now after John was arrested, Jesus came to Galilee, proclaiming the good news of God, and saying, "The time is fulfilled, and the kingdom of God has come near; repent, and believe in the good news."

Mark 1:14-15

The good news was that the kingdom of God was coming. The ancient struggles between good and evil, God and the devil, had reached a climax; the time was ripe, the last days were at hand—or so many Jews in the first century C.E. believed. Jews living in Palestine or dispersed through the Roman Empire looked for the start of God's reign over the world. Often they anticipated the appearance of a divinely connected figure who would liberate them from pagan domination. Sometimes the redeemer of Israel was depicted as God's anointed ruler ("Messiah" in Hebrew, "Christ" in Greek), or a new and greater Moses or David, or the king of the angels, or even God directly. The present age probably would end in wars, earthquakes, eclipses, plagues, and astral catastrophes. God's legions of angels and faithful people would fight against and vanquish the hosts of evil demons and those humans allied with them. After the last battles, the trumpet would summon the dead and the living to assemble before the righteous Judge's throne. There they would either be accounted worthy to enter the blessed kingdom or be condemned to eternal torment. The signs of the times, these devout Jews claimed, pointed toward God's decisive intervention in the cosmos. The message underlined the urgent need for humans to choose life or death, to be faithful to God or to adhere to evil; so repent, trust in the God whose kingdom is at hand! Whoever was coming and whatever would happen, the final result was that the nations that oppressed the Jews and the peoples who mocked their religion would see that Almighty God had chosen them to be a royal priesthood and a holy nation.

3

God's kingdom was more than an opportunity to punish Israel's enemies or the alternative to hell-fire. The Lord's new heaven and earth would be the realm of justice, joy, and peace. Sorrow, pain, and death would be wiped away, as would chaos and evil. Women and men would no longer exploit one another but would be transformed into what the Creator intended them to be, angelic images and likenesses of God. God promised to dwell with the redeemed, fulfilling the lives of worshipers and disclosing divine wisdom to them. There was no room in the kingdom for distinctions and privileges based on gender, class, or race. Neither would there be any need for human government or even a priesthood. As the prophets Micah, Isaiah, and Jeremiah promised, nations would turn their weapons into tools of peace, and every person would know the Lord's will in his or her heart.[1] Zechariah summed up the eager expectations for an Eden-like restoration of creation and the holy city: "On that day living waters shall flow out from Jerusalem. . . . And the LORD will become king over all the earth; on that day the LORD will be one and his name one."[2]

Such ideas about the kingdom are subversive, for they call into question a government's hold on its people's loyalty, a society's institutional and class structures, and any religion's claim to truth. Imperial officials and soldiers in the first century had reason to be wary of Jews who yearned for the kingdom of God. Not only did such longings contradict Rome's intention to endure for ages, but the Jewish people had a stormy relationship with the Empire. Ever since the 160s B.C.E., Jews and Romans had shown each other cautious respect, and emperors renewed the special status of Jews by which the Lord's people were permitted to exercise their religion and customs within the limits of the law.[3] Emperors and officials who insisted that the Empire's inhabitants reverence the symbols of its authority and even venerate the emperor were bound to encounter Jewish opposition. Already restive under foreign domination, Jews dedicated to Israel's God and their people's integrity reacted explosively against attempts to pressure them to adopt Greco-Roman religious and cultural practices. Rome had put down several actual and potential uprisings in the first century even before the massive revolts of 66–73 and 132–135.

CHRISTIAN BEGINNINGS

Among the Jewish wonder-workers and teachers who proclaimed God's will and power, Jesus of Nazareth (ca. 4 B.C.E.–? 32 C.E.) made the deepest and most lasting impression. John the Baptizer, another preacher of God's reign, evenhandedly denounced the elite and the common people for their sins, urged them to repent, and insisted that penitents be baptized as a sign of entering a renewed covenant community. After his arrest and execution, John's disciples gradually disbanded, and the movement around him faded within a few decades.[4]

Jesus, too, preached repentance and was executed. Apparently, he had challenged several circles of religious and civil leaders in his native Galilee and in Jerusalem. Apart from the animosity generated by these confrontations, some Jewish authorities realized that Jesus' message and personality could well lead to an insurrection and Roman reprisal. Herod Antipas, Emperor Tiberius's accredited ruler in Galilee, and Pontius Pilate, Rome's governor of the province of Judea, united with worried Jewish leaders; Jesus was crucified sometime between 28 and 32 c.e. Unlike John's followers, Jesus' disciples did not fade away. New Testament authors maintain that within days of the execution the disciples claimed that God had raised Jesus from the dead and exalted him to heavenly glory, and that he would return soon as God's mighty representative to begin the last judgment and inaugurate the kingdom. Now, they said, they knew that Jesus was the Christ, the Messiah. Among those who dedicated themselves to Jesus and his message were leaders who were convinced that God commanded and commissioned them to go through the Empire and beyond, announcing the good news of the kingdom, spreading Jesus' teachings, and convincing others that through Jesus they could be assured of a place in the kingdom. The people who accepted the good news of the kingdom in Jesus at first called themselves "the Way" or the "followers of the Way" and set out upon a new Exodus from death and bondage to peace and life in the kingdom that Jesus promised. Dubbed "Christians" by detractors sometime in the 40s, the followers took up that name as a fitting description of who they were and for whom they waited expectantly. Within two decades of Jesus' death, there were Christians in the regions we call Palestine, Syria, Cyprus, Italy, Egypt, Ethiopia, Greece, Turkey, the Balkans, and, some claimed, India.

ENTHUSIASM AND EXPECTATION

The first Christians were enthusiastic about their insights into God's will for themselves and for the cosmos. Jesus' crucifixion and resurrection meant that death was swallowed up in victory, and its sting, sin, was broken. The believer had been crucified with and raised in Christ, so now Christ lived in and transformed the person into a new creature. Put another way, the world had been crucified to the believer and the believer crucified to the world. In either case, the Christian was not trapped by personal problems or by evil forces, for the believer belonged to the triumphant Jesus. These Christians were convinced that Jesus had revealed God's righteousness to humans for their salvation not because they deserved such love, but because God was gracious. God's graciousness generated faith or trust in Jesus, devotion to God, and new ways to relate to society. Those who responded in faith to God's opportunity were liberated from spiritual bondage and became willing servants of Christ. Faith also drew believers into communities of dedicated persons so closely identified with Jesus that the communities were likened to his body. Faith promoted a mutual love and commitment among Christians that even opponents found remarkable. Some believers claimed to be specially influenced by God's Spirit in worship, when telling others about God's good news, or while facing hostile authorities. Often that influence showed itself in ecstatic speech and songs "in the languages of angels," and some claimed that the Spirit gave them further revelations about God's will. Zealous believers were active in doing good; they were to share the good news of Jesus with a world of potential fellow Christians.

Enthusiasm and expectation fueled each other. Christians fervently believed that Jesus' imminent return would trigger the final days of this age. In the twinkling of an eye, at the blast of the last trumpet, amid celestial shouts and creation's groans, Jesus would arrive in glory to judge the world. The living and the resurrected dead would put on imperishable natures as they entered their eternal existence. Nonbelievers, sinners, and demons faced everlasting punishment, and faithful Christians—and perhaps some others designated by God—were to enter the kingdom that had been prepared for them since the foundation of the world. With Israel's holy heroes and in the presence of angels, they would gather at the banquet table of Jesus the Messiah to feast and rejoice forever. All would be one in Christ, and Christ would be in all.

While they awaited their Lord's return, Christians had to live in the world, yet not be seduced by it. They were being transformed by God's Spirit so as to have among themselves the mind of Christ instead of being conformed to societies in which lust and violence seemed to prevail. Believers understood themselves to be reconciled to God through Jesus, created anew in baptism, and called to live in holiness as they looked for Jesus' second coming. Within their own communities, Christians exhorted one another to pray without ceasing, to bear one another's burdens, and, above all, to crown faith and hope with love. Expectations about Jesus and the kingdom led some Christians to advise others to avoid marriage, sexual intercourse, compromising social relationships with pagans, and political activism. They reasoned that since the end was coming and the new age would be free of such conventions and concerns, there was no need to bother with them now.

Anticipating the kingdom also made Christians confident and defiant. In the confidence that they were the earthly colony of God's heavenly kingdom, they defied scoffers and persecutors. Colony and kingdom would be united after the day of judgment; so, they said, sickness, peril, persecution, death, and evil angels were powerless to separate believers from the love of God in Christ. Caesars might call themselves conquerors of barbarian tribes and have triumphant parades in Rome. Christians knew, however, that their Lord had disarmed the cosmic evil powers, triumphed over them through his cross, and led them captive as part of his glorification. Christians knew themselves to be more than conquerors: they were heirs to imperishable heavenly riches; they were the adopted sons and daughters of the ultimate emperor, Almighty God.

As Christians assembled to praise God, thank Jesus, and pray for the coming of the new age they thought they saw in human and natural events signs that the time was ripe. They shared bread and wine in memory of Jesus, believing that his body and blood marked the start of a new covenant between God and humanity through which a people were called to be a royal priesthood and holy nation. Because their thanksgiving or eucharistic meal was a foretaste of the future messianic feast, they shouted enthusiastically and expectantly: "Maranatha! Our Lord, come!"[5] But he did not come, at least not as they expected, and the world kept going in ways they neither expected nor wanted.

FRUSTRATION AND ADJUSTMENT

Thorny issues, such as who decided what was appropriate teaching and practice, and on what basis decisions might be made, were raised from the church's earliest days and among its best-known leaders. Peter, the chief disciple; James, a brother of Jesus; and Paul, an apostle-missionary to the Gentiles, disagreed on central positions and policies. Personalities and theologies clashed, sometimes publicly, perhaps even dangerously.[6] Congregations were disturbed and individuals perplexed by questions that grew more pressing the longer Jesus' return was delayed.[7] Still, as long as Christians had a lively expectation that Jesus was about to come, they could bear a variety of attempts to understand God, Jesus, the world, and human destiny. In this age, they felt, we are like children—immature and seeing only partially the deep mysteries of God— but in the age to come, we will know truth fully.

The nonevent of Jesus' return provoked critical questions in the closing decades of the first century that are still being asked today. Were Jesus' critics and opponents right when they said that Jesus and his followers were wrong? Was Christianity a mistake or, worse, a fraud? Were the arguments within congregations signs of disunity, a telltale mark of error? Was there any truth

to the rumors that some Christians engaged in incest, cannibalism, drunkenness, and even cursing Jesus as part of their worship of God? What should
Christians do when those who spoke in the tongues of angels claimed that
the congregation's leaders were not valid authorities, or that Jesus was not
raised from the dead? How should believers regard sinners in their own ranks—
didn't baptism drown sinful desires among Christians? Where was Jesus now
that they needed him? Indeed, who was Jesus, and how did he relate to God
and humanity? What is evil, and what is God or Jesus doing about it? Who
are we—as humans and as believers? What are we doing in and through the
church? How do we live now? Is the kingdom still coming, is it here already,
or is another kind of future than we expected in store for us? Once the questions
started, they continued with increasing intensity.

PAROUSIA

The questions and responses that exercised Christians in the late first and
throughout the second century reflected, initially, the meanings believers gave
to the Greek word "parousia." The basic idea of parousia is "with-ness" or
"being there." Some usages of parousia stressed arrival or coming. Its Latin-
based English equivalent is "advent." Sometimes the word was used to describe
the arrival of a king or even a god.[8] Parousia in the sense of a royal or divine
arrival fit the expectation that Jesus would return in power to carry out
judgment and bring in the kingdom.

Those who desired to retain that meaning sometimes explained the nonoccurrence of Jesus' advent in terms of a difference between God's reckoning
of time and that of humans; a day in the Lord's calculations was like a thousand
years among humans.[9] Another explanation held that God delayed the parousia out of love and patience for humanity, for God wanted as many persons
as possible to hear and respond to the good news in Jesus.[10] A third approach
was to discourage speculation because it could lead to uprisings such as the
Jewish rebellion of 132–135 and shift attention to portents rather than concentrate on faithful expectation for God's actions.[11] A fourth reason given for
the delay depicted God as testing the faithfulness of Christians. As Job had
been tested, so believers were being probed by the devil. Through persecutions,
heresies, temptations to sin, and doubts about God's work in Jesus, they were
being sifted and purified.[12] Each form of explanation claimed that the parousia
was still in the future: Jesus will return, so be patient and be prepared.

"Presence," the more common pagan understanding of parousia, also was
used by Christians. In this case, parousia connoted a remaining or abiding
rather than an arrival or return. According to the Gospel of John, Jesus spoke

of his abiding in believers, and the Gospel's closing scene pictured Jesus in the midst of his community, breathing peace into them.[13] Jesus left the believers when he died, but after the resurrection he returned to be with them forever. His physical "with-ness" was transformed by the resurrection into a constant spiritual parousia. There was no need, then, to speculate about his return, for he had not left. Neither was there any need to look for a cosmic day of judgment and a future kingdom. By seeing, knowing, and believing in Jesus, a person was born again, or born from above, into eternal life. The judgment had already come into the cosmos, and if one walked in the light of Christ, one entered the kingdom now; but if one rejected Jesus, then one stood condemned already. Jesus was the resurrection and the life; those who believed in him might die physically, but they already lived eternally.[14]

Christians who emphasized parousia as presence tended to think about where and how Jesus was present now. During worship, while studying Scripture, and in making decisions, the church felt his presence and guidance. Some persons experienced a mystical union with Jesus, saying that they were "in Christ," or that Christ lived in their hearts and enlightened their minds. Other believers said that they made progress in becoming mature in Christ or that they advanced in Christ. Christians who took the parousia as continued presence did not need to look for a literal resurrection of the dead. They expected the soul to continue onward to its everlasting reward or punishment. Most Christians seemed to mingle both understandings of parousia so that they felt Jesus was present and coming, that eternal life started now and in the future, and that the soul continued on after death and was dormant until the last day of this age. When pressed to make choices or when confronted with the paradoxes and contradictions of their positions, believers realized that they had to deal with potentially divisive differences.

Frustrated expectations about Jesus' return and the kingdom's beginning pushed Christians to reconsider their identity, God's plan for themselves and for the cosmos, and their roles in society. Jesus' followers in the first and second centuries had no opportunity to explore those issues in calm circumstances. They developed responses more often in the course of controversy than in quiet reflection. If pressures for responses shifted as the second century opened, they also increased. Christians needed guidance as well as purpose and structure, yet in the name of order they risked limiting spontaneity and enthusiasm.

So when they had come together, they asked him, "Lord, is this the time when you will restore the kingdom to Israel?" He replied, "It is not for you to know the times or periods that the Father has set by his own authority. But you will receive power when the Holy Spirit has come upon you; and you will be my

witnesses in Jerusalem, in all Judea and Samaria, and to the end of the earth."
When he had said this . . . he was lifted up, and a cloud took him out of their
sight. While he was going and they were gazing up toward heaven, suddenly
two men in white robes stood by them. They said, "Men of Galilee, why do
you stand looking up toward heaven? This Jesus . . . will come in the same
way as you saw him go into heaven."

Acts 1:6-11

2

Jews and Christians

I am speaking the truth in Christ—I am not lying; my conscience confirms it by the Holy Spirit—I have great sorrow and unceasing anguish in my heart. For I could wish that I myself were accursed and cut off from Christ for the sake of my own people, my kindred according to the flesh. They are Israelites, and to them belong the adoption, the glory, the covenants, the giving of the law, the worship, and the promises; to them belong the patriarchs, and from them, according to the flesh, comes the Messiah, who is over all, God blessed forever. Amen.

Romans 9:1-5

Although Jewish-Christian relationships fell to gruesome depths during the twentieth century, tensions between Christians and Jews stretch back to the first two centuries of the Common Era. Although Christianity began as a movement among devout Jews in Palestine, within a hundred years it was a separate religious community spread across the Empire and composed almost exclusively of converts from pagan religions. Nevertheless, Christians were unable to detach themselves from Jews and Judaism.

From the Christian perspective, Jews are special. Other persons may be potential converts from religious traditions that Christians considered false or incomplete. Jews are different; they are God's covenanted people, the servant nation, the witnesses to God's faithfulness to the uttermost parts of the earth. Judaism, too, is different from other religious systems and ways of life. Christians might present their concepts of divine powers, humanity, and the world as alternatives to parallel positions in other religions. Jesus' followers naturally absorbed underlying concepts, Scriptures, and even problems that were taught, interpreted, and discussed in the Temple and the synagogue. Jewish persons as well as Jewish beliefs, traditions, and practices were at the center of the Christians' own movement.

YEARNING AND ANXIETY

Christians coupled their expectations for the kingdom's coming and Jesus' parousia with fervent missionary activity. Paul (d. ca. 65) wrote that all humans stood in imminent danger of God's wrath on judgment day and that only those who had faith in God through Jesus would be saved, for "we have peace with God through our Lord Jesus Christ."[1] The apostle always considered himself to be Jewish, and he believed that in Christ he had become a fulfilled son of Israel.[2] His background and zeal made him yearn for all Jews to become as he was: a true Israelite, that is, a person who saw, accepted, and trusted in God's plan to redeem humanity through the death and resurrection of Jesus. Paul was even willing to endure damnation if that were the price for his fellow Jews to turn to Jesus as their savior.

Paul and other Christians were active and disappointed yearners. They entered synagogues throughout the Empire proclaiming Jesus and the kingdom; they were usually cast out for disrupting worship and for spreading strange teachings. Occasionally, a Jewish person would subscribe to the Christian message and would assist in establishing a Christian community apart from the synagogue. More often, pagans who attended the synagogue service were attracted to the Christian teachings. These Gentiles had been drawn initially to Jewish monotheism, worship, and ethics, but not to the point of becoming official converts. They were reluctant to take upon themselves and their families the specificities of Jewish identity, such as male circumcision, observance of the Sabbath and other holy days, dietary restrictions, and abstinence from many public pagan ceremonies.

Paul and the Christian preachers who agreed with him offered Gentiles an open invitation to God's grace and kingdom without obligating converts to follow the Mosaic Law. It seemed to Jews and Gentiles that Paul's version of Christianity was Judaism without Jewishness, plus promises about salvation and the kingdom through Jesus. From the Jewish standpoint these subtractions and additions were totally unacceptable, because they distorted the cornerstone of Israelite faith (namely, the confession that God is one), broke morality down, and denied the unique place that the Jewish people held in God's world. It was no surprise that Jewish communal leaders reacted vigorously to Christian attempts to use synagogues as starting points for Jesus-centered missionary campaigns.[3]

Anxiety also motivated Christian relations with Jews. Bluntly, the Jew is the question mark who punctuates every Christian claim. The continued existence of Judaism and the Jewish people are radical criticisms of Christian assertions to be God's people and the bearers of divine truth. If the gospel, even when preached by Jesus, did not succeed in winning over the people to whom it was first proclaimed, then perhaps the messengers and the message were wrong. If God made covenants with Abraham and Sarah, Israel at Sinai, and the House of David, what need was there for another with a carpenter who gave odd interpretations of the Law? If Jesus came to his own and they refused to receive him, maybe they did so for good reasons. And if the descendants of those who rejected Jesus still do not receive his followers, why should anyone else believe in him or his movement?

The faithfulness of Jewish women and men to their religion led some Christians to search themselves and the Scriptures in order to discern more closely who they and the Jews were. Two responses were particularly relevant for second-century Christians: interpretations of the Scriptures and the identification of the true Israel.

INTERPRETING THE SCRIPTURES

The very word "Scriptures" is heavy with religious feeling and authority. A believing community designates as "Scriptures" only those writings that it considers special or holy. God or divine powers are thought to have been especially involved in disclosing the content and perhaps in writing and transmitting the literature. Most often these writings have remained meaningful and useful for many people over long periods of time, even centuries.[4] If God has been involved in the writing of the work, then it is thought to be holy and the author may be considered divinely inspired. Actually, designating some works as Scripture may indicate uncertainty on the part of the community about the sure and revelatory presence of God in the present. The past, not the present, is regarded as a time when God interacted with humans frequently and clearly. People in subsequent times have found it necessary to study how God and humans interacted and what the Holy One commanded and promised in the past in order to understand God's will so that they might be able to follow it in their time.

Jews and Christians interpreted the sacred texts that they held in common so as to apply principles, patterns, and directions from the past to their present circumstances; they also believed that God seeded divine meanings throughout the writings. The original readers and listeners certainly benefited from what was written, but the full meanings, the interpreters thought, had been reserved for the present or future generations.[5] God had somehow inspired the writers to put down what was yet to come. Sometimes a prophet was said to have been granted a vision of the distant future. A popular account described God commanding the scribe Ezra to drink a holy elixir and then to dictate to several stenographers the words that came to him.[6] In any event, the present generation needed not only the inspired writings and writers but also inspired interpreters to unravel the divine mysteries within the writings. Christians went about the interpretive task with remarkable intensity. They were certain that the Scripture they shared with Jews was divine and that it contained God's plan concerning Jesus. They had traditions in which Jesus not only interpreted the Law in the course of regular teaching but also used the Scripture to show that God planned for the Messiah to suffer, die, and be raised from the dead.[7] Their Lord had promised that he would send the Spirit to guide them into all truth, and that the truth would be about Jesus.[8] Fortified by such convictions, Christians applied their interpretive skills and discovered in Israel's Scripture what they already believed: Jesus the Christ and Redeemer who lived, died, was resurrected, and would come again as gloried Lord.

Jews, too, were busy interpreters. By the second century, Palestinian rabbis devised sets of rules that they used to understand and apply the Law.[9] The rabbis paid attention to the text and context of passages, then related the interpretations to daily life. They were particularly concerned about individuals and groups, including Christians, who used the text to speculate on divine mysteries or the end of the age. Others were not as restrained. The first-century Alexandrian, Philo (d. ca. 50 C.E.), probably learned some techniques of the allegorical method from pagan philologists in his city who sought to discern the moral excellencies of the gods in traditional Greek myths and epics. Theirs was a daunting task, for the accounts often depict the gods and goddesses in various love affairs, deceits, and conflicts. Allegory was a means of deriving "true" meanings.

An allegory interprets a text so that "persons and incidents become representative of abstract virtues or doctrines or incidents in the life of the soul."[10] Philo and other allegorists used the literal level of the passage as a springboard to two or three other levels. Philo moved quickly to the ethical level and more carefully to the spiritual or heavenly level. For example, when Abraham left Chaldea for Canaan (literal level), the divinity was urging every person to desist from doing evil and to start doing good (ethical level), and was encouraging the soul to leave behind the visible world to contemplate heavenly realities (spiritual level). The earthly Abraham, Chaldea, and Canaan merely represented what needed to be decoded through allegory. Jesus reportedly used allegories to explain his parables to the disciples, and Paul used one to berate the Galatians.[11]

Christians employed other interpretive techniques probably current among Jews as well. The most prominent was typology. Where allegory related to spatial realms by using an earthly sign for a heavenly reality, typology used the category of time. Through typology, the interpreter considered an event, person, or object described in the text as foreshadowing a subsequent time. For example, the Passover lamb (slain to achieve Israel's liberation from bondage) and the Yom Kippur lamb (slain for Israel's sins) were interpreted as "types" or forerunners of Jesus the Lamb of God who freed humanity by breaking the power of the devil and taking away the sin of the world through his death and resurrection. Real lambs were sacrificed, but they only pointed to what would be fulfilled by Jesus. Word studies (etymologies) were used to interpret numbers and names in the Septuagint to "prove" that Christian teachings were indeed Scripture-based.[12] If Jews rejected Christian conclusions as biased interpretive gymnastics, Christians proved to themselves that the holy writings supported their faith in Jesus and their role in God's plan.

IDENTIFYING THE TRUE ISRAEL

Christians affirmed that ever since Abraham left home for the land that the Lord was to give to him, God has had a people as a special possession. As long as they hoped that their version of God's purposes in Jesus for the salvation of humanity would become part of the Jewish faith, Christians worshiped in synagogues and in the Temple at Jerusalem. Gentile converts, Paul said, were like wild olive branches grafted onto the ancient, sturdy stock of Israel. Jews remained Jewish, however, and the tone changed. By the end of the first century c.e. many Christians no longer considered contemporary Jews to be the covenant people of God. As in the Gospel of Matthew, for example, Jews who did not become Christians were styled as the wicked tenants who killed the son of the owner of the vineyard (Matthew 21:33-46) or even the children of the devil (John 8:39-59). Christians came to identify themselves as the children of God, the heirs of the covenants made with Abraham, Moses, and David; and the community they called the church became to them the true Israel.

The drive behind such a switch in identities came from Christian exasperation with what they considered Jewish conceit and stubbornness, but what Jews called faithfulness to God and fidelity to holy traditions. To prove that they were the rightful heirs to the promises of the kingdom, Christians often felt compelled to denounce and demonize Jews and Judaism. Chains of passages from the Law and the Prophets were cited to show that the Hebrews and, by extension, the Jews of the first and second centuries c.e., rejected

God's mercy and truth and persisted in rebellion, faithlessness, and immorality. The Jews of past and present deserved God's punishment, and God justly replaced them with an obedient community that kept covenants made with Abraham, Moses, and their descendants. Traditions about Jesus' words, ministry, and death were handled in ways that made the Jews into hypocritical, hardened legalists, even children of the devil, murderers of the Messiah, and enemies of God.[13]

The true Israel was no longer the ethnic Israel, according to late first- and second-century Christians. The original people had forfeited their place to the followers of Jesus—the new Israel. As the prophets had warned centuries earlier, the Lord had made a new covenant with a faithful remnant in the old Israel and invited Gentiles to share in the promised kingdom. When Christians declared themselves to be the new and true Israel, they also attempted to work out understandings of the church's relationship to the synagogue, the Temple, and the Law.

EKKLĒSIA, NOT SYNAGOGUE

Christians called their community *ekklēsia*, a called-out people, the term we translate as "church." In Greco-Roman cities, it was the legal assembly of voting citizens called to debate issues, select leaders, and make decisions. Between meetings of the assembly, the city's affairs were managed by councils, courts, and officials. Since communal life and actions were under the auspices of the gods, the community's patron deities were called upon to guide and approve the deliberations of the *ekklēsia*. From a Greco-Roman perspective, *ekklēsia* referred to official assemblies of citizens in which there was discussion prior to the making of decisions. Leaders and administrators were subject to the community's review of their actions, praise, and discipline. Unauthorized gatherings were quite different from meetings of the *ekklēsia*. Participants in unruly mobs or disruptive factions risked punishment by the community's authorities and protecting gods.[14]

Although the word *ekklēsia* was well known and some of its connotations probably influenced Christians, it seems that they chose it for religious rather than sociopolitical reasons. The Septuagintal uses of *ekklēsia* appear to have informed Christian communities about what their life together under God's plan entailed. With scattered exceptions, occurrences of the word in the Scriptures that Christians applied to themselves show surprising continuity.[15] Three elements of that continuity helped Christians distance themselves from Jews.

The first element is a Deuteronomic basis for understanding the roles, the future, and the leaders of the *ekklēsia*. Those who left Egypt were a mixed multitude of Israelites and other ethnic groups.[16] When Moses reflected on the covenant made at Horeb (Sinai), the trek through the wilderness, his own impending death, and the people's entry in to Canaan, he referred to Israel as a community called out of bondage to hear God's liberating message, to fear and serve the Lord, and to teach God's ways to its children.[17] They were to give themselves gladly to the Holy One's instruction-discipline (*paideia*). God, Moses assured them, would never forsake them.[18] The elderly leader recounted times of sin and rebellion, and how he interceded with God to obtain forgiveness for them. He laid down jurisdictional boundaries, issued warnings and promises, and set up rules for excluding certain types of individuals.[19] The *ekklēsia* of Israel was no democracy, and anyone who challenged the divinely empowered leader risked God's wrath. As Moses prepared for his own death, God commanded him to commission Joshua as his successor. In an awe-inspiring scene before the tent of testimony, the Lord descended in a pillar of cloud, and Moses and God commissioned Joshua. Given the precedents of the establishment of the priesthood (Exod. 28:41 LXX) and the division of administrative tasks with the elders (*presbyteroi*) of the people (Num. 11:24-25 LXX), readers could infer that the commissioning of the new leader included the laying on of hands and the sharing of God's Spirit. Moses concluded his exhortation to the *ekklēsia* by teaching them a new song. The ode featured praise of the faithful God, warnings about divine wrath, and predictions of vindication for God's people.[20]

On the basis of the Deuteronomic tradition, the *ekklēsia* was considered to be a community with a past and future as well as a present. It was covenanted to obey God in all areas of individual and corporate life. The *ekklēsia* knew divine love and anger, and depended upon divine faithfulness. Called out from all nations, the *ekklēsia* was to reject all idolatry and immorality. Warned about assimilating idolatrous practices, the community was to protect against false spokespersons from within its own ranks. Leadership in the *ekklēsia* came through God's call and commission and was transmitted from one set of established leaders to others. Leaders such as Moses, the priests, and the presbyters were to proclaim God's will, interpret the Law, intercede for the community, offer sacrifices, and discipline members. Finally, the *ekklēsia* worshiped. Provision was made for a priesthood to preside over regular and special ceremonies in designated places of assembly.

A second group of Septuagintal instances of *ekklēsia* focused on worship, specifically in the writings of the chroniclers and psalmists about the Temple. David addressed "all the *ekklēsia* of Israel," together with military commanders and civil leaders, in order to gain their assent to move the ark of the covenant to Jerusalem. Later, and again after testing the will of the *ekklēsia* about building the Temple, the old king instructed Solomon about the future Temple's floor plans and furnishings. He behaved in a Moses-like manner by offering prayers, arranging the priesthood, and selecting his successor in the presence of the *ekklēsia*.[21]

Psalms in which the Septuagint used the word *ekklēsia* usually centered on worship in the Temple.[22] The psalmists stood in the midst of the *ekklēsia* to offer praise for God's acts of mercy and vindication, pay their vows, and celebrate God's presence and power. Priests, musicians, singers, dancers, various Temple functionaries, and other worshipers took part. Processions were held, incense was burned, and animals were sacrificed. The *ekklēsia* came to the Temple for all moods and modes of worship and to express its unity as God's called-out people. Psalm 88 LXX (= 89 MT) mentioned explicitly what may be implicit in other Psalms: the *ekklēsia* included heavenly beings (*hagioi*, holy ones, in verse 6) as well as the faithful people in Palestine. Even mountains joined humans in honoring God. Psalm 88 praised the king whom God anointed (*christon*, verse 39); the verse describes the monarch calling God "my Father" and God responding that the king will be made God's "firstborn."[23]

The *ekklēsia* was a community at worship, and its worship centered in the Temple. In that place, the Lord's name was present, and God acted to assure the called-out people of continued divine care, acceptance, and faithfulness. Worshipers recounted God's past saving acts, made new covenants, offered sacrifices of thanksgiving and for sin, and anticipated the future. Individuals testified to God's power, and groups of liturgists officiated. In the *ekklēsia*, God was present, kings were honored, and the people pledged to serve the Lord.

The book called 2 Esdras in the Septuagint (Hebrew: Ezra and Nehemiah) provided the third element, discipline and order.[24] Ezra expanded the *ekklēsia* to include all 42,360 Jews who returned to Judah and Jerusalem after the Exile.[25] But, following Moses' earlier advice, he purged nonethnic Jews from the *ekklēsia* and its priesthood. He also arranged for the reconstruction of the Temple and held celebratory liturgies as the work progressed. He performed the Moses-like tasks of presenting the Law to the community and interceding before God on behalf of the sinful people. Mixed marriages supposedly threatened to dilute Judaism with foreign cults and sexual promiscuity; Ezra wept over these marriages before the Temple in the presence of the "very great *ekklēsia*." His fasting and exhortation resulted in the *ekklēsia*'s decision to terminate the marriages of Jewish men who had taken foreign women as spouses. The elders (*presbyteroi*) and judges assisted in rendering the decision.[26] Postexilic concern over foreigners and their influences matched that of the pre-conquest period: the lure of idolatry, particularly fertility cults. A people covenanted to the God of the Exodus risked losing its integrity and identity in a polytheistic milieu. Leaders such as Ezra, Nehemiah, the presbyters, and the judges disciplined the community, provided for a purified priesthood, and exerted corrective authority in the *ekklēsia*. These steps were important if worship was to be pure and if the *ekklēsia* was to keep its part of the covenant as the holy people dedicated to the Holy One.

Septuagintal uses of *ekklēsia* indicate that it was a called-out, covenanted people that occasionally acted as a deliberative assembly and admonished or approved of its leaders. The *ekklēsia* was summoned to obey the God who repeatedly saved it and who could raise up oppressors to discipline it when it was disobedient. Internally, it was a community structured by the Law; externally it showed the nations God's power and justice. The *ekklēsia* repented of its sins through sacrifices and the intercessory prayers of its leaders. Assimilation to the surrounding societies and idolatry were temptations to which members often yielded. Such impurity needed to be rooted out by leaders and people, even at the cost of severe forms of discipline. Worship was central to the existence of the *ekklēsia* and required dedicated and holy leaders. The *ekklēsia* also extended to celestial beings who obeyed the Creator.

EKKLĒSIA AND TEMPLE

While the *ekklēsia* was not identical with the Temple, and one could exist apart from the other, they were closely associated. The Temple was the regular meeting place for the *ekklēsia*, and there the *ekklēsia* expected to encounter the One who had called it into being. The Temple was the successor of the tent of testimony or tabernacle used by Israel in the wilderness.[27] The ark of the covenant, brought to Jerusalem by David, was placed in the Temple's Holy of Holies by Solomon. Indeed, the Lord told Moses to instruct craftspersons about the fabric, furnishings, vestments, and adornments according to the pattern (*paradeigma*) revealed by God. In a similar way, David turned over to Solomon instructions for the Temple as detailed as those given by Moses to Bezalel and the other workers. The chroniclers reported that "David gave all to Solomon in the handwriting of the Lord according to the knowledge of the work of the model (*paradeigma*)."[28] The traditions that the tabernacle's and the Temple's plans and furnishings were revealed by God to Moses, David, and Solomon were continued in the Wisdom of Solomon. The sage-king rejoiced, "You [God] have given command to build a temple on your holy mountain, and an altar in the city of your habitation, a copy (*mimēma*) of the holy tent (*skēnē*) that you prepared from the beginning (*archē*)."[29] The earthly Temple, then, has a divine pattern. There is in the heavens a tabernacle or *skēnē* that served as the model for the building in Jerusalem. A heavenly sanctuary mentioned in the Septuagint spurred Christians to speculate on a celestial dimension for the *ekklēsia* as well.

The Temple and Jerusalem assumed eschatological importance, too. According to Micah and Isaiah, the mountain of the Temple of the Lord would be raised higher than all other mountains. As the nations came to it, they would learn the way of peace through God's Law. From his vantage point in the Exile, Ezekiel denounced the corruptions in the Temple and its priesthood. His visions of a city and a Temple set on a mountain included a restored priesthood, purified sacrifices, and a sanctified people.

Temple and *ekklēsia* belong together—in heaven as on earth, in the present age and in the age to come. Septuagintal elements, precedents, and associations were readily regarded by Christians as authoritative and as given to them for instruction and mission.

EKKLĒSIA AND CHRISTIAN CLAIMS

When Christians applied the term *ekklēsia* to themselves, they did more than seize on a term with extensive Greco-Roman and Jewish pedigrees; they made theological claims. The most obvious claim was that Christian communities, separately and as a whole, were not sectarians assembled to deliberate on their own issues, or even synagogues of people who believed that Jesus was the Messiah.[30] Instead, they claimed to be the *ekklēsia* of the Lord, the called-out people chosen to be saved through Jesus, to serve God in this age, and to live eternally in the kingdom that is coming—or might already be here—in Christ. The contents, contrasts, and nuances of that claim were debated among Christians, but the assertion held.

Second, if Christians were the *ekklēsia*, Jesus was analogous to the Temple. He could be the divine one who tabernacled or tented among humans, the one who raised up the Temple of his body after it was destroyed, the one in whom God dwelled and on whom the Spirit rested.[31] Jesus was high priest, lamb, intercessor, lawgiver, rejected stone which became the head of the corner. Especially after the destruction of the Temple in 70 C.E. by the Romans in the Jewish rebellion, the *ekklēsia* was free to think of the Lord's Temple in terms that were not tied to a geographic place. Wherever two or three gathered together, Jesus was with them—their Temple was present. God's dwelling place, at least in a preliminary manner, was among humans.[32] Christian descriptions and images of the church often reflected Septuagintal passages about the community of Israel, the Temple, and the Temple's furnishings: for example, royal priesthood, holy nation, temple, Israel, flock, vineyard. Other expressions included fellowship or association (*koinōnia*), body of Christ, bride, woman, mother, ark, lampstands, and tower.[33] But imaginative enthusiasm yielded to frustration in the wake of the delay of the parousia.

Third, by claiming to be the Lord's *ekklēsia*, Christians continued to distance themselves from Jews. Gentiles among the first generation of Christians may have regarded themselves as wild olives grafted onto the cultivated olive stock of Israel. By the end of the first century, however, terms such as "synagogue of Satan," words attributed to Jesus calling the Jews children of the devil, and writings branding Jews as superstitious, ridiculous, and conceited were becoming part of the church's discourse.[34] The claim to be the Lord's *ekklēsia* would also develop in painful ways. Fourth, by claiming to be the *ekklēsia*, Christians saw Jesus as the sign of the new covenant and the *ekklēsia* as the restored and purified community of God. As the community gained experience and found need, it felt authorized to develop liturgical and administrative structures analogous to Israel's to discipline members and thus avert God's wrath. Fifth, the Christian *ekklēsia* claimed that it was called to take up God's plan where ancient Israel supposedly left it. If Zechariah and Jeremiah sought to cleanse the Temple and to open the house of the Lord to all nations, then the church had a missionary imperative to go to the Gentiles. If Jeremiah and Isaiah said that God would instruct the covenant community inwardly, then the Christian *ekklēsia* was to be motivated by the mind of Christ. If Israel's Lord sent witnesses to God's justice and mercy to the ends of the earth, then the Christian *ekklēsia* would venture at least through the Empire and into its adjacent territories. If Moses ordered the ancient *ekklēsia* to teach its children the statutes of the Lord, then Christians would engage in moral training and gradually add higher studies. And if prophets saw a special role for Israel during the last days of the present age, then Christians saw the church as a cosmic salvational community that reached up to the heavens and down to the grave. The whole creation was being redeemed and fulfilled by Jesus— and the church had a role in that action—according to God's plan formulated before the beginning of time.[35]

CONTINUATION OR CONTINUITY?

Christian claims about Jesus and the roles his called-out people were to have in God's plan gave his followers a rationale that distinguished the church from the synagogue and provided incentives to convert as many persons as possible before Jesus' return. At the same time, separation from ethnic Israel led Christians to think of themselves as members of the true Israel in ways that disrupted the Christian community for at least two generations. Was the church the reformed and renewed continuation of Israel? Or was the church a development in continuity with, yet different from, Israel, carrying forward God's purposes on the basis of Jesus' fulfilling what had been prefigured by the old covenant and its people? How were Jesus' followers to understand themselves as people whom the God designated to be a holy nation and royal priesthood? Put in terms familiar to first-century Christians who struggled with their relationship to Judaism and one another, the question became, Was the Law that God gave to Israel through Moses binding in whole, or part, or not at all on Christians?[36] This was far from an abstract issue; at stake were the future identity and mission of the Christian movement, and the answers that the believers gave determined missionary methods and goals.

Those who claimed that the church was the continuation of Israel and insisted that the Law was binding on all Christians were called "Judaizers" by their detractors whether or not they were ethnically Jewish. They insisted that in the true Israel males would be circumcised and everyone would observe Sabbath and dietary regulations, celebrate the holy days prescribed in the Pentateuch, and avoid unnecessary associations with Gentiles. Outward obedience to the Law indicated that the person and the community were inwardly loyal to the God of Israel (and of all nations), were bound to the Ten Commandments, and responded to God with worship purified from pagan taint. Christians born Jewish and children born to Christian parents were expected to keep the Law as part of their adherence to the gospel. Judaizers insisted that converts to Christianity from paganism comply with the Law's requirements and, in effect, become Jews as part of their becoming members of the continuation of Israel in the church.

Paul was among those who argued that the church was not a literal continuation of Israel but its fulfillment. The whole range of prescriptions, requirements, and rituals related to the Jerusalem Temple, sabbaths, holy days, diet, and circumcision were but types that were fulfilled in and by Jesus. Paul could even write that the Law was given only as a custodian to keep the old Israel from becoming still more sinful than it already was until God sent forth the divine Son. Now that Christ had appeared, the old dispensation of the Law and the types were no longer binding on those who believed in Jesus. Christians were to live not by Moses' rules but by Christ's law of love—and bear the fruit of the Spirit.[37] The apostle claimed that the new age anticipated by prophets such as Isaiah, Jeremiah, and Zechariah was open to all nations and people. In the wake of Jesus' crucifixion and resurrection, the true Israel was empowered by the Holy Spirit; it was a community whose members' hearts were spiritually circumcised or covenanted to God, not one in which male organs were altered physically. Converts from paganism need not—indeed, must not—be required to keep the externalities of the Law. Insistence on the literal observance of the Law would amount to a denial that the types had been fulfilled in and through Jesus—a denial of the very gospel of God.

The controversy between Judaizing Christians and what may be termed "gentilizing Christians" wracked first-century Christianity.[38] The congregations in Jerusalem and Antioch disputed mightily with each other as they sent missionaries with conflicting messages into Syria, Asia Minor, Greece, and even Italy. Roman legions rather than theological debate settled the issue in an immediate sense. The destruction of Jerusalem and the Temple in 70 c.e. broke the heart of Judaizing Christianity. From 70 onward, speculative Christians and visionaries turned toward the heavenly model of the Temple.[39] During the second and later centuries there were occasional attempts to revive the view that Christianity was a continuation of Israel, but an increase in the number of gentile converts together with a decrease in the number of ethnic Jews and Gentiles sympathetic to a Judaizing view of the church effectively ended "Jewish Christianity" as a major movement in the church. Whenever it reappears, it is usually connected with a concern for the Old Testament, morals, and the expectation that Jesus will return soon to redeem those who have been most faithful and strict in keeping his teachings. During the years in which the controversy raged, those who opposed the Judaizers made comments that were not only hostile toward the Judaizers and their positions but also disparaged the Law; and they stressed Old Testament passages that condemned the old Israel for disobedience, hypocrisy, and legalism. Later generations of Christians have sometimes misconstrued this invective as referring not to a faction within the Christian movement but to Jews and Judaism.[40]

A generation after the fall of Jerusalem the church and the synagogue had separated into two distinct and mutually exclusive religious bodies. The members of the church understood themselves to be the new and true Israel in continuity with the faithful remnant of the biblical Israel, but not as a continuation of Judaism, and not as a people bound to the biblical Law. Jews and Christians persisted in opposing each other, each convinced that the other rejected the true God and distorted the Scriptures. Lurking beneath the Christian claims were tremors of doubt. Jesus' followers still yearned for the unification of ethnic Israel with their version of Israel. But Christianity's future lay neither in Palestine nor with synagogues dispersed through the Empire; the Christian future was in joining the gentile cultures, so as to reach out to the peoples of the Roman Empire.

But you are a chosen race, a royal priesthood, a holy nation, God's own people, in order that you may proclaim the mighty acts of him who called you out of darkness into his marvelous light. Once you were not a people, but now you are God's people; once you had not received mercy, but now you have received mercy. Beloved, I urge you as aliens and exiles to abstain from the desires of the flesh that wage war against the soul. Conduct yourselves honorably among the Gentiles, so that, though they malign you as evildoers, they may see your honorable deeds and glorify God when he comes to judge. . . . Honor everyone. Love the family of believers. Fear God. Honor the emperor.

1 Peter 2:9-12, 17

3

Imperial Visions
and Realities

Now the last age by Cumae's Sibyl sung Has come and gone, and the majestic role Of circling centuries begins anew: Justice returns, returns old Saturn's reign, With a new breed of men sent down from heaven. Only do thou at the boy's birth in whom The Iron shall cease, the Golden Age arise. . . . He shall receive the life of gods, and see Heroes with gods commingling, and himself . . . Reign over a world at peace.

Virgil *Eclogue* 4.5–13, 15–18

The good news was that the Golden Age was about to return. An ancient Greek view of the world and the human condition depicted a succession of eras that declined in quality from Gold to Silver, then from Silver to Bronze, and from there to the violent present Iron Age.[1] Humanity's hope lay in the restoration of that original time when justice and courage, honor and prosperity, wisdom and order prevailed as gods and humans lived in harmony. The Latin poets Virgil (70–19 B.C.E.) and Ovid (43 B.C.E.–17 C.E.) adapted expectations about the returning Golden Age to support the emergence of imperial Rome and its emperors as the renewers and preservers of the glorious epoch.

Virgil wrote that when the Trojan refugee, Aeneas, stood in the realm of the dead, his deceased father and the Sibyl of Apollo revealed to him the coming greatness of Rome and the glorious family of Julius Caesar. Julius's heir and adopted son, Octavian, later given the title Augustus, would be the "son of a god [who] . . . will renew a Golden Age in Latium in the fields where once Saturn was king." According to Virgil, the descendants of Augustus were destined to rule the world in the Golden Age. Other nations might be more skilled in philosophy, art, and divination, yet "yours will be the rulership of nations, remember, Roman, these will be your arts: to teach the ways of peace to those you conquer, to spare defeated peoples, tame the proud."[2]

Ovid's muse led him to rhapsodize over a creator who began the first Golden Age. In that time there was no need for lawyers or warriors, for "the peoples of the world, untroubled by any fears, enjoyed a leisurely and peaceful existence, and had no use for soldiers." Earth produced food spontaneously, so there was no private property or work or commerce, and "there flowed rivers of milk and rivers of nectar, and golden honey dropped from the green holm-oak."[3] In contrast, the Age of Iron was grim:

> All manner of crime broke out; modesty, truth and loyalty fled. Treachery and trickery took their place, deceit and violence and criminal greed. . . . War made its appearance. . . . Men lived on what they could plunder: friend was not safe from friend, nor father-in-law from son-in-law, and even between brothers affection was rare. . . . All proper affection lay vanquished and, last of the immortals, the maiden Justice left the blood-soaked earth.[4]

According to Ovid, the miseries of the Iron Age began to end with the rise of Julius Caesar. His assassins were not victorious, because the goddess Venus placed his soul among the stars of heaven, "so that deified Julius may ever look from his lofty seat" on Jupiter's holy city. Octavian was destined to beat back the barbarians, and "all habitable lands on earth will be his, and even the seas will be his slave. When the blessing of peace will be bestowed upon the earth, he will turn his attention to the rights of citizens, and will pass laws eminently just. By his own example he will direct the people's ways"—and he would ascend to the home of the gods when he died. Jupiter, ultimate ruler of the heavens, the earth, and the realm of the dead, had given Augustus and his successors sovereignty over this world.[5]

Expectations for the return of the Golden Age were more than the muse-driven hopes of poets; people longed for peace and were anxious about their futures. The poets were aware that ironies edged their visions of the Golden Age. Virgil seemed anguished that Rome could achieve justice and peace only through anger, deceit, war, and death. His descriptions of battlefield horrors, refugees, and failed attempts to reach settlements without conflict are poignant reminders that Rome's authority rested on the threat and reality of coercion. Ovid fawned over the imperial family, hoping in vain that Augustus would allow him to return from exile. His great work, *Metamorphoses* (Transformations), told how all existence and identities are subject to sudden, often calamitous, change. In the poem's ending, he defied his own view of persistent change and his own use of flattery by claiming that his fame as a poet would outlast that of the Empire and that his star would shine brighter than those of future deified emperors.

Irony about the Golden Age and anxiety that the Iron Age would decline even further were justified. Caesar Augustus's immediate successors clouded the vision for a future era of justice and peace under imperial auspices. Nero inadvertently and drastically altered the vision. Forecasts of a new age with new relationships between individuals, nations, and divine powers continued and even intensified in the late first century and throughout the second century of the Common Era. Those visions are inseparable from and may be recounted through the reigns of Rome's rulers.

NERO'S LEGACY

Nero's reign (54–68), once brilliant, unraveled as his conduct became increasingly bizarre and cruel. The great fire in Rome (64 c.e.) and the subsequent "most exquisite tortures" inflicted on Christians even turned many pagans against him.[6] The numerous unsuccessful conspiracies to overthrow him indicated that influential leaders were willing to move against the Augustan dynasty. At the end, generals turned on him, the Senate denounced him, the people of Rome rejected him, friends deserted him, and he botched his own suicide. No wonder he muttered in his last moments, "How ugly and vulgar my life has become!"[7] But Nero was more than the last of the Augustan dynasty; his end began a new, dangerous trend. The Roman historian Tacitus (ca. 56–120 c.e.) put it plainly: "Welcome as the death of Nero had been in the first burst of joy, yet it had not only aroused various emotions in Rome, among the Senators, the people, or the soldiery of the capital, it had also excited all the legions and their generals; for now had been divulged that secret of the Empire, that emperors could be made elsewhere than at Rome."[8] And they could be made and unmade by soldiers. The "Long Year," 68–69, had begun.[9]

Within eighteen months three men were acclaimed emperor, and each died violently. The crowd cheered first to see Galba's head stuck atop a spear, then Otho committed suicide in the face of certain defeat. Vitellius, caught in the palace by his rival's vanguard, had his hands

tied behind him, a noose was fastened round his neck, and amid cheers and abuse the soldiers dragged him, half-naked, with his clothes in tatters, along the Sacred Way to the Forum. They pulled his head back by the hair, as is done with criminals, and stuck a sword-point under his chin, which exposed his face to public contempt. Dung and filth were hurled at him . . . and his forlorn appearance occasioned loud laughter.

After mutilating and killing "Greedy-guts," the soldiers threw his body into the Tiber.[10] In that terrible year hundreds of persons perished, cities were plundered, treasuries were emptied, the Senate was threatened, military units fought one another on behalf of leaders who soon were killed, and the victorious divisions clamored for rewards. Authority was eroded, and piety seemed unavailing. Power had shifted; from 69 onward, the military decided who would be emperor and at what price.

Nero's legacy also included irrationality and cruelty. While these were not unknown in earlier reigns, people often cited Nero as the precedent for later tyrants. His instability seemed to infect future rulers. Nero had sent Titus Flavius Vespasianus, an experienced general, to Judea to quell the Jewish revolt (66–73). A soldier known for his courage, self-discipline, and pragmatism, he had already served in Germany, Africa, Britain, and Spain. Vespasian took with him his oldest son, Titus. When he saw an opportunity to make a bid for the *imperium*, Vespasian left Titus to finish the war with the Jews and moved on Rome. Titus destroyed the city of Jerusalem with its Temple (70) and set the stage for the mass suicide of the rebels at Masada (73). After his troops had dispatched Vitellius, Vespasian (69–79) set about to govern an exhausted realm from a city battered by civil strife and to reassert the orderly succession of imperial rule through the emperor's family. Peace was his goal, so when he rebuilt the Forum, he erected in it a temple to the goddess of that name. To maintain her favor and his own safety, he dealt cautiously with the military, retaining its support throughout his reign. He gave lip service to the theory that the Senate ruled the state while he centralized power in his office. Vespasian renovated Rome and stimulated public works in the provinces. After Rome's victory in Judea, the emperor established settlements such as Neapolis in Palestine and colonized them with loyal Greeks and Romans. (Justin's grandparents were among the new settlers in Samaria.) The emperor promoted reforms in the legal system, the Senate, education, and morals. Many began to have hope again about the Empire's stability and future blessedness.

Revolts continued, but the more serious problem was Vespasian's younger son, Domitian. Underneath Domitian's often charming demeanor lurked madness and cruelty. The test of Vespasian's attempts to reconstruct the government's stability came on June 23, 79; the old emperor died. Titus was rapidly acclaimed by the military and took over as ruler. Instead of progress toward the Golden Age, sixty-two days later the world seemed to break apart. Fire came out of the earth, death rained from the sky, and darkness spread over the land: Vesuvius erupted. Years later Pliny the Younger (ca. 62–113) remembered the awesome power of the explosions, the sheets of fire, the mushroom cloud, and the bewildered people.[11] The rest of Titus's principate was no better; a fire in Rome burned for three days, and the worst plague in memory raged in the city. Titus tried to maintain stability, but his health failed, and his brother schemed against him. When an animal he was about to sacrifice escaped and thunder clapped on a cloudless day, Titus knew what the portents signaled. Rumor had it that Domitian helped speed Titus's ascent to the heavens by poisoning his brother's dinner.

After a seemingly mild start, Domitian (81–96) exiled prominent persons and their families and executed others or forced them to kill themselves. Ever the lover of displays, Domitian rode a white horse when his brother and father celebrated their triumph over the Jews; later he held magnificent games and naval displays in specially built facilities. He had his name inscribed on monuments and structures originally dedicated to earlier heroes. The emperor's lust respected neither gender nor marital status. He was also given to sudden, shocking acts of brutality. Jews and Christians felt and remembered Domitian's suspicions and wrath. His animosity toward Jews was not unique—Tacitus was a master of stereotypes.[12] But the emperor had power. He increased the tax levied on Jews for the maintenance of the ruins of the Temple and executed several at court whom he suspected of being Jewish. Some Christians were banished or sent to the mines. Christian congregations in the province of Asia experienced sharp local persecutions as well.

Jews and Christians regarded Domitian as a blasphemer and agent of evil not only for his conduct but also for his claim to be god and lord, titles the Senate often bestowed upon a deceased emperor. The author of the Revelation (or Apocalypse) to John wrote of the contrasts and conflicts between God and the Lord Jesus on the one hand and Satan and the emperor-beast who served evil on the other. Many thought Domitian was a resurrected or returned Nero. Those closer to him gave him Nero's fate. The emperor was inordinately concerned about horoscopes. The plotters, including his wife, used his attachment to astrology to trick him into thinking that he had survived a supposedly fatal hour, only to surprise him with a bladeless dagger (his) and sharp swords (theirs). Instead of voting him the divine honors he craved, the Senate damned his memory. Twenty-seven years after the Flavians (the name of the dynasty of Vespasian, Titus, and Domitian) brought order out of the turmoil occasioned by assassinations, their dynasty ended in a blood-soaked bed chamber. The Age of Iron was proving to be dismally durable.

While the chaotic days of 68–69 threatened to recur, Marcus Cocceius Nerva, the new emperor (96–98), survived through adroit maneuvers and well-placed payments to wavering supporters. Nerva followed Julius's precedent of adopting a son to provide an heir presumptive to the imperial office. The choice fell on Trajan, the military governor of Upper Germany (roughly the area from Strasbourg to Koblenz). Four months later, Nerva died. With Trajan (98–117) a new and, in some ways, more stable, century opened.

TRAJAN'S VISION

Trajan's succession was unopposed, and he respected the Senate. When he arrived in Rome, he entered on foot as would a common citizen. In marked contrast to Domitian, Trajan gave the commander of his bodyguard a sword with the order to use it for the emperor if he ruled justly and against him if he was wicked. Over the few years he resided in Rome, Trajan moved freely through the city's streets, markets, and homes.[13] Born in Spain (ca. 53) to parents from distinguished Italian families, he was steeped in the Roman virtues of courage and loyalty. His father had commanded a legion in Vespasian's forces during the Jewish War and later became governor of Syria. While his father administered imperial affairs from Antioch, Trajan served with a legion stationed in the province. Probably he heard about the Christians there, and, if Ignatius was then in the city, the future bishop likewise heard about Trajan. The young soldier was given command over a legion in Germany and served with loyalty and competence, demonstrating that he respected the office of the *imperator* not as *dominus* (lord or master) but as *princeps* (leader).[14] The new emperor was a bold, yet careful, strategist and administrator. During his lifetime, the Senate honored Trajan with the titles "Father of the Fatherland" and "Best of Rulers." On the deaths of the emperor (117) and his daughter (119), the Senate declared them deified. Few considered Trajan anything but a just and clement ruler. Among the few with other opinions were the Jews and Christians who suffered in his reign.

Trajan had an expansive vision for the Empire, a vision related to his admiration for Alexander the Great and Julius Caesar. Almost immediately upon his accession to the *imperium*, he started a program of major public works in the capital. His forum included markets, baths, libraries, and a tower inscribed with the accomplishments of his reign. Engineers and laborers fanned out from Rome to build roads and to duplicate in the provinces what was being done in the capital. With the construction crews went inspectors and auditors to discourage cost overruns and corruption. He quietly enjoyed his wine and boys, but he had little time to enjoy the city. He began an extended campaign against the Dacians, eventually conquering them and turning their homeland into a province (100–102, 104–107). Other Roman forces subdued areas south and east of the Jordan to establish the new province of Arabia (106–112). Trajan sponsored lavish spectacles that featured gladiatorial combats and wild animal fights—and the deaths of criminals in the arenas. It is likely that Christians, including Ignatius, were among the festivities' victims.

Trajan appointed Pliny the Younger as governor of Bithynia with instructions to clean up the fiscal and administrative mess in the province and to improve the overall welfare of the populace. Pliny coped with scandal, shoddy construction, urban fires, and Christians. While it is clear that to be a Christian was a crime punishable by sentences including death, we do not know what actual charges generated such drastic actions.[15] Roman citizens condemned to death in the provinces were transported to Rome for confirmation and execution of the sentence. Ignatius may have been sent to Rome after being sentenced to death in Antioch and in prospect of his execution in compliance with this legal procedure. Pliny's reflections on the general situation in which Ignatius was enmeshed provide some insight into the more complex issues of the relations between Empire and church.[16] Local temples and shrines were half-empty, sacrifices to the gods neglected, and respect for the ancient ways undermined. Pamphlets and rumors circulated widely, probably accusing Christians of cannibalism. Pliny admitted, "I have never been at an examination [torture session?] of Christians. Consequently, I do not know the nature of the extent of the punishments usually meted out to them, nor the grounds for starting an investigation and how far it should be pressed." He complained that the persons accused of being Christians persisted in that confession, so "I am convinced that their stubbornness and unshakeable obstinacy ought not go unpunished." The governor did not think that those who sang hymns to Christ as if to a god were particularly menacing: "I found nothing but a degenerate sort of cult carried to extravagant lengths." Trajan and Pliny agreed to punish Christians, but not to search for them. The emperor advised his governor to ignore anonymous accusations against suspects as such procedures "create the worst sort of precedent and are quite out of keeping with the spirit of our age."

Trajan's version of that spirit led to war. The emperor went east in 113; only his ashes returned. Determined to conquer Parthia (roughly portions of modern Iran), he moved through the province of Asia and into Syria and nearly died in an earthquake at Antioch (115). In a series of hard-fought battles, the Romans conquered Armenia, Upper Mesopotamia, and Assyria and reached the head of the Persian Gulf. Trajan fulfilled a dream by sacrificing where Alexander had been. But supply lines were overextended, and conquered peoples resisted. Trajan secured what he could with understaffed garrisons and headed for home. Other troubles afflicted him on the return journey.

Resentment against the humiliating Temple tax combined with messianic speculation stirred Diaspora Jews to revolt against the government beginning in 116. The first insurrections took place in Cyrenaica (modern Libya), then Cyprus, Egypt, and some of the newly won territories in Mesopotamia. Dio Cassius's stories about Jews eating Greeks and Romans on Cyprus and his estimate that 220,000 died on the island are exaggerated, but they indicate the fury and the fear on both sides.[17] The emperor narrowly escaped a battlefield death in Arabia. During the struggle, according to Dio, rainbow-colored lightning bolts and hail fell on the Roman ranks. Given the signs, it was no surprise that Trajan sickened and died. Shortly before his death Trajan adopted a forty-two-year-old relative, Publius Aelius Hadrianus, as his heir.

HADRIAN'S REVISED VISION

Born in Italy and raised in Spain, Hadrian experienced the death of his father and the good fortune of obtaining Trajan as his guardian. Hadrian's enthusiasm for Greek literature, rhetoric, and philosophy earned him the nickname "Little Greek." Criticized for his provincial Latin accent, he practiced until even critics admitted that he spoke eloquently. Throughout his years in military service at various outposts, astrologers, oracles, and omens predicted that he was destined for the imperial title. He soon became governor of Syria and came to detest the people of Antioch. He received word that Trajan had officially adopted him two days before he was informed that his new father was dead; finally, he was emperor. The new ruler faced immediate challenges and responsibilities: "When he gained the imperial power he at once set himself to follow ancestral custom, and gave his attention to maintaining peace throughout the world."[18] And peace meant retreat from Trajan's frontiers.

From the start of his rule, Hadrian (117–138) realized that the Empire was overextended. Resources were spread too thin and borders too far-flung. Reversing Trajan's expansionist policies, Hadrian contracted the frontiers to make the Empire more manageable and defensible. Where possible, as in the East, he withdrew Roman garrisons, leaving well-disposed allies on the borderlands. Where this was not possible, as in Britain, he attempted to separate hostile peoples from each other and from imperial settlements. Hadrian envisioned the Empire as a commonwealth of ethnic territories in which each region had a broad measure of self-expression within the framework of loyalty to Rome. His version of the imperial vision represented more accurately the realities of the Empire's diversity than did Trajan's; it also demanded fealty to the Empire, commitment to commonly held practices and values, and a high degree of coordination. Given such loyalties, commitments, and coordination, plus the workings of providence and fortune, a renewed Golden Age or at least a mitigated Iron Age might have had a chance to develop.

Hadrian was a tireless coordinator committed to harmonizing provincial law codes with those of Rome and streamlining governmental bureaucracy. His personality and abilities suited the task. One of the most talented and cultured of the emperors, he encouraged art, philosophy, and literature by personal example and support. He was a poet, humorist, painter, sculptor, rhetor, lawyer, and author. He fancied himself a literary critic and engineer.

He befriended philosophers such as the Stoic Epictetus and sophists such as Fronto. Hadrian realized that religion was a potent force that could unify or split the Empire, so along with building new shrines and renovating existing ones, he performed with care and reverence the emperor's traditional roles as supreme priest. Aelius Spartianus observed, "During his times there were famines, plagues and earthquakes. . . . There was also a flood of the Tiber. . . . Roman rites he most carefully observed, foreign ones he despised." That proved ominous for Christians. He was realistic about the compliments and praises he received; styled by admirers as Liberator, Savior of the World, even Zeus, Hadrian knew enough not to be swayed by such accolades, since he remembered Nero and Domitian. He was not without fault or questionable habits. As a devoted hunter and competent warrior, Hadrian had the stalking instincts of both and was skilled with the weapons of death. He was a lavish entertainer, and some of his animal exhibitions included the slaying of a hundred lions at a time. His appetite for food and for boys was reputed to be enormous. His relationship with the Senate was ambiguous. His rule began and ended with a spate of unnecessary and fear-provoking killings. His biographers admired his intelligence and courage, yet realized that his cruelty made relationships with him difficult.

More than half of his nearly twenty-one-year principate was spent outside the capital. He traveled throughout the Empire, perhaps partially to avoid residence in a city he disliked heartily, but officially to reform the military. From 119 to 122 he was in Gaul and Britain, returning to the European mainland sooner than he expected because of riots in Alexandria. Next he journeyed to Asia and the Greek isles (123–125). While in Greece, he followed the tradition associated with Alexander and was initiated into the highest ranks of the Eleusinian mysteries. After visiting Sicily, he returned briefly to Rome and crossed the sea to Africa (128). Without a break, he took ship to Greece, and in Athens the emperor dedicated a new temple to Zeus and an altar in his own name. He traveled on into Asia again, returned to Syria, and passed through Judea.

If Hadrian disliked Antioch intensely, he soon had reason to add Judea to his list. According to Dio, he rebuilt Jerusalem as the pagan city Aelia Capitolina, "and on the site of the temple of the [Jewish] god he raised a new temple to Zeus. This brought on a war of no slight importance nor of brief duration, for the Jews deemed it intolerable that foreign races should be settled in their city and foreign religious rites planted there."[19] After the emperor left for Egypt, the rebels struck. The revolt spread to the Diaspora and wider conflict threatened. It was a war of attrition. The Roman commander "was able . . . to crush, exhaust, and exterminate [the rebels]. Very few of them in fact survived. . . . Five hundred and eighty thousand men were slain in various raids and battles, and the number of those who perished by famine, disease, and fire are past finding out." Dio's figures are astronomically high, yet clearly Judea was devastated. Hyenas and wolves stalked city streets. Justin had left Palestine before the war began, but the Jews with whom he later discussed theology and philosophy still reeled from the disaster. If the key rebel leader, Simon Bar Kochba, had messianic hopes, his defeat and the reality of Roman power were enough to discourage Jews who wanted to hurry the coming of God's kingdom through direct action.

The emperor's trek continued. Hadrian's travels through Egypt included a tour of Alexandria and a trip up the Nile. During the voyage, his favorite lover, Antinous, died under odd circumstances. Some say that he drowned in a boating accident, while others claim he offered himself as a sacrifice to further Hadrian's imperial aims. In any event, Hadrian had the Alexandrians deify his companion and build a temple for him. Toward the end of his reign, the streak of cruelty with which he began returned. When he considered whom to adopt, he passed over the son of the aged and respected Servianus. For some reason he feared that the old man would cause trouble, so he ordered both father and son to kill themselves. Servianus cursed the emperor with the prayer that he might long for death but be unable to die. The gods granted the prayer. Hadrian suffered from dropsy and perhaps cancer. His attempts to kill himself were thwarted, and he was in agony as he became a god.

Hadrian's first choice of a successor emerged from brief grooming in the provinces only to die on reaching Rome. Adopted by Hadrian, hailed as Caesar, and designated to be Augustus, Aelius Verus expired unexpectedly in 138 before he actually became emperor. A late-third-century biographer admitted that all that could be said of Aelius was that there was little for which he might be commended or blamed.[20] His reputation included observations that he dressed elegantly and discoursed eloquently. More attention was paid to his love of luxury than his pursuit of wisdom. Special beds with nets of perfumed petals to enhance his and his mistresses' enjoyment provoked critical comment. Still, a biographer commented that his practices, "if not creditable, at least did not make for the destruction of the state."[21] Aelius Verus provided an interlude between greater figures. He illustrated the propensities and tastes that marked the remainder of the century. Elegance, eloquence, prosperity, and luxury were regarded as blessings given by providence and made secure through prudent leaders. In their distinctive ways, Tertullian and Clement commented on the Verus-like life-styles of pagans and on luxury among fellow Christians.

THE ANTONINE EMPERORS:
RECOVERED VISIONS AND RELAPSES

Hadrian's time away from Rome and Aelius's failings in austerity were amply made up by Titus Aurelius Antoninus (139–161). Here was a person who recalled the hopes for an Augustus-like ruler who would guide the Empire on a steady and just course to peace. Adopted by the dying Hadrian after Aelius's demise and voted the title "Pius" by the Senate, he was, according to Julius Capitolinus,

> strikingly handsome, in natural talent brilliant, in temperament kindly; he was aristocratic in countenance and calm in nature, a singularly gifted speaker and an elegant scholar, conspicuously thrifty, a conscientious landholder, gentle, generous and mindful of other's rights. . . . Almost alone of all emperors, he lived entirely unstained by the blood of other citizens or foes, so far as it was in his power.[22]

Even after applying a generous discount for the biographer's obvious bias, Antoninus was outstanding. He added his substantial personal fortune to the imperial coffers and handled the Empire's finances so well that he left his successors a sizable surplus. His relations with the public and the Senate were open and respectful, and his reform of the legal system favored women and slaves. Antoninus's concern for education led him to elevate the social status of philosophers and teachers. While he had the means to live in luxury, the emperor preferred dignified simplicity and tranquillity. Throughout his twenty-three-year reign, Antoninus never left the capital or its immediate environs. On his deathbed, at the age of seventy-four, he gave the watchword for the day, *aequanimitas*, and quietly passed on.

Aequanimitas means evenness of soul, mind, and temper. Equanimity is calmness, composure, steadiness, self-possession. It means the ability to discipline one's emotions and actions in trying circumstances so as to be undisturbed. *Aequanimitas* was a fitting watchword for the emperor's last day. But what did he mean by it? Was it a reflection about himself and what he tried to accomplish? Or a comment on what he expected from the Empire's inhabitants? Or a hope for his successors in prospect of what he realized they would face?

Upon examination, Antoninus's reign was largely free from major military or civil conflicts, but it was scarcely placid. Revolts in Dacia, Achaea, and Egypt were suppressed with little difficulty, but unrest was building, for the Empire's borders remained vulnerable. By persuading political foes to remain peaceful and by negotiating differences among rivals on the eastern frontiers, he only postponed hostilities. Troops were dispatched to assist hard-pressed allies on the Black Sea, and German tribes were becoming aggressive. Natural disasters, considered portents of greater catastrophes, troubled his reign. Rome suffered a fire that destroyed nearly 350 homes; the Circus collapsed, crushing over a thousand persons; and the city suffered both famine and flood. Earthquakes devastated the islands of Cos, Lesbos, and Rhodes, the cities of Smyrna and Ephesus, and towns in Bithynia. On top of these calamities, fires scorched Narbonne, Antioch, and Carthage, and a plague struck Arabia. Antoninus left his successor a fine example of a ruler but a tense realm.

If ever an emperor needed decisiveness along with *aequanimitas*, it was Marcus Aurelius (161–180). He possessed *aequanimitas* perhaps overmuch, and he was short on the ability to make critical decisions. Justly celebrated as philosopher, scholar, and soldier, he was a lackluster statesman, reluctant persecutor, and ineffectual family leader. When twelve years old, he took the philosopher's robe, committing himself to the study and discipline of Stoicism. He was duly saddened when Antoninus adopted him as son and heir; he knew that imperial duties would draw him away from the life that he would have chosen for himself, but he undertook his tasks with dedication and austerity. He also showed admirable but ultimately misplaced generosity and patience. Marcus not only took Antoninus's family name, he also accepted as co-ruler the son of Aelius Verus, a man known popularly as Verus. Verus acted as his father might have. Talented and charming, he fancied himself a poet and orator, but he was a dismal leader. Verus's love of luxury and his disdain for discipline were as notorious as his irresponsible conduct when heading a military campaign. Marcus, however, would not criticize his colleague, but tried to work around him. The emperor was doubly fortunate; competent generals won battles while Verus dallied with mistresses, and then Verus died before he could do further damage.

Marcus longed for tranquillity and divine wisdom but spent his reign in almost constant combat. From the start, he faced invasions from the north and east, uprisings in Britain and Spain, Germanic incursions into Italy, Parthian breakthroughs in Armenia, and revolts in the Balkans. On top of these troubles, he had to cope with rebellions of officers and peoples in the midst of the Empire. These disruptions forced a fiscal crisis and unpopular austerity. Tales of Verus's lavish banquets and expenses undermined the emperor's credibility. To propitiate the gods, he ordered people throughout the Empire to participate in sacrifices for divine favor. Then, feeling threatened and realizing that some secret societies spawned opposition movements, Marcus banned such groups under threats of banishment and death. Christians were put in a painful position. If they sacrificed, they would be guilty of betraying their Lord, but, if they did not offer sacrifice, they would be accused of atheism and treason. Further, the Christian movement was widely considered to be a potentially subversive organization of the sort proscribed by the emperor. The emperor's policies left his subordinates little choice but to punish Christians. Ironically, the philosopher resorted to persecution, the scholar to suppression. During Marcus's reign, Justin taught a Christian version of philosophy in Rome and was beheaded for his efforts.

The emperor's troubles included his wife and son. Faustina's rumored liaisons with gladiators cast doubt on Marcus's paternity of his heir, Commodus. True to his philosophy, personality, and public image, the Stoic ruler ignored the reports. Commodus, however, lived up to the gossip and died in its shadow more than he lived by his legal father's ideals. Dio Cassius, the tale-telling and perhaps tale-creating senator, reports that as a youth Commodus was known not for cruelty or wickedness but for cowardice and a slavish attachment to friends. Julius Capitolinus reported that Marcus Aurelius realized Commodus was so apt to become another Caligula, Nero, and Domitian that he wished Commodus would die with him. The expiring emperor was not the last to desire such a fate for the next ruler.[23]

Dio and Lampridius agreed that few rulers were more feared and detested than Commodus. His reign (180–192) featured unrelieved imperial arrogance, debauchery, extravagance, treachery, and murder. Whether out of genuine megalomania or warped humor, he styled himself as Mercury and Hercules, played the role of a gladiator, humiliated aristocrats and ordinary folk, and gave himself grand titles. He insisted, so claimed Dio, that henceforth Rome was to be called Commodiana and his reign revered as the Golden Age. Even the months of the year were to be renamed in his honor. Claims to divinity and authority did not translate into reality. Commodus deferred defending the Empire's borders, for in such struggles he might have had to risk himself on the battlefield. He also failed to secure Italy's Egyptian food supply, so while he and his three hundred male and female concubines fared sumptuously, the populace hungered. The city and the Empire weakened. The emperor stifled opposition by engineering purges and killings. Although he seemed more indifferent than hostile toward Christianity, Commodus continued the policy of persecuting Christians and members of other secret societies.

Clement's response during the years of Commodus's Golden Age was characteristic of the teacher; he internalized a zeal for martyrdom, linking its courageous faithfulness to the soul's progress to spiritual fulfillment. Tertullian, just as characteristically, summoned believers to reject publicly and vehemently all blandishments and temptations to comply with the wiles and ways of evil rulers. Bishop Irenaeus ministered to his suffering flock and attempted to cull dissidents from among them, because he sought to lead the faithful according to God's plan for redemption.

Whether by chance or by providence, Rome was afflicted as well with fire and pestilence. Predictably, Commodus's reign ended with violence. The plotters left little to chance. They fed him a poisoned dinner and bribed his personal wrestler-confidant to strangle him as he bathed. Pent-up hatred roused the Senate to condemn his memory and a mob to desecrate his body. The heir of the philosopher-emperor was accorded the treatment of Nero and Domitian. The first months after Commodus's overthrow also resembled the aftermath of those earlier emperors. Commodus had depended on the army for support, and now the Praetorian Guard determined who would replace him. Pertinax, a sometime soldier with a reputation mottled by tales of greed and vacillation, promised the troops near Rome generous bonuses in return for their support. They responded accordingly. Time, however, was not on his side. Others were acclaimed *imperator* by their military units. Never popular with the people and supported only halfheartedly by the Senate, he was decapitated by the Praetorian Guard less than four months after Commodus was strangled. Next, the Praetorians auctioned the emperorship, and Didius Julianus was brash enough to make the highest bid. Julianus was insulted and opposed for three months by a city afraid of approaching forces led by an African, Septimius Severus. When Julianus's assassins failed to strike down the invading general, the Praetorians struck again, beheading Julianus in his bathroom. Severus, camped near Rome, was accepted as emperor by a fear-filled city.

THE SEVERANS: IRON AND BLOOD

Lucius Septimius Severus (193–211) made the Praetorians' acceptance prevail until his death eighteen years later. In the course of defeating the other serious claimant to the imperial authority and thwarting a rebellion, Severus broke the power of the Praetorians and humbled the Senate. Since he could ill afford to let regicide go unpunished, he had Commodus's assassin thrown to the lions and ordered the Senate to deify both Commodus and Pertinax. From the day he entered Rome to his death at York, the emperor made it clear that he would brook opposition from no one, least of all from Italians. To back his authority, he recruited only non-Italian soldiers, paid them handsomely for their loyalty, and sought to ensure that future emperors would be selected solely by provincial legions.

Severus was a complex man who sought power, often hesitated to grasp it, yet when he did, held it tenaciously. His family came from the land of Dido and Hannibal but had been admitted to the Roman knight class. Severus never lost his African accent, a cause for snide and necessarily whispered comment among the Roman aristocracy. From his youth onward he was intellectually inquisitive yet uncommonly given to dreams and omens. He studied in Athens, was equally proficient in Greek and Latin, studied philosophy and rhetoric, and practiced law in Rome. All the while he had recurring dreams, cast astrological projections, and was given omens indicating that one day he would be emperor. He began his public career under Marcus Aurelius, serving with distinction in spite of being accused of adultery. Under Commodus he survived charges that he consulted treasonably with astrologers regarding his becoming emperor. He held military-administrative posts in Sardinia, Africa, Spain, and Germany. After his first wife's death, and guided by another omen, he married Julia Domna, daughter of Elagabal, a priest of the sun deity in Emesa. Whether Julia was the mother of his sons is not clear, but she became an important figure. She provided a salon for literary favorites, spice for gossip, and access to Rome for syncretistic eastern cults.

Severus was unpretentious, determined, and shrewd. He ate, dressed, and behaved plainly—and worked constantly. One of his favorite watchwords was "let us toil." And toil he did. With less than happy results, he tried to reform the currency, applied African landholding policies to Italy, constructed public buildings, and furthered the codification of the laws. His travels, mostly for military purposes, took him through Palestine and Egypt. In the former, he supported some Jewish foundations but forbade conversions to Judaism and Christianity. The monuments, sacred animals, archaic wisdom, and religions of Egypt impressed the western North African deeply. He traveled through Clement's city to Memphis and Thebes. His two sons were probably in the entourage. He allowed Alexandria a local senate and worshiped in the city's great temple to Serapis. Yet he also was a conniving, often ruthless man whose anger could be fatal to others. He continued the Antoninian policy of sporadic persecutions against Christians. Sharp outbursts against them occurred in Egypt and Asia Minor during his reign. Severus crushed purported rivals, often with scant legal pretext and great bloodshed. Twelve of his eighteen years as emperor were spent commanding troops in the field. From Parthia to Britain, from the Tripolis to Germany, he and his men attempted to safeguard the borders. At the end, exhausted and hobbled with gout, he advised his sons, "Make your soldiers rich, and do not bother with anything else." His bitterness, sharpened by catching one of his sons unsheathing a dagger against him, led him to comment, "I have been everything, and it is worth nothing." At least he died of natural causes, something no other emperor was to do for eighty years.

Marcus Aurelius was Severus's model. After he dreamed that his successor would be named Antoninus, he gave his sons that surname. The elder, Julius Bassanius, was renamed Marcus Aurelius Antoninus, but preferred the nickname "Caracalla" after the Gallic cloak he popularized. His model definitely was not a Stoic emperor but his own version of Alexander the Great. Within a year of his father's death, he had his brother brutally murdered. The new sole emperor (211–217) inherited a troubled, changing realm. Caracalla's policies led to inflation and the impoverishment of small landholders. Taxes were high, discontent rife, and pressures on the borders more serious than the emperor calculated. His extension of citizenship to most freeborn men actually gave them more taxes to pay and responsibilities to fulfill than privileges to enjoy. Even before he began to rule, Caracalla already had a reputation for jealousy, wantonness, cruelty, and perhaps incest. The people of Alexandria mockingly referred to him and Julia as Oedipus and Jocasta. The emperor was not amused. Suspecting a revolt in Egypt and despising the Alexandrians, he massacred many who bore the traditional Egyptian royal name, Ptolemy, forced others into the military, and damaged the city as a warning. Since he also despised and persecuted Christians, believers who were in Alexandria probably suffered, and many fled. But nature and the gods caught up with Caracalla. While he was on a campaign in Parthia, he dismounted from his horse in order to urinate, and members of his personal staff stabbed him to death.

Sometime during the reign of Severus or his successor, Clement dropped out of sight, perhaps finding safety in Palestine or Cappadocia. Tertullian continued to fume against church, state, heretics, and other forms of demonic treachery.

VISIONS OLD AND NEW

In the beginning, when the Empire's shape was still emerging, news about the Golden Age was indeed welcome. After a century of sporadic tumult and civil war, Caesar Augustus's consolidation of authority and power in the office of the *princeps* raised the hope that Rome would provide the order necessary for an era of prosperity, justice, and peace for Rome and for those states and peoples associated with it. The Augustan pattern featured a regular succession of authority through a divinely sanctioned family. Not only did poets such as Virgil and Ovid expect and pray for the coming of a Golden Age ruled by Augustus's sons, so did many others in Asia and Africa. And neither Augustus nor his descendants discouraged pious persons in the provinces from offering sacrifices and building temples to Rome and the current emperor. After all, an age in which gods and humans commingled was one in which a holy family was needed to provide a connection between humanity and the gods as well as continuity from one generation to another.

The Long Year was traumatic for those who saw Rome as the center for and preserver of order, culture, and peace. Tacitus was right; the secret of the Empire was that emperors could be—and would be—made elsewhere than in Rome. Since the army controlled the selection process, the emperors were usually military men who, in turn, depended on the support of the legions to remain in power. Some who ruled the Empire after Nero were remarkable and talented persons. Several, whether talented or not, were caught in bloody repetitions of the Long Year. Deviations from the Augustan pattern of succession and the Augustan vision for the Empire might have been expected, but persistently cruel and erratic conduct was scarcely expected of competent and cultured persons such as Trajan and Hadrian. They seemed capable of leading humanity into a reasonable facsimile of the Golden Age. The still darker and longer years under Domitian, Commodus, and Caracalla underscored the ability of irrational and brutal persons to keep power, that is, until the iron of others deigned otherwise. Tacitus, reflecting on the events of 68–69, wrote what many victims, survivors, and observers of those and subsequent grim years probably thought: "Never surely did more terrible calamities of the Roman people, or evidence more conclusive, prove that the gods take no thought for our happiness, but only for our punishment."[24]

Visions for a hope-filled Golden Age were out of the question for Tacitus and like-minded second-century pagans. They looked back to pre-Augustan times, thinking that then leaders had integrity, the populace discipline, and the gods good will. Others were attracted to philosophical and religious teachings, communities, and rituals from Egypt, Asia, Syria, and Palestine. Often such groups blended their messages about truth and the future of humanity, the divine powers, and the order of the cosmos with Greek and Roman traditions. Obviously, Jews and Christians were among those whose messages and visions were being heard by Greco-Romans who longed for justice and peace or at least escape from the present.

Could the good news of the Golden Age be translated into the messages of these groups? Could Christian good news be rendered into terms understandable to other longing, searching women and men in the Empire? What issues and questions had to be addressed? What traditions and precedents from Greco-Roman culture could be continued? Was there still time and hope for a restored Golden Age or for a change toward a safer, more just, more promising life? Or was it too late? Was the Iron Age all that one might expect? Often while in the commander's tent, Marcus Aurelius reflected on order, life, and meaning. Perhaps his views were not good news, but he sought to make sense of the ambiguous prospects and realities that he and his fellow citizens confronted:

It is no evil for things to undergo change, and no good for things to subsist in consequence of change. Time is like a river made up of the events which happen, and a violent stream; for as soon as one thing has been seen, it is carried away, and another comes in its place, and this will be carried away too. Everything which happens is as familiar and well known as the rose in spring and the fruit in summer; for such is disease, and death, and calumny, and treachery, and whatever else delights fools or vexes them. In the series of things those which follow are always aptly fitted to those which have gone before. . . . so the things which come into existence exhibit no mere succession, but a certain wonderful relationship.[25]

4

Greco-Roman Dilemmas

All good things . . . sensible men must ask from the gods; and especially do we pray that from those mighty gods we may, in our quest, gain a knowledge of themselves, so far as such a thing is attainable. . . . For we believe that there is nothing more important for man to receive, or more ennobling for God of his grace to grant, than the truth. God gives to men the other things for which they express a desire, but of sense and intelligence, he grants them only a share, inasmuch as these are his especial possessions and his sphere of activity. For the Deity is not blessed by reason of his possession of gold or silver, nor strong because of thunder and lightning, but through knowledge and intelligence.

Plutarch *Isis and Osiris* 1

By definition a dilemma is a forced choice between two or more seemingly unsatisfactory alternatives. The opening centuries of the Common Era were dilemma-laden times. The Empire's geographical breadth and ethnic diversity promoted a profusion and confusion of cultural traditions, intellectual speculations, and religious expressions. Teachers of rhetoric and philosophy, preachers of Asian and African religions, and defenders of Greco-Roman traditions jostled with astrologers, proclaimers of new revelations, and outright swindlers to offer their versions of the truth and their ways of life to eager and anxious people. Those versions of truth and ethical patterns combined with visions and ironies to produce frustrating predicaments for pagan men and women. The horns of second-century dilemmas were exemplified by Plutarch of Chaeronea (ca. 45–120) and Lucian of Samosata (ca. 125–185).

Lucius Mestrius Plutarchus lived geographically between Athens and Delphi and symbolically between reason and revelation. An intelligent man with broad interests, he studied philosophy in Athens, lectured in Rome, and visited Egypt.[1] He held a variety of local public positions and was connected with influential persons in the Empire's capital. His dedication to reasoned discourse complemented his piety; Plutarch was a priest of Apollo, probably serving Zeus's son at the renowned shrine at Delphi. In addition, he was devoted to the Egyptian goddess Isis, and he and his wife may have been initiated into the Asian-influenced cult of the dying-rising god, Dionysus.[2] He was the very model of Greco-Roman propriety. His responsibilities and travels did not prevent him from being one of the most prolific and influential of all pagan authors. Plutarch frequently wrote about religious, philosophical, and historical subjects; and morality was his consistent theme. In his best-known work, *The Lives of the Noble Greeks and Romans*, he employed history to cite models of good and evil conduct among the famous and the powerful. The collection of his essays and treatises called the *Moralia* shows him to have been an earnest and devout person who attempted to maintain what he considered excellent in the Greek intellectual tradition and infuse it with the spiritual depth and respected antiquity of Asia and Africa. He was highly critical of those philosophers and sophists who carried on word-wars in which arguments took precedence over what he considered to be sound reason, divine inspiration, and ethics. Disdainful of philosophical fussiness and rhetorical jargon, Plutarch was committed to sensible, open, and essentially optimistic discussions.

During the last century B.C.E. and the opening centuries of the Common Era, rival philosophical schools and religious groups moved toward a general monotheism that understood one divine power to have been revealed under different guises in various cultures. While the philosophical and religious theories differed, many persons saw ethics as providing a common basis for teachings and rituals. Plutarch attempted to express that unity in diversity in his philosophical and religious writings. Although he criticized the Stoic school and disparaged the Epicureans, he and they took the intellectual and spiritual challenges seriously, debating earnestly what truth was, and how one attained it, together with how God revealed knowledge and truth to humans and how humans were to live before God and with one another.[3]

If Plutarch presented an approach to pagans that stressed the traditional and the new, the theological-philosophical and the moral, Lucian offered another option. He left his native Mesopotamia to establish his reputation and fortune throughout the Empire. Like Plutarch, he was soundly educated and well traveled, but unlike his earlier Greek counterpart, Lucian treated his audiences with discomforting satires. He became a performing public speaker whose appearances delighted and tweaked those who heard him. Relentlessly, Lucian examined popular notions about religion, philosophy, education, life after death, and the whole range of human emotions and relations, and found them all scatterbrained. His eloquent addresses, copied and imitated widely, depicted philosophers hawking their ideas much as shopkeepers extolled their wares, showed humans taking themselves with utmost seriousness while behaving in laughable ways, and cast doubt on cherished values.[4] Nothing seemed sacred, and his criticisms could leave thoughtful persons not only skeptical but cynical about gods and humans.

Both Plutarch and Lucian questioned and criticized their societies and cultures. Plutarch attempted to offer intellectual, religious, and moral possibilities that accounted for familiar and different understandings of truth and ethics. His blend of mystical piety and philosophy was attractive, but could it stand up under the harsh pressures of the second century? Lucian, on the other hand, was satirical and sharp-tongued. From the Euphrates to France and from Italy to Africa, he poked at obvious foibles, contradictions, and superficialities that have counterparts in most societies. Claiming that his only purpose was to amuse his listeners, he nevertheless engendered a wry skepticism toward all claims to truth, a skepticism too plain to avoid and too thorny to embrace wholeheartedly. The approaches represented by Lucian and Plutarch indicate the span of alternatives with which sensible and sensitive Greco-Romans struggled as they faced four significant dilemmas: unity and pluralism, human nature, *paideia*, and religious diversity.

THE DILEMMA OF UNITY AND PLURALITY

The basic philosophical problem is "the one and the many." Expressed in fields such as philosophy, politics, religion, and science, the issue raised by ancient Greek thinkers still challenges thoughtful persons. Put succinctly, the question is whether a single principle or many different principles undergird existence. Behind the old, perhaps original philosophical problem were questions such as: from what element or elements was this world made? These questions were readily transposed to cultural, intellectual, and spiritual levels. Do we live in a universe or a multiverse? Are humans of the same essence regardless of their ethnic and cultural differences? Does one moral law bind all societies, or are cross-cultural resemblances only coincidences? Is there one way, or are there many ways, to know the truth about humanity, divinity, and their destinies?

If the answer to these questions is "many," then the prospects for enduring harmony, mutual understanding, political stability, religious sharing, and intellectual growth are indeed dim. In such a world, power rules and life makes no sense. Perhaps because Greco-Roman society was immensely varied as well as multiethnic, the issue of the one and the many could not be resolved, but Greco-Roman philosophy, religion, and politics tried to find unity and order in the cosmos, the state, the soul, and the gods in spite of the evidence of bewildering pluralities.

"Logos," a central and many-faceted ingredient in the ways thinkers responded to the dilemma of the one and the many, defies definition.[5] Coming from a Greek root meaning "speak," logos carries the basic meaning "word." Speech as logos is distinguished from the sound of the voice (*phōnē*) what passes through the mind (*phantasia*). Word is spoken, thought, written; arranged in discourses, treatises, laws; and expressed as theories, formulas, and reflections. "Logos" is used for words spoken before an audience and between persons, e.g., talk, rumor, argument, debate, legal case. It may be translated as order, reason, tangible thing, subject, calculation, explanation. Rhetoric and grammar employ logos as logic, that is, how to put words together as premise, thesis, and conclusion. Knowledge and wisdom are forms of logos, so too are divinely given oracles and insights.

"Logos" implies a relationship between reasoning beings. On the one hand, Greeks had few hermits; on the other hand, they had little patience with monologues. They were thinkers and talkers, logos people. Logos seemed to dwell in all, giving order, balance, and unity to things and processes. In short, logos made *kosmos*, harmonious arrangement, possible. The one-in-many-meaninged logos was reason, a sense of comprehensibility in which boundaries and purposes could be discerned. For people who experienced geographical, cultural, ethnic, and political fragmentation, logos offered a means to understand and structure individual and communal life. Since Greeks did not have a monopoly on logos, it provided a bond between the many peoples of the Empire. Logos could express the one that undergirded the pluralisms of human existence. Plato (ca. 428–347 B.C.E.) reflected that when it came to logos the Greeks were but children in comparison to the Egyptians.[6] Logos also offered a link to the realm of the divine. From the earliest philosophers, such as Heraclitus (ca. 540–480 B.C.E.), logos was considered a divine principle that ordered existence and made knowledge possible. Heraclitus perceived the possibility that a fundamental unity or primal element, fire, was the origin of all diversity.

Plato's discussions of logos were particularly important for Greco-Roman pagans, Jews, and Christians. At a basic level, he linked logos to orderly statement, the reasoning activity within a person, and that which transcends opinions and appearances. He held that logos accounted for the truth of statements and made statements possible about the parts that constitute a thing. Logos dealt with complex matters rather than with first principles. First principles are simply there; they are given, and we cannot probe behind them. Implicitly in most and explicitly in several of his works, the Athenian philosopher used "logos" to describe the great cosmos (macrocosm) and its parts, including humans. Logos, then, was a power that related to order in the universe and the ability of humans to comprehend its parts.

Plato moved to another level when he broached the role of logos in the inner workings of the state and in a human being. The well-ordered state was a magnification of the well-ordered soul; both were ruled and moved by logos.[7] A human, he held, was part of the great cosmos and was a mini-cosmos (microcosm). Within a person, logos was the means, action, and power that brought about order, knowledge, and proper conduct. The soul contained the capacities to reason, to will, and to desire. In the well-ordered soul, the reasoning capacity ruled the other capacities as a chariotcer controlled the horses. A properly governed soul was characterized by understanding, forti-tude, and temperance, all harmonized by justice. The reasoning capacity's rule could be overthrown, however, making the soul subject to the lurchings of will and desire. The disordered soul's reasoning capacity was harnessed by the other capacities and made to rationalize greed and lust, cowardice and arrogance, injustice and cruelty.

A third level opened the way for the soul to be healed and for its order to be restored. At this juncture Plato linked logos to the one and the many in relation to the soul. Plato held that reality, knowledge, and order were possible only where there was no change. Change made the cosmos slippery; a chang-ing cosmos eluded the grasp of certainty, leaving people with only appearances and opinions. There must be, Plato reasoned, a changeless and divine realm of eternal forms or universals, the principles which united all. Briefly, the forms are the universal concepts (*ideai*) that people perceive in the presumedly objective world of sense experience. For example, many particular things are considered beautiful, so there must be a constant model—beauty itself—which is somehow reflected by or in the objects humans see. Plato was convinced that these overarching forms were not simply mental constructs but resided in transcendent constancy.[8] Further, beyond that divine realm and in remote, all-knowing serenity was the One, the Being—God.

Souls, according to Plato, were immortal, and their home was in the eternal realm where they contemplated the divine forms. When a soul was summoned by divine decree to enter the world of change and to reside in a body, the soul's direct vision of the forms was suppressed and lodged in the reasoning capacity's memory, whence recollections of the vision might be retrieved through the promptings of logos employed by someone such as a teacher. Memories of the eternal order were suppressed even more in disordered souls, and such souls were damaged and stained by their earthly experiences. Plato described the human condition in the world of change and opinion by likening people to prisoners facing the rear of a dimly lighted cave.[9] They saw only the flickering shadows of the divine forms projected on the wall, not the forms themselves. Mistaking the shadows for the forms (that is, confusing the eternal realities with the objects they experienced), they saw pluralities rather than unity and engaged in arguments about reality on the basis of sense perception and appearances. Occasionally, someone was enabled to leave the cave, see the light shining outside, and gain insight into the true nature of the cosmos. That person, on returning to the cave, informed the others of the vision granted to him or her. The light was logos, and the discourse about what was seen in that light was framed and expressed in reason-logos. Plato used this allegory to teach that logos was the divine light that assisted the soul in understanding the complexities and issues of the world of change, illumined it about the eternal realm of truth, goodness, and beauty, and opened the way for the soul to probe and receive insights about the One. Death was the means through which the immortal soul was delivered from the weight of the body and the corrupting changes of appearance and opinion. On the way back to its true home, the soul went through a sometimes harsh cleansing process, through which it was purged of the stains and corruptions it incurred during its earthly course. Restored to its true self and its true home, the soul contemplated the divine forms until it was called upon to descend into another body.[10]

Plato's speculations about logos, the forms, and the soul reflect complex developments. In the *Timaeus*, Plato spun a "likely story" about the origins of the cosmos. The myth included a creator-shaper (the Demiurge) who fashioned the gods and the world while keeping a metaphorical eye on the divine forms or models. The Demiurge, in turn, was subject to the distant Supreme Deity, and the cosmos was animated by a soul–life power.

At his school, the Academy, Plato and the teaching staff, like the sophists and the other philosophers in their schools, taught public (exoteric) and confidential (esoteric) courses.[11] The master left his successors with some unresolved questions and several avenues to pursue the answers. Among the critical areas were how to bridge the perceived gap between the changeless dimension of reality and the world of change; how to relate both realms to the Deity; and how to understand the origin and destiny of the soul. The later Platonic tradition expanded his positions in ways that he probably would have accepted at some points and rejected at others. One consistent mark of the various forms of Platonism was a preference for the contemplative and mystical sides of religion over public worship and sacrifices. By the second century B.C.E., many within Platonic schools identified the divine logos and the eternal forms with thoughts in the mind of God and envisioned these thoughts as emanating from God's mind so that they made, harmonized, and provided for the cosmos. By 230 C.E., philosophers systematized these emanations still further. Consequently, historians of philosophy recognize three broad periods in the Platonic tradition: Platonism (ca. 400–200 B.C.E.), Middle

Platonism (ca. 200 B.C.E.–230 C.E.), and Neo-Platonism (after 230 C.E.). Plutarch was a major popularizer of Middle Platonism and melded it with his Delphic piety.

Attempts to resolve the problem of the one and the many using logos concepts were not unique to the varieties of Platonism. The ancient mystical-philosophical guild founded by Pythagoras (ca. 580–500 B.C.E.) influenced Plato and the Academy profoundly. The Pythagoreans, an erudite if somewhat elitist and obscure school, saw number as the underlying reality of the cosmos. The Peripatetics or Aristotelians disagreed with the major Platonic positions, denying the forms an existence separate from particular objects. Stoicism adapted ideas from these positions, as well as from the highly critical and deliberately eccentric Cynics, in a system centered on logos.

From its start, Stoicism reflected its Asian origins and syncretistic tendencies.[12] Its founder, Zeno, first attached himself to an Athenian Cynic and then entered the Academy. While he was duly impressed with the Socratic method of seeking truth by asking and answering questions, he rejected the Platonic view of the immaterial realm of the forms and Plato's dismissal of knowledge based on experience. Instead, Zeno adapted Heraclitus's ideas on fire and logos along with the Socratic method when he established his own school in the *Stoa Poikilē* (the Painted Porch, a public colonnaded area). Either he or his successor, Cleanthes, divided philosophy into logic, ethics, and physics, an arrangement that was critical for later schools of philosophers and sophists. The cosmology advanced by the Stoics held that all things originated from and returned to a divine logos-fire. The cosmos came into being from fire and was returned to fire on a regular schedule of cycles, each of which lasted for thousands of years.

More important for the widespread influence of Stoicism was its logos-concept, which it used to promote human ethics and understanding of cosmic unity. Logos was synonymous with divinity, reason, law, and nature. Because all came from the divine fire, logos was present in whatever existed. Sometimes the presence was described as different qualities of logos-seed (*logos spermatikos*) planted in and capable of being germinated throughout all things. Stoics suggested understanding that logos in several dimensions. First, the cosmos was permeated with divinity, reason, nature, or law. Anything that happened naturally, then, was divine, reasonable—and therefore good. Logos was the divine providential power that was responsible for making and running the cosmos. It was the law and directive principle within all existence. Humans were to accept what logos-nature gave them; the willow, which bent with the wind, endured, while the oak, which resisted, was toppled.

Second, because logos was everywhere, men and women were at home in all places and with all people in the world. The world was depicted as a great city (*polis*) in which all persons were citizens, that is, cosmopolitans. Stoicism thereby offered a human unity that transcended geography and ethnic particularity. A corollary was the presence of the divine logos-seed in each person: humans had within themselves a divine entity. No matter what their social status might be, slave or free, they were all one in the logos. Stoic ethics enjoined people to recognize and respect the logos within themselves and all others. It would be an irrational error to allow the logos in oneself to suffer disgrace either at the hands of someone else or through one's own actions. It would be equally wrong to dishonor the logos in someone else. Tyrants were able to kill the body, but they could not harm the logos within. A Stoic was to seek apatheia. Far from being apathy in the modern sense of lethargy or indifference, apatheia was a resolute imperturbability, the equanimity sought by Antoninus. It was the avoidance of passions such as greed, lust, and pride. Instead, the Stoic was to be zealous for justice, moral excellence, and integrity. The early second-century C.E. Stoic, Epictetus, summed up Stoic courage and steadiness by urging his followers to be purple, that is, to be that touch of noble logos-brilliance in the middle of an otherwise gray society.[13]

A third dimension returned to the theme of cosmic recurrence. Death was simply the restoration of one's own logos to the cosmic logos. Death was not to be lamented but accepted as part of the divine and reasonable natural law. Sorrow over another person's death resulted from an attempt by the bereaved to hold on to, to possess, the one deceased. In one's own case, death was neither to be feared nor avoided; the logos went on. Martyrdom and suicide— especially of the aged and infirm—were acceptable because each was in harmony with logos-nature.

Due to their use of logic and their bent toward organization, Stoics were voluble speakers and energetic arrangers. Chrysippus made logic into a complicated philosophical discipline, and Stoic ethical terms passed into general usage in the Empire. From ca. 200 B.C.E. to the beginning of the Common Era, Stoicism entered a period (the "Middle Stoa") during which it was open to Platonizing tendencies and Platonists often absorbed Stoic views, especially in matters of ethics and curricular structure. While it is debated whether Epictetus and Marcus Aurelius continued to blend Middle Platonism with Middle Stoicism, they reflected the debates about proper Stoic teaching and practice. In the latter part of the first century and through the second century C.E., Stoicism underwent an internal turmoil in which many pressed for a return to the original teachings of Zeno, Cleanthes, and Chrysippus. The rise of "Late Stoicism" with its rejection of Platonizing elements demonstrated to many that even a philosophy to which emperors adhered might be susceptible to fragmentation and conflict.

Stoics and Platonists were not alone in sharing ethical and theological categories. Jews, especially those living in the Roman Empire, held analogous ideas about one God, the divine Logos, the Law (which was known as Wisdom and identified with the special revelation given to Israel), the soul, and the end of the age. Platonists, Stoics, and Jews were not intellectual strangers as the Common Era opened. They adapted and developed ideas with reference to one another as well as separately. Still, the dilemma of the one and the many resisted resolutions, especially when those resolutions seemed tantalizingly close. As in Socrates' time (ca. 469–399 B.C.E.), philosophical attention turned toward basic questions about human nature and conduct.

THE DILEMMA OF HUMANITY

Aretē is the key to Greek views of humanity. Often translated as virtue, *aretē* is more accurately rendered as excellence and goodness. "One and many" style questions were raised about *aretē*. Was there one *aretē* common to all, or many *aretai* depending on factors such as race, gender, social class, and occupation? Was *aretē* one, and were the different excellencies in crafts and intellectual pursuits part of an overall unity, just as the nose and the eye were parts of a single face? Was *aretē* innate or was it acquired—that is, did a human come equipped with a set quantity of *aretē* or could it be taught and learned? Could *aretē* be increased or diminished? If so, by what means—and if not, what accounted for differences in character and ability among persons of similar backgrounds and experiences? Did a community's ideas about *aretē* remain the same or change? Answers to questions such as these were critical to Greek and then Greco-Roman perspectives on human nature, sociopolitical institutions, and religious-intellectual developments. These questions and answers eventually confronted Christians and influenced them powerfully.

Whether or not *aretē* changed, Greek concepts of and expressions about it contained two consistent themes: *aretē* was the excellence a person needed in order to fulfill his or her role in society with competence and honor, and the person of *aretē* was one who spoke wisely and well and whose actions brought renown to the person and the community. Neither the *Iliad* nor the *Odyssey*, attributed traditionally to the poet Homer (ca. 750–650 B.C.E.),[14] was much concerned with ordinary people and slaves; each centered on a male-dominated, warrior-oriented aristocracy in which few women were given more than passing attention. The ideal Homeric man was someone of noble birth, preferably with a god or goddess in his lineage, who spoke wise, persuasive words in the council of warrior-leaders as well as did deeds that brought honor to his family and community. The ideal woman was modest, hospitable, and faithful to her husband, and managed his household competently.[15] By the fifth century B.C.E., *aretē* as excellence in speech (logos) and valor in deeds of battle was transformed into integrity and conduct in the affairs of the community or *polis*. The playwright Euripides (ca. 485–406) often reversed the roles of the traditional heroes with commoners, women, and slaves.[16] The supposedly noble were seen to be knaves, and those whom society marginalized were persons of moral strength and human decency.[17] In the process, he also called into question the *aretē* of the gods, asking if the stories about them were only tales concocted by humans to justify human actions, or whether perhaps the gods willed the misery of humanity.[18]

Characteristically, Plato approached *aretē* with intellectual rigor even in the heat of controversy. Conflicts with various sophists pushed him to explore *aretē* thoroughly, and in so doing, he developed themes that helped shape second-century debates between and among pagans and Christians. Briefly, the founder of the Academy held that *aretē* was one, innate, and not subject to being taught or learned as if it were something external to the soul. Plato's version of Socrates has the philosopher liken *aretē* in the soul to vision in the eye; it is innate but capable of being improved and directed. For Platonists, *aretē* was a moral-ethical excellence that a person could externalize in disciplined words and deeds. The teacher did not insert *aretē* into the soul but helped bring forth the excellence that was already there. *Aretē* in the Platonic tradition involved the soul's right ordering of understanding, fortitude, justice, and temperance.

Plato's conflicts with various sophists were reflected in a series of dialogues in which Socrates deflated those who claimed that they were able to teach their students all they needed to know in order to be wise, articulate, happy, and prosperous.[19] He accused them of lacking morals, for they not only charged for their lessons but also taught their students how to make the worst case look better. Plato, Euripides, and others caricatured the sophists, extending the root meaning of *sophos* ("wise and skilled") to "clever and cunning."[20] The sophists, however, had a better account of *aretē* than Plato reported.

Isocrates (ca. 436–338), one of Socrates' long-lived followers, also studied under the sophist Gorgias of Leontini (ca. 485–380). Gorgias derided those who disdained knowledge derived from experience in the changing realm of space and time. From Gorgias, Isocrates absorbed a love for the sound of words and the poetic quality of language, and from Socrates he gained insight into the necessity of plain, accurate speech. He established a school in which he determined that education (*paideia*) would be practical and aimed at right conduct in private as well as public life.[21] Refusing to separate the functions of philosophy from rhetoric, he claimed to be a philosopher and a sophist. Throughout his career, he combined these roles with that of statesman. Isocrates understood the sophist to be a wise person who was expert in teaching students not only eloquence but also citizenship and statecraft. He was especially critical of two types of sophists.[22] The first were the eristic sophists, that is, teachers who claimed to debate ethical issues but who were in fact more interested in stirring up controversies, making logic-chopping distinctions, and arguing merely for the sake of arguing. He was no less harsh on rhetorical sophists. One branch enjoyed making bombastic and sensational speeches in public. In reaction to this type of orator, Isocrates developed a precise style with balanced, if long, sentences. The other branch of rhetorical sophists—those who set themselves up as flamboyant courtroom professionals, the ancient equivalent of shyster lawyers—also felt his ire.

Still, Isocrates and other sophists had a view of humanity markedly different from that of the Academy. For Isocrates, the one quality that distinguished humans from other animals was that humans could be persuaded to change their ways of thinking and acting. Humans had reason (logos), and they could be taught. They were able to learn the skills or excellences *(aretai)* that made for well-ordered lives and well-ordered states. Human beings might or might not have *aretē* as an innate quality, but they could be persuaded to learn excellent ways, to shape their conduct justly, and to do honorable deeds. Logos as reason and speech was essential in the task of educating students to their full humanity. The teacher was required, he said, to cultivate rigorous, creative, and disciplined minds. Rhetorical rules and procedures were helpful and necessary, but these were not the goals of the sophist-teacher. *Aretē* was the goal, that is, excellence in being and acting as human beings in the *polis*. Timotheos, one of his grateful students, placed a statue of Isocrates in the temple at Eleusis, indicating that the old teacher's gifts came from and were directed toward the divine sources of all harmony and order.[23]

Isocrates' practicality, emphasis on the world of sense and change, and flexibility about logos and *aretē* may have helped bridge the differences among later Platonists, Stoics, and sophists. Stoics linked the logos within humans to *aretē*. Humans had the *aretē*-logos within them, yet it could be as dormant as an ungerminated seed. The task was to germinate the seed so that the *aretē*-logos would come to life and be manifested in actions and words. Epictetus reflected that bulls that lolled about the meadow or chased after insubstantial annoyances did not develop the ability to defend their herds against attacking lions. So it was with persons who did not consciously train their wills and who jumped at trivial concerns; they easily strayed into irrational and shameful conduct.[24] All persons needed the discipline, training, and incentive to externalize their divine excellence. Theoretical differences that ought to have separated the Platonic Academy, the Stoic Porch and the sophists' schools of rhetoric blurred as they joined in common approaches to morals, divinity, the soul, ethics, and society's ways of improving or externalizing the soul's *aretē*-logos. Rhetorical sophists joined by declaiming the need for logos and *aretē* to reform the morals of the Empire and its cities.[25]

Nevertheless there were dilemmas. A double-edged tension disturbed considerations of *aretē* and human nature. One was the implication that *aretē*, in spite of Euripides, was the possession of an elite. Only a few had the position and leisure to cultivate their *aretē*. Stoicism was popular, and its vocabulary became part of people's conversation; but, as with Platonism, only members of the upper class could pursue it consistently. The schools of the sophists, like those of the philosophers, charged substantial sums for their insights and training. People who had opportunities to develop their *aretē* or gain it through study and practice produced mixed results, especially if they were in positions of power. Nero, Domitian, Commodus, and Caracalla came from good, virtuous stock, but they would hardly win awards for excellence. Others who seemed to develop their *aretē* included Seneca and Servianus—and they paid with their lives for the effort. *Aretē* seemed more a wish or delusion than an innate, universal excellence.

The other edge of the tension was the widely held idea that a person was born with a fixed character, an unchangeable set of dispositions, or stamp, to her or his personality. No matter how one might try to hide or alter that disposition, it was bound to come out. Astrologers studied the birth signs and historians the childhood traits of persons, convinced that these would govern the adult's later behavior. Nero, Domitian, Commodus, and Caracalla opened their principates with clement words and acts, but soon they reverted to their true character. If character was dominant, then were persons fated to live out their types no matter what they might intend? Was there no room for change or regeneration? Many of the Empire's women, poor, slaves, and aristocrats yearned for new views of human nature and destiny. They were open to philosophical and religious messages that transcended cultural differences and class barriers. They wanted assurances of peace, not the prospect of continued struggle.

THE DILEMMA OF PAIDEIA

If *aretē* was the key to Greek and Greco-Roman understandings of human nature, then communities had to develop ways to express and form *aretē*. *Paideia* encompasses the activities and patterns a society uses to develop persons fully and form them into responsible members of the community.[26] Through *paideia*, a community transmits its values and expectations to future generations. Taken broadly, *paideia* is aptly translated as "culture." The community's public rituals, plays, dances, orations, assemblies, and even executions are elements of its *paideia*. Through these activities members learn about their society's distinguishing principles and ideals. Persons or groups that refuse to join in the community's spectacles, sacrifices, and ceremonies are suspected of subverting or opposing those principles and ideals.

The institution that most intentionally and specifically passes on the community's culture is its educational system. *Paideia*, then, is also rendered as "education." A species ensures its continuance through biological reproduction; a society reproduces itself through its *paideia*. Educational systems are a community's way of giving birth to and raising up the next generation of its members. Logically, problems in *paideia* are extensions of the wider problems and challenges that vex a society. As might be anticipated, Greco-Roman *paideia* was not exempt from the dilemmas of the Empire.

Greek and Greco-Roman *paideia* had a broad threefold structure: *propaideia*, encyclical *paideia*, and higher studies. *Propaideia* was preschool education for girls and boys. Usually, it was undertaken in the home by mothers and, depending on the family's circumstances, women servants. The children were instructed in basic religious, family, and civic traditions. Girls born to families willing and able to provide instruction in the home were able to continue their educations. At any rate, they were expected to know the principles of household management and wifely devotion. The second form, encyclical *paideia*, involved sending the family's sons to a nearby school. If the family had adequate social status and financial means, it employed a tutor-slave (*paidagōgos*) to escort the boys to school, monitor their intellectual progress, and discipline them. The curriculum in encyclical *paideia* took two major emphases. One, associated with *mousikē* and *grammatike*, embraced the disciplines associated with mental agility and intellectual development through the use of words in writing, speaking, thinking, and singing. The other dealt with *gymnastikē* and concerned bodily disciplines and dancing. It attempted to lay the foundation for speaking wisely and persuasively and for acting bravely and gracefully. The "music" curriculum included basic literacy, study of the Homeric epics, logic, arithmetic, and harmonics. Those who completed the program of general studies and who were able to go further had a pair of options for higher studies: rhetoric and dialectic.

In a formal sense, rhetoric was the province of sophists and dialectic that of philosophers. Actually, schools dedicated to rhetoric also taught courses in philosophy and philosophical methods, and schools of philosophy gave instruction in eloquent and persuasive speech. Plato distinguished sharply and harshly between his school and those of the sophists, arguing that rhetoric and dialectic were rivals in the pursuit of knowledge. Behind his animosity toward rhetoric and sophists were his understandings of *aretē* and logos, as well as his experiences with particular sophists. Philosophy or dialectic was superior to rhetoric as a way to knowledge, he claimed, because philosophy was a theoretical discipline and did not appeal to the emotions as did rhetoric.

Isocrates and the rhetorical tradition insisted that they aimed to teach persons to persuade others to make right decisions and to undertake proper actions. Rhetoric, then, was a practical way to knowledge and thus was useful in the political life of the community. Aristotle (384–322), Plato's student and founder of a rival school, altered the terms of the discussion by recognizing that dialectic and rhetoric were complementary skills or arts (*technai*) needed in daily life and formal discussions.[27] By the second century C.E., the lines between schools of rhetoric and philosophy remained, but each used the other's art. In schools of philosophy, for example, dialectic was expounded in the morning and rhetoric in the afternoon.[28] Philostratus (ca. 170–245 C.E.) signaled the shift away from the old battles when he coined the term "New Sophistic" for the period after Plato to his own time.[29]

The purpose in rhetorical education was to present as many persuasive arguments as possible about an issue so as to urge the listeners to take appropriate actions. Aristotle delineated three types of rhetorical discourse: forensic (judicial), deliberative, and demonstrative.[30] While the audiences and specific purposes of each type of speech differed, a speaker would follow the same general pattern in developing each kind of speech.[31] Forensic speeches were either accusatory or defensive. The latter category included a type called the *apologia*, or apology. The different forms of apologies were determined by the attitude of the audience and the judges toward the defendant. Demonstrative speeches praised or blamed, and deliberative speeches dealt with proper (*protreptikē*) and improper (*apotreptikē*) conduct.[32]

Although sophists were harshly criticized and also engaged in self-criticism, they were respected as experts in addressing social issues, advocating moral change, and in presenting cases in court. Frequently they adapted their techniques to Stoic ethical terms and concerns. To be sure, sophists also used increasingly complicated grammatical and euphonic devices intended to please and surprise listeners and readers. For some in the first two centuries of the Common Era, these permutations became sources of intellectual delight and sophistication, but for others they were evidence of pomposity and trickery. From the first century B.C.E. through the second century C.E., rhetoric underwent a popular revival, and a leader who did not speak clearly, persuasively, and eloquently was diminished in the eyes of those whom the leader sought to influence. Aristotle's was not the only rhetorical schema available in the Empire. Hegesius of Magnesia (ca. 275–220 B.C.E.) attempted to go behind Aristotle's structure and Demosthenes' long, balanced sentences to an earlier tradition. He stressed short sentences (even fragments), vivid expressions, and multiple examples. In its oral and written forms, the Asianic style, as it came to be called, lent itself to theatrical declamations. Asianist or Asianic rhetoric spread westward and was taken up by some lawyers in first-century B.C.E.

Rome, including Cicero's (106–43) forensic rival, Hortensius. Although it faded in Rome when Cicero won cases decisively using the disciplined traditional Western rhetoric, the style was common in Syria, Asia, and Palestine from 100 B.C.E. to 200 C.E. Among the surviving works in this style are 4 Maccabees (first century B.C.E.) and letters of Ignatius of Antioch.[33]

Dialectic differed from rhetoric in organization and intention. Aristotle held that dialectic was the theoretical art that advanced understanding through deductive reasoning.[34] Philosophers attempted to resolve issues by using reason. Consequently, Aristotle wrote that dialectic was a form of reasoning built on premises accepted by society or at least by those involved in a discussion. There were different modes of philosophical discussion, such as the dialogue, the treatise, and the lecture. Whatever the mode, the purposes were the same: intellectual training in argumentation, wide-ranging discussions to determine the truth of a particular matter, and the study of various intellectual disciplines.[35] A dialectical exercise began by posing a question or series of questions. The question was then divided into constituent parts, terms were defined, and various hypotheses tested. If possible, a conclusion was reached or at least implied.

To attract students to their schools, philosophers had to be as eloquent and persuasive as sophists. The philosopher delivered a public exhortation, sometimes called a *protreptikos*, which called upon listeners to make the proper choice for future educational development. Actually, the speech advertised what students could expect if they enrolled and studied in that school, its superiority over other rhetorical and philosophical schools, and the wisdom that advanced students would gain. The curriculum had three stages. Most persons, however, did not complete the full course.

The first stage centered on advanced logic, or the proper use of words in formulating arguments. *Logistikē* featured an intense study of syllogisms and the use of reason. Since the proper use of reason involved conduct, the new student began to deal with matters related to ethics as well as dialectics. At the entry level, the student was designated as a *phaulos* or beginner. Ethics was the next stage, and the student was called *prokopos* or progresser. Students were expected to gain mastery over their habits, passions, attitudes, and actions as they learned and practiced the school's ethical teachings as modeled by the teaching staff. Many schools followed the Stoic practice of dividing ethics into a study and practice of specific rules of conduct or duties (*kathēkonta*) and the underlying precepts or principles (*katorthōmata*). Some teachers, such as Seneca (ca. 4 B.C.E.–65 C.E.), debated which should be taught first or whether they should be taught together.[36] *Katorthōmata* engaged subjects that concerned divine matters and the school's private or esoteric teachings, and the advanced level of ethics involved oral, secret instruction. Most students probably stayed with the curriculum through *kathēkonta* and some *katorthōmata*. Those who had the ability and resources and wanted to become teachers went further. The third stage, often called *physikē* or *cosmologia*, engaged the highest studies: theology, cosmology, physics, and mathematics. Teaching in this field was considered so special that it was to be kept a secret from those who were either outside of the group or not yet able to bear its content of divine truths. To commit such wisdom to writing risked its falling into the hands of unworthy persons; therefore, the leaders of the schools insisted that the lore be imparted only orally. A person was initiated into the final stage and became a *sophos* (sage) or *philosophos*. A philosopher remained at the school if there was an opening on the faculty or he opened a school elsewhere.

The structure and process of *paideia* contained problems within itself and elicited others. Obviously, both rhetoric and dialectic thrived on debate, argument, intellectual and verbal gymnastics. Each became more and more complicated and detailed and so became more distant from most people, including those who sought guidance from teachers. Rivalries between the competing schools of the same *technē* probably were more confusing and contentious than the already existing tensions between rhetoric and dialectic. Mutual criticism undermined informed opinions about all of the schools. Furthermore, the schools underwent startling changes, so that Stoics disagreed with Stoics, and Platonists squabbled among themselves. Which carried on the honored traditions of the founders? Which, if any, was capable of transmitting the identity of the polyglot cultures of the Empire into the future? Did the custodians of the society's *paideia* still convey the community's values and traditions to the next generation? Were those values and traditions still viable? And what was the result of all the intellectual activity? Whether the emperor was a Stoic like Marcus Aurelius or a blunderer like Galba did not seem to matter. If not, what would reinvigorate or replace the Empire's identity?

THE DILEMMA OF THE DIVERSITY OF RELIGIONS

When the apostle Paul addressed philosophers in Athens, he observed that the Athenians must be very religious since they had many shrines to and statues of the gods.[37] Whether he was using rhetorical irony or a ploy to gain attention, the missionary was right; pagan society was intensely and publicly religious. Like most people until the eighteenth century, Greco-Roman pagans, Jews, and Christians lived in a "full world"; there were no gaps or spaces in the cosmos. The very word *kosmos* meant an artfully, hierarchically arranged network within which the divine powers as well as humans had their proper places. All existence, in the heavens, on earth, and in the underworld, was suffused with divine beings and powers. The divinities guided all activity.

The traditional Olympians under varying names were the divine authorities in the Empire. Their altars were in homes, on highways, and at stadiums as well as in temples. Animals in marketplace butcher shops were dedicated to them before being slaughtered for food, and libations were poured to the gods at mealtimes. The divine names were invoked at birth and death, their doings were pictured in sculpture, painting, public and private art, graffiti, whorehouses, and chaste bedchambers. The Greek gods proved their amazing adaptability by assimilating their approximate counterparts from Africa, Asia, and other parts of Europe.

As if the array of traditional gods and the introduction of deities from Asia were not enough to maintain and encourage piety, the cults of the city of Rome and of apotheosized emperors gained popular and official recognition. Veneration of the eternal city and the emperors spread particularly in the provinces of Asia, Syria, and, after the Bar Kochba revolt, even Judea. Officials called Asiarchs supervised temples and altars dedicated to the holiness of the capital and its rulers. Few emperors considered themselves divine while they lived; most of those who did were dispatched by their associates. The Empire-emperor cult attempted to establish a common base for devotion and loyalty among the different and competing claims of gods and cults in the Empire. People could hold their many rites and beliefs, yet participation in the imperial cult—no matter how superficial—acknowledged the oneness of the Empire as a community in which there was order and continuity.

The traditional religion of Greece and Rome had serious problems in the first and second centuries. Critics from within had long raised difficult questions. Euripides' characters not only asked if the stories about the gods were actually fictional tales meant to justify human actions, but also observed that people often seemed more decent than the gods. How could tales of divine lust and treachery inspire people to temperance and justice? Philologists in Alexandria interpreted the accounts of Hesiod and Homer allegorically so as to teach morality for the improvement of the soul and the state. Plutarch advised readers not to take accounts literally, but to search for deeper meanings. Reinterpretation was inevitable, yet it raised questions over whose interpretation was correct. It also raised such profound issues as whether the gods were adequate to guide such a diverse and troubled Empire. Tales of immoral priests and crooked preachers shocked and dismayed believers—and made many even more skeptical about traditional religion.[38]

Other gods from other lands had always been imported into the Greco-Roman pantheon. Herodotus (ca. 484–420 B.C.E.) reported favorably on the Egyptian deities, Osiris and Isis; Alexander was awed by the cultures of the

Nile and Euphrates, and Julius Caesar literally sought to marry East and West in his ill-starred venture with Cleopatra. The deities of Egypt and Asia provided people in the Empire with much of what they missed in the worship of the Olympians and the imperial cult. African and Asian gods made gray-eyed Athena, white-armed Hera, golden Apollo, and even Father Zeus seem small in stature and local in influence. Adonis-Dionysus-Bacchus encouraged women and men to express and purify themselves in song, dance, and even orgy. Mithras and Orpheus called upon potential converts and their devotees to struggle with the powers of darkness and death in order to make ethical commitments. Isis and Osiris, perhaps more than any of the others, promised wisdom, life, prosperity, harmony with nature, and purposeful existence now and beyond the gates of death.[39] Isis absorbed all the Great Mothers, divine virgins, and loyal spouse deities both male and female. Their names were many, but she was the One, the essence of all existence and the divine power whom the entire cosmos worshiped and glorified.

Some Egyptian and Asian cults had public ceremonies and processions in which whole cities joined and from which the municipal communities benefited. Those who entered these cults bound themselves to ethical rules, were initiated into profound mysteries, experienced rites of life and light, and discovered causes to hope and live joyfully. Through syncretistic associations of common ideas and expressions, Greek holy places such as Eleusis and Delphi were linked with Isis and Eastern gods. As adaptation and absorption progressed, questions were raised about Asian influences on Roman life and manners, *paideia*, and politics. When people were longing for truth and hope, would such a conglomeration of religious ideas and groups bring clarity or confuse matters even further? Could the traditional religion and the ideals it fostered, even the Roman identity of the Empire, survive? Indeed, should the traditional religion and the Empire itself survive?

Intellectually and spiritually, Greco-Roman society was a bundle of dilemmas. The alternatives were many and bewildering, involving risks with no assurance that the results would resolve any problems. A new cult from the Eastern provinces entered an already crowded and heated scene. It fixed on a divine human who was reputed to have imparted heavenly wisdom, who died but was proclaimed as having been raised from the dead, and who promised eternal life in a glorious realm for those initiated into his community. Sophisticated pagans saw the newcomer as a clumsy alloy of Dionysus, Mithras, and Isis, and its adherents were scarcely drawn from the leading classes of society. Yet, Greco-Romans were groping for intellectual, religious, and social moorings in an age that was anything but golden. Did God really give sensible men and women a share in knowledge and intelligence as Plutarch hoped, or was Lucian right in describing the human condition as fogbound and uncertain?

[Ignorance] is really a terrible thing, a cause of many woes to humanity; for it envelops things in a fog . . . and obscures the truth and overshadows each one's life. Truly, we all resemble people lost in the dark—nay, we are even like blind persons. Now we stumble inexcusably, now we lift our feet when there is no need of it; and we do not see what is near, but fear what is far away and extremely remote as if it blocked our path. In short, in everything we do, we are always making plenty of missteps.

Lucian of Samosata Slander 1

Part II

Challenges for Christians

Now the eleven disciples went to Galilee, to the mountain to which Jesus had directed them. When they saw him, they worshiped him; but some doubted. And Jesus came and said to them, "All authority in heaven and on earth has been given to me. Go therefore and make disciples of all nations, baptizing them in the name of the Father and of the Son and of the Holy Spirit, and teaching them to obey everything that I have commanded you. And remember, I am with you always, to the end of the age."

Matthew 28:16-20

Written during Domitian's mad and bloody reign, the Gospel of Matthew began with wise Gentiles who, following an astrological sign, found and worshiped the infant Jesus. The Gospel closed with Jesus, the risen *Dominus*, being worshiped by his followers and proclaiming that he had authority in heaven and earth. He sent his now-wise disciples to the Gentiles, charging his representatives to teach humankind all that he had commanded and to incorporate others into the promised kingdom of heaven through baptism. Finally, he assured them that he would be present among them even to the end of the age. Between the accounts of the coming of the foreign sages and the sending out of Jesus' sages, the evangelist told the story of the Messiah-Teacher who was greater than Moses. Jesus' death and resurrection were types of the end of the age, and his community both fulfilled the type of Israel and foreshadowed the fullness of God's reign. He interpreted the Law anew and summoned those who received his instruction to be wise scribes of the kingdom. At the same time, and in terms as menacing as those attributed to Moses in the wilderness, Jesus warned about false teachers who would attempt to corrupt God's truth and lead the faithful astray. He admonished them to keep from being distracted by the cares and delights of the present age, to guard their conduct, and to watch for his return. The initial responses by the disciples to their first encounter with the resurrected Jesus were awe and great joy. Yet

63

even in the Gospel's powerful *epilogos*, the author admitted that "some doubted."[1]

Who doubted? What did they doubt? Perhaps the evangelist was addressing problems and problem-makers in late-first-century Christian congregations. Throughout the Gospel, the author emphasized the need for Jesus' followers to be subject to the discipline of the church, surpass the piety and righteousness of their Jewish critics, forsake pagan behavior, and be willing to bear the brunt of persecution. "Matthew" gathered many sayings attributed to Jesus into what sound like teaching discourses more appropriate to church members of the eighties than to Palestinian Jews living a half century earlier. Doubts reported on the Galilean mountain reflected questions and frustrations about the presence of Jesus in the life of the church, the delay of the kingdom's coming, the reality of Jesus' resurrection, sins among the baptized, Jesus' role in God's plan for the cosmos, authority in the church, and relationships among Christians, Jews, and Gentiles. Similar issues about Christian theory and practice had surfaced in the fifties among Christians in Corinth and Galatia. From 80 to 100 the authors of James and the epistles associated with John struggled with Christians who disagreed with them about the human and divine aspects of Jesus, the role of wealth and the place of the wealthy believers, and the proper way to handle dissent. As the second century opened, the authors of the Pastoral Epistles (1 and 2 Timothy and Titus) and Jude were clearly on the defensive about doctrinal, ethical, organizational, and social issues. The Christian movement appeared to be in disarray, a bundle of slippery and clashing opinions.

Originally "heresy" (*hairesis*) denoted a choice or opinion, and then it came to mean a religious group, a philosophical school, or a common way of thinking. It was a short step to regarding opinions distinctly different from those held by the majority or the authorities of a larger group as heresies in the sense of odd, rejected notions. The majority, or those who had authority to speak for the majority, took the heretics to be obstinate misbelievers and subverters of what the group considered to be true.[2] Paul used the word both for the factions that threatened the unity of the Christian community but led to the recognition of genuine believers (1 Cor. 11:19) and also as a sin comparable to wrath, strife, and rebellion (Gal. 5:20). The author of 1 Timothy warned against those who taught "a different doctrine . . . and the teachings of demons" (1 Tim. 13 and 4:1). Remembering reports of Jesus' prediction that there would be troublesome claimants to the truth, the author of 2 Peter (ca. 110–15) wrote that there

will be false teachers among you, who will secretly bring in destructive opinions [heresies]. They will even deny the Master who bought them—bringing swift destruction on themselves. Even so, many will follow their licentious ways, and because of these teachers the way of truth will be maligned. And in their greed they will exploit you with deceptive words. Their condemnation, pronounced against them long ago, has not been idle, and their destruction is not asleep.

2 Peter 2:1-3

The Christian movement entered the second century with internal diversity, dissent, and disunity. It was vulnerable to both superficial and incisive criticism by Jews and pagans. Even under the best of circumstances, Christians had much material for thought and debate. The issues clustered mainly around five challenges: creation, humanity, Jesus, the church, and culture. Part II takes up each by considering the issues at stake and some Christian responses, including "minority opinions." The Matthean *epilogos* was far from the end of doubting or learning; it was the prologue to a frustrating and creative era.

There are also many rebellious people, idle talkers and deceivers . . . they must be silenced, since they are upsetting whole families by teaching for sordid gain what it is not right to teach. . . . For the grace of God has appeared, bringing salvation to all, training us to renounce impiety and worldly passions, and in the present age to live lives that are self-controlled, upright, and godly, while we wait for the blessed hope and the manifestation of the glory of our great God and Savior, Jesus Christ. He it is who gave himself for us that he might redeem us from all iniquity and purify for himself a people of his own who are zealous for good deeds. Declare these things; exhort and reprove with all authority. Let no one look down on you.

Titus 1:10-11; 2:11-15

5

The First Challenge:
Creator and Creation

> In the beginning when God created the heavens and the earth, the earth was
> a formless void and darkness covered the face of the deep, while a wind from
> God swept over the face of the waters. Then God said, "Let there be light"; and
> there was light. And God saw that the light was good; and God separated the
> light from the darkness.
>
> Genesis 1:1-4

Who created the world, and who governs it now? From what was it made
and for what purpose, if any? The word "creation" assumes that there was a
time when the world as humans recognize it did not exist. Perhaps before the
beginning a primordial matter or an array of forces brooded or churned in
the space which the world now occupies. Perhaps there was a vacuum-like
nothing instead of a chaotic something. "Creation" implies a shaping or making from what was present as raw material or a coming into existence of the
raw material. Creation is not accident; it implies an entity that fashioned the
material and forces in a purposeful manner. The purposes and their results
do not have to be good, at least as humans might reckon goodness. The
"entity" might be elemental forces just as much as it might be a god. As the
Timaeus indicated, a creator does not need to be the highest power or intelligence in existence.

Questions about creator and creation deal with more than how time and
space started. Accounts about origins reflect a community's understanding
and experience of life's beginning and purpose. This understanding, in turn,
is fundamental to the community's religious beliefs and rituals, identity, and
relationships with other peoples. Often the same group has several stories

about the way things began. The different myths, even when logically contradictory, correlate experiences and attitudes from the community's past with
its present hopes and anxieties.

Because their community grew in, and then out of, the Jewish community,
Christians absorbed and adapted Jewish accounts of creation in the Septuagint
and other writings. Christians also were influenced by creation stories from
Greco-Roman and Egyptian sources. Under pressures such as those generated
by frustration over the parousia, persecution, and internal debates, members
of the church began to raise questions about the Creator and the creation.
Speculation, discussion, and outright argument about creation immediately
raised the problem of the origin of evil and led further to questions about
human nature, Jesus, the church, and society. In other words, the challenge
of understanding the Creator and the creation was the basic theological issue
facing the church throughout the second century—and is still an issue for the
Christian community today.

OLD TESTAMENT ANSWERS

Who created and governs the world? Clearly enough, the Bible said that God
created the world. But the Bible was not clear about how God created the
world and whether God controlled the world. There were four, perhaps five,
distinct accounts of the world's creation in the Old Testament. Each affirmed
that God was the Creator, and none described God making the world out of
nothing. Something was there, but how that something came to be was not
considered by the biblical writers.

The first chapter of Genesis described God gradually calling forth a harmonious, interdependent heavens and earth from the watery, formless mass.
God's command was a sufficient cause for matter to respond obediently and
constructively. At each step in that account, God pronounced the results good;
finally, the totality was judged to be "very good." The Deity's dignity and
power were never questioned, nor was there any hint that the divine will was
anything but benevolent. Human beings were made in God's image and likeness, given authority to rule creation, and enjoined to have offspring.

The second account dealt less with creation itself than with the origins of
human relationships with God, other humans, and the world.[1] Beginning with
a desert, the Maker shaped the first human from the dust of the ground,
breathed God's own life-breath into the creature, and gave Adam authority
over the garden in which the human was placed. Eventually the primal being
was differentiated into a male and a female, and the couple enjoyed close
fellowship with God until an act of disobedience led to their expulsion from

their first home. The wily serpent had triggered the human desire to be like divinities, knowing all things. According to the author, human transgression of God's command was catastrophic. The earth lost its naturally generous fertility, women were afflicted with pain in childbirth and men with burdensome fatigue in toil—and soon brother murdered brother.

The third and fourth accounts, if they are separate myths, reflect Israel's assimilation of some of its neighbors' stories. Mesopotamians described the created world as the result of a battle between the dragon-forces of the ocean depths and the champion of the sky gods. The victorious heavenly deity killed the serpent-dragons who sought to preserve the primordial chaos of the seas. The world was often described as made out of the corpse of the matriarchal leader of the forces of destruction and the celestial bodies from the blood of her consort. A world built on such foundations might degenerate into the disorder out of which it came. Canaanites, too, regarded the ocean as a menace. It was the power of sterility and death, a monster that only a more powerful sky deity could keep within its bounds.[2] Psalmists and prophets referred to the Creator's slaying a dragon and commanding the raging sea to stay in its assigned place and even ordering the waters to be still.[3] God, in these accounts, battled hostile forces within the material from which creation was wrestled. Death, destruction, and evil lurked almost as unfinished portions of the world that resisted God's creative design.

Proverbs, Wisdom of Solomon, Sirach, and Baruch differed from the other biblical stories. Perhaps reflecting Egyptian traditions, these accounts gave God a female colleague, Wisdom. Regarded in the first instance as "skill" or "intelligence" piously used, Wisdom was also hypostasized, that is, transformed into a principle or power with personal attributes and existence. She was the firstborn of all creatures and the master worker who carried out God's creative plans.[4] Sirach, Wisdom of Solomon, and Baruch also emphasized the role of Wisdom in creating the world and guiding humans. In her was a spirit

> that is intelligent, holy, unique, manifold, subtle, mobile, clear, unpolluted, distinct, invulnerable, loving the good, keen, . . . all-powerful, overseeing all, and penetrating through all spirits that are intelligent, pure, and altogether subtle. . . . For she is a breath of the power of God, and a pure emanation of the glory of the Almighty. . . . For she is a reflection of eternal light, a spotless mirror of the working of God, and an image of his goodness.[5]

Whatever existed, then, was formed in her presence and could be guided and fulfilled by her. Wisdom was the "one" in the "many" of the world's diversities.

She also was identified with a personalized version of God's Word. Genesis described the Creator speaking the world into existence. The Word, often connected to the prophets' oracles and pronouncements, was described as a powerful force, a fire, an agent of judgment, a revealer carrying out God's will. The Wisdom of Solomon described the Word as God's angel of judgment who leaped from the heavenly throne to destroy Egypt's firstborn (18:15). Obviously, Wisdom-Word could be joined with Stoic-Platonic understandings of logos.

If the question "Who created the world?" was still answered "God," the answer was nuanced with diverse traditions and ideas about the presence of another with God and the response of the material from which the world was made. Diversity also entered the biblical understanding of God's control of the world. Certainly, the thrust of the Old Testament was to underscore the Lord's sovereign power over all. The Creator and Redeemer of Israel was regarded as one, the sole deity to be worshiped and obeyed by the covenant people. Sometimes Old Testament writers took for granted the existence of other divinities but subjected them to Israel's Lord. Nations apart from Israel might be described as assigned by God to be ruled by lesser divinities.[6] By the mid–sixth century B.C.E., the claim was made that other gods did not exist at all. A theoretical and practical result of such a thoroughgoing monotheism was the affirmation that the Lord was responsible for more than punishing the faithless and disobedient; God made light and darkness, peace and evil.[7] The concept of an evil being or beings hostile to God appeared in late writings that were incorporated into the Old Testament. The accuser (śāṭān in Hebrew, diabolos in Greek) in the prologue to Job and in Zech. 3 was still God's servant, but the śāṭān-diabolos who led David to make a census of the people (1 Chron. 21:1) seemed to act apart from God's will.[8] The visions concluding the mid-second-century B.C.E. book of Daniel indicated that Israel was protected by a national guardian angel–prince, Michael, and that perhaps other nations were governed by guardians hostile enough to the Ancient of Days that they opposed God's people. Did God govern the world? Was God responsible for all that happened, even the unmerited suffering of those who were faithful to the Lord's ways?

By the second century B.C.E., Jews were thinking through their plight as a people caught between the major powers of the Mediterranean, seeking to be faithful yet being dominated by pagans. Even when they achieved a measure of self-determination under the Maccabees, their rulers divided and the resulting civil war brought them under Roman control. Something was radically wrong with events and relationships in God's world.

AN INTERTESTAMENTAL ANSWER

What went wrong? Perhaps God had relinquished authority over the world temporarily and would resume sovereignty according to some plan humans did not currently understand. Or the Creator might be malignant or defective.

Several attempts were made to explain the disorder and evil in the world. A fragment of story preserved in Gen. 6:1-4 was more important to many Jews and first-century Christians than the account about Adam and Eve.[9]

> When people began to multiply on the face of the ground, and daughters were born to them, the sons of God saw that they [the daughters of men] were fair; and they took wives for themselves of all that they chose. Then the LORD said, "My spirit shall not abide in mortals forever, for they are flesh; their days shall be one hundred twenty years." The Nephilim [LXX "giants"] were on the earth in those days—and also afterward—when the sons of God went in to the daughters of humans, who bore children to them. These were the heroes [LXX "giants"] that were of old, warriors of renown.

The account was elaborated by several authors from about 160 B.C.E. to 200 C.E. One of the writings, *Enoch*, was considered Scripture by some first- and second-century Christians.[10] The complicated account in *Enoch* may be summarized briefly. God created the world, arranging hierarchies of angels, beings, and things. An angelic rank, the Watchers, was assigned to oversee human affairs. Many leading Watchers lusted after "the daughters of men" and left their celestial places to have sexual intercourse with women. These rebels became the "fallen angels," or devils. Their descent caused horrendous cosmic disorder as some stars and astral beings joined them. The displaced astral beings became wandering deceivers (planets) and other malignant luminaries. As serious as this was in the heavens, the situation on earth was worse. The fallen angels paid the cooperative women and their menfolk with stolen, distorted heavenly secrets. Using the purloined knowledge, humans developed idolatry, philosophy, music, dancing, cosmetics, war, poetry, drama, witchcraft, jewelry making, adultery, fornication, lust, city life, murder—in short, all the evils, corruptions, and sins of humanity, plus key features of humanity. But the worst was yet to come. The women gave birth to semi-divine giants who tyrannized the earth. They became the demons. Eventually, God's faithful angels defeated and imprisoned the devils and demons in a waterless pit at the edge of the world. For some reason known only to God, God allowed one-tenth of the demons and devils to roam the earth, testing humanity, until the terrible day of judgment. On that day, all evil beings would be condemned to eternal punishment. In the meantime, however, the evil ones wandered the earth, possessing human and animal bodies, setting up pagan worship, raising storms, causing natural disasters, and tempting, as well as persecuting, God's people. Until the last day and the establishment of God's rule over a re-created earth, the marauding Watchers and their offspring seemed to control the world. Creation and its human inhabitants needed to be saved.

Saved? Salvation carried a double meaning. In light of the *Enoch*-style demonology, salvation meant escape from demonic bondage and from God's wrath upon those who gave themselves to the devils. Yet not everyone was ready to accept the implications of the Enochian view that, in effect, the devil was the god or ruler of this world, at least in the present. Others saw salvation as the fulfillment, or consummation, of God's creative activity. For them, life now was a process of growth, an educational discipline, a journey to a glorious destiny willed by the Creator. They attempted to see a benevolent God working within the threats and disasters of life, drawing all to fruition in a heavenly future.

PHILO OF ALEXANDRIA'S ANSWER

Rome was the Empire's political capital, Alexandria its intellectual center. Located on the outcropping of the wide Nile Delta, Alexandria was a crossroads for merchants and thinkers from Britain to India and from Europe to Ethiopia. The city's large and well-established Jewish population experienced sporadic hostility from local as well as imperial authorities. One leading figure, Philo, wrote treatises that presented Judaism as the original and truest philosophy.[11] According to him, Abraham taught the Egyptians the basics of philosophy, and Moses—God's specially endowed philosopher—revealed to the Egyptians, and then to the Hebrews in the first five books of the Scripture, as much of the heavenly philosophy as they were able to bear. Various Gentiles, chiefly the Greeks, derived their versions of the truth from the Egyptians. In the process of transmission, the Egyptians and other Gentiles misunderstood and perverted the truth received from Moses. The different schools of philosophy and sophistry as well as the poets and dramatists were correct when they agreed with Moses but fell into corruption when they departed from him. From his own perspective, Philo did not borrow from or develop a synthesis of Middle Platonism, Stoicism, Pythagoreanism, and Judaism; he merely returned to the divine truths on which the pagan systems were dependent and from which they had strayed.

He opened his study of creation by observing that "for the sake of the God-beloved author [Moses] we must be venturesome even beyond our power. We shall fetch nothing from our own store, but, with a great array of points before us, we shall mention only a few, such as we may believe to be within reach of the human mind when possessed by love and longing for wisdom."[12] Philo's "few" points from the great array stretched into two interpretive treatises on Gen. 1–3.[13] He claimed that Moses opened his exposition on philosophy with the creation in order to set the context for the revelation of the divine Law. The description of the beginning echoed Stoic views of law, nature, logos, and divine harmony: "It consists of an account of the creation of the cosmos, implying that the cosmos is in harmony with the law, and the law with the cosmos, and that the man who observes the law is constituted thereby a loyal citizen of the cosmos (cosmopolitan) regulating his doings by the purpose and will of nature, in accordance with which the entire cosmos itself is also administered."[14] His themes were present in Middle Stoicism and in Middle Platonic interpretations of the *Timaeus*.

Philo depicted not one but two interrelated worlds. The first and superior cosmos was the one that existed in the mind of "the Being" (God). Just as the plan for a city was shaped in the mind of an architect before a stone was laid, God conceived a faultless, eternal, intelligible pattern. The pattern reposed in the Mind of God. Middle Platonists would recognize this intelligible plan-city as the realm of the eternal forms. According to Platonic and Philonic logic, because it was in the divine Mind, the plan could be discerned only by enlightened minds. The second cosmos was the realm perceived by the senses: "So when [God] willed to create this visible cosmos, he first fully formed the intelligible cosmos, in order that he might have the use of a pattern (paradigm) wholly God-like and incorporeal in producing the material world, as a later creation in the very image of an earlier, to embrace in itself objects of perception of as many kinds as the other contained objects of intelligence."[15] Philo held that the cosmos of the forms had "no other location than the divine Logos, which was the author of this ordered frame."[16] The Logos, for Philo, was the Mind of God, in which resided the divine patterns; and the Logos was also the artificer or direct maker of the visible world. From a Platonic view, the Logos had Demiurge-like functions, while from a Stoic view logos permeated the world. Philo's fellow Jews could take his Logos as an expression of Wisdom, especially as expressed in Proverbs and the Wisdom of Solomon. The Alexandrian did not make clear, however, whether the Logos was related to God as a beam of light to its source, or was a superior angelic creature below the supreme God, as Wisdom was according to Prov. 8. That ambiguity would be raised repeatedly among Christians in later generations.

Philo continued the metaphor of a city. An architect thought not only about buildings and streets, but also about the various inhabitants of the projected city. God also conceived of those who would live in the cosmopolis. In the Logos-Mind, therefore, are the incorporeal beings, that is, the orders and ranks of angels and other celestial powers. The Logos employed these in the actual construction and care of the visible cosmos-city. Present as well in the Logos-Mind was the pattern or paradigm of humanity. The pattern was in the image and likeness of the Logos, and the rational portion of the souls of earthly women and men reflected the likeness of the heavenly human pattern.

When Philo dealt with issues related to the governance of the world, he relied on understandings based chiefly in the Septuagintal Wisdom literature and Middle Stoicism. While the analogy has limitations, it appears that Philo considered God to be like the architect, and the Logos like a contractor who engaged a network of divine subcontractors in the construction of the visible world. The Logos then entered into the visible cosmos as the divine reason, arranging all things through nature and law, so as to guide the cosmos according to God's plan. Because humans were related to the Logos through the heavenly pattern by means of reason (logos), humans could know some things about the eternal cosmos and God through the Logos. Indeed, the role of Scripture, interpreted through allegories, was to link the earthly human mind with the divine patterns and from that realm to relate humanity to the Being, for allegories were "modes of making ideas (forms) visible," lifting the earthly human mind to ponder the realities of the divine and timeless world.[17]

Who was the creator, from what was creation made, and who ruled it now? Philo described a hierarchical system that reached from the supreme unknowable Deity through the Logos and divine powers into the structures of the visible world and the minds of humans. The eternal realm provided paradigms for the things and relationships of the earthly world, and the whole was compassed about and permeated with divine Reason, God's Logos. There was no room for absolutely evil entities, for whatever existed on earth had its paradigm in the Mind of the supremely good God. Distortions of reason and disordered relationships within the soul were the sources of misfortune and immorality.

SOME CHRISTIAN ANSWERS

Platonists, Aristotelians, and Stoics held that there was a "something" from which all was made. For them, the creator was the molder, crafter, and shaper of some raw or undifferentiated stuff. Logically, however, the primeval matter would then be as eternal as God was; and matter might be understood as a hostile co-deity with the good God of creation. The Jewish emphasis on the sovereignty of Israel's God led to the conviction that before any matter existed, God formulated and planned all that would come into existence, so that even the raw material that formed the basis of all else came through God and not through another power.[18] Works such as Philo's and the first-century writings 2 Esdras and 2 Apocalypse of Baruch were among those that implied that God created the world out of nothing. The first clear reference in a Jewish writing to a "creation out of nothing" occurred as a passing comment during a torture session described in 2 Macc. 28:7. To claim that the Lord called into existence even the matter and forces of the cosmos was a confession of faith about the supremacy of God's power from the beginning through the fulfillment of the world; it was not originally a reasoned statement about cosmology. First-century Christian authors whose works came to be part of the New Testament appear to have agreed with the position that prior to the beginning of the divine creative activity, there was only God. Characteristically, the Christians connected Jesus to the creation of the world, and just as characteristically, they expressed that connection in different ways.

First, Paul used the idea that God created the world out of nothing to emphasize the promise of the resurrection of the dead when Jesus returned in glory.[19] The same point seems to have been in the mind of another author, who, writing of the sufferings of Jesus, said, "It was fitting that God, for whom and through whom all things exist, in bringing many children to glory, should make the pioneer of their salvation [Jesus] perfect through sufferings."[20] Second, and more important, Christians identified Jesus with the divine principle and action whereby the cosmos was made—obviously, long before Jesus was born in Palestine. As was the case with creation out of nothing, assertions about the role of Jesus as a preexistent being or emanation from God who was the actual artificer of the world began as confessions of faith and not as philosophical statements about cosmology. In a letter attributed to Paul, Jesus was described in terms Jews used for Wisdom: "He is the image of the invisible God, the firstborn of all creation; for in him all things in heaven and on earth were created . . . all things have been created through him and for him. He himself is before all things, and in him all things hold together."[21] In a similar but even more developed manner, themes about God speaking the world into existence, Wisdom, and logos became prominent in the Fourth Gospel:

In the beginning was the Logos, and the Logos was with God, and the Logos was [a?] God. He was in the beginning with God. All things came into being through him, and without him not one thing came into being. What has come into being in him was life, and the life was the light of all people. The light shines in the darkness, and the darkness did not overcome [understand] it. . . . And the Logos became flesh and lived among us . . . full of grace and truth.[22]

When expressing themselves about the power or powers that governed the world in the present, Christians relied upon Jewish responses. The *Enoch*-style demonology ran through the Gospels of Matthew, Mark, and Luke as well as the letters of Paul. The Fourth Gospel put the diabolical powers in even sharper focus by calling the devil the "ruler" of the world.[23] Throughout the New Testament, the present age is looked upon as a time of warfare between the authority of God and the claims of the demonic. Life, clearly, is a struggle in which humans are caught in the warfare between powers and beings beyond human comprehension.[24] Christians and Jews believed that the outcome of the struggle was not in doubt, for God had a plan under which even evil was used to work the divine will. The plan, Christians insisted, included Jesus as the one through whom God would overpower the forces of evil, defeat death, and inaugurate the kingdom of God. Given the delay of the parousia, however, second-century Christians posed the questions about Creator and creation with urgency and with different results.

An early second-century respondent, Marcion of Pontus (flourished ca. 140), proposed a radical answer based on his study of Scripture, the emerging New Testament, and human experience.[25] Marcion probably was a wealthy merchant, and his travels led him to Rome and into membership in the Christian congregation there.[26] According to Tertullian, Marcion's *Antitheses* (or *Opposites*) juxtaposed passages of the Septuagint against sections of his edited versions of the Gospel of Luke and several Pauline letters. Although only snatches of his own words survive and these are quoted against him by opponents, some of Marcion's leading ideas may be accurately discerned.[27]

Apparently Marcion was deeply impressed by the disparities of regions and conditions in the visible world. Some places were hot and others cold. In some areas people starved, while in others food was abundant. The state of humanity probably troubled him, too. Men and women suffered, were cruel to one another, and seemed to have no peace in their lives or relationships. His readings of the Scriptures of Israel and other documents that were used widely in the church confirmed his sense that there was a split between creation and redemption, a split that could be accounted for only on the basis of the existence of two gods. He concluded that the supreme God did not create the visible world. Some low-level bungler, a Demiurge-like shaper, made—rather, mismade—the visible world. The god of this world was not deliberately evil but harsh, legalistic, and capricious. So one part of the world suffered with drought and heat, while other parts experienced floods and freezing. As for the effects of this god's efforts among humans, the Old Testament, said Marcion, was evidence enough. He may have pointed to Job as the victim of a bet that involved death and humiliation, to Psalms that hymned God's destructive power even in the lives of those who sought to be righteous, and to Isaiah's report that this deity created both peace and evil. The creator was the master of atrocities, wars, punishments, and hateful passions. He was also the master of the Jews and selected them to be his people. He gave them the harsh Law through Moses, sanctified lust through marriage, planned to gain more subjects by means of procreation, ordained the custom of killing animals for food, and entrapped humans by praising greed. It appears that Marcion's creator also had a son, apparently a figure who fulfilled the expectations of Israel's Messiah.

On the other hand, Marcion taught that there was a supremely good, life-enhancing, and loving God. This God is the Father of Jesus, the God of redemption, of escape from the creator and the creation. Marcion's Jesus did not have a fully human body and was not born; he came down from the supreme God's realm to call women and men to salvation in the form of escape from the creator's rule to the life offered by the supreme God. Those who had ears to hear the message of radical love were enjoined to be celibate, gentle, vegetarian, self-denying, and disciplined. They were to reject the Old Testament as the creator's book and read as Scripture Marcion's expurgated version of the Gospel according to Luke and epistles of Paul.[28] And Marcion, together with his followers, claimed to be Christians.

Other responses to the questions about the creator and the creation were made by groups often collectively called "gnostics." *Gnōsis* is one of several Greek terms for knowledge. *Gnōsis* came to have a meaning distinct from knowledge as sight, experience, investigation, perception, and understanding. It was the specially revealed knowledge of the transcendent realm that was believed to exist beyond and behind the corporeal world of sense perception. The transcendent realm was considered to be indescribable and invisible except to those who were granted insight into the eternal mysteries.[29] Whatever else it came to include, *gnōsis* concerned knowledge of the heavenly realms, the wisdom that pervaded nature, and the divine purposes within and beyond the cosmos. The secret things, as Deuteronomy put it, belong to God; there are mysteries in the swings of the seasons and the stars, according to the Wisdom of Solomon; and the ways of God are beyond the normal attainments of the human mind, said Isaiah. The apostle Paul wrote of *gnōsis* as the meat rather than the milk of Christian teachings, the mysteries of which designated church teachers were the stewards. The Gospels presented Jesus as giving his disciples private instruction about the mysteries of the kingdom.[30]

Several Christian teachers, including Clement of Alexandria, used *gnōsis* and terms related to it as a normal component in Christian teaching. Other second-century teachers, notably Valentinus, Basilides, and Carpocrates, advanced ideas that sparked controversy and generated challenges. Generally, this trio and those related to them held that a supreme and unknowable God had produced a complex heavenly realm, the "Fullness" (*Plērōma*) of God. Valentinian systems, especially, spread through the Empire. Tertullian wrote with grudging admiration about Valentinus (flourished ca. 150).[31] According to Valentinus, the Pleroma was the realm of life and reality, the home of numerous pairs of angels who depended upon the unknowable God. Something went awry when the last-emanated angel, Sophia, attempted to become a creator herself and was expelled from the Pleroma. While wandering in the emptiness and unreality outside of God's Fullness, she gave birth to a monstrous being (Ḥoḥmah), with whose aid she made the Demiurge. The Demiurge, in turn, arranged the cosmos as well as a clumsy, ignorant worker was able. Nevertheless, Sophia and Ḥoḥmah implanted in a few persons sparks of *gnōsis*, and made some others capable of faith and good works; but they were unable to do anything for the majority of humans. The Valentinians taught that Jesus had called those who had ears to hear and wills to respond to the message of the real world of the Pleroma. Persons who responded were to live in the greatest possible freedom from the Demiurge's customs, rules, and authorities. The cosmos, then, is the result of a defect in the heavens, made by a demiurge, governed by forces that are at best ignorant of the true God and, at worst, in opposition to God. And these believers also claimed to be Christians.

Who created and governs the cosmos? From what was it made and for what purpose? These questions challenged Christians as they waited for Jesus' parousia. Christians were profoundly influenced by Plato's *Timaeus* and the Stoic logos. Septuagintal and intertestamental responses to the questions were even more important in the forming of first-century Christian responses. In affirming their faith in Jesus, Christians involved him in the process of creating the world as well as in bringing in the kingdom of God. Second-century Christians struggled with the challenge of creation and the Creator, and they were led to consider surprising answers. As they asked, searched, and knocked, they moved into another challenge: what is humanity, and what is its destiny?

> You brought into being the everlasting structure of the world by what you did. You, Lord, made the earth. You who are faithful in all generations, righteous in judgment, marvelous in strength and majesty, wise in creating, prudent in making creation endure, visibly good, kind to those who trust in you, "merciful and compassionate,"—forgive us our sins, wickedness, trespasses, and failings. Do not take account of every sin of your slaves and slave girls, but cleanse us with the cleansing of your truth, and "guide our steps so that we walk with holy hearts and do what is good and pleasing to you" and to our rulers.
>
> *1 Clement* 60:1-2

6

The Second Challenge: Human Nature and Destiny

When I look at your heavens, the work of your fingers,
the moon and the stars that you have established;
what are human beings that you are mindful of them,
mortals that you care for them?
Yet you have made them a little lower than the gods,
and crowned them with glory and honor.
You have given them dominion over the works of your hands;
you have put all things under their feet.

Psalm 8:3-6[1]

Who are human beings and where are they going? What motivates their actions and emotions? How are they related to the divine and to one another? Questions such as these challenge and haunt individuals and societies. The questions engage anxieties and aspirations that lead to the hearts as well as heads of religious persons. The study of the origin, nature, and destiny of human beings, termed "anthropology" by students of religion, is inseparable from theology (the study of God and of religious teachings and practices). A community's anthropology influences its understanding of God, and vice versa. To ask whether theology or anthropology came first is to pose the old chicken-or-egg conundrum.

Different societies gave different answers to the anthropological-theological questions. Ancient Babylonians, often beset by invaders, blistering winds, floods, and droughts, expressed their conviction that the world was built on chaos through creation stories about sea dragons and sky gods. That fundamental myth depicted humans as the slaves of the gods. The neighboring Assyrians said that once upon a time drunken gods created humans as slaves to care for the unkempt divine garden.[2] In the Gilgamesh Epic, a semidivine hero lost the gift of immortality for all humanity when a passing snake ate the plant of eternal life. The anxiety and irony reflected in those tales seemed justified when a suffering Babylonian convinced his erstwhile comforter that the gods favored the sly and punished the good.[3] Such myths, epics, and poems expressed a theology of wariness toward the gods and an anthropology in which people were dominated by forces that could not be trusted. One of the oldest Greek accounts of the creation of the world, Hesiod's *Theogony* (ca. 700 B.C.E.), told the story of a world made through divine power, love, treachery, and agony. Castration, murder, and even cannibalism among the divinities signaled a view of the cosmos that was hardly harmonious and peaceful. Zeus punished men in an insidious way for an offense committed on their behalf by the god Prometheus. The father of the Olympians commanded that woman be fashioned out of nonhuman matter and that she deceive and trouble man. Yet sculptors, potters, and painters celebrated human beauty in their statues, urns, and murals. Philosophers and sophists taught about *aretē*, and dramatists such as Aeschylus, Sophocles, and Euripides presented noble though tragically flawed heroes.

From the death of Alexander the Great (323 B.C.E.) onward, anthropological questions sharpened as Greeks tried to understand themselves and others in their culturally expanding world. Old Mesopotamian and later Greco-Roman anthropological questions often fixed on the aristocracy and disregarded the masses of slaves and workers. The Old Testament, Philo, and first-century Palestinian Judaism handled anthropological questions in ways similar to and different from pagan writings. Challenged and influenced by Jews and pagans, Christians attempted to work out their own responses.

OLD TESTAMENT ANSWERS

A psalmist asked who humans were that God should lavish such extraordinary care on them. As quickly as the question was posed, the poet answered that the Lord regarded men and women as slightly below the highest rank of angels and crowned them with honor and glory. Another psalmist, awed by God's creative engagement with humankind, wrote that people are shaped in wondrous and secret ways by the Lord, who knitted their various parts together in their mothers' wombs. The authors of the creation stories in Genesis seemed to write in deliberate opposition to the Babylonian and Assyrian versions of humanity and divinity. One described God making humans as the culmination of creation and the most precious of creatures. Women and men were not merely just below the angels; they were in the image (*eikōn* in the LXX) and likeness (*homoiōsis*) of God, and they had dominion over all the earth. The other writer said that humanity was the first of all God's creatures, and that the Lord personally shaped the human form, then breathed the divine breath of life into that form to make humanity a living being. That author, too, insisted that humans had authority and responsibility over all that happened in the beautiful garden God gave them as a home. Wisdom's sages maintained that humans were capable of learning, responding to, and doing the will of the Lord.[4]

The dominant traditions in the Old Testament emphasized that the created world was good, and that humanity had special, even intimate, connections with God and an exalted place in the cosmic order. Divine malice and drunkenness were as absent from the Old Testament views as were indications that humans were made to be God's slaves. Rare exceptions to that motif were rooted less in God's will or human nature than in human attitudes and deeds. David, for example, lamented his adultery with Bathsheba and cried out that he was conceived in sin.[5] The author of Psalm 14 pictured God looking down from the heavens and saying of humanity, "They have all gone astray, they are all alike perverse; there is no one who does good, no, not one."[6] The Jewish experience of being conquered by foreigners and caught in civil wars pushed them to raise questions and complaints about human nature and God's sovereignty.[7]

PHILO'S ANSWERS

From his vantage point in Alexandria, Philo saw humans putting reason to noble uses, and he saw people indulging their passions. He responded to the anthropological issues by interpreting the Pentateuch allegorically, lacing those interpretations with Middle Platonism and Stoicism. Two dimensions of Philo's treatment of humanity were especially germane to developments in first- and second-century Christianity. The first grew from Philo's cosmology and the other from his handling of *paideia*.

Philo's cosmology depicted two major realms that were separated and yet linked to each other by an intermediate sphere, *aēr* or "air," in which dwelled the various divine powers that assisted the Logos in creating the world of space and time. Beyond these, according to Philo, was God. The first realm, that of the forms or paradigms, took its rise in the Mind of God. Logically, it existed before space and time. Although Philo was ambiguous at points, perhaps deliberately so in his exoteric works, the Logos was the first of the divine powers in the Mind of God and could be called God's Mind, the beginning (*archē*), the pilot, the leader, the supporter of all, and the image (*eikōn*) and likeness (*homoiōsis*) of God. It seems that Philo also identified as the Logos the creator figure in Genesis 1:26: "Then God said, 'Let us make humankind in our image, according to our likeness. . . .' "[8] In any event, the heavenly Man was Mind and had neither an earthly body nor specific sense perceptions. The heavenly Man had, in a general manner, the patterns through which sense perceptions could be properly arranged and balanced.[9] When he turned to Genesis 2, Philo distinguished between the heavenly and earthly realms by means of allegory. His highest or "philosophical" interpretation of the garden portrayed it as a heavenly pattern in which a single river, *Aretē*, flowed in four branches, that is, the traditional *aretai* of understanding, self-control, courage, and justice. United as one *aretē* or deployed separately as circumstances required, these chief excellencies were the paradigms to be employed in the earthly realm. Except for the tree of life, the trees in the heavenly garden were the patterns for the other *aretai* or specific skills that were useful in the realm of space and time.

The realm of this world began with God, through Logos and the angelic powers, creating matter out of nothing, then mixing the elements of water, fire, air, and earth into a doughlike mass. The paradigmatic forms were impressed upon the material of the tangible cosmos to make the visible world and, in the process, to implant seeds from which later plants and animals sprang up. Humans were different. They were molded in the image and likeness of their heavenly model. The human mind with its reasoning capacity (logos) derived from the divine Logos. Philo contrasted the heavenly and earthly figures: "There are two types of men; the one a heavenly man, the other an earthly. The heavenly man, being made after the image of God, is altogether without part or lot in corruptible and terrestrial substance; but the earthly one [Adam] was compacted out of the matter scattered here and there, which Moses called 'clay'."[10] When the Logos breathed life into the earthly man, man became a living being encumbered with a body.

Philo's allegorizing biology regarded Logos, mind, and reason as the active and male principles, while earth, Eve, and passion were the passive and female principles. Recognizing the account of Eve's creation to be a myth, the Alexandrian wrote that she represented sense perception and passion. He maintained that existence in the corporeal world required desire, emotion, and pleasure in order to guarantee God-willed reproduction. He assumed that the female elements, if unchecked by the male, could lead to disordered passions and actions. As he switched from considering the heavenly to the earthly realm, Philo said that the paradigmatic garden was impressed upon the human mind. The *aretai*, represented by trees, became the inner models that motivated men and women to be disciplined and skilled in life, and the river or rivers encompassed the soul to protect it from the assaults of external passions and to confront internal emotions that prompted improper responses and actions.

The soul, which was the human factor in the compacted creature of the earthly garden, was intended to dwell in the heavenly garden. Physical death—the disengagement of the soul from the body—was seen as a birth or liberation. If, however, a soul was too weighed down and damaged by its irrational surrender to passion and disorder, it was not liberated by death but entombed in the world of sense perception and wickedness; such a soul was truly dead. If liberated souls needed some purification on the way to their heavenly home, the way was open through repentance and knowledge.

This purification was Philo's version of the Greek notion of *paideia*. Because he taught that the soul was capable of being improved as well as corrupted, he understood the couple in the earthly garden and all subsequent humans, with the exception of Moses, to be immature and in need of discipline and instruction (*paideia*) if they were to participate in heavenly *sophia*. Philo developed *paideia* in four ways. First, it was the necessary disciplinary agent that brought order to and corrected the soul in its stages of *phaulos* (beginner) and *prokopos*. He allegorized Aaron's rod, melding it with the serpent held aloft in the wilderness (Exod. 4–7 and Num. 21). The rod impressed stubborn Pharaoh and bit the Israelites to discipline them. *Paideia*, then, was the instrument of Logos that chastened the wayward soul so that it sought self-control.

Second, Philo allegorized Abraham, Hagar, and Sarah. In Philo's reading of the literal level of the biblical accounts, Abraham, unable to have offspring with his true spouse (Sarah), was given Hagar the Egyptian handmaiden in order to have a child. After being with Hagar, he was eligible to engage with Sarah, and Sarah gave birth to Isaac, the child of promise. Sarah thereupon dismissed Hagar from her service. In the allegory, Abraham represented the soul, the offspring were *aretai*, Hagar represented encyclical *paideia*, and Sarah was divine *Sophia*. Philo interpreted the account to mean that the soul was too immature and disordered to relate immediately with divine Wisdom just as the *phaulos* was unready to handle advanced studies. The soul required the preliminary training of encyclical *paideia*, which produced the *aretai* of specific duties (*kathēkonta*). Yet, the soul ought not stay overlong with such studies, for encyclical *paideia* was only the vestibule to Wisdom's house. To confuse the vestibule with the inner chambers was to fall into the trap of becoming a word-mongering sophist. Only when the soul reached the level of self-control was it able to enter a relationship with divine Wisdom.[11]

Philo's third account allegorized *paideia*, a feminine noun, as the soul's mother and the wife of Logos.[12] Noah's inebriation and the responses of his sons (Gen. 9:20-28) allowed Philo to involve Deut. 21:18-21, the punishment to be inflicted on a rebellious son. According to Philo's allegory, the marriage of Logos and *Paideia* produced the daughters of *mousikē* and four sons or types

of humans. Mother *Paideia* was identified with disciplinary ethics—the culmination of encyclical studies and the prokoptic stage of ethics. She enjoined
her sons to follow acceptable human customs that were common to all peoples
in order for them to be properly prepared to be led by Father Logos into
esoteric divine truths. The first son obeyed both parents, was initiated by
Father Logos into the divine mystery, and was clothed in the vestments of the
high priest. The obedient son had moved through the stages of beginner, in
which he learned from his sisters, and progressor, in which he received instruction from his mother. Finally he was admitted to the ranks of the sages
by his father. The second son disobeyed both parents and became a truant
and wastrel who deserved to remain steeped in immorality and wickedness.
The remaining sons obeyed only one parent and disobeyed the other. He who
obeyed *Paideia* and learned from his sisters but declined to follow his father
was the model for the sophists. The other son followed his father only, so he
had little rhetorical and intellectual practice to withstand the critics of the
truth or guide others to the truth.

In the final allegory of humanity and *paideia*, Philo described humanity's
origin and goal as the heavenly realm. Life in the world of space and time
was a disciplinary and educational process in which God, through the *paideia*
offered by the Logos, drew those who were willing to improve their souls
through the stages of beginner, progressor, and sage.[13] Philo worked out a
pattern of two triads, that is, Enosh, Enoch, and Noah, plus Abraham, Jacob,
and Isaac. Topping these was the most perfect human, Moses.[14] He was God's
loan to the world of time and space, was never swayed by passions, and had
all knowledge. He was the living law, the lawgiver, the educator (*paideutikos*),
and the initiator (*hierophantos*) of humanity into divine *gnōsis*. It seems that
Philo verged on identifying Moses with a manifestation of the Logos in his
attempt to show that Judaism was the truest, most divine, and most universal
philosophy that humans could follow.

What was humanity and its destiny? Philo answered the anthropological
questions in his characteristic, many-faceted way. Humanity could be identified
in terms of the Logos as well as humans being in the image and likeness of
the Logos, or just the soul, and even the mixture of soul and matter. The
heavenly patterns of the realm of the Mind of God were impressed upon the
mind of humans, so giving humans incentive to improve their souls and to
progress toward their true goal of being in the image and likeness of the Logos.
God was not a fearsome judge; God did not make anything that God hated
or wanted to destroy, and God always opened the means for souls to repent
and be purified. *Paideia* became a divine power pulling willing souls to their
fulfillment. In developing and even personifying *paideia*, Philo attempted to

incorporate what he considered to be the truest and noblest elements of Greco-Roman culture by attributing them to divine revelation through Israel's patriarchs and Moses. History, however, played little, if any, role in Philo's philosophical theology. He internalized events, making them events of the soul rather than of the struggles of flesh-and-blood merchants, slaves, soldiers, or rebels. He died before 70–73 C.E., so he did not have to explain or allegorize the destruction of the Temple and Jerusalem; that task was left to others.

TWO PALESTINIAN JEWISH ANSWERS

The writers of 2 Esdras and *2 Apocalypse of Baruch* faced the questions Philo did not have to handle, questions which had been raised on the level of individuals by the authors of Job and Ecclesiastes but which became wrenching issues for Jews living in the aftermath of 70–73 C.E.: Is God righteous? Is human existence futile? What is humanity destined to be?[15] In their wrestling with these questions, 2 Esdras and *2 Baruch* made incisive comments on human nature and destiny. The comments, often poignant and searching, disclosed ideas and issues among Jews, especially those living in Palestine in the aftermath of the destruction of Jerusalem and the Temple in 70 C.E.. Indeed, the overriding concerns of these Jewish writings were to understand how the Lord could allow the holy city and the Temple to be destroyed and what role the Jewish people had in the sweep of history. The authors expressed anxieties and concerns among Jews during the period (ca. 70–100) when the Christian Gospels, Acts, the Pastoral and Catholic Epistles, the pseudonymous writings attributed to Paul, and Revelation were written.[16] Some second-century Christians knew those ideas and concerns, and they knew and used 2 Esdras as a respected, perhaps holy document.[17]

"Ezra" put eloquent and hard questions to God through the angel Uriel. In the course of their conversations, visions, and explanations, an anthropology based on Adam unfolded. The Creator had made two worlds, the present age and the age to come. Generally, the current world was intended for the many and was likened to a contest in which those who competed successfully would be welcomed into the future age.[18] More specifically, the first world was created for the sake of Israel. Ezra and Uriel said that God placed the Law in the heart of Adam from the beginning—along with a tiny grain of evil. Adam had the ability to obey God and live, but almost immediately Adam disobeyed the only commandment that had been enjoined on him. Ezra lamented that it would have been better that Adam had never existed: "Adam, what have you done? For though it was you alone who sinned, the fall was not yours alone, but ours also who are your descendants."[19] People had the opportunity to obey the Law that God had put within them, but, through Adam, almost all humans germinated and cultivated the evil seed or impulse within them.

2 Esdras is the earliest extant Jewish source for the concept of the two impulses in humans.[20] In its more developed form, the concept included the view that a good and an evil impulse resided in the human heart or flesh. Persons who allowed themselves to be motivated by the evil impulse headed toward death, and they could not readily, if at all, change their plight. In 2 Esdras, the good impulse was the Law, renewed and expressed plainly in the covenant made with Abraham and the revelations disclosed through Moses and the prophets. Ezra complained bitterly that it would have been better if the earth had not yielded the dust out of which Adam had been made, for through Adam's fall many have come into the world and perished. Although Ezra's concern centered on the Jewish people, he observed that some individuals might be blameless and sinless in their lives; nations, however, could never escape sinning against God.[21] Ezra even reversed Ps. 8:4 and 14:3:

> But what are mortals, that you are angry with them; or what is a corruptible race, that you are so bitter against it? For in truth there is no one among those who have been born who has not acted wickedly; among those who have existed there is no one who has not done wrong. For in this, O Lord, your righteousness and goodness will be declared, when you are merciful to those who have no store of good works.[22]

Ezra did learn that in the coming catastrophic end of the present age "It shall be that all who will be saved and will be able to escape on account of their works, or on account of the faith by which they have believed, will survive the dangers that have been predicted, and will see my salvation within my borders, which I have sanctified for myself from the beginning."[23]

The deep sorrow and helplessness expressed by Ezra was answered in Uriel's revelations about death and the age to come. When women and men died, for seven days their spirits saw revelations about the end of the present age and the future of humanity, and then they went to their respective habitations, where they remained until the end of the age. Those who had followed the way of destruction and death in the present age grieved about their sinfulness in seven ways, while those who had striven to overcome the evil impulse rested in seven orders or states. Among the latter states was one in which angels cared for and guarded the spirits of the righteous from all harm, and the righteous spirits were shown in the future "how their face is to shine like the sun, and how they are to be made like the light of the stars, being incorruptible from then on." The intermediate state after death and before the beginning of the new age involved disclosures of heavenly knowledge, discernment of the spirits' destiny, and manifestations of the mercy as well as the justice of God. The germinating evil seed, according to God's plan in the present age, was to grow, and its fruits would be harvested on the dreaded day of judgment.[24] Ezra was warned not to focus on the punishment of the wicked but rather to consider the mercy of God in saving any humans.

After lengthy discussions with his revelatory angel about the timing and terrors of the end of the present age, Ezra learned of some of the wonders in store for the cosmos and for humanity. The wicked who were alive at the end of the age would perish or be sent into eternal punishment. A heavenly city and a new land not previously known were to be revealed for the righteous who lived in the last days. Then God was described as saying, "For my son the Messiah shall be revealed with those who are with him, and those who remain shall rejoice four hundred years. After those years . . . the Messiah shall die, and all who draw human breath."[25] After seven days, the new world was to be created, all the deceased raised, and the resurrected either cast into the "pit of torment" or welcomed to "the place of rest," either the furnace of hell (Gehenna) or the "paradise of delight."[26] In the final stage of blessedness in the age to come, the righteous "shall behold the face of him whom they served in life and from whom they are to receive their reward when glorified."

On the whole, 2 Baruch shared with 2 Esdras the same thought world and even snatches of poetry. One difference was 2 Baruch's view of Adam: "For though Adam first sinned and brought untimely death upon all, yet each of those who were born from him . . . has prepared for his own soul torment to come, and again each one of them has chosen for himself glories to come. . . . Adam is therefore not the cause, save only of his own soul, but each of us has been the Adam of his own soul."[27] Adam, then, was a negative example for all, including the Watchers.[28] 2 Baruch commented briefly on the Messiah: he would arrive, summon the nations for judgment, spare those who did not know "Jacob" or trample the seed of Jacob, slay the wicked, and establish the glorious reign of peace on a fabulously renewed creation.[29] Not only would life in the new age be pain-free and sinless, but to

those who have been saved by their works, and to whom the law had been now a hope, and understanding an expectation, and wisdom a confidence, shall wonders appear in their time. For they shall behold the world which is now invisible to them, and they shall behold the time which is now hidden from them . . . for in the heights of that world shall they dwell, and they shall be made like unto the angels, and be made equal to the stars, and they shall be changed into every form they desire, from beauty into loveliness, and from light into the splendor of glory.[30]

In the late first century C.E., two Palestinian responses to the anthropological issues attempted to account for three factors: the created glory of humanity, the present misery of humanity and especially the desolation of the Jewish people after 70, and the promises of the new age. In describing the plan of God, the authors dealt with questions about the ability of humans to know and do God's will, God's plan for history and the cosmos, hidden and revealed knowledge, and the prospect of an ongoing existence for the human spirit or soul. Christians were listening to and reading Jewish conversations and writings such as 2 Esdras and *2 Baruch*, factoring in their understanding of God's actions in and through Jesus. Sometimes the conversations and writings contradicted each other or went in unusual directions; the same, then, may be expected to have occurred when Christians responded to the anthropological challenges.

SOME CHRISTIAN ANSWERS

The anthropological questions were literally cosmic in scope. Jewish writers who answered them sometimes allegorized traditional accounts, internalized events, employed powerful images, envisioned souls ascending into the heavens, and saw cities descending from celestial realms. The first Christians shared aspects of those answers and furnished others that were just as inspiring and satisfying—and sometimes even more menacing than those of their pagan and Jewish contemporaries. Greco-Romans may be described as struggling with anthropological versions of the problem of the one and the many. Jews puzzled over the sovereignty of God and Israel's plight in the present. Of the various Christian answers to anthropological questions, one focuses on the human will, sin, and divine intervention.

First, matters of the will. Do persons have free will? Although the terms are often used interchangeably in daily conversation, theologically speaking, free will and free choice are different. Free choice deals with matters in individual and community affairs which may be vitally important in the present but which do not directly concern a person's destiny or a community's achieving its highest fulfillment. Whether a man selects one pair of shoes or another, or a woman decides to buy a car or a station wagon, or two persons decide to marry or not are matters of free choice. So, too, are decisions by generals over strategy, scientists about experimental procedures, children with games. Freedom of choice might not be total, because it could be hedged by economic factors, social customs, physical strength, and mental abilities. To deny it absolutely is determinism, the claim that persons are unalterably set or programmed to think or act in a particular way. The determinants may be external forces such as the Fates of Greek mythology, the celestial powers of astrology, the inexorable rhythms of history, or the manifest destiny of nations. The determinants could also be internal, e.g., the results of genetic factors, cranial capacity, race, and gender. Jews and Christians have affirmed, at least in theory, that humans have freedom of choice. Free will, on the other hand, deals with goals and destinies. It asks whether humans have the ability to shape or control, in whole or part, what they ultimately will be. In theological terms, free will is concerned with the question, Are human beings able to think and do those things which are pleasing to God? Do we, to some degree, merit God's love or God's saving action? Free will, then, has to do with the meaning and achieving of salvation. Answers to questions about free will spread across a spectrum from a vibrant affirmative to a despairing denial.

Generally, those who respond that we do have free will agree with the author of Ps. 8 and highlight human dignity and responsibility. Often, the anthropology behind the affirmation of free will refers to humans as being in God's image and likeness. If Adam and Eve are mentioned, they are sometimes styled as being immature in the garden, and often life in the present age is described as an educational process toward a higher state of existence, such as being an angel or shining among the stars. This belief may or may not entail the position that after death the soul continues to make progress toward its ultimate goal, so that a resurrection of the body and world judgment are unnecessary. Among supporters of human free will, God is the Creator who still engages in completing the cosmos, including its human members. Salvation, then, is the completion or fulfillment of the creative process begun by God at the beginning. Clearly, Philo and 2 Baruch, as well as numerous Old Testament writers, were among those who stressed the freedom of the will.

But if humans are such noble and responsible creatures, what is sin? Related terms include transgression, trespass, debt, error, missing the mark, iniquity, and ignorance.[31] These expressions imply that while sinners act contrary to God's will, they still have the capacity to obey God, pay for their offenses, correct their conduct, practice to improve their ways of life, and learn to love God and their neighbors. If sinners set themselves to those goals and tasks, then God may forgive and restore them to fellowship with Godself. The Scriptures described God's providing various means of discipline, reparation, and instruction: nature, events, the Law, rituals, Scripture, teachers, prophets, the voice of conscience, and the community of believers all provide ways to set sinners back on the paths of righteousness. The human problem is the misuse of free will, and salvation can be offered through moderate degrees of divine intervention. The maximum level of divine intervention might be an angel-instructor who reveals divine knowledge and provides fitting direction for those who seek to please God.

To deny that humans have free will leads to different understandings of human nature, sin, God, and divine intervention. The authors of Psalms 14 and 51 and 2 Esdras were among those who claimed that something was fundamentally wrong with human beings, not because God made mistakes, but because sin penetrated to the core of a person's will. Adam's sin ruined the wills of all his offspring—or almost all—and sentenced them to pain and death. As the author of Psalm 14:2-3 (53:1-3) reflected, when the Creator looked upon humankind to find any who seek after God, the Living One saw that "They have all fallen away, they are all alike perverse; there is no one who does good, no, not one." The grim result of this line of reasoning is that because of Adam or for some other reason, people are born sinful or are distorted by the society at birth or soon afterwards. Accordingly, sin is an inner rebellion, sickness, or stain that contaminates the whole person.[32] Even thoughts and acts that appear decent manifest the desires and orientations of sinful humans. Sin, then, is a condition of being human, not a matter of decision; it is bondage to evil, being overcome by dark impulses within one's heart. Specific acts are merely symptoms of the internal, death-directed state of persons. What can be done about such a sorry state? Knowing the rules, hearing the Law, trying to change, paying back, or seeking to return to God are all unavailing. Even attempts to repent are tinged with sin. There is nothing that anyone can do except sin more; humans are lost and condemned creatures. How can a person be saved from a destroyed will, or slavery to demons, or impending divine wrath?

The answer is radical divine intervention to rescue or forgive some humans. God is experienced not so much as a Creator or Helper but as Savior-Liberator. Perhaps humans need a God-pleasing sacrificial victim, high priest, new Adam, redeemer. At the very least, people need an angel—the higher in the celestial hierarchy, the better. Indeed, persons desperate for assurance that there was more to life than waiting for eternal punishment hope that God or a power directly associated with God will enter the human situation to rescue at least some persons. Again, whether one thinks of the soul continuing after death or holds that there will be a bodily resurrection varies. The souls of those elected by God to be saved experience judgment when death separates them from their bodies, and those souls will need a period more of purging than of education. Persons who look forward to a resurrection of the body then anticipate a great time of judgment in which there will be anguish by all as the sovereign Lord pronounces condemning judgment or gracious acceptance of humans. Those who denied human free will often felt a tension between the identity of God as Creator and God as Savior, for they were convinced that God was mighty but that the present age was dominated by evil.

Most believers do not live on either extreme of the spectrum of free will, but move along the spectrum according to their dispositions and conditions.

Those who stress free will, God as Creator, and human dignity minimize the gravity of sin and the need for divine intervention. They find ready evidence for their positions when they experience growth, prosperity, and success. Those who take the opposite position minimize free will and maximize the gravity of sin and the need for divine intervention. Logically, their position will be supported by disasters, frustrated expectations, and feelings of helplessness.

First-century Christians held positions across the spectrum about the freedom of the will. They adapted some Greco-Roman ideas on the soul, assumed that the Septuagint's version of human nature and destiny was authoritative, and absorbed much from Jewish thinking on the cosmos and history. As far as we know, Paul's was the earliest Christian attempt to present an anthropology that related Jesus to the human situation, and even the apostle gave mixed answers. He wrote the congregation in Rome that the God left enough traces in the creation about God's existence and will that humans ought to have known that they were to worship and serve God as well as live decently and harmoniously with one another. Either because people willed to worship creatures instead of the Creator, or because Adam sinned, the nature and situation of humankind became corrupt and deadly. By exchanging the truth about God for a lie about themselves and the world, people fell into idolatry and moral degradation. From another angle, Adam's rebellion resulted in a pervasive sinfulness, which in turn led to death. "All, both Jews and Greeks, are under the power of sin."[33] The good that a person might want to do, she or he was unable to accomplish, while the evil that one sought to avoid was exactly what one did. People no longer understand themselves because sin lived in and controlled them. The wills of all humans were distorted, if not altogether ruined. Paul, speaking for a desperate humanity, called out, "Wretched man that I am! Who will rescue me from this body of death?"[34]

The apostle answered immediately that the solution of the human plight was in God's hands. Since humans could not be justified through obeying God as Lawgiver, they all faced God as stern Judge unless God also could be merciful Savior. Salvation, then, was first and foremost escape from the coming wrath of God and only secondarily fulfillment of elect humans to be in the divine image and likeness. In Jesus, the righteousness of God was revealed apart from the Law. Jesus' death and resurrection were the vital factors that renewed humanity and opened the way to reconciliation with God. As he wrote to several congregations, those who were in Christ had Christ living in them, and through Christ they were constituted as new creatures, even being conformed to the *eikōn* of God's Son. Jesus was the new Adam and the heavenly Man through whom earthly humans were reconciled with God and adopted as children of God.[35] Through baptism, men and women were initiated into the death and resurrection of Jesus and incorporated into the Body of Christ, the church.

But what happened next? Paul, possibly because he was convinced that the parousia was imminent, appears to have thought at times that baptized Christians were able to exercise free will. They were to bear one another's burdens and work out their salvation with fear and trembling.[36] It was just as possible for Christians to fall back into slavery to sin and to betray their calling to holy living as it was for them to advance in knowing and doing God's will, although evil forces could not separate faithful Christians from the love of God in Christ Jesus.[37] Paul certainly did not believe that he was stalked by a corrupt will or continued to be in a sinful state during his career as an apostle.[38] Paul and others struggled to understand and cope with sin, dissension, and corruption among Christians. Perhaps the persistence of sinful behavior among Christians indicated that Christians were not fully liberated when they were initiated into Christ and nourished in his sacred meal. For those who denied free will, at least before baptism, the anthropological questions were only pushed back to be raised once more in light of the delay of the parousia. The delay meant that the anthropological responses had to include considerations about Jesus' power, God's plan for the church, and problems of discipline and authority in the Christian communities.

The Gospels, too, do not have a single view on anthropological issues. The writer of Matthew indicated at some points that persons who did not believe in the true God were to be saved if they acted kindly toward God's people. In that case, salvation was earned through doing good deeds rather than by accepting particular teachings or trusting in a certain deity. The same Gospel warned that being part of the people of God did not guarantee salvation, for "many are called but few are chosen."[39] On the whole, the Synoptic Gospels can be used to support the ideas that sinful humans still can do God's will and are responsible for their actions. The Gospel of John presented a more mixed picture in which sometimes persons seemed to have free will but on other occasions did not.[40] The Epistle of James gave a strong affirmation of free will, and the author came down harshly on the wealthy Christians and their flatterers.

The anthropological questions were not resolved among first-century Christians. In their enthusiasm for the kingdom of God and in their concentration on Jesus, the first two generations of believers combined both affirmation and denial of free will, both salvation as escape and salvation as fulfillment. They thereby set their successors a formidable task: responding to the old questions under the new pressures of the failure of the parousia and the problems arising in the church over the identity of Jesus, discipline within the ranks of Christians, and relations with the rest of God's world. During the second century, Christians such as Valentinus provided responses that heightened tensions but also gave opportunities for other Christians to develop alternatives.

Valentinians and related groups had accounts about God, humanity, and the cosmos that are still being translated and studied.[41] It appears that Valentinians divided humanity into three groups.[42] The first, a small minority, were the Gnostics or "spirituals" (*pneumatikoi*). Unknown to the Demiurge, a divine seed of *gnōsis* had been implanted in the souls of these persons. That seed may be compared to a receiving set. Gnostics were by nature tuned to hear the pleromatic call and to receive the messages of divine knowledge. As they grew more able to respond, they advanced in wisdom and were initiated by more advanced Gnostics into higher degrees of *gnōsis*. When the cosmos was dissolved, the Gnostics would enter the Pleroma and be united with their angel consorts. As one Gnostic was reported to have said, the Gnostics know from where they have come, into what they have fallen, and to where they are returning.[43] The second category were the "soul-people" or *psychikoi*. They had the capacity to be saved but lacked the gnostic seed. It is as if they had the antenna and the connections, but not the receiving set itself. They were aware that there was more to life than entrapment in this cosmos, but they were limited in their ability to respond. Their salvation depended on whether or not they had amassed enough evidences of faith and good works by the time the cosmos was destroyed. Those who failed expired with the world, and those who were saved entered the Pleroma as angels of a lower rank than the Gnostics. The third class, the *sarkikoi*, were just "flesh-folk." They had neither the seed nor the capacity, neither the receiving set nor the antenna. When the cosmos was terminated, they would be destroyed.

Whether a person belonged to one category or another was not a matter of human or demiurgic will, but of pleromatic intervention. The divine powers in the Pleroma determined how a person was classified. One more turn: the categories were related to Christian missionary efforts and membership in the church.[44] Those who heard and did not respond to the Christian message were the *sarkikoi*: they did not have the capacity to hear with discerning ears. Unresponsive Jews and pagans, therefore, followed the Demiurge, and they were hostile or indifferent to *gnōsis* and the community in which *gnōsis* was present. Those who responded were the Gnostics and *psychikoi*. The church, therefore, was composed of the spirituals and the soul-people. The *psychikoi* were the rank-and-file members who stayed at the level of diluted knowledge and milklike doctrines, that is, the basics. They were given to literal interpretations of Scripture and superficial understandings, and they were saved by faith and good works. The Gnostics were the advanced teachers and their students. They were "in the know" about the divine realities or meaty, higher mysteries. They were saved by the *gnōsis* given them from the Pleroma. The Gnostics might even be exempt from the normal ethical restrictions that bound the soul-people.

Behind the creation myths of Valentinians and similar Gnostics was a sense of profound alienation from the world of time and space. Some persons felt within themselves that they did not belong to the realm of pain, confusion, disorder, and death; their home was elsewhere, in the Pleroma. The very rules of society and the ways of nature were not permeated with some *logos spermatikos* but with defects and anguish. They longed to be their true selves in their true home beyond the cosmos misruled by the Demiurge. They had to escape in order to be fulfilled, and Christian messages about humans and Jesus allowed room for the interpretations that Valentinus and his fellow Gnostics could put on the Scriptures and experience in this world. Others in the second-century church reacted differently to the claims of such teachers and their followers.[45]

As Christian believers awaited the parousia, they struggled with divergent understandings of human nature and destiny. In this struggle they worked toward a clearer understanding of Jesus' identity and work.

> But they who have the fear of God, and inquire concerning the Godhead and truth, and have their hearts towards the Lord, perceive quickly and understand all that is said to them, because they have the fear of the Lord in themselves; for where the Lord dwells, there also is great understanding. "Cleave therefore to the Lord," and you shall understand and perceive all things.
>
> *Shepherd of Hermas, Mandate* 10.1.6.[46]

7

The Third Challenge:
Identities for Jesus

"You are from below, I am from above;
You are of this world, I am not of this world.
I told you that you would die in your sins,
for you will die in your sins unless you believe that I am he."
They said to him, "Who are you?"
Jesus said to them, "Why do I speak to you at all?"

John 8:23-25[1]

The name of Jesus is familiar, yet when people were asked who he was and what he did their answers seemed to be a bundle of identities tied together by the fears and hopes of those who were convinced that somehow God had acted through him to save humans, perhaps even to save the cosmos. His story was and is experienced in many ways by women and men. A person who overcame political and demonic powers appealed to those who felt marginalized by oppressive forces. For them, Jesus was the Victor, and to follow him meant sharing in his triumph. Another interpretation emphasized him as the innocent one who gave himself as the victim on the altar of the cross and through whom people were forgiven by and reconciled to God. Jesus' resurrection showed, they said, that the divine Judge accepted Jesus as the substitute for guilty humanity. As a result of his sufferings and exaltation, humans now were offered life instead of death. "Jesus the redeemer" was a variation on the theme of the victim. Whereas in the "victim" view God accepted Jesus as the offering for sinners, in the "victor" view the demonic powers took him as the ransom or redemption price for humankind. Men and women, in this view, were slaves to evil until Jesus bought them with his own blood. But Jesus broke the power of sin and death through the resurrection. A number of Christians said Jesus restored to humanity the immortality that the old Adam lost through disobedience. If the first man contaminated his children, Jesus, the new Adam, began the process to renew human nature and fulfill creation according to God's plan. Still other Christians found most meaningful the identity of Jesus as Teacher. His exoteric lessons and example taught a life of harmony and joy. He also gave to those who progressed in his community an esoteric *gnōsis* consisting of the heavenly secrets through which believers were drawn into eternal communion with God. To know Jesus' *paideia* meant knowing God's wisdom and mind.

This bundle of identities met emotional and spiritual needs and fostered intellectual speculation. Those ideas were accompanied by strings of metaphors, e.g., hope, truth, life, way, peace, wisdom, and knowledge of God; vine, door, branch, fruit, rock, light, and bread; and king, lamb, shepherd, pioneer, high priest, Servant, and even God and Lord. But, who—which one of these—was Jesus? Could a Palestinian peasant be these and more? The impact of Jesus' personality, tensions in people's lives, and hopes for the future made people receptive—even to the point of gullibility—toward divine solutions to their predicaments. As expectations for Jesus' parousia waned, questions about him became more complex. Christians, pushed to articulate their faith before pagans and one another, used the language and thought categories and literature of their Jewish origins, Greco-Roman philosophy and culture, and their own *ekklēsia*. The books of the Septuagint and a few other writings that some Jews and Christians considered sacred took priority over all other documents and traditions. Far from being a straitjacket, the Scriptures allowed room for creative and searching interpretations. Three christological options emerged to challenge the church's unity and Christian identity: Jesus was a human raised to divine stature, or an angel visitor, or a revelation of God in human form.

THE FIRST OPTION: THE MAN WHO BECAME DIVINE

When 2 Esdras and *2 Baruch* envisioned humans shining like stars and living among angels, they tapped hopes already current among Greco-Romans and Jews. Greco-Romans did not think that apotheosis, or promotion to divine rank, was simply a political act granted by or extorted from the Senate. The Christian claim that Jesus was a human whom God exalted to a heavenly position made sense to Jewish and pagan audiences. Each audience heard and responded to the claim in its own context and terms. In the Hebrew Scriptures, Enoch and Elijah were said to have been transported to heaven. Writings attributed to Enoch described him as the scribe of righteousness who heard and saw the secrets of righteousness, myriads of angels, and the future, and was transformed into an angel. Elijah defied monarchs, championed the poor, fed the hungry, raised the dead, encountered God on a mountain, and chose his successor before being transported to heaven in a fiery chariot. A later prophet predicted that he would return before the Day of the Lord to "turn the hearts of parents to their children and the hearts of children to their parents, so that [God] will not come and strike the land with a curse."[2]

Intertestamental and first-century C.E. Jewish traditions mentioned four others who were glorified. Ezra seemed to have been so rewarded, and Isaiah was said to have been taken into heaven after his martyrdom. Levi, the patriarch of priests, toured several of the seven heavens and saw God. An angel promised Levi a place in the higher heavens where he would be God's minister, mediate the Lord's mysteries to humans, and intercede with God for humanity. Jacob's son was assured that his descendants would be priests, prophets, judges, and scribes. Exceeding all others in importance and holiness, Moses was the defender of the oppressed, shepherd, liberator, interpreter of the Law, orator, writer, organizer, prophet, priest, servant, strategist, architect, provider of sustenance for his people, and recipient and source of the Spirit of God. His special relationship to God was summed up in the comment, "the Lord used to speak to Moses face to face, as one speaks to a friend." Moses' death was handled with mystery and tenderness; no one knew where on Mount Nebo God's friend was buried. Given that finale, it was natural for later writers to reopen his case and his grave. Sirach knew a tradition that Moses had become "equal in glory to the holy ones, and . . . allowed him to hear [God's] voice, and led him into the dark cloud, and gave him the commandments face to face, the law of life and knowledge, so that he might teach Jacob the covenant, and Israel his decrees." A tradition developed that God commanded the archangel Michael to bear Moses' body to heaven, where he was presumably revivified. Apparently, the devil disputed such a blatant despoiling of death's domain but lost the argument. Philo extolled Moses as the greatest and most perfect human. Although he scarcely needed instruction from them, sages from far-off places came to share their wisdom with Moses when he was but a boy, and they recognized his greatness and understanding. According to Philo, God made him partner and heir in the world of sense perception, a god and king with the privilege of entering the sacred darkness of God, that is, the realm of the forms. Finally:

> When [Moses] had to make his pilgrimage from earth to heaven, and leave this mortal life for immortality, summoned thither by the Father who resolved [Moses'] twofold nature of soul and body into a single unity, transforming his whole being into mind, pure as sunlight. . . . for when he was already being exalted

and stood at the very barrier, ready at the signal to direct his upward flight to heaven, the divine spirit fell on him."[3]

Old Testament and later Jewish precedents were few but important for Christians. Those who were welcomed into the precincts of heaven were holy figures who had a special relationship with God, were divinely endowed, and revealed God's will to the elect. For Christians, these heroes served as types that supported their claims about Jesus, who, they said, fulfilled and surpassed all his forerunners. Old Testament and other Jewish examples of humans who went to heaven were supplemented and even surpassed by a number of terms widely used among Jesus' followers. These expressions, which came directly out of the human dimensions of Jesus' identity, may be grouped roughly into two categories: messianic language and the language of sacrifice.

"Christ," the main term used by Christians for Jesus, connoted among Jews a human leader who had divine connections. The Hebrew "Messiah" or anointed one made little sense to Gentiles because they did not put sacred oil or salves on the heads of their leaders. Originally a name plus a title, "Jesus the Christ" or "Jesus the Messiah" was shortened by Gentiles to "Jesus Christ," as if "Christ" were one of his names. Before the end of the first century, he was referred to simply as "Christ."[4] But what did that mean, and how did it help Christians identify Jesus? Among the Hebrews, the title applied to the elect people of God, to prophets, to priests, and to rulers. In each instance, the bearers of the title were protected by God. First, the Israelites were the anointed people because of their covenantal relationship to God. As the people of the Lord, they were to be faithful, keep the Law, show justice and mercy to all, and be the Lord's witnesses to the world. Those who harmed the anointed people without being led to do so by God were doomed because of their arrogance and folly. Second, the Spirit of God authorized and empowered prophets (at least figuratively) to speak the word of God, whether or not they were literally anointed with oil.[5]

Third, priests were anointed when they took office. The precedent, amplified by later writers, was God's vesting Aaron in the sacred garments and Moses' anointing his brother. The postexilic prophets, Haggai and Zechariah (ca. 520 B.C.E.), described God's vindicating the high priest, Joshua, in spite of an angel's accusations. Joshua became a sign of the coming prosperity and glorification of God's people. In the *Testaments of the Twelve Patriarchs* a writer described Levi's heir, who would begin a new priesthood for the kingdom of God. His star, like that of a king, would be noted in the heavens. Through its light and the new priest's revelations of the Lord's word, all persons would come to know the true God. The new priest's ministry would reach to the origins of humanity and into cosmic disorder: he "shall open the gates of paradise, and he shall remove the threatening sword against Adam. And he shall give to the saints to eat from the tree of life, and the spirit of holiness shall be on them. And Beliar shall be bound by him."[6]

Rulers, the fourth category of those called the Lord's anointed, often were associated with David. His reign was idealized as a time of glory and faithfulness in spite of his well-known failings. God, it was said, established an "eternal covenant" with the house of David which guaranteed that a descendant of David would always rule the elect people. Subsequently, "Son of David" described a ruler through whom God maintained the covenant. The designation of rulers as Messiah or "christ," found mostly in the Psalms, indicated their special status. Ps. 2 named the anointed the "son of God," and the one through whom God determined to rule other nations. By applying "son of God" to the king, the Hebrews meant neither that the king was a projection of the deity, as the Egyptians thought, nor that he was apotheosized, as the Romans believed some of their emperors were. The person became "son of God" when he was anointed king of the anointed people. Clearly, status as son of God and anointed did not confer upon the monarch sinlessness or a heavenly home, let alone a trouble-free reign. The christ-king could come before God in repentance and hope, claim the Lord's attention, and ask God to save and prosper the covenant people. A unique reference to a Messiah-ruler appeared in the writings of an author whose poems and oracles were included in the scroll of the prophet Isaiah. The poet-prophet looked forward to the deliverance of the Jewish people from Babylonian captivity and called the expected Persian liberator, Cyrus, the anointed or "christ" of the Lord.[7] While a reference to a foreigner's being empowered to liberate God's elect was odd, its placement close to a series of poems about the Lord's servant allowed eager Christians to combine typologies about a "christ" to the servant, and then to apply both to Jesus.

Many Jews grafted expectations about a Messiah onto their anticipation of the kingdom of God. Hopes for relief and a reliever grew as the plight of the Jewish people worsened from 200 B.C.E. to 135 C.E. The *Psalms of Solomon* (ca. 100 B.C.E.) described a messianic son of David who would defeat Israel's enemies, punish faithless Jews, purge Jerusalem of Gentiles, and shepherd the purified nation with justice. Reflecting the traditional Ps. 2, the Solomonic psalmist described the messianic son of David judging and ruling all nations. In the *Testaments of the Twelve Patriarchs*, dying Judah repented, warned about women in general, and predicted that a great leader would rise like a star from his descendants. The anointed son of Judah, a subordinate partner to the anointed son of Levi, would lead humanity in justice and gentleness, pouring the divine Spirit on God's people to make many children of truth. As God's kingdom began, the patriarchs would rise, Babel's confusion reverse, evil's misery cease, and those who suffered and endured poverty for the Lord's sake glorify God forever. Descriptions of the messianic age and the human Messiah became more elaborate in 2 Esdras and *2 Baruch*. The former predicted that the Messiah, "whom the Most High has kept until the end of days, who will arise from the offspring of David" to denounce and punish sinners, would deliver God's faithful people and "make them joyful until the end comes, the day of judgment." *2 Baruch* said less about the Messiah than about the messianic age. The Messiah's origins were not specified, but he was to judge all nations and rule over a peaceful world. Those who lived in his age apparently married, had children, and died, but without pain or sorrow.[8]

In early Christian reflection about Jesus, messianic language was combined with and modified by the language of sacrifice. Sacrifices were rituals through which an object or animal was offered to the divine for a number of purposes. Sometimes the offering involved thanksgiving for a harvest, a birth, deliverance from illness or danger, the initiation of a project, or the dedication of a building or of children. At other times sacrifices were part of rites related to vows, memorials, festivals, and prayers for help by the community and individuals. The Hebrews expended substantial energy and livestock for sin offerings to obtain forgiveness and reconciliation. The item sacrificed paid for an offense and often substituted for the offender. The merging of messianic and sacrificial language proceeded less by logic than by combinations of ideas and images. Three animal and four human offerings were applied to Jesus.

First, the Passover lamb. Prior to the escape from slavery, the Lord instructed those who intended to leave to slay lambs, put the victims' blood on the tops of their doorposts, and eat the lambs' flesh as their last meal in Egypt. During the night, an angel killed the firstborn males in houses and stables not marked by the lambs' blood. The lambs were the sacrifices that liberated God's people from bondage and offered them new life. Oxen slaughtered when the covenant was made between God and Israel at the foot at Mount Sinai were the second type. After Moses read the Ten Commandments and the other laws, the people responded enthusiastically that they would obey and be the Lord's covenant nation. Moses splashed blood from the sacrificed animals against the altar and on the people, thereby binding them and God together in a covenantal relationship. The third featured two goats sacrificed on the annual Day of Atonement (Yom Kippur) for Israel's sins. After becoming ritually pure by sacrificing a bull and a ram, the high priest brought forward two goats. One was heaped symbolically with the people's sins, which had offended a desert demon, Azazel, and was driven into the wilderness. Presumably, Azazel killed and accepted it as a substitute for Israel. The other was sacrificed to God for the people's sins. Its blood was sprinkled in the sanctuary and on the altar to cover or remove the "uncleanness of the people of Israel." Again, the blood of victims canceled the power of sin and satisfied God's justice while also discharging any claims that evil forces might have had on the people. These sacrifices led first-century Christians to understand Jesus as the fulfillment of the liberation lamb who died at Passover, the one who gave his blood to establish a new covenant, and the victim who took away the sins of the world, or at least of those who believed in him.[9]

Christians also found christological meaning in four Old Testament figures who were portrayed in terms that suggested human sacrificial victims. The first was Isaac, the son of Abraham. According to Genesis, God ordered Abraham to sacrifice "his only son" on Mount Moriah. Originally, the account may have explained the Hebrews' banning human sacrifice, or it may have described Abraham's punishment for expelling Hagar and his firstborn son, Ishmael. Whatever its origin, the story described a father's intention to sacrifice his child, the child's obedience, and the substitution of a ram for the child. Christians styled Jesus as a type of Isaac, the "son of Abraham" (Matt. 1:1), who was offered to God (Gen. 22), and themselves as "the children of [God's] promise, like Isaac" (Gal. 4:28-29).

The second human was not explicitly a sacrificial victim but a righteous sufferer. Ps. 22 (Ps. 21 LXX) opened with the cry, "My God, my God, why have you forsaken me?" The complainant was surrounded by jeering enemies who gloated over the sufferer and cast lots for the person's clothing. Even though the individual appeared grotesque, thirsted, and was wounded, he or she trusted in God and was confident of being vindicated.[10] The lament ended with the person standing in the midst of the great *ekklēsia* (LXX), feeding the poor, and promising to proclaim the Lord's deliverance to future generations. Obviously, Christians crafted their narratives of Jesus' sufferings, death, and mission with this psalm in mind.

The other two human victims that were interpreted as types of Christ were "servant" figures. The servant of the series of poems in Deutero-Isaiah was ready-made for Christian typologists.[11] In the initial poems the servant is identified as Israel, the covenant people. Chosen, shaped, and named by God while in the womb, the servant has had the Lord's Spirit poured upon him. This singular origin meant that the servant was God's personal possession and did not have to fear any foe, for the Lord promised to guide and be present with him. The Holy One made the servant a covenant to the nations, God's witness to all humankind, and the one through whom scattered Israel would return to the homeland. As God's light to the nations, the servant declared God's redemption and salvation to the ends of the earth, opening the eyes of the blind, liberating prisoners, and establishing God's rule even to the far-off coastlands. Through the servant, God's will was done, deserts blossomed, and the hungry were fed. The servant's tenderness toward the weak was balanced by a swordlike tongue and arrowlike sharpness in battles with God's enemies. Naturally, those opponents attacked the servant, for they despised him and sought to eliminate him. Temporarily discouraged, the servant—like the sufferer of Ps. 22—recovered his confidence in God and proclaimed that the Lord honored him. As a result, even kings and princes prostrated themselves before the servant. The servant's posterity would benefit from his faithful service, for the Spirit of God would also be poured upon them, and they would prosper in the age of justice. In the midst of the poems, the poet called Cyrus the Lord's shepherd and "christ." The fourth poem (52:13—53:12) explicitly called the servant a sin offering through whose suffering and death God forgave others their sins. The servant was mocked, marred, and made abominable in the sight of others, a man of sorrows and acquainted with griefs. Compared to a sheep in front of its shearers and a lamb led to slaughter, the innocent servant went to his death with steadfast confidence in God. After his execution, he was counted among the sinners and entombed with the wicked and the rich. But God vindicated the servant, giving him a portion with the great, letting him see his offspring, and prolonging his days. Why? The poet responded that the servant was a sin offering. God used the malice of those who plotted against the servant so that the servant's suffering and death became the punishments that others deserved for their iniquities. By his self-sacrifice others were healed. He took upon himself their transgressions and trespasses; he bore their sins. Sheeplike he died, and priestlike he interceded for sinners. As a result of his anguish, light shines, many are made righteous, and his knowledge satisfies him. While the vicarious suffering of one person for others to expiate sins is almost unique to this passage in the Old Testament, Christians seized on this poem, making it basic to their understanding of Jesus' identity and mission, and the identity and mission of the church.[12]

Wisdom of Solomon opened with another servant. For "Solomon's" servant, righteousness rather than forgiveness was the issue. The poem recounted the struggles of the Wisdom-endowed servant against sinful fatalists who believed they were accountable neither to human nor to divine authorities. Unwittingly, they made a covenant with eternal death. God's righteous servant opposed their lawlessness by his existence as well as his words and deeds. Little did they know that he had the *gnōsis* of God and was not boasting when he claimed that God was his father. Sounding like the wicked of Ps. 22, and the perverters of justice of the fourth Isaiah poem, they humiliated, tortured, and killed the servant. But, because God cherishes the souls of the righteous, the servant died only physically; he was preserved in peace. The righteous were compared to a sacrificial burnt offering accepted by God, and the sparks from the flames that consumed them ignited the punishments that awaited evildoers. The full bitterness of death, the product of the devil's envy, would strike those who were of the devil's company, but God would exalt the righteous in God's own image so they would "govern nations . . . and the Lord will reign over them forever. Those who trust in [God] will understand truth, and the faithful will abide with [God] in love."[13] The servant is God's righteous son, whose sacrificial death will bring judgment upon evildoers, and through whom the Lord's reign will come. The exemplar for all who seek to be loyal to God and are oppressed by wicked humans, the servant will shine forth with the other righteous souls who have endured to win the wages of holiness.

Solomon's righteous servant, his opponents, and the Lord's people were interpreted by first-century Christians as types of Jesus, his foes, and the church. The servant's triumph was a type of the resurrection, exaltation, and parousia of Christ. In short order, Christians identified Jesus as the righteous and suffering Servant. His Isaac-like obedience, his anguish (like that in Ps. 22), and his sacrificial death brought liberation, procured forgiveness, and inaugurated the new covenant. At the same time, Jesus was the anointed high priest who was in the heavenly tent making intercession, and who obtained redemption by his blood, and who mediated an eternal covenant for his followers. To be sure, he was the worthy lamb who was slain and raised to reign in heaven, and the anointed ruler, the Son of David and Son of God who silenced demons and promised to return as judge, savior, and king. During his earthly career, Jesus fulfilled and surpassed the righteous and revelatory scribes (Enoch and Ezra), was seen to outshine Elijah, and surpassed Moses in revealing God's gracious Law and judgment. Then he joined the exalted heroes in the heavens. In this way other Old Testament themes were bound together with the messianic and sacrificial motifs and applied to the Christian understanding of Jesus.[14]

Pagans drew some lines between divinities and humans, yet many felt that gods and humans were physical beings. While their blood and life spans differed, they could communicate, mate, and live together. Platonists and Stoics contributed to the widespread belief that the true human home lay beyond this world: the philosophers described an immortal portion of a human returning to transcendent heights after the individual's physical death. To the delight of Christian critics, some pagans held that gods such as Zeus originally were humans who died but were believed by others to have been divinized after their deaths. Some of the heroes exalted in Greek tales were characters of dubious virtue and sanity.[15] At least three divinized human figures provided pagans and Christians with models for discussions about Jesus.

The first was Asclepius.[16] Zeus's son Apollo had taken a special interest in the mortal Arsinoe. When she became pregnant, Apollo transfixed her and her lover with a lightning bolt. As they were being burned on a pyre, the god removed the baby Asclepius from Arsinoe's womb and then ensured his future by making Chiron the centaur his guardian and teacher. From Chiron he learned the secrets of therapeutic herbs and elixirs, ways to discern illness and health, and the arts of healing and surgery. After he left his teacher, Asclepius traveled, taught, became a famous physician, and did wonderful deeds. He cured the sick, healed the blind, restored the limbs of the crippled, and raised the dead. Zeus objected to the latter. Again, a lightning bolt was thrown, this time by Zeus. After it struck Asclepius, Apollo apotheosized him as a star in the constellation Scorpio. Humanity's healer and benefactor could not be kept from his rounds. Throughout the Empire temples were established in his name, and he appeared to patients and doctors, prescribed treatments, and enlightened researchers. While one temple was at Epidauros, he also practiced at Apollo's shrine at Delphi. Many thought of him particularly as the divinized friend of the needy. (Perhaps a combination of these factors moved Socrates to remind Crito to offer a cock to Asclepius.) His cult spread through Greece and Asia, then to Rome. Ovid told an awesome story about Asclepius's serpent's arrival in the capital to end a plague in the city and add to Rome's glory. Asclepius was venerated as a savior, healer, and compassionate god who had once been a human. Inevitably, he and Jesus were compared.[17]

Apollonius of Tyana, the second figure, lived from around 4 B.C.E. to around 98 C.E., that is, during the same time as Jesus and almost all the writers of the New Testament; and he was far better known than they. Tyana (modern central Turkey) was near Tarsus, Paul's city, and Aegae, the site of a major temple to Asclepius. Apollonius's story began when the god Proteus announced to a married woman that she would bear the god in human form. Apollonius was born in a blooming meadow, surrounded by dancing swans as a lightning bolt somersaulted through the skies to show that the child would be exalted to the heavens as an adult. The boy was brilliant and knew all human and animal languages, but when he began encyclical studies in Tarsus he "found the atmosphere of the city harsh and strange and little conducive to the philosophic life, for nowhere are men more addicted than here to luxury: jesters and full of insolence are they all." So much for Paul's city! Soon he located in Aegae, took the vows of a Pythagorean adept: he became a vegetarian, rejected animal sacrifices, foreswore sex and possessions, abstained from wine and haircuts, and maintained strict silence for five years. Wherever he went, he lodged in Asclepius's temples and depended for food on the generosity of others. The god-doctor visited him often to instruct him in medicine and provide him with insight about patients. In a short time, Apollonius was famous for his wisdom, sanctity, and ability to cure people as well as predict the future. He traveled eastward to share esoteric knowledge with Babylonian *magoi* and Indian Brahmins and Buddhists. He exorcized demons, healed the blind and the lame, and aided women in labor. Once he stopped a funeral cortege, whispered in the corpse's ear, and raised her from the dead. He halted a demon-spread plague in Ephesus, predicted earthquakes, and startled conceited leaders with his pithy sayings and insights. He criticized Athenians for their superstitious veneration of divinities they could not understand, and visited (as well as wrote to) cities such as Antioch, Smyrna, Sardis, and Alexandria. During the Long Year, Vespasian asked and received Apollonius's advice about becoming emperor. A philosopher's life was not without travail. During Domitian's reign, rivals charged Apollonius with cannibalism, human sacrifice, treason, claiming to be divine, and consorting with evil spirits. His *apologia* won him an acquittal, and when Domitian tried to question him further, Apollonius vanished. He reappeared, assured his disciples that he was not a ghost, and told them to touch him to prove it. For two more years he traveled, taught, and healed. Although accounts vary, it was said that when he entered a temple, possibly that of Apollo in Ephesus, the doors closed by themselves while bystanders heard a heavenly choir sing— and he disappeared. Exaltation did not mean absence; he still appeared in visions and dreams to his disciples and those who needed his correction.[18]

Accounts about Asclepius, Apollonius, and Jesus share common patterns: they had unusual nativities, were visited by divine beings, healed people, encountered opposition, died in mysterious circumstances, and were believed to be taken into the heavens after they died. Death and exaltation did not stop them from appearing in visions and dreams, and they were worshiped by disciples who carried on the missions of their apotheosized leaders. Other details could be added, such as contacts with sages or *maqoi*, the roles of temples, and abilities to vanish and reappear.[19] In Acts, Jesus' followers see him in visions, receive revelations, heal, and even raise the dead in his name.

A third analogue is Alexander the Great (356–323 B.C.E.). As was appropriate for a descendant of Hercules, Alexander's birth was accompanied by omens of greatness. Teachers, including Aristotle, instructed him in logic, ethics, and metaphysics. Whether or not he believed that he was divine, he certainly used evidences of it to his advantage.[20] A man of great and even foolhardy courage, he was a daring strategist and ferocious drinker with a temper to match. Alexander dreamed of carving out a multiethnic empire either by force or by negotiation. His marches led him to the temple of Apis at Memphis, where he was crowned pharaoh, that is, identified with the god Horus, son of Isis and Osiris (332). By that Egyptians meant that Alexander was the legitimate ruler who spoke with the authority of the god when he sat upon the throne, and that he was to be accorded public worship and private veneration. The Macedonian pushed for more. At the holy oasis, Siwah, seat of the sun-god Amun (known to the Greeks as Zeus), the priest greeted him as Amun's son and revealed that he would be invincible on the battlefield.

Confident of success, he set out to conquer what is called today Iraq, Iran, and Afghanistan, and moved into India. His conduct changed, and he seemed obsessed with power. He insisted on receiving Persian-style obeisance, which smacked of worship; he dropped objections to being considered divine and may have insisted that conquered peoples sacrifice to him. Alexander conquered, as Amun had predicted; but a sudden fever brought on his death. Worship of him was promoted gradually by two of his successors, Ptolemy and Seleucus. Ptolemy (d. 282 B.C.E.) entombed Alexander's body in Alexandria and decreed that the Egyptians must worship the son of Amun-Zeus. Seleucus (ruler of Syria, d. 281 B.C.E.) likewise determined that Alexander was a god; and he added divine veneration for members of the Seleucid family.

While earlier Greeks and Romans sometimes regarded their deceased leaders as divine, usually those claims extended only to the area the person ruled and expressed public approval more than devotion. The cult of Alexander drew on that tradition but shifted it to match his imperial stature. The syncretistic climate of 200 B.C.E.–200 C.E. brought together god-kings of Egypt and Asia with the local chiefs of the West, giving a cosmic depth to the Greco-Roman piety associated with previous hero-leaders. Later emperors were touched by the aura of divine power generated by Alexander's precedent. It was scarcely coincidental that Julius Caesar's conquest of Egypt and liaison with Cleopatra evoked visions of empire and divinity, or that the Golden Age sometimes sounded like the fulfillment of Alexander's dream. Neither was it a coincidence that emperor after emperor went to Alexandria to sacrifice at Alexander's tomb. With only a few exceptions, emperors did not claim divine honors during their lifetime; they could assume that many in the Empire venerated them and that divine authority was accorded the imperial office and the holy city. Domitian added to his titles one that had an odd ring at first to Roman ears, "Lord." The Greek *kyrios* was rarely applied to the Olympians before 200 B.C.E.[21] From Nero's time onward, "Lord" was used broadly to refer to gods, heroes such as Asclepius, emperors, officials, owners of property and slaves, and teachers, and it was used generally as a term of respect for a free man. Obviously, "Lord," like "Christ," became central to Christian understandings of Jesus.

Whether people came into Christian communities with Jewish or pagan backgrounds, they were ready to identify Jesus as a person who had been adopted by God and raised to heaven. Critics, defenders, and curious bystanders who heard about Jesus and his followers recognized patterns and themes in his career and in the ministry of the early church that were readily adapted to Jewish and Greco-Roman precedents. Adoptionist tendencies are clearer in Mark and Acts than in other portions of the New Testament, but Matthew and Luke could also be read as supporting an adoptionist Christology. Groups of Christians, perhaps Jewish in orientation, understood Jesus the Messiah as Jesus the human who was raised to heaven.²² The adoptionist Christology has roots in an anthropology that emphasizes human free will and in a theology that sees God as the Creator. Adoptionists held that Jesus, born a human being, exercised his free will to obey God and "was made Christ and Lord" on the basis of his exemplary conduct and faithfulness to God. In brief, Jesus was worthy to be apotheosized to angelic status. The adoptionist version of the gospel, then, encouraged believers to see Jesus as a human in the heavens who supports and draws people to himself. His teachings and example guide believers now and into the future. The exalted Jesus will return to judge all and send humans to their proper eternal rewards. But the adoptionist option was vulnerable to shifts in the prevailing anthropologies in society and in the church. As long as there was a generally positive disposition to human nature and free will, the option could hold its own against others. To perceive the human will as twisted or ruined or enslaved, on the other hand, undermined the idea that Jesus began as a noble and righteous human who merited exaltation. Under those conditions, a thoroughly human Jesus could not be the victor, victim, redeemer, restorer, and teacher whom men and women needed in order to be saved.

THE SECOND OPTION: THE ANGEL WHO REVEALED SALVATION

Christians who doubted any human's ability to know and do God's will perceived the forces of evil and the warped condition of human nature so acutely that they were convinced that a human could not save the cosmos and that God had sent Jesus to save persons from bondage to demons and the divine wrath. For them, Jesus came "from above."²³ Such an affirmation was inconsistent with Jesus' being Christ and Servant and with his fulfilling types involving sacrifice and heroes. Consistency, however, is not a characteristic of most religions, and Christianity was adept at transferring expressions from one line of development to unrelated or even contradictory lines. Naturally, the practice created problems when options became rival positions. One option based on the inability of humans to follow God's will expected divine intervention in the form of an angel who would reveal the way to salvation. An angel christology was congenial to many pagans and Jews interested in Christianity. Greco-Romans knew that while one God might be supreme, there were subordinate divinities who appeared in human form to advise, help, and save people. Middle Platonism and Stoicism likewise had divine powers create the cosmos and then guide people. A pagan expected to hear that a god in human form healed, revealed secrets, or rescued persons, but would be puzzled to think of that divinity as spending years in human guise and would regard it as foolish to believe that the god died and was raised from a tomb in human form.

In the Old Testament and later Jewish literature, angels were intermediaries between God and humanity. Some Old Testament authors, reluctant to impute emotions or a human shape to God, substituted angels as the Lord's emissaries to men and women. So angels comforted Hagar, saved Isaac, and guided Israel. They were God's avengers who brought destruction on Egypt, Sodom, Assyria, and even Israel. They stood close to God and counseled with the Lord about doings on earth. And they appeared in human form to enjoy Abraham's hospitality, show Lot's family an escape route, announce Samson's birth to his parents, and feed Elijah in the wilderness. The "commander of the army of the Lord" revealed to Joshua the tactics that toppled Jericho's walls, and another angel goaded Gideon into being a liberator. Angels in human form were teachers and guides for prophets and sages, showing them God's hidden will and purposes. They interpreted visions and encouraged the faithful to be patient in suffering. Nations and even individuals had guardian angels, and the warrior angel Michael was Israel's special protector.[24] Two titles applied by Christians to Jesus could support an adoptionist and an angelic identity for Jesus. The first, "son of God," might mean Israel or the king, and so could be connected to "Christ." On the other hand, "sons of God" also meant angels, such as those who mated with women, gathered in the heavenly council to report to God, and protected Daniel's companions in the furnace.[25] But more important was "son of man."

"Son of man," too, admits of two meanings. It can be used for humans in general, prophets, and perhaps the covenant people. Expressions such as "son of man," "man," and "having the appearance of a man" can also describe a heavenly being. Usually such figures performed various tasks in visions given to Daniel or Zechariah or interpreted visions to seers. On one occasion the "man" was a spectacular being who appeared to have an emerald torso, bronze limbs, a lightning-bolt face, torchlike eyes, and a roaring voice, all enhanced by linen and gold clothing. The same figure may be the one who appeared before the Ancient of Days to receive eternal dominion over all kingdoms and peoples, and whose raised hands signaled the coming judgment.[26] Figures in *Enoch* and 2 Esdras were more spectacular. Enoch saw a number of figures who seemed to blend into one super-angel. Called variously the elect one, the righteous one, the Messiah, and the son of man, he was hidden under God's wings until God sent him to destroy evildoers, raise the dead, judge all humans, and start his reign over the earthly kingdom of God.[27] His human face was gracious and his form dazzling white. All righteousness and dominion belonged to him, and wisdom went before him. In a description that echoed Daniel, *Enoch*'s son of man was given honor, power, and a new name by God as he set forth on his mission to destroy evil and preside over the day of judgment. The son of man was scheduled to come to earth surrounded by angels and, apparently after a fierce battle, overthrow the mighty and the treacherous. Humble and faithful persons would rejoice in his day, for he would vindicate their loyalty and service to God. The wicked shepherdlike leaders of the nations would be broken and destroyed by the victor sent out by the Lord of the sheep. Seated on his glorious throne after the dead were resurrected and with the living assembled before him, the son of man would judge the hearts and deeds of humans. Sinners would be cast into everlasting flames, and the righteous would be granted eternal life on the renewed earth. After carving out a new holy mountain, the son of man would place there a new Temple in which all the saved would worship with great joy.

2 Esdras's Man from the sea (13:1-13) shared much with *Enoch*'s king-angel. This man was hidden by God in the depths of the sea until the time was fulfilled. Flying on the clouds of heaven, he looked at the struggles waged by the righteous against evil. His glance and his voice melted mountains and panicked the hosts of wickedness. After making his own mountain and taking a stand on it, he was attacked by evil hordes. He did not need to carry weapons because flames and storms roared out of his mouth to destroy all enemies. He would welcome the burdened and sorrowful righteous into the kingdom which he was to rule.

Descriptions of Jesus in the Gospels and Revelation were influenced by the angelic figures in Daniel, *Enoch*, and 2 Esdras. Although some "son of man" passages were applied to Jesus in the human sense, many point to the extraordinary angelic figure. Whether or not Jesus considered himself to be the Son of man in the heavenly sense is debated, but Christians certainly took him to be the one who was disclosed as the celestial Son of man in the Transfiguration and who would return on clouds of glory to judge the world. Again, whether or not Jesus said that he was the divine Son of man who came to serve and give his life as a ransom for many, numerous followers of his held that he was the Son of man who appeared first on earth in the form of the suffering and righteous Servant and who would return in full heavenly regalia on the last day. Paul pointed in the same direction when he wrote that Jesus existed in heaven before descending into this world in the form of a servant. The Gospel of John quoted Jesus as saying that the Father was greater than he but that Abraham rejoiced to see Jesus' day.[28] Marcionites, Valentinians, and other Gnostics used different terms but insisted that Jesus was an angelic emanation from the Pleroma who summoned *pneumatikoi* to their heavenly places and offered *psychikoi* salvation as escape from the Demiurge's world.

To understand Jesus as a superior heavenly being or as king of the angels made sense given some of the popular cosmologies in the Empire. Although awkward to express in English, the general scheme could be stated in Greek, which has a definite article ("the" is *ho*) but not an indefinite article (that is, no "a" and "an"). The highest or supreme Deity is *ho theos* or "the God," and the highest rank of angelic beings just below the God is *theoi* or "gods." Numerous sets of lesser angels, spirits, astral powers, humans, animals, and plants are positioned beneath the two top orders:

the God (*ho theos*)
|
gods (*theoi*)
|
various angelic ranks
|
astral and other beings
|
humans
|
animals, plants, etc.

One problem is that a single member of the highest angelic rank is *theos*, a god—the same word which, with the definite article, means the supreme Deity. Greek-writing authors sometimes dropped "the" when they meant "the God," thereby making it unclear to readers if the author meant the Most High or "a god." In the Fourth Gospel Jesus was declared to be the Logos in human form. But what was the meaning of the Gospel's very first words, "In the beginning was the Logos, and the Logos was with *ho theos*, and the Logos was *theos*"? Was the Logos a member of the highest rank of angels, or was the Logos a manifestation of the supreme God? And if the human situation was even more desperate than those who looked for an angel-savior, was it possible that the supreme God or a manifestation of the supreme God would intervene?

THE THIRD OPTION:
THE GOD WHO CAME INTO THE WORLD

Some believed that not even an angel could overcome the demonic forces and distortions afflicting humanity; the Most High had to be directly involved. Popular pagan traditions occasionally depicted Zeus coming in human form to liberate persons and to change the balances of power in human struggles. Again, they would question an account in which Zeus really felt human pain, underwent the humiliation of being beaten, and died on the cross. Zeus might take the shape of a person, but he never became human. In the Old Testament, the Lord became personally involved in the plight of the slaves in Egypt and visited them during their trek through the wilderness. The Holy One also appeared in human form to speak with Abraham at Mamre, wrestle with Jacob at Peniel, be seen by Moses and the elders at Mt. Sinai, and awe Ezekiel in his first vision.[29] Perhaps the starting point was the conviction that the Lord God creates and gives life, and that through the breath of God, humanity came into being. The Living One also guided, preserved, judged, reconciled, and forgave those who were in covenant with God. Salvation, whether as fulfillment or escape, came from the holy Lord. Logic and consistency aside, the real enemy of sin, death, and the devil was not an angel but the supreme God. Only God could destroy God's enemies, save humanity, and transform the whole creation. The God who freed slaves from Pharaoh and struggled with Jacob certainly would not send a substitute in the war with cosmic evil and human degradation. Wisdom and Logos also were cited. To be sure, both terms could refer to angelic beings, but they also applied to God. Wisdom of Solomon described Wisdom as an emanation of God, and, if the Word was within God, then Jesus could be identified as originating not just in heaven but from within God. The Almighty was the One who spoke the Word and was the Mind from which Wisdom emanated. At times, first-century Christians said that Jesus and God were one; that God's glory could be seen in the face of Jesus for God was in Jesus, reconciling the world to Godself; that Jesus was the visible image of the invisible Deity; and that as Creator, God willed the world into existence and as the Logos accomplished the task. At the conclusion of John, Thomas clarified the Gospel's opening by stating Jesus was *ho kyrios mou kai ho theos mou*, that is, "My Lord and my [supreme] God."[30]

An early Christian confession, "Jesus is Lord," seemed to indicate that Jesus was God. Applying "Lord" to Jesus in itself could mean that the speaker regarded Jesus as the master of the person's life or emperor, or revered teacher, even angel. "Lord" even expressed to Greco-Roman pagans what Jews meant when they said "christ" or "Messiah." But it also was the title that Jews used for the Holy One of Israel, YHWH, the Creator and Redeemer of all. Christian authors whose works became the New Testament readily called Jesus "Lord," and then applied to Jesus Old Testament texts that referred to the supreme God. Psalm 107 shaped the Gospel writers' presentation of Jesus' ministry. The psalmist wrote that the Lord nourished the hungry and thirsty in the wilderness, liberated captives, gave light to those who were in darkness, broke bonds, and healed the sick by the divine word. When the Lord's people went down to the sea in ships and were caught in such a violent storm that they cried out in terror, the Lord rescued them by commanding the seas to be still. The Lord raised up the lowly and humbled the proud, so that all who were wise were urged to heed these deeds and consider the steadfast love of the Lord. Other Psalms were also readily applied to Jesus: the Lord is a shepherd, friend, judge, teacher, lawgiver, redeemer, ruler, and savior. Given Christian interpretive methods, the Scriptures were read by some Christians to mean that Jesus was not a human adopted to be an angel or an angel who visited the earth, but was part of and "in" the supreme God. Because divinity at the highest level acted in and through Jesus, salvation, evil's defeat, and humanity's renewal were certain. What humans and angels were helpless to accomplish, the Lord God did by becoming human.

Frankly, the "full God Christology" has problems. More passages in the New Testament reflect adoptionist and angelic positions than the full God option. It may assure those who are convinced that human free will is unable to obey God, but it makes no philosophical sense, invites forced interpretations of the Scriptures, and raises questions. For example, the Gospels reported that Jesus prayed, but if he was *ho theos* to whom did he pray? If God is one, how could a section of God be sent out on an earthly mission? Is God divisible? In the event that Jesus was a manifestation of the supreme God, does that mean God is subject to change with all the philosophical risks such a view entails? If God became enfleshed in Jesus, did God-as-Jesus sweat, hunger, and have bowel movements? Doesn't such a view degrade the holy and transcendent God? If the enfleshed God did not participate in human grubbiness as well as nobility, then what kind of humanity did Jesus-God have? As serious and far-reaching as the questions are, the position became increasingly acceptable as growing numbers of persons inside and outside Christian communities felt that the human situation was so desperate that nothing less than God's personal intervention could save even a remnant in the last days. The message that Jesus was a part of God was welcomed by persons who felt that they had little or no free will, and were polluted with sinfulness. For them, the good news was that God entered the cosmos and took human form in Jesus to enlighten and save people. Those who responded tied together identities and titles from the adoptionist and angelic christologies in spite of the tensions and contradictions between the options.

DOCETIC UNDERTONES

Both the angelic and fully God christologies asked, "Was Jesus really human or did he only appear to be human?" The issue still vexes Christians. One solution regarded Jesus as a divine visitor temporarily disguised as a human but not really flesh and blood. The Greek word for "appear" or "seem," *dokein*, provided the labels docetic, doceticism, and docetists for teachings, approaches, and persons who denied the reality of Jesus' humanity and held instead that he only appeared to be human. Many believers held this view implicitly, and Gnostics and Marcionites claimed it explicitly. Doceticism attempted to preserve the transcendence of the divine and the dignity of Jesus. It also denied or severely limited factors such as Jesus' suffering, death, and resurrection. The docetic position implied that the created world was a mistake, a place of anguish and terror. The docetic challenge was to get out of this world and to ascend to God, and not to pull God down into the mess. But other Christians said that only God-become-human could save the world, so they branded docetists "antichrists."[31]

Who was—is—Jesus? Was he one or some or all or none of the identities that believers considered him to be? The bundle of identities loosened toward the end of the first century and showed signs of breaking apart through the second century. The failure of the parousia, contending Christian factions, and cultural pressures pushed Christian communities to make decisions, decisions that led to questions about the church and its place in God's will and world.

> Jesus said to his disciples, "Compare me to someone and tell me whom I am like."
>
> Simon Peter said to him, "You are like a righteous angel."
>
> Matthew said to him, "You are like a wise philosopher."
>
> Thomas said to him, "Master, my mouth is wholly incapable of saying whom you are like."
>
> *Gospel of Thomas* 13

8

The Fourth Challenge: The Church's Place

I reprove and discipline those whom I love. Be earnest, therefore, and repent. Listen! I am standing at the door, knocking; if you hear my voice and open the door, I will come in to you and eat with you, and you with me. To the one who conquers I will give a place with me on my throne, just as I myself conquered and sat down with my Father on his throne. Let anyone who has an ear listen to what the Spirit is saying to the churches.

Revelation 3:19-22

People are community-makers. They draw together in groups ranging in size from couples to worldwide associations. One way to view communities is to regard some as natural and some as intentional. A natural community develops from normally occurring relationships such as kinship and shared territory. Such a community's *paideia* and religion usually are rooted in traditions handed down from ancestors and modified slowly by changing circumstances. Intentional communities, on the other hand, are formed deliberately for reasons ranging from convenience to conviction. A combination of seminal ideas, heroes, events, and practices tells members and outsiders why the group exists, what it stands for, and where it is heading. Such a community's *paideia* and religion reach beyond the boundaries of natural affinity and often depend on incorporating persons from different groups into its fellowship. The greater the commitments the founders made when beginning the community, the sharper are the lines distinguishing it from other groups. With time, however, lines between the types blur. As one generation succeeds another, not only do those who come after moderate the founders' fervor, but the intentional community slides into being a seminatural community united by kinship, *paideia*, and evolving patterns of communal life. When persons in the intentional-becoming-natural community feel that its original identity is menaced, they may seek to return to their version of the group's first ideals. Successful movements may be hailed as reforms; unsuccessful attempts risk being branded heresies. If members of the rejected faction are not expelled, they may assume lower profiles for a time or split from the original body to become a new intentional group. In effect, the community is challenged by its members and often confronts its members.

The Christian *ekklēsia* began as an intentional community, but within two decades after Jesus' physical departure, the church became a problem to itself as it moved from being an intentional to a seminatural community. Expectations of the parousia had allowed flexibility in understanding Jesus and the church as long as essential principles and goals were maintained. In light of the delay of the parousia, who decided that some versions of those principles and goals were right and some were not? On what basis was the decision made? While they waited for the kingdom, Christians still married and raised children, and converts entered the community. How were they to be told about and raised up in the Christian way? The *ekklēsia* needed its own *paideia* to guide the young and instruct converts, and to continue to learn more about God's will. Obviously the content of Greco-Roman *paideia* was unacceptable because it promoted a culture that Christians believed was demonic, but could its expressions and structures nevertheless be used for the sake of the kingdom?[1] But who would do the teaching and guiding, how were the teachings to be monitored or even agreed upon, and what would happen if teachers disagreed? And then there was the matter of disciplining errant members. Who had the authority to penalize sinners? What, indeed, were the standards of conduct? Behind these and similar questions were basic issues about the place of the *ekklēsia* in God's plan. One writer (ca. 95) envisioned Jesus locked out of a congregation. He knocked for entry, promising his life-giving fellowship to those who obeyed him and warning those who persisted in their own ways. That picture epitomizes the challenge the church became to its founder as well as to itself. During the second century, the *ekklēsia* struggled with three closely related problems: the church's role in God's plan for salvation, key positions in the Christian community, and the organizational patterns of the *ekklēsia*.

THREE ROLES FOR THE CHURCH

Christians insisted that their *ekklēsia* was neither an assembly of citizens nor a synagogue for fulfilled Jews. God Almighty, they claimed, willed this *ekklēsia* into existence as part of the divine plan for all creation. Septuagintal types and precedents, transformed by faith in Jesus, led Christians to describe three linked roles for the church: cosmic, communal, and individual.

The church's cosmic role stems directly from God. The Living One is the source and goal of all goodness and order; indeed, goodness and order are synonymous. According to Genesis 1, when God spoke, chaos obeyed immediately, and God called the results of that obedience good. Disobedience results in sinful disorder and cosmic catastrophe. Eve and Adam not only fouled their descendants' wills, but their disobedience moved God to curse the earth so that it would not be freely productive in this age. The activities of the sons of God, or Watchers, magnified the disaster by disrupting God's order and jolting celestial beings out of their proper places, and so spread misery and disorder from heaven to the earth. War in heaven was matched by hostilities waged by devils and demons against humans and nature. No longer the harmonious arrangement that God designed and made, the cosmos was aimed toward destruction; only a restoration of God's order could save it. Enter Jesus and the *ekklēsia*.

Jesus—the obedient, righteous, and sacrificed servant—was the Victim whose redemptive suffering paid the price demanded by the forces of evil and the justice of God. His actions set the stage for the restoration of humanity and the world to their God-intended fulfillment. Jesus established and heads the *ekklēsia*, making it the instrument for God's new order. He, the Wisdom and Way, taught its members even what angels did not know and what Israel's inspired sages only glimpsed about the purposes of God. While the new order would not be fully implemented until the kingdom comes, human and celestial beings could see the beginnings of its goodness, harmony, and unity in the *ekklēsia*. Neither the gates of hell nor the devil's deceit would prevail against Jesus' church. Still, its members needed to be vigilant and disciplined. The fate of their Israelite types warned them that they would be overthrown if they strayed from proper worship, refused to obey God-given leaders, and fought among themselves. So the earthly *ekklēsia* and the individual believer were urged to put on the whole armor of God, "For our struggle is not against enemies of blood and flesh, but against the rulers, against the authorities, against the cosmic powers of this present darkness, against the spiritual forces of evil in the heavenly places."[2]

Even though the church was on the defensive, it had a positive role. The writer of Ephesians described Christ and the church as being as inseparable as husband and wife. Through God's power, Christ was raised from the dead and enthroned above all beings (except the supreme God) for all ages. He was the head of all existence, uniting the whole cosmos into the *ekklēsia*, "which is his body, the fullness of him who fills all in all." Put another way, the cosmos is like a column of numbers on a page which the accountant adds from the bottom up, setting the sum at the top. So, the sum of all that exists is totaled in Christ, and his *ekklēsia* is the manifestation of that totality.[3] A yo-yo provides a modern comparison. Sent downward, the yo-yo spins aimlessly until tugged from above. Once tugged, it climbs up the string to its owner. Similarly, the downward fall of the cosmos is reversed by God's pull in Christ through the *ekklēsia* to restore the cosmos to its Head. Whatever the metaphor, the church is the living, harmonious, intentional community headed and animated by Christ, through whom the cosmos will be raised to its fulfillment. The cosmic role was a natural topic for speculation and esoteric teaching about heavenly activities and beings, angelic hierarchies, hidden purposes, and the consummation of all things in the fullness of God. Teachers and philosophers in the first and second centuries pondered the origin of evil, the will of God, and the drama of creation and salvation. Preachers and writers shared exoteric doctrines on the same topics with congregational audiences. By setting the *ekklēsia* in a cosmic context, members gained a perspective on their local fellowships and their individual lives that emphasized the unique God-given origins and goals of the church.

The role of the *ekklēsia* as a community had local and universal dimensions. Paul reminded congregations that each was the Body of which Christ was the head and with which Christ shared his mind. On the basis of those partnerships with their Lord, Christian associations ought to express their trust in God through worship, reconcile differences between members for the sake of unity in Christ, support those who proclaimed the gospel, help needy fellow believers, instruct new and present members about God's will, and witness faithfully to Christ in the general society. The congregation gave its members a sense of belonging, a shared destiny, and a common hope. When Paul and the writer of James addressed local problems related to ethnicity, class, and wealth, they appealed to God's purpose to save persons through incorporating them in Jesus' *ekklēsia* and by threatening cantankerous and sinning Christians with eternal punishment. The body of Christ was not restricted to individual communities; it embraced the whole *ekklēsia*. One evidence of that breadth was a congregation's hospitality to Christian travelers, itinerant ministers, and those who relocated from other places. To be sure, some leaders branded a few new arrivals as troublemakers who held unsettling ideas, but Christians were to regard one another as sisters and brothers within the *ekklēsia* and heirs of the kingdom through Christ.[4] First-century Christian communities seemed to be associated with one another or at least connected to traveling preachers designated as "apostles" or ambassadors.[5] Some, like Paul, gave their opinions about matters through correspondence or direct visits. Comments about, recommendations for, and greetings to persons were exchanged and read aloud in meetings of congregations. A number of congregations in

Asia Minor and Greece demonstrated their solidarity with their coreligionists in Palestine during a famine by contributing funds. Congregations, such as those in Philippi and Colossae, sent aid to imprisoned apostles. By the middle of the first century a loose network of relationships, concerns, and communications existed among congregations in the Empire. In the late nineties, the congregation in Rome presumed that it had the authority to send representatives to restore order along the lines outlined in its letter to the Corinthian congregation.[6] The *ekklēsia* included particular fellowships and extended to the broader union of the body of Christ wherever believers gathered to be Christ's worshipers, reconcilers, contributors, learners, and witnesses.

The church's role in the lives of individuals was profound. While the first believers became Christians through conversions in which they felt themselves grasped by the power of God's Spirit and made into new persons, they confessed that God had called them out of darkness into light, out of chaos to new order, out of death to life. Through the initiation rite of baptism, women and men were buried with Christ and raised to be his servants, free from the devil's claims. The corollary to that freedom was their incorporation into the body of Christ, the *ekklēsia*. To be a Christian was to be a member of Christ's community in its local, earthly, and cosmic dimensions. And membership put the person under the authority and discipline of the Spirit of Christ at work in the church and in the person's life. Some metaphors for the Christian life included athlete, soldier, servant, virgin, saint, and martyr. The community aimed at empowering, edifying, and building up the saints through worship, instruction, service, fellowship, and discipline. Risks for the individual were great; Jesus summoned followers to leave their families to join his community, and he warned that they would be tested and even killed for his sake. Their rewards in the kingdom, however, would surpass any offered in the present age. Yet believers had to be wary of the devil, who prowled about looking for Christian prey. The *ekklēsia* as the local and universal fellowship offered the individual a home, shelter, and kingdom—if the believer and the community had ears to hear what the Spirit was saying to the church. As the second century opened, the Spirit seemed to address the *ekklēsia* increasingly about its officers and organization.

THREE POSITIONS EMERGE

The issue of who was in charge of the regular functions of the local Christian community loomed large as questions and controversies developed. Dissent seemed to invite demons, so questions about authority and power pressed increasingly for answers as expectations for the parousia dulled. The initial generations of believers did not draw organizational charts, and they mentioned officials and offices mostly in the context of other issues. Probably duties and posts evolved on the precedents of Scripture and synagogue as well as need and local circumstances. Jesus, of course, was regarded as a key source.

He appears to have gathered persons around himself in ways shared by other rabbis. He was the center of a series of concentric circles of followers. The twelve whom he called to be a core group to travel with him on a regular basis were his disciples and apostles.[7] Within the core were several who posed the questions of others as well as their own, served their master, and became messengers for him. A surrounding circle of some women and men traveled with him consistently, and from their ranks Judas's successor was chosen. The outermost circle consisted of persons who followed him secretly (as did Joseph of Arimathea) or only while he was in their area. As later Gnostics were quick to point out, Jesus interpreted his parables and sayings privately, relating their hidden meanings to the "mystery" of the kingdom of God. After his resurrection, Christians claimed that the exalted Christ disclosed to them the proper meanings of the Scriptures, authorized them to go into the world to teach others his Way, do wonders, and initiate them into the *ekklēsia* through baptism. In anticipation of the kingdom, Jesus advised his followers to avoid using honorific titles and to shun exercising any form of authority over one another except that of service (*diakonia*). He would be present spiritually, most claimed, until the end of the age, when he would return in glory to judge the world.

Christian communities had different forms. In Jerusalem, there may have been a centralized structure that included key apostles or "pillars," that is, James, Peter, John, and possibly one of Jesus' brothers, along with others who served as an advisory council.[8] In Antioch and other Diaspora congregations, the offices and arrangements seemed to involve the congregation more directly. Paul and the author of Acts reflected severe tensions between some Christians in the Diaspora and the Jerusalem officials. The New Testament mentions several organizations: e.g., guilds of widows and virgin women, and perhaps another for virgin men. These groups helped poor and sick members and probably provided solace for the bereaved. Paul wrote about the kinds of ministry (*diakonia*) for which the Spirit gave special gifts (*charismata*), such as speaking wisdom and *gnōsis*, having faith, healing, working wonders, uttering prophecies, distinguishing between good and evil spirits, speaking in angelic tongues, and interpreting what was said in those tongues.[9] He named several charismatic ministers in what seems a priority order: apostles, prophets, and teachers (*didaskaloi*), then wonder-workers, healers, helpers, administrators, and speakers and interpreters of angelic tongues. The lists indicate that Christians expected the power of God to be present and active in their worship and daily lives. Paul's letters and other New Testament writings indicate still other offices, but are not clear about the duties involved. Three offices emerged as particularly important in first-century congregations: bishop (*episkopos*), elder (presbyter), and deacon.

The multiple meanings of *episkopos*—overseer, guide, supervisor, shepherd, and teacher—had overtones of ruler, leader, and benevolent provider. A faithful *episcopos* or bishop showed the qualities of loyalty, self-sacrifice, governing authority, and watchfulness. The Septuagint could be quoted to show that the Lord exercised *episkopē* or guiding oversight to Israel during the wilderness trek, set watchmen (*episkopoi*) over the house of the Lord, promised to give the covenant people *episkopoi* who were righteous, and was the true observer (*episkopos*) of the heart. Jews associated the term with God, angels, and prophets.[10] It seemed natural for Christians to call Jesus their shepherd (*poimēn*) and *episkopos* and to use the word for the supervisory officers in local congregations. Some congregations may have had more than one bishop.[11] Bishops administered, disciplined, made decisions, and taught. The author of Titus indicated that a bishop installed presbyters in congregations that were under the bishop's jurisdiction. According to the writer of the Pastoral Epistles, bishops exhorted members to do good and avoid evil, taught the proper doctrines, looked into their members' home lives, and modeled the godly life. It also seems that persons became bishops and other types of leaders through an act that involved the laying of hands on their heads, perhaps an echo of Septuagintal themes. No extant first-century documents describe the selection of bishops, relationships among bishops of different congregations or itinerant apostles, and the discipline or deposition of bishops. Such matters became issues in the second century.

Presbyter, the second position, is another multifaceted term. Greco-Romans used it for a prince, foremost leader, elder, and ambassador. Common threads in those meanings relate to age or maturity and governing authority. In the Septuagint, the word was related to councils of local or tribal leaders, and priests. It referred to the leaders who assisted Moses in making decisions, joined him on the mountain, and received a portion of the divine Spirit that had been given Moses, and prophesied. In the first century C.E., the Jewish presbyters or elders along with the scribes and priests were the preservers and interpreters of legal and ritual traditions. They also were connected to the Temple and to teaching and administering in the synagogues. Early Christian congregations commissioned men to be part of a council of presbyters. In Jerusalem, they were closely associated with the apostles in setting policy for the whole *ekklēsia*. Their ministry is described in several references as involving teaching, preaching, administering, disciplining, praying for and anointing the sick, and confirming charismatic leaders. An unnamed presbyter toward the end of the first century wrote "the elect Lady" and her children (a congregation and its members) to warn them of false teachers and advised them to expel a rival to his authority.[12]

Deacons and deaconesses filled a third office. They carried out the congregation's ministry of distributing food and other forms of assistance to needy Christians, and they may have guided the guilds of virgins and widows. They may have been included as helpers in Paul's catalogue of charismatically gifted persons. Their personal qualifications emphasized faithful, selfless service, "Deacons . . . must be serious, not double-tongued, not indulging in much wine, not greedy for money; they must hold fast to the mystery of the faith with a clear conscience. And let them first be tested; then, if they prove themselves blameless, let them serve."[13] Once again, there is no information about their selection or deposition, but apparently some moved from one congregation to another (Rom. 16).

The three positions gained prominence in the second century. Some doctrinal and organizational struggles within and between first- and second-century congregations derived from the church's attempts to balance and harmonize these positions in the midst of internal tensions and external pressures.

THREE PATTERNS FOR THE EKKLĒSIA

Because the *ekklēsia* was of cosmic, eschatological significance, its structures and leaders assumed increasing importance for believers as they waited for Jesus' return. Three patterns of church polity emerged and struggled for dominance in the second century.

The earliest was probably the congregational pattern. Culturally it had direct ties to the Greek *ekklēsia*, at which citizens debated and decided issues and assessed and selected leaders. Among the Septuagintal precedents were David's and Ezra's putting matters before the *ekklēsia*. Supporters of the congregational position might point to Jesus' criticism of disciples who jockeyed for positions of authority over others. Advocates of putting maximum authority in the hands of the congregation also might recall that Jesus breathed peace on all those in the upper room and stayed with the community. They might even remember that women had important roles related to Jesus: for example, Mary bore him, and Mary Magdalene was the first to know about and spread the news of his resurrection. They remembered that Jesus said that his Spirit would guide them into all truth, and that he would be present when as few as two believers gathered in his name. The Spirit was not limited to inspiring the disciples or the apostles, for the Spirit also was given to unbaptized foreigners such as the Roman soldier Cornelius. There was no indication, they could claim, that Jesus made some of his followers superior to others, save a curious comment to Peter.[14] Revelation came from God when and where God willed to give it. And that made sense out of the Antioch congregation's selecting and sending out apostles. The array of precedents was complemented by the theological claim that God was present in the worship and the deliberations of the called-out people. The presence of *charismata* showed that the Spirit ratified God's approval of the congregation that sought to be true to its calling to be a community of saints. Authority in matters of doctrine and discipline, therefore, was vested in the whole fellowship of believers and not in a few leaders. Behind the congregational position was confidence in the presence of the Spirit and of the ability of humans to discern the will of God. The position allowed for a distinction of functions but minimized the need for a leadership caste such as the Levites or a hierarchical governance structure as in the Empire. Within the *ekklēsia*, Christians were one in Christ, regardless of sex, social status, race, or educational level. Such a stance encouraged believers to exert their enthusiasms and insights, especially in being receptive to the inspiration and gifts of the Spirit. And if the congregation's leaders seemed spiritually lethargic or ready to compromise with the world, God would raise up charismatic leaders from the congregation just as the Lord raised up deliverers from within Israel of old.

Around 130–150 C.E. interest in the parousia welled up in Phrygia (modern northern Turkey) and spread later to western North Africa. The Phrygian leaders included Montanus, Priscilla (or Prisca), and Maximilla. They claimed that the Spirit moved mightily in them and in the congregations associated with them in what the New Prophecy as they called their movement. Their goal was to recall the church to its enthusiasm about the parousia and the *charismata*. Jesus' return, said the Spirit through the prophets, was at hand. Christians were urged again to detach themselves from worldly pursuits, sexuality, and possessions. The prophets exhorted Christians to be faithful, even if faithfulness led to death. In fact, many who were moved by the message deliberately sought the crown of martyrdom. The New Prophecy, or as its opponents called it, Montanism, sounded much like the earliest Christian expectations and enthusiasms. Some congregations in Europe, including Rome for a time, were well disposed toward it. The movement did not have doctrinal problems as such, but it ran into political and organizational resistance from fellow Christians. New revelations, calls for martyrdom, women prophesying, and spontaneous charismatic outbursts drew criticism from congregations and leaders who saw in Montanism the prospects of disorder. When leaders of other congregations objected to claims made by the new prophets, the Montanists accused their critics of being spiritually cold and of conforming to the world. Neither side was ready to compromise, and the Montanists were discredited by the larger, more centrally organized congregations. Some Montanist sympathizers, as in North Africa, stressed that only a spiritually pure *ekklēsia* was worthy to meet the Lord on his return. Given the option of being silent or being rejected, many Montanists formed their own congregations or became dominant in existing congregations.

Charismatic movements such as Montanism thrive in the congregational pattern because they appeal to a broad range of members, especially those who feel marginalized in Christian communities run by a hierarchy. Yet, as Paul learned at Corinth, there are different spirits blowing in the church. Disorder is a constant risk in a congregation that stresses *charismata*. Disorder, Christians often discovered, was the prelude to disgrace and failure. Some others, convinced that they had the *charismata*, set up spiritual hierarchies, thinking that those who did not speak in angelic tongues were deficient or second-class believers. The Montanist movement also underscored the persistent problem of who had authority to decide doctrine, morals, and worship. When the congregation cannot reach a consensus or when the spiritual elite disagrees with the consensus, or when the consensus conflicts with previously accepted positions, who speaks as a new Amos, Jeremiah, Ezra, or Nehemiah? A related theological challenge to the congregational position asks, Is the *ekklēsia* more than a collection of congregations? Is there one Lord, one faith, one baptism, and one *ekklēsia*?[15] A congregation, then, would be a member of a larger organism, and the larger whole would be present within even the smallest fellowship of believers. If so, then congregations are interdependent and responsible to one another for their worship, teaching, order, leadership, and social witness. If the *ekklēsia* is the body of Christ, then what one congregation does brings joy, concern, sickness, or praise to the whole Body. When there are divisions or disputes within a congregation, when doctrines are questioned or persecutions cripple communal life, should other congregations and leaders intervene to restore harmony? As a result of the controversy over Montanism, Christians in the late second and subsequent centuries became uneasy when they heard about new bursts of prophecy, new revelation, manifestations of the Spirit, speaking in tongues, fervent expectations of the parousia, women in leadership positions, and the congregational pattern.

The council of presbyters provided the second pattern. Septuagintal and synagogal precedents indicated that members of the Christian councils had the authority to administer, lead worship, teach, and discipline members. In the Jerusalem congregation, the council and apostles deliberated and decided issues together. In the Diaspora and after 70, the presbyters, perhaps on the basis of their associations with apostles, could be regarded as the leaders and teachers of congregations. Functions cited for presbyters coincided with some oversight duties connected to bishops, e.g., administering, teaching, and disciplining. At certain points it seems that when first-century authors referred to "bishops," the reference was to presbyters as overseers.[16]

Gnostics such as Valentinus found this form of organization congenial. Neither the *psychikoi* majority nor the *psychikoi* bishops and deacons, Gnostics could argue, ought to interfere with the teachings and practices of the spiritually superior *gnōstikoi*. It is likely that persons such as Valentinus, Basilides, and Carpocrates headed independent schools and that some of their students were presbyters of congregations. They must have been pained by what they saw and heard from the *gnōsis*-deprived soul people who led worship, spoke in tongues, or attempted to explain the mysteries of Scripture. They would have reacted with disdain when presbyters and bishops whom they considered their spiritual inferiors criticized gnostic interpretations and commentaries. Teachers, whether on the doctrinal fringes or at the center, could claim that informed, biblically knowledgeable, articulate leadership was critical for the *ekklēsia*'s preaching, teaching, witnessing, and administration. Ezra and his scribes taught the Law, purified the remnant, restored true worship, and provided for the *ekklēsia*'s continuance in God's plan. The council of presbyters were like the scribes and Pharisees who Jesus said sat on Moses' seat and who brought forth treasures from the storehouse of God's wisdom: they were to be obeyed.[17] But teachers often disagreed, and administrators differed over both methods and goals. Teachers such as Valentinus could not find wide acceptance—although some officials thought Valentinian Gnostics were all too widely accepted. Who among the teachers or among the members of a board of administrators decided what proper teaching was and what sanctions were to be imposed on erring members? On what basis were such decisions made? Presbyters might be sound advisers, but ought they be the decision makers?

The third pattern picked up momentum, theological justifications, and supporters as controversies disrupted numerous congregations in the late first century. Although significant ambiguities cloud the argument, an episcopal or bishop-oriented polity seemed to many to be the solution to the problems of authority and order. The Pastoral Epistles described Paul selecting Timothy and Titus as the overseers, preachers, teachers, and discipliners of congregations with the responsibility to ensure the appointment of other proper leaders. *1 Clement*, the letter written from the Roman to the Corinthian congregation, used "presbyter" and "bishop" interchangeably as it addressed the revolt against the presbyters at Corinth. The letter described Jesus and the apostles establishing a procedure in which Jesus called the apostles, and the apostles appointed bishops and deacons to lead congregations. The first bishops and deacons were to be succeeded by other worthies as needed. While the actual arrangements are not specified, a structure involving supervisory officers called bishops was attributed to and sanctioned by Jesus and the earliest followers. *1 Clement* stated that opposition to these officials was "exceedingly disgraceful, and unworthy of your Christian upbringing. . . . the Lord's name is being blasphemed because of your stupidity, and you are exposing yourself to danger." To stand against the bishops was to stand against the apostles, Christ, and God. During the argument for proper discipline and order in the church, *1 Clement* used *laikos*, the term associated with average or "lay" members, for the first time in the sense that such persons were the lowest rank in the *ekklēsia* and were to take orders from the officials.[18]

The Christian community began as an intentionally formed fellowship united by commitments to Jesus and the Kingdom of God and not one that was based on ethnicity or family. By the second century, it had become an ongoing organization. Tensions and conflicts among the roles and positions within the church became woven into the challenges Christians faced concerning creation, humanity, and Jesus. As pressures within and among congregations increased, Christians also faced the wider culture.

The intentional community became a seminatural community and thus became a problem to itself. By the second century, tensions and conflicts among the roles, positions, and patterns of the church wove through the challenges concerning creation, humanity, and Jesus. As pressures within congregations pushed believers to seek and find adequate responses, Christians also faced the wider culture.

> Remember, Lord, your Church, to save it from all evil and to make it perfect by your love. Make it holy, "and gather" it "together from the four winds" into your Kingdom which you have made ready for it. For yours is the power and the glory forever. Let Grace come and let this world pass away.
>
> *Didache* 10:5-6

9

The Fifth Challenge: Christians and Society

Do not love the world or the things in the world. The love of the Father is not in those who love the world; for all that is in the world—the desire of the flesh, the desire of the eyes, the pride in riches—comes not from the Father but from the world. And the world and its desire are passing away, but those who do the will of God live forever.

1 John 2:15-17

Christians are at odds with one another over attitudes toward and participation in the societies in which they live. Both bold and muted contrasts appear in their public rhetoric and actions. Pagans overheard the intrachurch debates, listened to the external statements, and observed Christians' behavior. Critics and mobs formed their own opinions about the gospel and Jesus' followers, thereby pushing Christians to make responses. A series of challenges and counterchallenges rotated around Christians in society: the challenges within the church, by the church to the society, and from the society to the church.

CHALLENGES WITHIN THE CHURCH

The challenges within the church over society came from conflicting thoughts about the nature and destiny of the creation and of humanity. Most Christians operated with a theology that moved between two poles or extremes. At one pole, often showing the influences of *Enoch* and the *Testament of the Twelve Patriarchs*, some Christians were convinced that demonic forces had seized control of the present age and that humanity had fallen from its lofty origins. Society and its cultural expressions, then, were shot through with evil. The

127

demonic distorted art, literature, and intellectual pursuits. Government, *pai-deia*, entertainment, religion, and morality had fallen under the sway of God's enemies. Cosmetics, dance, jewelry, clothing styles, sexuality, and related social conventions were snares set by the devil. Christians ought to be forbidden to be actors, musicians, dancers, tax collectors, soldiers, sculptors, and teachers of Greco-Roman rhetoric and philosophy because these and other occupations recognized and supported devotion to the gods, who were demons in disguise. In a similar manner, Christians were to heed to warnings of Sirach and Solomon about wealth and commerce, for the love of money was the root of all evil. Love for God and love for the demon-corrupted world were contradictory. That world was perishing, and Jesus' resurrection-victory over evil would be fulfilled in the coming judgment on the present age and on those who dedicated themselves to it. Christians exhorted one another to be ready in holiness, unspotted by the societies around them. Jesus-Moses led the new Israel out of Egypt-bondage, made a new covenant with them at Sinai-Calvary, and was still with them in the wilderness–present age. The promised land–kingdom beckoned to them; but golden-calf-like-temptations, Balaam-like false prophets, and Moabite-like oppressors lurked in that wilderness. When moving toward the pole which emphasized the fallenness of the age and of society, Christians branded pagan culture as evil and human nature as corrupt. Consequently, Jesus' people, individually and communally, were to avoid contact with society and its cheap, dangerous pleasures.

The other pole, anchored in a positive evaluation of creation and humanity, emphasized that God created the world, provided for it out of love, and guided it to its ultimate fulfillment. Divine Wisdom and Logos were often cited by supporters of the positive pole as God's agents in creating the world and humanity, guiding the whole toward its glorious fulfillment. If the world-creating and enlightening Logos-Life had entered the cosmos and become a human, then human nature and will were capable of being holy again. And if God's Logos really dwelled in the physical structures of the present age, then the creation had the capacity to be holy. If God loved the cosmos so much that God sent the Only-Begotten into the world to die for its salvation, then the cosmos was God's precious possession and the very work of the Lord's mind and will. If Jesus was the restorer of immortality and the renewer of humanity, then the world was where restoration and renewal were at work. Surely, a world made by Logos-Wisdom contained the seeds and traces of the knowledge and goodness of its Creator and the Creator's agents. God was not without adequate witnesses and just persons in any time or culture—even in the first and second centuries and even in the Roman Empire. Christians needed to be present in society, for they were the salt of the earth, the leaven in the lump, the light set upon the lampstand to inspire, guide, and show others the way to the God who is truth and life. Christians, obviously, had to be careful in maintaining moral discipline and in using the objects and institutions of the world. Yet they ought not be afraid to address and participate in their societies, for Christians had the insight to discern the seeds and traces of God's wisdom scattered throughout the world. The world was like a school in which Christ's *gymnastikē* was exercise in moral excellence and his *mousikē* prepared them to speak God's message accurately and persuasively. With the proper teachers and curriculum, believers could engage philosophy, literature, art, even social life so as to be educated in ethics and prepared for the higher revelations that God had in store for them. As Jesus promised to prepare heavenly mansions for his followers, Christians could look forward to the ascent of their souls after death to their proper heavenly homes. There was room, then, to encourage Christians who sought to join with their societies, when the societies tolerated their participation.

Most Christians could carry on their daily lives and worship regularly using the categories of the two poles but without exalting one over the other. They both prayed for the coming of the kingdom and opened businesses, accepted both Gen. 1 and *Enoch* as Scripture, both steeled themselves against persecution by the demonic government and exhorted one another to obey the emperor. Two sets of circumstances generated conflict between the two poles within the church. One came as a result of external pressures, such as persecution and mob actions. The church closed ranks and emphasized the need for discipline and massive divine intervention. The powers of evil and the corruption of humanity seemed strong under those conditions, and the world's hatred of Christians appeared tantamount to hatred of God. The other set of circumstances featured problems within the church. When the community was split by rival factions, hotly contested doctrinal positions, and scrambles for power, various parties appealed to various understandings of the Christian's relationship to society. The Montanists, Marcionites, and Valentinians, for different theological reasons, looked for the dissolution of the present society and its rules and the church of the majority and its structures. By the end of the first century, and in light of the nonoccurrence of the parousia, Christians were giving each other mixed signals about the legitimacy and extent of their participation in society. Paul denounced Greco-Roman rhetoric and philosophy—and used both. *1 Clement* used Greco-Roman examples and traditions to describe Christian teachings while advocating the development of a Christian *paideia*. The Pastorals condemned the use of myths and Greco-Roman sources, yet employed the vocabulary of Middle Platonic–Stoic ethics to describe appropriate Christian behavior. James denounced the wealthy, but the author of Acts emphasized successful merchants who became Christians. 1 Peter agreed with Paul that Christians were to respect the state, not be subversive, and even to pray for the emperor, but John of Patmos damned the government to an eternity in the lake of burning sulphur. Perhaps as long as the church was in a minority position and lacked social power, the contradictions and challenges would remain. Even then, both poles provided rallying points for future supporters, and both poles could appeal to Scripture, tradition, and worship patterns. Both sides could unite on their criticisms of Greco-Roman society.

CHALLENGES BY THE CHURCH TO THE SOCIETY

Men and women became Christians mostly because they felt that the traditional religious expressions failed them, while the gospel met their needs. Christianity entailed a rejection rather than a renovation of the gods, their worship, and the social structures which they sanctioned. People who went through the waters of baptism to be buried with and raised in Christ understood themselves to be born anew in God's reign. Intent on sharing that new life and fellowship with others, Christians spoke frequently and sometimes fervently of the shortcomings, hollowness, and distortions that they claimed characterized Greco-Roman society. Criticisms and denunciations of pagan principles and goals were staples in Christian rhetoric. When seeking to convert others or to explain the Way to pagans, Christians highlighted as many inconsistencies, dilemmas, and corruptions as they could in order to discredit the old and validate the new religion. Within their own congregations and schools, Christians reinforced their decision to follow Jesus by reminding one another of the life they had left behind, the holiness to which they had been called, and the kingdom that awaited them. The Christian critique of pagan society was sharp, effective, and, to a large extent, accurate. Two commonly cited themes were moral and spiritual degeneracy.

The charge of moral degeneracy was neither new nor unique. Earlier Greek dramatists and poets were blunt in exposing flaws in individuals and their own society. Latin satirists such as Horace (65–8 B.C.E.) and Juvenal (ca. 55–127 C.E.), the historians Tacitus (ca. 55–120) and Suetonius (ca. 70–125), and moralists such as Plutarch exposed and warned about moral conditions. Apuleius (ca. 124–170) took every opportunity to illuminate the ethical bankruptcy of persons and institutions. Pagan and Christian criticisms struck mostly at the same subjects: corruption, drunkenness, gluttony, greed, violence, and especially sex. There was no need to ferret out or invent evidence to prove that immorality was rife in society; most people were aware of scandals from emperors' courts to local brothels. Rhetorical and philosophical schools concentrated on ethical concerns in hope of educating persons to control their passions, habits, and actions. They devised lists of conduct to be encouraged and avoided. Christians sometimes adapted items from the catalogues of pagan ethical *paideia* to describe the depths into which Greco-Roman society had fallen and the virtues toward which Christians should strive. Following Deuteronomic patterns, Christians lumped the way of death with the works of the flesh and devil, setting these against the way of life, fruits of the Spirit, and the law of Christ.[1] They cited the traditional heroes and divinities depicted in public art, the theater, literature, and lessons in encyclical *paideia* as shameful praises of adultery, fornication, deceit, murder. If moral degeneracy can be found in most societies, Christians in the first and second centuries not only found it but used it to dislodge persons from their traditional ways so that they would become and remain fellow Christians.

The charge of spiritual degeneracy also challenged pagan society. Again, there were pagan critics who called for reinterpretations of the divine and religion. The trend toward ethical monotheism in Middle Platonism and Stoicism and the success of Asian and Egyptian mystery cults indicated that the educated and the aristocrats knew that the old religion needed to be revitalized if it was to survive. The cults of Isis, Mithras, Dionysus, Orpheus, and Serapis offered new visions for the emotions, the intellect, and life beyond death. The Isis cult proposed that the many deities were really other names for Isis.[2] The tales about the gods, if taken literally, clearly embarrassed many thoughtful pagans. Accounts about divine castrations, infidelities, jealousies, and conflicts needed to be reinterpreted, if they were to be used as resources for a religion that was seeking to guide an ethical and pious society. Christian critics obviously were interested not in rehabilitating the old religion but in replacing it with the gospel of God in Jesus. They saw the myths as the devil's tools. The moral degeneracy of society and individuals was the direct product of the spiritual degeneracy of traditional pagan religion. *Paideia* at all levels was contaminated by demonically inspired treachery and disorder. The devilish origins and distortions of the pagan culture were evident in society's corruption and despair as well as in the attempts of scholars to find noble meanings in immoral texts. The multiplication of new religious groups and philosophical schools claiming to possess the truth seemed to many Christians to be further proof that the wider society was rife with evil influences. Christians repeated the pagan criticisms of paganism and offered in its stead the one who they claimed was the Way, the Truth, and the Life. Criticism and rejection, however, ran in the other direction, too.

CHALLENGES BY SOCIETY TO THE CHURCH

As far as pagans were concerned, Jesus' followers advocated the violent overthrow of all forms of human government, commerce, society, and culture. They prayed in the name of an executed criminal, longed for his return, and refused to recognize Rome's divine mission. Pagans who read the Revelation to John might be baffled by the imagery that cloaked Christian hostility to the imperial government, but they would not be able to miss the animosity toward the whole culture, including its merchants and musicians. No wonder Tacitus, John's contemporary, regarded the Christian religion as one of the hideous evils that had flowed to Rome.[3] Pagans responded to Christianity with two sets of moral accusations and three serious challenges to Christian claims to have the truth.

The most cogent set of accusations charged Christians with atheism and treason. Educated pagans often came to regard the deities of the various nations, even the Olympians, as names given to a unified divine power. Christians, however, derived their monotheism from Judaism and not through philosophy. Biblical prophets such as those who were in the book of Isaiah denied that the gods of the nations existed at all. Jesus' followers repeated and stressed Isaiah's mocking comments about the idols and idolatry—a tactic that had inflamed the populace. Christians went further and relegated the gods of the Empire to the status of demons in the sense of evil beings. Since Christians denied the existence or the goodness of the traditional gods and refused to sacrifice to them, pagans naturally accused Christians of being atheists. To deny the gods due reverence was further evidence that Christians were treasonous. The gods protected the state, and Rome was the eternal, divinely endowed city. Logically, those who rejected the gods rejected the Empire's claims to be sanctioned by the gods. Traditions such as those associated with Oedipus showed that a citizenry that did not root out persons who mocked the gods would be punished. When disasters struck and people sought to determine what had offended the gods, fingers could be pointed toward Christians. Even when Christian criticism and ridicule of the traditional cult did not gain converts it led to a decline in public pagan worship—a decline that could well evoke Olympian retaliation.[4] The litmus test for an atheist and traitor was whether or not the person sacrificed to the gods. In the case of Christians, officials sometimes added that the person also was to curse Christ. Refusal to comply indicated punishable obstinacy and impiety. If the individual performed the required sacrifice, she or he was restored to the larger social community. The church, obviously, considered those who offered the sacrifices to be apostates, that is, deserters from the ranks of Christ's saints.[5] The New Testament tract, Hebrews, declared that apostates could never be forgiven; they were like thorns and thistles, good only for burning.[6] While any Christian might be ordered to sacrifice, prominent members such as bishops, presbyters, and deacons were likely targets. If the authorities could regain such a person, the validity of pagan ideals was vindicated and the church weakened. If the Christian refused, then fines, confiscation of property, prison, servitude in the mines, or death could be ordered. The church would lose a leader, and potentially susceptible pagans were discouraged from following such a dangerous course. Or perhaps the blood of the martyrs would be seed for even tougher believers who admired such courage. Many government officials did not relish persecuting Christians. Like Pliny, they preferred to avoid disruptive confrontations and impassioned crowds. Yet officials knew that they were responsible to enforce the law and to punish the obstinate. Christians knew that they were charged by God to be faithful to their Lord, even if it earned them the martyr's crown.

The other set of charges, Thyestean feasts (cannibalism) and Oedipal intercourse (incest), developed largely on the basis of rumor. Christians, like members of other sects, opened their rituals only to initiated members. Baptism, the initiation, or entry rite, qualified persons to participate in the central act of worship, a sacred meal or meals.[7] If there was one meal by the late first century, it covered themes such a love feast or fellowship (koinōnia) meal among the brothers and sisters in Christ, a remembrance of the new Passover-covenant made by Jesus on the night in which he was betrayed, an appropriation of Jesus' action as the lamb that took away the sins of the world, and a foretaste of the messianic banquet in the kingdom. The meal was probably shared at night because most believers worked or were unable to attend meetings in the daytime. Probably, as Pliny reported, the community sang hymns to Christ. First Corinthians and the Synoptic Gospels indicate that Christians shared bread and wine, quoting to one another a version of Jesus' words, "Take; this is my body," and "This is my blood." Persons who only overheard the words or who wanted to defame the Christian community reported that Jesus' followers ate and drank human flesh and blood. Since Christians prohibited abortion and did not expose their unwanted babies, the report about cannibalism sometimes modulated into the charge that Christians devoured their excess infants. For pagan listeners that rumor recalled Thyestes, the king who ate his children. The charge of cannibalism was repeated throughout the second century and served to arouse pagan opposition toward Christians.

Charges of incest were based on reports that at a signal during the sacred meal the lamps would be put out and an orgy would take place. Since one would not be able to see one's partner in the dark, brothers and sisters, parents and children were rumored to have sex with each other. Probably widespread use among Christians of terms such as love, brother, and sister, and night meetings helped clothe the charge with credibility. Greco-Romans would also recall that Thebes suffered terribly for Oedipus's sins. Some Christian groups, such as the followers of Carpocrates, may in fact have been sexual libertines. Apparently members of several congregations believed that freedom from the

Law meant freedom from all restraints on conduct. For them, being in Christ entailed being liberated from the taboos of society. Paradoxically, pagan men sometimes denounced Christians for alienating the affections, or at least the obedience, of their wives and daughters, for often women who became Christians refused to have sexual relations with their husbands.[8]

Accusations about cannibalism and incest seemed farfetched to pagan intellectuals; they took a more incisive line. At the intellectual and spiritual level, pagans challenged Christians at three points: novelty, ignorance, and barbarism.

First, novelty. The older, the truer; the oldest, the truest was the conventional wisdom of the Empire and other societies. The more ancient a school's or an idea's pedigree was, the closer it was to divinely revealed and sanctioned truth. Branding persons, groups, or ideas as new or as harboring new tendencies amounted to calling them shallow and false. The basis for the principle that linked antiquity to truth was the view that the divine powers disclosed truth in a powerful manner at the beginning (*archē*) or in events closer to the beginning than the present. Since then, the truth has been seen and heard with decreasing intensity and clarity.[9] In order to perceive the divine truth as accurately as possible, people need to find the oldest teachings, read the most venerable texts and traditions, and associate with the most ancient communities. Practices, ideas, and communities that are new are ipso facto seen to be seriously deficient in or devoid of truth. The gods and lore of Egypt, Greece, Asia, and Syria-Palestine were impressively ancient. Greeks and Romans were awed by the antiquity of the Nile, the pyramids, and the gods of Egypt. Persia enticed Alexander and his imitators to adapt their comparatively crude customs to the high culture of Mesopotamia. The Jews were especially intriguing. They had outlasted the ancient Mesopotamian empires, and accounts of Moses outclassing Pharaoh's wizards and leading Egypt's armies into a watery trap attracted the attention of many. Solomon was reputed to be a sage, and he certainly antedated the Greek philosophers by four centuries. Philo claimed that Abraham taught the Egyptians philosophy—and they passed it on to the Greeks. Josephus argued that Judaism was the oldest and best route to knowing God's truth. What about Christianity? Was it old or new? Was it novelty or truth?

Since Christians insisted on the historical specificity of a person born during the reign of Caesar Augustus, they had to admit that the founder of their religion lived only recently. Other religions that entered the Empire claimed connections with older cultures.[10] They were new only in the sense that they were introduced recently, not in the sense that they were new chronologically. Moreover, they featured deities who were not limited to a time or place. Isis and Mithras, for example, transcended the limitations of time and geography.

They were described in personal terms, but really they were more like cosmic principles than persons. Christianity's origination in a set place at a particular time was taken by pagans as a clear indication that its claims to truth were shaky at best.

Initially, Christians responded that they actually held to the oldest form of divine revelation. That response relied heavily on their claim to be the true continuation of God's chosen people, Israel. As long as Christians were associated with synagogues, pagans might be willing to consider such a rationale. Jews, of course, rejected such claims by Christians. Christians not only read the Septuagint as predicting and prefiguring Jesus as the Messiah, they also read Jesus' teachings into Greco-Roman literature and philosophy. Socrates and Plato, the dramatists and poets were, said some Christians, proto-believers in Jesus. Paul used pagan poets, and *1 Clement* referred to the self-sacrificing, dying-rising phoenix as evidence that God prepared pagan culture for the coming of Christ. The Stoic logos was especially important in "proving" that Christianity was ancient, for, as the Gospel of John said, the logos became human in Jesus and lived among us. But pagan critics were scarcely deflected by such Christian special pleading.

Pagan intellectuals leveled a second criticism: Christianity was steeped in ignorance. Rhetoric sought to arrive at knowledge through persuasion and philosophy through reason. Both used argument, experience, and demonstration. Analyzing carefully, testing positions, and taking little for granted were all basic to the pursuit of knowledge and truth. Even then, pagan thinkers realized that their conclusions were tentative. They arrived at likely statements that could be revised and corrected. For them *pistis* meant probing and testing, weighing and sifting factors. An unprobed conclusion was like an unexamined life, not worth holding. By the same token, a position that was contrary to reason and experience, flew in the face of the ancient values and traditions of the community, and could not or would not submit to probing was suspected of being shaped in ignorance. Those who held it must be superstitious, obstinate, and deluded. The more the Greco-Roman pagans applied reason and the more they pointed toward Jesus' nonreturn, the more they saw serious inconsistencies in Christian claims and teachings. And the harder pagan critics pressed their objections to Christian claims to truth, the more insistent and defensive Christians became about Christian doctrines. Pagans took that response as further evidence of stubborn ignorance.

From the pagan point of view, Christianity was foolishness and its adherents were determined ignoramuses. The teachings attributed to Jesus were not in themselves superior to the ethical insights of Greco-Roman, Egyptian, and Mesopotamian sages. Wonders attributed to Jesus were the standard stuff of wonder accounts about great teachers and heroes such as Asclepius and Apollonius. Pagans knew that heroes often inspired others by dying and being apotheosized or praised for their exemplary actions. Pagans could make little sense out of the proposition that one person's ignominious death might benefit even those who followed that person, never mind all humanity. The resurrection was a bigger problem. Christians admitted that only those who already believed in Jesus saw him after the resurrection. It would be difficult, then, to probe that assertion because the alleged witnesses had a special interest in using the story to prove their points. Further, while pagans could understand a soul leaving a body on death, they could not take seriously the idea that dead bodies—even mutilated ones—would rise from the grave. Resurrections made neither philosophical nor experiential sense. Claims about the coming end of the age and the future kingdom were inherently unverifiable hypotheses. Christianity, pagans concluded, did not stand up to the rigorous inquiries of rhetors and philosophers—and Christians knew it.

Paul failed at Athens when he addressed philosophers, and he apparently developed hostile feelings toward them and rhetors.[11] He took pride in saying that Greeks viewed Christian teachings about Jesus' crucifixion as foolishness. In a grand reversal, he argued that God's wisdom was regarded as foolishness by the so-called wise of the world when really human wisdom was foolishness in the sight of God. *Pistis*, Paul held, was not probing inquiry but faith, faithfulness, trust, and trustworthiness. He wrote that humans were saved not by knowledge but by trust and faithful adherence to the faithful God who revealed divine trustworthiness in Christ.[12] Christian-style *pistis* was the starting point for knowing truth, an echo of the biblical maxim that the fear of the Lord is the beginning of wisdom. Pagan thinkers could not see how Jesus was the Wisdom of God. They took Christian *pistis* to be unthinking acceptance of nonsense. The charge of ignorance rankled Christians. Some believers wanted to jettison *paideia*, philosophy, and rhetoric. Others were convinced that the pagan disciplines could be used for Christian self-understanding and mission.

The third challenge was the criticism of barbarism. Originally a barbarian was a foreigner, specifically, someone who was not Greek or who mangled the Greek language. Since Rome understood itself to be the successor to and custodian of Greek culture, Romans included themselves among those whose language and ideals were the standard for cultural acceptability. A derivative and more popular definition of barbarian was someone who was uncultured, crude, inferior in class and background. Isocrates provided a bridge between ethnic Greeks and persons of other groups when he wrote that whoever had a Greek *paideia* could be considered a Greek, that is, whoever participated in the public and academic *paideia* that characterized Greek society and its values would be considered a cultured person.[13] Conversely, those who did not have or who rejected that *paideia* were cultural barbarians. The pagans had good reason to brand Christians as barbarians. Plainly, the first Christians were barbarians in the ethnic sense. Palestine was on the eastern edge of the Empire, and it was considered an odd place populated by odder people. As far as Tacitus was concerned, the Jews were a "nation prone to superstition but hating all religious rites," a race "detested by the gods." Their worship and customs were "perverse and disgusting, [and] owe their strength to their very badness." In his opinion, "the Jewish religion is tasteless and mean."[14] When pagans heard Christians lay claim to antiquity through Judaism, the pagans could counter that since Jews were cultural barbarians, so, too, were Christians. Pagans then asked, what kind of people would join a movement that was accused of atheism, treason, cannibalism, and incest, denied the public *paideia* of society, and was a novelty marked by ignorance? The pagan answer was: only those who were uncultured, gullible, ill-mannered, and low-class. Christianity, then, was a cult and way of life for barbarians. As such it scarcely merited the respectful hearing its devotees desired—or the protection of the Empire's laws.

Christians were also regarded as barbarians for reasons peculiar to themselves. Pagan intellectuals were quick to point out that Christianity appealed largely to the lower ranks of society, that is, the poor, slaves, women, and recently emancipated slaves (freedmen). The marginalized were welcomed into congregations, just as Jesus had welcomed them. Paul reminded the Corinthians that not many of them were wise, highborn, or wealthy. To be sure, there were rich persons such as merchants and government officials in some early congregations, and as the first century closed, wealth and the wealthy became problems for the church.[15] Still, pagan critics linked the validity of the message to the social status of those attracted to it. The uncultured and the underclass responded to the gospel more frequently and fervently than the cultured elite. Another reason to label Christianity as barbarous was its apparent rejection of Greco-Roman *paideia*. Joining in public rituals and events was part of a cultured person's responsibility in society. So, too, was being educated in the Homeric literature and the principles of a school's ethics. Christians protested that participation in public and academic *paideia* were religious acts prohibited by their loyalty to Jesus. Pagans took such objections as further proof of Christian barbarism.

Novelty, ignorance, and barbarism were criticisms that ran through the objections intelligent pagans raised against Christianity. When added to charges of atheism, treason, and gross immorality, these criticisms of the church constituted a formidable indictment.

THE RISKS OF RESPONDING AND SEARCHING

How should Christians respond? To whom should they respond? Who was authorized to respond? To ignore or admit some of the accusations risked leaving the impression that they were true, but to offer explanations and to make defenses was no easy task. To explain even some aspects about the Eucharist—for example, to refute the charges of incest and cannibalism—entailed opening the church increasingly to the prying eyes of a public that could be expected to remain hostile. What could and should be disclosed? Was there sufficient agreement among Christians to offer a generally common view of what the members of the *ekklēsia* believed and taught? Would faith become "the faith," that is, a compilation of teachings rather than an active personal trust in and loyalty to God? Who would respond and what purposes would be served when responses were made? Mobs and pagan officials did not want to discuss theology; they wanted Christians to stop being Christians. If there were interested pagans, how could Christians address them except in the language and thought forms of Greco-Roman culture? It was, felt many Christians, a seductive culture, one that might infiltrate and change basic Christian beliefs about God, humanity, and salvation.

As the first turned into the second century, energies spent earlier on Jesus' imminent return were redirected partially to responding to challenges within the church, challenging pagan society, and responding to pagan accusations and criticisms. The community was learning to seek answers to critical questions within its own ranks, to develop organizational patterns, to formulate its own *paideia* so as to transmit its identity to future generations. Christians might tell themselves that they were in the world but not of it, but still they began to settle down, answer their critics, and to develop deeper understandings of God and themselves. Responses to the challenges were not made in vacuums or by faceless entities. People in particular times and places searched and reported on their quests. They did so at considerable risk—inside as well as outside of the church. Still, the leaders who knocked were convinced that they had received insight, and they shared what they discovered with supporters and critics.

> What the soul is in the body, that Christians are in the world. The soul is dispersed through all the members of the body, and Christians are scattered through all the cities of the world. The soul dwells in the body, but does not belong to the body, and Christians dwell in the world, but do not belong to the world.
>
> *Epistle to Diognetus* 6:1-3

Part III
Five Leaders Respond

Remember your leaders, those who spoke the word of God to you, consider the outcome of their way of life, and imitate their faith. Jesus Christ is the same yesterday and today and forever. Do not be carried away by all kinds of strange teachings. . . . Obey your leaders and submit to them, for they are keeping watch over your souls and will give an account.

Hebrews 13:7-8, 17a

The decades that began with the reign of Trajan and ended with Caracalla's death were wonderfully and miserably unbalanced. It was a time for philosophy, art, and commerce—and passion, crassness, and fraud. One emperor walked the streets unmolested, others were cut down by their friends. Legal codes were reformed and made more humane, but hundreds perished in arenas as gladiators and victims of persecution. Religious and philosophical groups multiplied, yet their basic principles and ethical concerns seemed more similar than different. Throughout the messy century people longed for balance, equanimity, and direction. The author of Hebrews told readers to remember their leaders and the outcomes of those leaders' lives. For pagans, the memories were decidedly mixed, and the outcomes ranged from apotheosis to denunciation. Jews had different memories; they lost leaders and people in rebellions and persecutions. Partly in response to failed apocalypticism and perhaps to counter Christianity as well as to express Judaism in a new time, Palestinian leaders began to collect and use rabbinic interpretations and discussions. The results, the Mishnah and eventually the Talmuds, became fundamental for later Judaism.

When remembering their leaders and the results of their lives, Christians recalled Jesus, his associates, and some other first-century figures. Jesus, in his several identities, and those who lived—and died—for him were models to be emulated and guides to the kingdom. The writer of Hebrews also wanted fellow believers to obey their present leaders. Along with the perennial problems of order and discipline, the church was being unbalanced by conflicting teachings and interpretations. Leaders in Christian schools labored to express the Christian message and way of life to those who accepted and those who rejected the gospel. Minor variations and sharp disagreements were linked to power struggles in congregations and impressions the church gave to the general society. Christians were struggling to find balanced ways to organize their own schools, congregations, ideas, and actions while remaining faithful to the enthusiasm and the expectations that energized the movement from its beginnings. Christians needed leaders who could give clarity about the past, promote harmony in the present, and point the way to the future.

The five leaders considered in Part III are different in several senses. They were different first because they were uncommon. Each is important for the contributions he made to the church and its subsequent development and for the leadership he gave or made possible. Second, they are different from one another. While there are some resemblances and overlap, the five contributed distinctive nuances and insights about the Christian belief and life. Finally, they are different in the sense of being offbeat. They were scarcely pedestrian individuals. They are sometimes odd, often frustrating, but always challenging in their own ways. Each chapter in Part III opens with a biographical sketch, then tells how the leader handled the five challenges, and concludes with some summary comments. Taken together, these responders covered specifically Christian issues that also have had important connections to broader religious, social, and political concerns. They reflected and furnished accepted and rejected positions for their contemporary and later believers. In an unbalanced century and in an unbalanced church, these individuals attempted to be guardians of the tradition, guides for the community, and faithful witnesses in the world.

> Again, and yet again, I beseech you: be good lawgivers to one another; continue faithful counsellors of one another; take away from among you all hypocrisy. And may God, who rules over all the world, give you wisdom, intelligence, understanding, knowledge of his judgments, with patience. And be taught of God, inquiring diligently what the Lord asks from you; and do it that you may be safe in the day of judgment.
>
> *Barnabas* 21:4-6

10

Ignatius of Antioch

What a thrill I shall have from the wild beasts that are ready for me! I hope
they will make short work of me. . . . May nothing seen or unseen begrudge
me making my way to Jesus Christ. Come fire, cross, battling with wild beasts,
wrenching of bones, mangling of limbs, crushing of my whole body, cruel tortures
of the devil—only let me get to Jesus Christ.

Ignatius Romans 5:2-3

Some persons seem to be larger than life. Ignatius was just such an individual.
His flamboyant Asianic rhetoric captured the attention of admirers and critics.
The man who said that the prospect of being eaten by beasts in the arena
thrilled him claimed that neither torture nor the devil could separate him from
Christ. Whether he was a hero or a madman or something in between is still
debated. It is certain that his seven letters were collected soon after his death,
that his reputation grew, and that he has been appealed to as an authority at
important junctures in the church's history. Pious legends about Ignatius frequently cloud questions and answers concerning him. If popularity were
measured by associations with holy heroes, Ignatius would outrank other
second-century figures. Still, there are those who discern latent heresy in his
writings, others argue that he is a forerunner of orthodoxy, and some others
simply focus on his use of materials that became part of the New Testament.
Criticisms, praises, and legends aside, who was he, and how did he respond
to the challenges that faced second-century Christians?[1]

IGNATIUS THE PERSON

Almost nothing is known about him biographically. I think Ignatius neither
came to Christianity through Judaism nor had Jewish-Christian roots; there
is no way to know whether he was a convert or was born into a Christian

family. His being sent to Rome after being condemned to death in Antioch for being a Christian indicates that he held Roman citizenship and was entitled to have the sentence confirmed as well as carried out in the capital. He probably became a martyr during a celebration marking Trajan's victories in the east (ca. 110). A military escort (Ignatius called them "leopards") marched him through Syria and Asia to the port of Troas.[2] News of his arrival at several stopping points spread among the congregations, and the "leopards" allowed him to meet with delegations of believers along the way. Ignatius wrote four letters while at Smyrna and three more from Troas—all within two weeks—before taking a ship to Italy.[3] As thin as the information is, the letters disclose four personal themes: inspired believer, sacrifice, martyr, and bishop.

First, inspired believer. Each letter began with Ignatius calling himself "the God-bearer" (*theophoros*), and once he referred to himself as "full of God."[4] Ignatius and others were convinced that he was specially inspired by God and spoke under the Spirit's influence.[5] He, his visitors, and his readers knew him to be a charismatic, and they accepted charismatic persons without reservation. Second, Ignatius described himself as a sacrifice for the restoration of God's peace in the church.[6] Certainly Old Testament precedents, Jesus' sufferings and death, Paul's descriptions of his own ordeals, and pagan practices supplied him and his readers with familiar images. The sacrifice could also be a condemned criminal who functioned as the *peripsēma* offered to restore a community to wholeness and well-being. Ignatius indicated that he was being sacrificed for problems within the whole church, especially in the congregation at Antioch. He prayed not for pagans to stop hounding Christians, but for Christians to stop fighting one another and for them to recover unity and harmony.[7] When he learned of the restoration of peace in Antioch, he celebrated not the end of persecution but the renewal of communal life and increases in membership. Writing from Troas, he urged the congregations in Asia Minor to send representatives to Antioch to underscore the need for unity and harmony.[8] Indeed, peace among Christians in Antioch signaled to the condemned prisoner that God had accepted him as a *peripsēma*, and so he pleaded with Roman Christians not to prevent his execution.

Third, martyrdom fulfilled his discipleship. His passion for death, colored by Asianist rhetoric, derived from 4 Maccabees. The author opened the gory tale of nine martyrdoms with the philosophical question whether devout reason ruled the emotions. If reason ruled, then it was possible for disciplined and faithful persons to live before God justly, rationally, courageously, and temperately. An old man, an unnamed mother, and her seven sons provided imminently rational and philosophical models that showed that loyalty to God was the way to attain pure and immortal souls in heaven. Descriptions of the instruments of torture and of the tortures themselves left nothing to the imagination, and the torturers were described as "leopard-like beasts."[9] The Maccabean martyrs' sufferings and death purified the land and caused the downfall of tyranny, substituted for the punishment their people deserved, served as a blood ransom for the sin of the community, and gained peace for the community by reviving God's law in the homeland.[10] As in Isa. 53, death for the sake of God and God's people worked forgiveness, renewal, reconciliation, and peace for the people and pointed the way toward God's ultimate victory over evil. Ignatius transposed the Maccabean idea that perfection was following the Jewish Law into perfection as imitating Jesus' sufferings in order to become a real disciple. The journey to Rome was a disciplining struggle that culminated in fighting with the wild beasts just as Jesus fought evil and death on the cross. With Jesus as his paradigm, Ignatius held that full discipleship included a pilgrimage through suffering and death before winning the victory of being with Jesus. As the Maccabean martyrs engaged in a divine contest to gain the prize of immortality and membership in the heavenly choir, so did Ignatius.[11]

As a bishop, Ignatius knew the human dimensions of being a shepherd and the needs of other pastors. His comment, "Let all things be done to the honor of God," reflected his view of the Christian life and his pastoral style.[12] For Ignatius, the pastor-bishop's relationship to God, leadership in the congregation, and witness to the general society affirmed and extended God's honor. He relished images drawn from Stoic sources, using them to describe the bishop as a sailor and a ship's pilot. His favorite, however, was the Pauline example of the athlete. He wrote others that the bishop was to exhort others to run in the race for salvation, to run himself, and to set the goal in front of all and help them attain it. He emphasized the bishop's responsibility to lead in worship, guard the faithful, and meet their physical as well as spiritual needs. Patience, aiding the widowed and orphans, being kind to critics, and discerning remedies for the troubled in heart—all were part of the pastor's ministry. He urged the stuffy bishop of Smyrna, Polycarp, to call members by their first names, know their family life, and treat slave members with respect. Bold and persistent prayers were essential for a bishop to handle daily issues and understand divine mysteries.

Ignatius's Antioch was known as a target of imperial disfavor. Its multi-ethnic, often divided, Christian community was highly visible, at least for other believers. The congregation initiated direct missions to Gentiles; sent missionaries through the Empire; and heard Paul argue with Peter and Barnabas. Were the old divisions between Jewish and gentile Christians healed? Had dissidents challenged Ignatius's leadership and contributed to his arrest? Had he failed to resolve doctrinal and political conflicts? Those whom Ignatius considered troublemakers were fanning out through Syria and into Asia, spreading their teachings as they went. His letters warned Christians that they must be vigilant and support their leaders, because a storm was headed their way. Ignatius's identity as a charismatic, sacrifice, martyr, and bishop largely determined how others received his responses to the challenges that the church faced.

IGNATIUS ON THE CREATOR AND CREATION

Although Ignatius died before Marcion and Valentinus flourished, he, too, struggled with the issues of the Creator and creation, evil's origins, and God's will. Given the nature of his writings and the problems he addressed, his ideas on the Creator and the world are scattered through the letters; yet his theology was determined by a cosmic-creation framework in two senses. First, his theology was cosmic in scope; he ranged from the heights to the depths, from primordial beginnings to the age without end. Every aspect of existence was engaged in his understanding of the Creator and creation. Second, and most important, his theology was cosmic in design; he depicted God making the world as an interrelated whole. Order was the key to the cosmos and to his theology.

Ignatius rooted creation's origin and fulfillment in the reason, will, and power of the supreme and unbegotten Creator. All life and goodness reflected God's plan for order and unity. The bishop agreed with those who understood the creation to be a cosmos, a beautiful harmony with God at its transcendent pinnacle. Below God stretched the rest of the cosmos, arranged from angelic ranks and astral powers to humans, animals, and things. Each had its proper place and function, and each—in its own way—was capable of worshiping and serving God. Knowing and filling one's place in the cosmos was the way to be at peace with God and the rest of the cosmos. God willed unity, harmony, and love through order. Accordingly, God made the cosmos so that each of its parts had an affinity, a built-in energy, that pulled it toward the God-designed order. The design for order and the promises of its benefits of fulfilled life were mirrored in the structures of the cosmos and among its creatures. The cosmos was like a choir singing to God while deepening in its mutual love and unity. But the world did not remain a cosmos; it fell into disorder and toward death. Ignatius did not blame humans for starting sin and corruption. He assumed the *Enoch*-style explanation about angels who broke rank and caused cosmic disarray. The planets and other astral spirits were knocked out of their orbits, and some longed to return to their proper places. Disobedience to the supreme divine authority equalled rebellion; rebellion was the same as schism or division; and those heavenly rebels would be saved only by obeying God. The fallen heavenly powers refused to end their schism but became the leaders of schismatics and heretics among humans. Salvation is more than escape from the coming wrath of God; it is the restoration of proper cosmic order, the recovery of the unity and harmony willed by God. The devil's plot to thwart God's plan involves dividing whatever seeks to be united and ordered to do God's will.

Ignatius had neither the time nor perhaps the inclination to launch full tilt into Enochian denunciations of cosmetics, philosophy, and clothing styles. He was convinced that as the present chaotic age was drawing rapidly to a close, and as God was acting to reintroduce order into the world, demonic forces were bent on maintaining misery and multiplying the numbers of those who would be damned in the final judgment. Evil attacked Christians because they and their message menaced discord and death. In pointing his readers to God's plan for order and threats against it, Ignatius addressed the challenges of humanity, Jesus, the church, and culture.

IGNATIUS ON HUMAN NATURE AND DESTINY

Ignatius wrote hurriedly about problems that were already troubling or soon would trouble congregations in Asia. Human nature and destiny were not yet the controversial issues they would be by mid-century, so his comments on anthropology were more implied than stated. One surprise is Paul's role in the letters. Ignatius was the bishop of the congregation in which the apostle had ministered and which the author of Acts regarded as his base of operations; and Ignatius knew Paul's letters, corresponded with congregations familiar with Galatians, and even wrote to Ephesus and Rome. Yet Ignatius did not employ distinctive Pauline ideas such as law and gospel, justification by faith through grace without works, human corruption, or the conflict of flesh with spirit. It seems that Paul was regarded as a hero but disregarded as a shaper of Christian teaching, at least in Syria and Asia. Instead of drawing on Paul's thought about human depravity, Ignatius stopped short of depicting people as enslaved by demonic forces. Indeed, his anthropology depended on humans responding either positively or negatively to God's plan for salvation. Four anthropological factors may be culled from his letters.

First, humans could be convinced to obey or disobey God. Ignatius operated on rhetoric's principle that women and men could be persuaded and dissuaded about thoughts, words, and actions. His Asianic rhetoric was purposeful as well as passionate. He employed demonstrative and deliberative arguments to convince fellow believers about praiseworthy and appropriate beliefs, worship patterns, ecclesial relationships, and ethical acts. The bishop was exuberant and his writing rough, but his thinking was coherent. He realized that others would try to present counterarguments just as convincing as his because they too were convinced that their audiences had the ability to decide between competing ideas and practices. The second factor follows logically; Ignatius connected the human mind to the body. He did not consider the "flesh" to be evil or prone to resist God, but used "flesh" and "body" interchangeably. The physical dimensions of humanity and the cosmos were part of the Creator's domain and plan for salvation. To be sure, Ignatius warned about unethical conduct and immoral desires, but he did not disparage the body, sexuality, or the physical creation. The flesh even was essential in God's design to reorder the creation in Jesus.

Next, humans were capable of receiving and worthy to receive God's *charismata*. The gifts of the Creator to inspire, reveal secrets to, and establish communion with humans were neither beyond creaturely grasp nor restricted to an elite. Finite humans were capable of bearing the infinite *charismata* and were enabled to share the insights and fruits of those gifts with others. A Christian was a God-bearer as a charismatic and as a believer who carried the image and likeness of God. But, finally, in spite of the positive dimensions of human nature, people needed divine intervention in order to be saved. The rebellion that caused evil, heresy, and destruction could not be quelled by pious persons. The devil, too, was persuasive and had a rhetoric that led many to their eternal death. As wonderful as humans were, they needed divine intervention to overcome the disorder in the world and in themselves. Humans were destined, Ignatius indicated, for orderly, united eternal life. The old racial-ethnic split of Greek and barbarian would be overcome in the identity of a new people—Christians. Only God, however, could make that new brand of humanity. As God spoke once before to make the world, so God spoke again, uttered Logos anew—and the new cosmos began to take shape in the action of the re-spoken Logos.

IGNATIUS ON THE IDENTITIES OF JESUS

Cosmic design was the framework, order the key, and Jesus the organizing principle of Ignatius's theology. His views of Jesus were clear except, at least for later readers, on one point. The bishop insisted that Jesus was the enfleshed divine being but was not clear about Jesus' being either an angel or fully God. Although the evidence is mixed, I think that he leaned toward an angel Christology in which Jesus was the highest of the rank called gods. In his setting, the critical issues dealt with Jesus' relationship to humanity rather than to the supreme Being. If the line between the angel and fully God

Christologies was not sharply drawn in the opening years of the second century, it is noteworthy that Ignatius did not consider the adoptionist position. His own view of Jesus may be termed "incarnationalist," and he posed it directly against his most pressing problems: docetism and docetists. Exactly who the opponents were and what their teaching entailed is murky. Apparently they insisted that Jesus was an angelic being who only seemed to have a human body and physical needs but did not in fact suffer and die and so was not actually raised from the dead.[13] Further comments indicate that these docetists did not make caring for needy Christians a priority but appealed to well-placed members of the congregation for support in toppling the congregation's regular leaders. The docetists' interpretation of the Scripture (that is, the Septuagint) led them to affirm that Christians were obligated to keep precepts about sabbaths, new moons, and dietary rules. In brief, they were Judaizing Christians who held a docetic angel Christology. Whether they cited Peter and Barnabas and the earliest Jerusalem leaders as their authorities and whether Pauline positions were in good odor in Antioch are not demonstrated from the letters. Perhaps old tensions between gentilizing and Judaizing versions of Christianity erupted at Antioch and Ignatius engaged in a power struggle with the docetic Judaizers, who put him on the defensive theologically and ecclesiastically. In countering his foes' case on Jesus and the church, the convict-bishop first centered Jesus' identity in an incarnationalist Christology that made Jesus the organizer of the new cosmic order. Next he responded to the christological challenge with more than rhetorical fervor; his life's purpose was at stake. Finally, he returned to heavenly beings and cosmic order. In the process, he branded the docetists as vicious beasts, rabid dogs, atheists, and wicked branches that bore poisonous fruit. The heat of those terms lingered long after the controversy faded and fueled later attitudes toward those who disagreed with church authorities.

Fury aside, what light did Ignatius attempt to shed on Jesus' identity? Both incarnationalist and docetic Christologies could share Ignatius's metaphors for Jesus, such as physician of the soul, crane that lifts humans to God, and leader of the cosmic choir. The core of Ignatius's Christology, however, was unsharable; Jesus was "of flesh yet spiritual, born yet unbegotten, a god incarnate, genuine life in the midst of death, sprung from Mary as well as God, first subject to suffering then beyond it—Jesus Christ our Lord."[14] Although Jesus was the preexistent Logos who served as God's agent to create the world, in restoring the cosmos to harmony and unity Jesus had to be a full-fledged human being. As Ignatius construed it, Jesus was the only being who participated naturally in heavenly and earthly existence, so

Be deaf, then, to any talk that ignores Jesus Christ, of David's lineage, of Mary; who was really born, ate, and drank; was really persecuted under Pontius Pilate; was really crucified and died, in the sight of heaven and earth and the underworld. He was really raised from the dead, for his Father raised him, just as his Father will raise us, who believe in him, through Christ Jesus, apart from whom we have no genuine life.[15]

Ignatius did more than hammer at readers with the incarnational theme; he made it the energy of his theology. The bishop claimed that God planned to restore the disheveled cosmos to order, unity, and harmony through the incarnate "god" Jesus. Three secrets that escaped the devil's notice activated the plan. The first secret was Mary's virginity and Jesus' conception.[16] That conception fulfilled promises in Isaiah about God's plan to restore the cosmic order through the Holy Spirit and the family of David. Israel's rituals, observances, and laws, then, foreshadowed the incarnation, so Judaizing Christians who insisted on keeping them denied the plan's actualization. Any form of docetism was inadmissible also in light of the second secret, the birth of Jesus. Evil forces, distracted by their noisy disorder, did not hear God speak the creative Word anew to reunite and reorder the cosmos. Obedient powers and astral bodies, however, heard and responded to the secret:

A star shone in the heaven brighter than all the stars. Its light was indescribable and its novelty caused amazement. The rest of the stars, along with the sun and the moon, formed a ring around it; yet it outshone them all, and there was bewilderment whence this unique novelty had arisen. As a result all magic lost its power and all witchcraft ceased. Ignorance was done away with, and the ancient kingdom [of evil] was utterly destroyed, for God was revealing himself as a man to bring newness of eternal life. What God had prepared was now beginning. Hence everything was in confusion as the destruction of death was being taken in hand."[17]

The third secret was Jesus' death and resurrection. Ignatius implied that the death of Jesus allowed God's life-power to gain entry to evil's citadel, death. That was the beginning of the end of chaotic disorder because the resurrection of Jesus brought life out of death, unity out of terrible fragmentation. God's order is evil's confusion, and God's life is evil's death. Life from God entailed a new creation that began with a new human, Jesus. Believing in and loving Jesus included trusting and hoping in his passion and resurrection.

The incarnationalist note that the believer's victory over death depended on Jesus' dying and being raised is not surprising; but Ignatius went further. He personalized his theology by using himself as a paradigm. The inspired man who was preparing to die for Christ insisted that he had not dedicated himself to a feelingless angel who pretended to be human. The docetic Jesus was a fraud proclaimed by those who only pretended to be Christians. So he wrote, "And if, as some atheists (I mean unbelievers) say, his suffering was a sham (it is really *they* who are a sham!), why, then, am I a prisoner? Why do I want to fight with wild beasts? . . . [If the docetists are right] I shall die to no purpose. . . . It is through the cross, by his suffering, that he summons you who are his members."[18] Ignatius pushed his point into Jesus' post-resurrection appearances:

> Even after the resurrection he was in the flesh. . . . [The disciples] touched him and were convinced, clutching his body and his very breath. For this reason they despised death itself, and proved its victors. Moreover, after the resurrection he ate and drank with them as a real human being, although in spirit he was united with the Father. . . . If what our Lord did is a sham, so is my being in chains. Why, then, have I given myself up completely to death, fire, sword, and wild beasts? For the simple reason that near the sword means near God. To be with wild beasts means to be with God. . . . To share in his Passion, I go through everything, for he who became the perfect man gives me the strength.[19]

From his conception through eternity, Jesus bears human flesh. Because he is enfleshed, humans are able to have fellowship with him, imitate him, be drawn to him, and unite in the church that shares his body and blood through the Eucharist.

Yet the other side argued from the accepted Scriptures. Ignatius countered that "the gospel" took priority over the "prophets." While it is uncertain whether he included written documents in "the gospel," the bishop applied a new hermeneutic to the Old Testament: "Pay attention to the prophets and above all to the gospel. There we get a clear picture of the Passion and see that the resurrection has really happened." The prophets' writings—and here he meant the "Old Testament"—were holy but subordinate to the gospel because the prophets "anticipated the gospel in their preaching and hoped and awaited [Jesus], and . . . were in Jesus Christ's unity. Saints they were, and we should love and admire them, seeing that Jesus Christ vouched for them and they form a real part of the gospel of our common hope." Challenged by his biblically oriented detracters, Ignatius responded:

> When I heard some people saying, "If I don't find it in the original documents, I don't believe it in the gospel," I answered them, "But it *is* written there." They retorted, "That's just the question." To my mind it is Jesus Christ who is the original documents. The inviolable archives are his cross and death and his resurrection and the faith that came by him. . . . But there is something special about the gospel—I mean the coming of the Saviour, our Lord Jesus Christ, his

Passion and resurrection. The beloved prophets announced his coming, but the gospel is the crowning achievement forever.

The incarnate Jesus served as the organizing principle of the Scripture and its interpretation.[20]

Ignatius capped his incarnationalist identity for Jesus with some quick comments about the celestial hierarchy and the accountability of heavenly beings. God arranged the heavens so that the supreme God was over all, apparently with Jesus immediately below, yet linked to God as God's Mind and Word. Jesus' relationship with the Creator was comparable to that of the fruit to its tree or the hand to the will of the person. An assemblage of angelic councillors, serving spirits, and the heavenly choir, among others, filled out the heavenly court. Jesus functioned as the connector between God and the rest of the heavenly host, so obedience to the Creator entailed a right relationship with Jesus the Logos.[21] And from the celestial hierarchy, only Jesus became enfleshed as a human. Since the incarnation of Jesus and the work of reordering the cosmos began, the eternal hosts have been commanded to accept the enfleshment and its results: "Let no one be misled: heavenly beings, the splendor of angels, and principalities, visible and invisible, if they fail to believe in Christ's blood, they too are doomed."[22] The docetists were not only in conflict with Ignatius, they also separated themselves from the heavenly beings who were loyal to God. Logically, then, they were lumped together with the rebellious angels responsible for evil and death. There could be no genuine life apart from the incarnate, suffering, triumphant god, Jesus, who shared in both the life of the Creator and the life of the human, and through whom came order for the cosmos and the church.

IGNATIUS ON THE CHURCH

Ignatius's letters are so woven into the church that to deal with any aspect of his theology is to involve his whole ecclesiology. Images for the *ekklēsia* tumbled from him in Asianic style, yet each has been thought through by an intense believer. He likened the church to an army, a bank, an athletic team, a procession, and a choir. He often used temple language to refer to Christians and the church. Sometimes he seemed to agree with Ezekiel that there was a heavenly temple and with Hebrews that Jesus was the High Priest in the celestial sanctuary. At other times he recast themes in Ephesians and Corinthians: Christians were being hoisted by Christ and the Spirit into the church as a derrick might fit stones into a temple; Christians were to "run off to the one temple of God, as it were, to one altar, to one Jesus Christ . . . "; and

Christians "shall be his temples and [Jesus] will be within us as our god." And Ignatius seems to have been the first to write about a "catholic church." By that he may have meant that Jesus and the heavenly and earthly dimensions of the church in general were present in local congregations that were properly ordered and harmonious.[23] Ignatius relied on the Septuagintal, intertestamental, and first-century C.E. Christian treatments of the *ekklēsia* but took them further. For him, God designed the church to be the locus and the means of Jesus' reorganization and extension of the divine order to renew—to save—the cosmos. Ignatius spoke of this ecclesial project as fulfilling God's will for order and unity versus the devil's will for disorder and disunity.

First, God's design for order and unity through the *ekklēsia*. Ignatius was firm and clear: the church reflected and derived its order, unity, and polity from heavenly models. God designed the proper order for the cosmos and established it in the heavenly realm through relationships among its beings. Naturally, the supreme God was at the zenith, and Jesus, as the Mind of God, was in unity and harmony with the Deity. Councillor angels were united, too, and were in accord with Jesus as they knew and obeyed his mind. They, in turn, were over and were linked with the serving spirits, and below them were this world's humans. With some variations, Ignatius described the earthly *ekklēsia* and congregations as reflections of the heavenly pattern. As the Creator is the head and God of the cosmos, Jesus is the head and god of the church. The roles of bishops, presbyters, deacons, and members mirror the pattern:

HEAVENS (OR COSMOS)	EKKLĒSIA (OR CONGREGATION)
God	Christ
Christ	Bishop
Councillor angels	Presbyters
Serving spirits	Deacons
Humans	Members

The *ekklēsia* (or congregation) was linked to the heavens (or cosmos) through the incarnate Jesus because he participated fully in both realms. On the basis of the heavenly pattern and its earthly reflection, Ignatius exhorted members to obey their bishops because the bishops were in harmony with the mind of Christ, and that mind was the Mind of God; to do nothing apart from their bishops because where the bishop is, there is the *ekklēsia;* to recall that to be on God's side is to side with the bishop; and to "follow the bishop as Jesus Christ did the Father . . . [and to follow] the presbytery as you would the apostles; [and to] respect the deacons as you would God's law."[24] He told members of the congregation in Ephesus that the bishops, "appointed the world over, reflect the mind of Jesus Christ. Hence you should act in accord with the bishop's mind. . . . Your presbytery, . . . a credit to God, is as closely tied to the bishop as the strings to a harp. Wherefore your accord and harmonious love is a hymn to Jesus Christ." The unity and harmony of congregations worked toward God's plan to reorder and retune the cosmos. The *ekklēsia*, as a catholic whole and as manifested in individual congregations, was essential to fulfilling God's saving design. Obedience to due authority was at the heart of God's action in Christ. To achieve perfect unity, humans in the church were to stand firmly by the orders of the Lord and the apostles doing everything with the bishops, presbyters, and deacons.[25]

Given Ignatius's parallel cosmology and ecclesiology, bishops were indispensable to divine authority and saving order. Christ was present positively in the community only as the community was unified under the bishop. To be a valid act of worship, every Eucharist had to have either the bishop or his approved representative present. If members heeded their bishops, then God would be favorable toward the congregation. As Ignatius considered his future, he wrote about his relationship to the church's members and the teamlike relationships among the officeholders: "I give my life as a sacrifice . . . for those who are obedient to the bishop, the presbyters, and the deacons. . . . Share your hard training together—wrestle together, run together, suffer together, go to bed together, get up together, as God's stewards, assessors, and assistants."[26]

Ignatius's fixation on unity and harmony through obedience and submission to God, Christ, and the church's officials was developed in light of his response to the opposite of the divine plan: demonic disorder. The great tragedy of the cosmos was the fall of the angels through disobedience. That disobedience fractured unity and concord. The healing of the cosmos could only be accomplished through a restoration of peace and unity through obedience and order. By becoming incarnate, Jesus entered the chaotic world to set it back toward life. He used the church and its congregations to enlarge and continue his mission. From Ignatius's perspective, the demonic powers, of course, counterattacked by sowing discord, schism, heresy, confusion, and rebellion in the Christian training camp, the church. Ignatius experienced the devil's assault at Antioch and on the road to Rome through the docetic teachings and challenges to the authority of bishops.

The docetists seem to have attacked the bishop-structured church at two points. First, their denial of Jesus' humanity led them to criticize and then separate from the congregation's worship. It was senseless for docetists to participate in the Eucharist as Ignatius presented it. He indicated that somehow the bread and cup were related to the physical body and blood of Jesus, and were to be considered the "medicine of immortality." Any self-respecting docetist would consider that offensive to divinity, scripturally warped, and open to the charge of cannibalism or at least crudeness. An incarnationalist Christology could be argued with, but when worship centered on it, the dissenters withdrew to form their own subgroups for worship and prayer—an act that Ignatius recognized as the prelude to open conflict and schism. Second, they supported their docetic views largely through interpretations of the Scriptures contrary to Ignatius's. They saw Christianity as the continuation of Judaism and the church as the reformed synagogue. Perhaps they wanted a more open and questioning structure similar to that of a rabbinic school as part of the congregation's life. Instead, they experienced a tightening hierarchy that stifled debate and diversity. Debate and diversity were just what Ignatius and his associates considered to be a demonic trick to introduce heresies and schisms to foil God's plan for salvation. The dimensions of worship and interpretation apparently erupted in a challenge to the emerging hierarchical structure of bishops, presbyters, and deacons. The heavenly model was loaded with implications about earthly authority figures, and the laity was at risk of being subjugated in an oppressive polity. Ignatius sought order and direction in a cosmos stalked by chaos and wandering, but his opponents recognized that their views could be stifled, and they could be driven from the community of believers.

By the time he wrote his letters, Ignatius had stopped arguing about doctrine and polity; he spoke against the menaces of the evil forces that were attempting to destroy God's plan and Christ's church: "I warn you against wild beasts in human shapes. . . . You must not only refuse to receive them, but if possible, you must avoid meeting them. . . . The right thing . . . is to avoid such people and to talk about them neither in private nor in public. . . . Flee from schism as the source of mischief."[27] As for Christianity's being a continuation of Judaism, he fumed:

> Get rid, then, of the bad yeast—it has grown stale and sour—and be changed into new yeast, that is, into Jesus Christ. . . . It is monstrous to talk Jesus Christ and to live like a Jew. For Christianity did not believe in Judaism, but Judaism in Christianity. . . . Now, if anyone preaches Judaism to you, pay no attention to him. For it is better to hear about Christianity from one of the circumcision than Judaism from a Gentile. . . . Flee, then, the wicked tricks and snares of the prince of this world, lest his suggestions wear you down, and you waver in your love."[28]

Later generations would hear those harsh condemnations both as directed toward those who opposed authorities in the church and as directed, in part, at Jews. The church, then, had an indispensable place in God's plan for the healing and salvation of the cosmos. In developing his positions, Ignatius used his multifaceted authority as a charismatic, prospective martyr, and bishop.

The fervor of his rhetoric added to the message, and the message would influence Christians from his own day to the present.

IGNATIUS ON CHRISTIANS AND SOCIETY

Ignatius advised and warned congregations in Asia about fellow Christians, not about the society around them. Nevertheless, his comments and allusions disclose a paradoxical view of that society and the world. On the one hand, his commitment to God the Creator and the cosmos-shaping action of the Logos prevented him from denouncing the world as such; it was still God's creation. At the same time, he was painfully conscious of the disruptions and turmoil of present creaturely existence. He did not think that the social structure could be reformed or turned into the kingdom. The man who complained about his ten leopards did not criticize the government or the laws that condemned him, and he did not rail against the gods and their worshipers. He reserved his condemnations for other Christians. Perhaps he held his fire because it would have been inept to denounce or mock the authorities with whose representatives he had to travel. He expected the present created structures to end soon in a final judgment on angels and humans, but was silent on whether the saved would live on a re-created earth or in a heavenly realm. He wrote in eschatological terms: "Everything is coming to an end, and we stand before this choice—death or life—and everyone will go 'to his own place.' One might say similarly, there are two coinages, one God's, the other the world's. Each bears its own stamp—unbelievers that of this world; believers, who are spurred by love, the stamp of God the Father through Jesus Christ."[29]

Ignatius pointed to a positive approach to the cosmos when he hinted at God's greater plan for the world. He knew esoteric "heavenly mysteries" about angels and celestial events that took place before creation or will occur after the judgment.[30] The undisclosed part of the plan dealt with "the New Man Jesus Christ." Given his incarnationalist Christology, use of heavenly models, and longing for unity, he might have depicted the preincarnate Logos as the celestial model for unified and well-ordered humanity. The incarnation might have served as the means to engage humanity in its own renovation so as to restructure humans into God's order and to obliterate the divisions of race, class, and ethnos. The church would then be the forerunner of the New Age, the people who would be in the image and likeness of the incarnate *theos*, Jesus. If Christians learned from Ignatius the prospects and risks of hierarchical structures in the church, they also learned from him that the cosmos was not to be rejected out of hand. Divinity became incarnate, and the church carried out its role, in God's world.

Charismatic, martyr, bishop—and struggling believer. Beneath his passionate rhetoric was a thinker who expressed himself succinctly and articulately. Clearly, his description of the church's place in the cosmic hierarchy was expanded by others to become part of a worldwide structure with claims to authority that he could never have imagined. He offers insight into the struggles still current in the church, such as the nature and responsibilities of ministries, the interpretation of the Bible, the problems and opportunities of Christian diversity and unity, and christological development. In a time when there were no agreed-upon orthodoxies, Ignatius indicated some of the options that might be pursued. He emerges from his hastily composed letters as a courageous and determined leader.

> Stand your ground like an anvil under the hammer. A great athlete must suffer blows to conquer. And especially for God's sake must we put up with everything, so that he will put up with us. Show more enthusiasm than you do. Mark the times. Be on the alert for him who is above time, the Timeless, the Unseen, the One who became visible for our sakes, who was beyond touch and passion, yet who for our sakes became subject to suffering, and endured everything for us.
>
> *To Polycarp* 3:1-2

II

Justin Martyr

[My] spirit was immediately set on fire, and an affection for the prophets, and those who are friends of Christ, took hold of me. . . . [It] is my wish that everyone would be of the same sentiments as I, and never spurn the Savior's words; for they have in themselves such tremendous majesty that they can instil fear into those who have wandered from the paths of righteousness, whereas they remain a great solace to those who heed them. Thus, if you have any regard for your own welfare, and the salvation of your soul, and if you believe in God, you may have the chance . . . of attaining a knowledge of the Christ of God, and after becoming perfect, of enjoying a happy life.

Justin *Dialogue with Trypho* 8[1]

Christians' enthusiasm for Jesus and the coming kingdom rarely persuaded devout Jews or intellectual pagans to repent and believe in the gospel. Although there were notable exceptions in the first century, converts generally came from the edges of Judaism and the ranks of unsophisticated Greco-Romans. Most Jews considered the cross to be a scandal, and educated pagans regarded talk of resurrections as foolishness. Paul was routinely cast out of synagogues and failed to get beyond the protreptic introduction when he addressed Athenian sophists and philosophers. Exasperated, he demanded to know, "Where is the sage? Where is the interpreter? Where is the critic of this age?"[2] Jews and pagans were not alone in probing Christian statements and practices; from the start of the movement, believers, too, raised issues that had to be considered. By the opening decades of the second century, Christians wanted to know where their sages and interpreters of the Scripture were. Justin was among the first to retain the fervor of the faith and still cope persuasively and intelligently with outside analysts and internal questioners.

JUSTIN THE PERSON

Born around 90 C.E. to a Greek family settled in Flavia Neapolis (modern Nablus), Justin knew little or no Hebrew and Aramaic and had only a passing acquaintance with Judaism. Although he probably traveled through Judea and Galilee, he did not reflect on places connected to Jesus. His spiritual rather than geographical pilgrimage became a model for Christian intellectuals. In his journey to truth and faith, Justin made the rounds of schools and teachers: a Stoic taught him nothing about God, an Aristotelian's tuition was too high, and a Pythagorean rejected him as insufficiently prepared to enter higher studies. Despondent, he turned to a Platonist, and the combination of teacher and seeker clicked. Justin made such rapid progress that he assumed he would reach the Platonic goal, "to gaze upon God." One fateful day, the brash student was accosted by an old man. Whether the ensuing dialogue was internal to Justin or an external event, the "old man" functioned as a Christ-Wisdom figure for Justin. As a result of the stranger's questions and Justin's fumbled answers, the student discovered inadequacies in Platonism and asked plaintively what philosophy he should follow. The old man directed him to the study of Scripture and the fellowship of those who interpreted it faithfully, that is, Christians. Confident that he was finally on the right track, he sought out Christ's friends and the holy writings. In the process, he also became an admirer of Christian martyrs, for he reasoned that those who died so honorably must be giving themselves for a noble cause. Growth in wisdom, enlightenment in the meaning of God's inspired books, fellowship with Christians, and the examples of the martyrs combined to persuade Justin emotionally and intellectually that Christianity was the only true philosophy and guide to God as well as to proper conduct; he became a philosopher of and for Christ.

His school, established in Rome, offered Christianized rhetoric and dialectic. The reigns of Hadrian, Antoninus, and Marcus Aurelius were auspicious for such intellectual enterprises—and for governmental suspicions of secret societies and foreign cults. Justin knew Marcion personally, learned about Valentinus and others whom he considered heretics, and disagreed with several he still accepted as Christians. He ranted against a Samaritan named Simon and carried on a word-war with a Cynic from a rival school.[3] Perhaps the latter denounced him to the authorities, and around 165 he was martyred. Several plausible and implausible traditions surround his death.[4] Some Christians considered him to be the Christian Socrates; he questioned society's values, taught youth about a strange divinity, debated with other scholars in a dialectical manner, composed apologies, and was put to death for his persistent criticisms. He appears to have been a lay member of an expatriate Syrian-Palestinian congregation, and he headed a school that educated some who later became bishops, presbyters, and schoolmasters throughout the Empire. These alumni carried his ideas and writings into their ministries and schools. Curiously, Justin, like Ignatius, knew Paul's letters but did not rely upon the apostle's ideas. Unlike Ignatius, Justin did not address issues concerning the church's order and structure, although he described its worship. Justin is credited with writing several influential treatises that are now lost and two surviving apologies and the *Dialogue with Trypho, a Jew.*[5]

Although a number of second-century Christians have been called "apologists" and several rhetorical apologies have survived, there is no record that any were heard or read by Roman authorities.[6] Justin's *First Apology* is cast as a forensic address to an audience that is prejudiced against the defense, while the *Second Apology* appears to be a rough draft appropriate for delivery between the announcement of the guilty verdict and the pronouncing of the sentence. Both presented Christian teachings, practice, and worship forcefully and even defiantly while attacking pagan morals and intentions. By composing these apologies, Justin signaled that Christians were sufficiently cultured to use rhetoric and ought to be treated with respect even if the authorities disagreed with them.[7] In the *Dialogue with Trypho,* Justin put on the philosopher's robe and engaged in dialectics, supposedly with Jews.[8] In his mostly monological "conversation" with a young Jewish scholar and his friends, Justin became an "old man" who attempted to lead his interlocutors to Christian truth. That search for truth centered on the Scripture. The *Dialogue,* then, combined Socratic-Platonic dialectical forms with a basis drawn from Septuagintal wisdom literature. In the process, he reflected on the nature of Christianity, the condition of the church, and most of Christian theology.[9]

I hold that the extant works were not intended for the audiences to which they were formally addressed but were in-school models prepared by the master teacher for use by his students. By working with the documents—both in form and content—students learned not only the techniques of rhetoric and philosophy but also their master's theology. His works probably were used and preserved by his students when they became presbyters and bishops in congregations and by those who established their own schools of Christian philosophy. Polemics and insults in the three works were used against pagans and Jews by Christians in later generations. On the positive side, Justin's works (both those that survived and those that did not) provided Christian students and leaders with a respectable *paideia* in Christ that could be adapted and emulated elsewhere in the Empire. Justin, then, was what he claimed to be: a Christian philosopher who based his teachings on the Bible. His extant works conform to Greco-Roman literary types and fit those types and their Scriptural analogues. In brief, he responded to challenges thoroughly and thoughtfully by using rhetoric and dialectic based on Scripture.

JUSTIN ON THE CREATOR AND CREATION

The supreme God, insisted Justin, deliberately created all that exists. The Christian philosopher rejected cosmologies about the Demiurge and the production of the traditional deities. As an interpreter of Scripture, he repudiated Marcion's splitting the Creator into two separate gods ruling distinct realms. And in his role as sage of Christ, Justin denied gnostic speculation that the visible world is the product of an angel's ill-begotten yearning. His version of the Creator and the creation included a divine plan, a celestial hierarchy, and an explanation for evil based on *Enoch*. He worked chiefly with the first creation account in Genesis, augmenting it with Prov. 8 and John 1, then wove into it themes from Philo, Middle Stoicism, and Middle Platonism. Out of disparate sources, Justin developed a coherent account about creation and the Creator that served as the framework for his responses to the challenges he faced.

First, the Creator. Justin knew the limits of language. In good philosophical style informed by biblical emphases on divine transcendence, he noted that no word or title adequately expressed the Being people call "God." Indeed, terms such as God, Father, Creator, and Lord were human attempts to communicate what people say God is and how God is experienced. The God who is unbegotten (without beginning) and timeless (without change and end) is infinite and beyond the concepts of origin, development, and end. Logically, the unbegotten and timeless one is completely unknown and unknowable apart from divine self-revelation. This God wills to be revealed, and the revelatory agent is the Logos. The Logos is the Mind, Word, Wisdom, and messenger of the supreme Deity. Whatever is properly and truly disclosed of, enacted on behalf of, and done by the God is channeled through the Logos. The Transcendent One is the Creator as initiator because that One determined that the cosmos was to be and how it was to be arranged. The Logos is the Creator in the sense of effecting the will of the transcendent God, because Logos is the actual maker and shaper of the world.

Now, the creation. The Logos made the cosmos to be orderly, harmonious, and responsive to God. At the same time, the creation was structured for the sake of humankind; angels, heavenly bodies, and the rhythm of planting and reaping were arranged by a divine law to direct care and love toward people. According to God's command, all earthly things were under human dominion. So far Justin's comments reflected standard themes derived from Gen. 1 and Philo and were opposed to Marcionism and Valentinian Gnosticism. His position became more imaginative and far-reaching when he folded into it John 1 on the Logos and Middle Stoicism's *logoi spermatikoi*. Justin's few comments concerning these "seed-words" appear to have been part of a fuller teaching to the effect that the Logos sowed the logoi of reason, justice, courage, and temperance throughout the cosmos. The Word imparted the seeds as receptors of God's will and generators of devout response in all humans. The world, then, was good and able to return praise and obedience to God through the Logos. The "seed-word" could be germinated in any human being and in every human culture because the Creator-Word made people and nature, and because the Creator-Word cast the holy seeds into all that was made. As reason within the cosmos, logos linked the cosmos to the Logos-Creator who in turn related the whole to the supreme God-Creator. The Christian philosopher's emphasis on a Logos cosmology took a decidedly negative turn when he explained evil's origin and its role in fomenting sin, persecution, heresy, and rejection of Christianity. Justin rehearsed the fall of the Watchers and the subsequent distortion of both the rebel angels and of humanity. As a result of losing their heavenly position, the wicked angels became slaves of their own lustful passions and needed sacrifices, incense, and libations. The cultus of paganism resulted directly from the fall, as the evil angels

> engendered murders, wars, adulteries, all sorts of dissipation, and every species of sin. Thus it was said that the poets and writers of legends, unaware that the bad angels and the demons begotten by them did those things to men and women, to cities and nations, ascribed them to [their] god himself [Jupiter] and to those whom they thought were sons of his seed and to the children of those whom they called his brothers, Neptune and Pluto, and to the children of their children. For they called them by the name each of the bad angels had bestowed upon himself and his children.[10]

The destiny of the cosmos, however, is not everlasting disorder and evil. God will reassert authority and power over all through the return of Christ in glory. Justin adopted the eschatology of Revelation and claimed that prior to the general resurrection and judgment of the dead Christ's followers would live for a thousand years in a divinely rebuilt Jerusalem. Justin actually appears to have been one of only a few who held to the millennialist views of Revelation.[11] Upon the glorious return of Jesus, the disobedient angels and their followers would be condemned to eternal flames. With his eschatological vision for the future blessedness of the faithful celestial and earthly beings, Justin's view of the Creator and creation came full circle. What began with the supreme God and the Logos is completed in the fulfillment of those for whom the cosmos was created, and the fulfilled humans will be the equals of angels.

JUSTIN ON HUMAN NATURE AND DESTINY

Justin's anthropology fit his personal faith journey. He did not have a sudden conversion experience as did Paul. Instead, he became a Christian through searching for truth, finding traces of the presence and seeds of the Logos in the wider culture, studying Scripture, and being with Christians. *Paideia* enlightened him about God, the cosmos, and himself. His operative anthropology was based in Gen. 1 and Septuagintal Wisdom literature. He held that angels and people have free will, can be persuaded, and are capable of reasoning so that they are responsible for their attitudes and actions. Neither celestial nor human beings can excuse themselves by claiming that fate or chance or a Demiurge or anything other than themselves kept them from obeying God. Both angels and persons are responsible for how they obey God and what they do in God's cosmos. Given his comments on the *logoi spermatikoi*, he took the seed of reason as present in all persons and not just in a handful of *pneumatikoi*.

Since humans and angels have free will and are persuadable, they may be misled by evil forces. In *Enoch*, those Watchers who convinced themselves and others to rebel continued their wickedness by stealing and distorting heavenly secrets so as to make evil masquerade as goodness, idolatry as worship, ignorance as wisdom, greed as satisfaction, and lust as love. Pagan *paideia*, tainted with such distortions of God's goodness, truth, and beauty, beguiled men and women to praise what was blameworthy and to accept as appropriate conduct what was reprehensible. Adam and Eve were involved in the deception of humans, because

> from the time of Adam [humans] had become subject to death and the deceit of the serpent, each man having sinned by his own fault. For God, in his desire to have the angels and men (who were endowed with the personal power of free will) do whatever [God] had enabled them to do, created them such that, if they chose to do the things pleasing to him, he would preserve them immortal and free from punishment, but if they preferred to do evil, he would punish each one as he pleased.

At another point, Justin linked the fall of one Watcher to that Watcher's deception of Eve and hinted he had further teachings on the subject.[12] Adam and Eve's disobedience, then, led to human subjugation, physical death, and openness to deception, but not to the loss of free will. Justin's emphasis on free will at the beginning of human existence pointed toward humanity's destiny in God's plan; humans were intended to live eternally as equals to the angels in a re-created cosmos or at least on a re-created earth. The process of getting from the deceptive snares of the fallen Watchers to the new Jerusalem involved unlearning the ways and customs of the demons. Instead, people were to learn the Law of God given through the Logos and the *logos spermatikos* implanted within them. Humans and angels still were able to exercise their free will to please God by calling upon God and exerting themselves in the struggle to be saved. Justin's insistence on free will stressed both responsibility and hope. The critical difference between humans and evil powers is that the latter know that eternal punishment is the penalty for disobedience, but they refuse to repent. Indeed, they are determined to drag as many humans as possible into damnation with themselves.

Given his understanding of human nature as persuadable and human destiny as subject to judgment on the basis of obedience to God in attitude and deed, Justin placed a high premium on education. *Paideia* in Christ is critical in the salvation-journey of men and women. The wicked demons have conspired to pollute society with perverted, stolen knowledge and with worship distorted into veneration of the fallen Watchers, who pass themselves off as life-giving divinities. Justin discovered that the wholesome work of the Logos in creating the world and sowing the seeds of logos in all persons made salvation through education possible. Women and men needed to leave the demonic teachings and habits that enslaved them and instead to turn to the Law of God, that is, Logos. Because people could still be swayed by rhetoric, dialectic, and example, and because the Scriptures contain the clear statements and teachings of God, Christian teachers such as Justin were essential to God's plan to reorder the cosmos. This perspective on human nature and its destiny explained how love caused the Logos to enter the cosmos in the flesh to be the teacher and enlightener of humanity.

JUSTIN ON THE IDENTITIES OF JESUS

With only a hint of ambiguity, Justin asserted that Jesus was an incarnate angel. He was the first-begotten Son, the Logos, the Wisdom, Covenant, and Law of God. The universal Father did not speak to Abraham at Mamre or to Moses on Sinai. "the very Son of God who is styled Angel and Apostle" did. In the earlier times, the Logos appeared in different forms to reveal the supreme Deity's will, but in recent days, claimed Justin, the Logos became incarnate through being born of a virgin, and, as Jesus, suffered, died, and was raised from the dead. The initial incarnational appearance will be succeeded by Jesus' return in glory to judge humans on the basis of their deeds and their loyalty to God, and then Jesus will reign over the new age. Pagans especially ought not be surprised by that message because Christians "propose nothing new or different from that which you say about the so-called sons of Jupiter" such as Apollo and Bacchus. Even if Jesus were an apotheosized human, Hercules and Asclepius were pagan analogues for Christian truth. Justin acknowledged the legitimacy of an adoptionist Christology, admitting to Trypho that some Christians held an adoptionist view with Judaizing tendencies. The philosopher, however, regarded the incarnationalist-angelic identity for Jesus as standard among Christians.[13] In identifying Jesus, Justin did more than meld Stoic,

Platonic, and biblical words and ideas. He set up a pattern for hermeneutics and an attitude toward Jews that helped shape later theological positions, interpretive procedures, and interfaith relationships.

Justin came to Christianity through searching for the true philosophy and finding it in the Septuagint, so interpretation was vital for him. He applied the tools of rhetoric and dialectic—and his own creativity—to figure out what a passage might mean for the present. His hermeneutic was single-minded: all Scripture came through the Logos, centered on the Logos, and led back to the Logos. Since Justin assumed that the Septuagint was divinely inspired, his assertion that the Logos was the effective source of the Scriptures under-scored his rejection of Marcionism and promoted his claim that the Scripture belonged to those, past, present, and future, who listened to the Logos. The centrality of the Logos in the Scriptures encouraged Justin to regard every passage as testimony to the Logos. The Septuagint, then, was a coded message about the Logos to be deciphered through typology and allegory: both it and whatever Christian works Justin considered sacred led properly instructed persons back to the Logos and God's truth about the cosmos and its future. In other words, Scripture contained clues as to what was yet to happen. The sage-dialectician went on to provide three hermeneutical rules. First, some passages were intended only for the Jews because God knew that they were stubborn and rebellious. Second, other portions were part of God's plan of salvation, which would be manifested in the new covenant made in Jesus for people from all nations. Third, God's gift of grace was needed for anyone to understand the Scriptures properly. Justin adroitly relegated Trypho's objec-tions about Christian disregard of the Mosaic regulations about circumcision, diet, and Sabbath to the first rule.[14] The second hermeneutical rule is crucial for Justin's handling of the biblical texts. Through it he claimed that Christianity was the most ancient and true school of God's truth, that Christians and not Jews were the rightful possessors of God's sacred writings, and that those within the church who opposed his views about the Creator and Jesus were in serious error.

Justin's comments about Jews ranged from the vituperative to the amiable. In the apologies he wrote that the Jews failed to recognize the Messiah when he came, continue to reject him now, and "hate us who declare that he has come, and who show that he was crucified by them as foretold." He dealt at length with passages from the prophets that criticized Israel for being stubborn, disobedient, and unfaithful to its Lord. In the hands of a second-century C.E. Christian, the words of seventh- and sixth-century B.C.E. Hebrews had om-inous overtones. He described the Jews as sneering at the crucified Jesus. Justin's comments on the sacrifices performed in the now-destroyed Temple—sacrifices that the prophets said God did not want—echoed comments he made about demonically inspired pagan rites. The Christian apologist cited another prophet to the effect that the Jews would not repent until the day of judgment, and then it would be too late. Demonic connections were implied also in his accusation that the Jews rejected the self-evident truth of the Christian interpretation of Scripture because they were vain and slaves of passion, characteristics associated with the demons and their supporters. The implications became explicit: Jesus "bore all the torments which the demons prompted the rabid Jews to wreak upon him." If Jews were slaves to their passions, were proud, denied God's self-evident truth, practiced sacrifices not acceptable to God, rejected Jesus, sneered at him while he died, carried out the will of the demons in tormenting him, hated and opposed Christians, and would not repent before it was too late to be saved from hell-fire, Justin's Christian readers would conclude that the Jews were inspired and led by the forces of evil. Standard passages about Jewish stubbornness, rebellion, and rejection of God appear even sharper in the face-to-face contact reported in the *Dialogue*. Jews, he said, continue to blaspheme God by rejecting Jesus; therefore, they will be condemned. Justin's list of accusations is long and often heated; but sometimes his tone was friendly as he tried to draw his interlocutors into conversion oriented discussion. For whose consumption was this dia-tribe? It seems unlikely that it promoted philosophical discourse between the followers of Moses and Jesus. Was Justin reflecting problems in the schools and congregations he knew? Was he trying to give his students the interpretive and dialectical practice they needed in order to debate, reason, and teach when they left his classes?[15]

What were some results of Justin's interpretive steps as he attempted to identify Jesus? Justin's hermeneutic helped make possible the church's reten-tion of the "Old Testament" in the face of Marcionite criticisms, yet he vitiated the integrity of the biblical material by homogenizing its richness and diversity so it "proved" his theological positions. Second, he not only displaced Jews as the covenant people, he demonized them and made them appear to be God's enemies. Third, Justin's explication of Jesus' identity lacks the flesh-and-blood verve seen in some first-century authors and in Ignatius. Justin said that Jesus is incarnate, yet Jesus seems to be more a theological principle than a historical person.

JUSTIN ON THE CHURCH

Justin's treatment of the church is surprising. The Septuagint spoke enough about the Temple and the *ekklēsia* to provide material for fulsome typologies and allegories regarding the Christian community. The Pauline and deutero-Pauline writings and Revelation contain images (e.g., body and bride of Christ) that are ready-made for further development. *1 Clement* and Ignatius's letters, part of Rome's ecclesial source materials, made precedents available for the authority and the cosmic role of the church, but Justin's apologies and *Dialogue* reflect almost nothing resembling those works and the opportunities they offered for speculation.[16] Judging from the titles of works now lost, they probably did not expand on the church any more than the surviving writings did. If Justin wrote for his students, then his exoteric teachings naturally dealt with matters more pertinent to rhetoric and dialectic than to the self-understanding of Christians and their congregational organization. In spite of his silence about the cosmic side of the church and its polity, he dealt with three important areas.

First, worship. Worship, proper conduct, and intellectual illumination were indivisible. Those who were misled by demons were mis-worshipers and misbehavers. They misinterpreted the *logoi spermatikos* within themselves and the cosmos so that they accepted distortions as truth and idolatry as piety. Christians, on the other hand, began to be enlightened when they approached membership in the congregation because they were enabled to discern God's Logos-given truth in culture, Scripture, and the conduct of believers. Baptism was the initiatory illumination that washed away sin and ignorance and regenerated the baptized by giving them a new understanding of God's truth and will. Participants in the community increasingly harmonized their lives with the Logos. In natural birth, argued Justin, the newly born had no choice about parents or society. After their first birth, children were raised and trained into a society "of wicked and sinful customs," becoming victims of necessity and ignorance. Baptism, however, depended on the candidates' assent. Baptism, then, was a liberating enlightenment that enrolled newly reborn Christians in the community nourished by and united to the Logos through the Eucharist. Members of the properly worshiping and intellectually enlightened *ekklēsia* joined together to regulate their individual and corporate lives according to the "principles laid down by Christ."[17] Justin described in considerable detail the congregation's worship, mentioning deacons and a presiding leader but not presbyters. He noted that the reading and interpretation of the Scriptures and the "memoirs of the apostles" were prominent as were exhortations to proper conduct. Worship, he insisted in agreement with Ignatius, included aiding sick and needy Christians.

Second, Justin regretfully admitted that some Christians considered Jesus to be a good man who was raised to divine status by God because of his singular obedience to the Mosaic Law. These adoptionists held that since Jesus was so rewarded, those who wished to be saved ought to obey the Law as well. The adoptionists' anthropology was consistent with Justin's views on free will, and he made no attempt to argue with them directly on biblical, dialectical, or ethical grounds. He did warn that they ought to refrain from making their views the only way to salvation.[18] The adoptionist position actually undermined Justin's theological hermeneutic, dialectic, and rhetoric. By necessity, an apotheosized Jesus could not be the preincarnate Logos who sowed the *logoi spermatikos*. In addition, adherence to the Mosaic Law in itself denied the typological program whereby Justin distinguished Christianity from Judaism, that is, Jesus would not have ended the Law in the ceremonial sense. Justin's admission that the Judaizing adoptionists were considered members of the church and his restraint in mentioning them may indicate that they were a significant force, at least among Christians in Rome. Justin also made passing reference to a group that denied that Old Testament figures had any share in Christ's millennial rule and believed that the souls of the saved went immediately to heaven on physical death. He did not consider people who held such views "real Christians."[19]

Third, heretics. Justin's breaking point between acceptable and unacceptable diversity was over the Creator's identity. Marcion and a list of gnostic deviants earned Justin's scorn and enmity because they claimed that the creator of the world was not the supremely good and purposeful Deity who sent the Logos-Son to make the cosmos. He wrote extensively against heretics, outlining their positions in a work now lost but highly influential in the second and third centuries. The time and energy he expended indicates that these were more than schools that rivaled his own for students and attention. Justin insinuated that the heretics were moral deviants who brought shame and persecution upon right-believing Christians. As he did with the Jews, the philosopher identified demonic forces as the real culprits behind those who opposed the true version of God's truth: "These spirits whom we class demons strive for nothing else than to alienate men from God their Creator, and from Christ, his first-begotten. . . . Besides, they even try to trip those who rise to the contemplation of divine things, and, unless such persons are wise in their judgments and pure and passionless in their life, the demons will force them into ungodliness."[20] In response to Trypho's question about those who call themselves Christians but eat meat sacrificed to idols, Justin retorted angrily that they were not of the communion of believers; even though they confessed the crucified Jesus as Lord with their lips, they were really impious atheists and wicked sinners who professed the teachings of the spirits of error. They were called after the names of the founders of their sects: Marcionites, Valentinians, Basilidians, and Saturnilians. He reserved particular ire for Marcion, perhaps because Marcion's hermeneutic competed with Justin's: "The evil demons also introduced Marcion of Pontus who even now urges men to deny that God is the Creator of all things in heaven and on earth, and that the Christ foretold by the Prophets is his Son, and he proclaims another god besides the Maker of all things, and likewise another son. Many have believed this man."[21]

Right worship, right conduct, and right belief were critical ingredients for the church. Justin did not expand images or engage in speculation about the church, and he did not offer new insights on the hierarchy of congregations. The alumni of his school, however, carried his ideas into the congregations they served and blended those ideas with the positions of others. In comparison to some who followed him, Justin's typologies and allegories were conservative. His demonization of Jews and heretics, on the other hand, contributed to later animosities and atrocities.

JUSTIN ON CHRISTIANS AND SOCIETY

Justin answered pagan challenges to Christian participation in society vigorously while selectively rejecting and accepting Greco-Roman culture. His apologies critiqued the wider society, pointing out what was inappropriate and blameworthy. When Justin turned the tables on Christianity's detractors, his sarcasm strained Aristotle's advice regarding decorum. He accused the Stoic Antonine emperors of being unphilosophical and potential tools of the demons in that they punished innocent and decent people simply because they were called "Christians." In fact, he argued, Christians were far from being traitors, atheists, cannibals, or immoral. Those charges stemmed from the demons, who were desperate to discredit God's truth by causing suffering for those who believed rightly and lived rationally. Paganism was the height of atheism in spite of its many gods because those gods acted immorally and cruelly, as one might expect from evil spirits. The fallen angels camouflaged Logos-given truth by devising wicked myths and rituals to lead humans to condemnation. Christians were the emperors' best subjects because they told the emperors the truth about evil's plots and disguises. Christians were presented as the most moral of all persons in the Empire because they honored God rightly and knew that eternal punishment awaited all who persisted in sin.

Justin turned the slurs of barbarism and ignorance against the pagans. Christianity's origins were more ancient than those of Greece and Rome because the teachings of Christ came from heaven to Moses and then were transmitted through the prophets until the incarnate Logos revealed them fully to all humanity. As for the charge that Christians were ignorant and low-class persons, the apologist and teacher argued that since the Logos gifted all humans with *logoi spermatikos*, uneducated yet illumined Christians knew God's truth: "You can hear and learn these things from persons among us who do not even know the letters of the alphabet, who are uncultured and rude in speech, but wise and believing in mind; some, too, have been disabled and have lost their eyesight. So you can readily see that things are not the result of human wisdom, but are the pronouncements of the power of God."[22] In his rejectionist mode, Justin threw down the challenge to the emperors and the culture they promoted: "As far as we [Christians] are concerned, we believe that no evil can befall us unless we be convicted as criminals or be proved to be sinful persons. You, indeed, may be able to kill us, but you cannot harm us."[23]

While Justin's demonology undergirded his rejection of pagan culture and provided his students with arguments against those who claimed that Christians deserved to be suppressed, he also claimed Greco-Roman intellectual achievements for Christianity. The Logos was his operative principle in affirming whatever was good, true, beautiful, and noble: "We have been taught that Christ was First-begotten of God and we have indicated . . . that He is the Word of whom all mankind partakes. Those who lived by reason are Christians, even though they have been considered atheists: such as, among the Greeks, Socrates, Heraclitus, and others like them; and among the foreigners, Abraham, Elias, Ananias, Azarias, Misael, and many others. . . . So also they who lived before Christ, and did not live by reason were useless men, enemies of Christ, and murderers of those who lived by reason. But those who have lived reasonably, and still do, are Christians, and are fearless and untroubled."[24] Several claims follow upon Justin's emphasis on the Logos. First, as the Logos had already made God's truth known in pagan culture before becoming incarnate, whoever spoke and acted in accord with logos was a proto-Christian. Thus the apologist turned Socrates and Plato into Christians with clouded visions of the truth that was to be revealed and manifested in the incarnation of the Logos. Instead of being a latecomer on the intellectual scene and having as its central figure an unlettered carpenter, Christianity was the oldest of the philosophical systems; it counted the noblest Greco-Roman minds among its supporters, and its teacher surpassed both Moses and Plato. Pagan and Jewish sources could be used to plumb the depths of God's will and to foster rational and ethical living. Second, by extension, all truth and goodness now resided in the community of the Logos, the church. Arguing as had Philo and Josephus before him, Justin maintained that the Greeks received philosophy from the Egyptians, who, in turn, had been taught it by Moses and Abraham. The incarnate Logos, spurned by the Jews, established a new people, the church, to be the heirs and continuers of the true philosophy. Any who behaved irrationally and opposed the Logos and his people unjustly, whether before, during, or after the incarnation, faced destruction. Third, the Scriptures became the authoritative texts to be interpreted under the guidance of the Logos in the community of the faithful and by Christian sages such as Justin.

Justin pushed the Christian faith to fruitful and dangerous positions. With Justin, Christianity entered the intellectual mainstream of the Empire, and Christians were enabled to use the methods, language, and concepts of rhetoric and philosophy to defend, advance, and deepen their faith. Christians used Greco-Roman *paideia* to present the Christian message to the broad public and to fellow believers in ways that were relevant to current intellectual developments and cultural patterns. His extension of Logos theology combined and adapted Stoic and Johannine concepts and led him to harmonize classical culture and Christian particularity. Through his development of the Johannine side of the Logos, he emphasized the universality of the work of God in Jesus. Along with the church's missionary dynamic, Justin contributed a philosophically and biblically based structure for Christians to develop their intellectual mission to the nations. His Logos theology opened the way for later generations to frame christological debates in terms of the Logos, adding to heat of the later conflicts about Jesus' identity that split the church and the Empire for decades in the mid-fourth century.

There were risks, however, in Justin's appropriation of non-Christian culture. In opening their discussion, Trypho observed that Christians bore no distinctive physical marks and behaved just as did their pagan neighbors. By Christianizing culture, did Justin prepare the way for culture to paganize Christianity? In his eagerness to claim the brightest and best of paganism for the church, Justin risked diluting Christian ethics and teachings. Perhaps his use of pagan intellectual forms was a charade, for he turned, even twisted, the Greco-Roman materials toward his already assumed conclusions. Did this appropriation set a pattern for other Christians, leading them to think that only the hardhearted and demon-controlled would not agree with them? Perhaps it inspired a persecuted community to withstand the opposition and ire of pagan society. As developed by Justin, it also contributed to a narrowing of the Christian mind and fueled arguments between Christians. By lumping persecuting pagans, Christ-rejecting Jews, and adamant heretics together as demonically inspired and enslaved, Justin helped ensure that believers would become oppressors when they gained power.

On balance, Justin was a fervent believer who sought to be a Christian sage. He struggled to understand his faith. His "old man" started him on the way to life and truth, and he became like that old man in sharing Christ's philosophy. Even though he and Trypho exchanged some heated comments, they parted friends. The Jewish scholars went on to ponder the philosophy they had just debated and the philosopher went on to his martyrdom. His last words in the *Dialogue* show him ever the believer and the searcher:

And I in turn prayed for them, saying, "I can wish you no greater blessing than this, gentlemen, that, realizing that wisdom is given to every man through this Way, you also may one day come to believe entirely as we do that Jesus is the Christ of God."

Trypho 142.

12

Clement of Alexandria

Education is a word used in many different senses. There is education in the
sense of the one who is being led and instructed; there is that of the one who
leads and gives instruction; and thirdly, there is education in the sense of the
guidance itself, and finally, the things that are taught, such as precepts. The
education that God gives is the imparting of the truth that will guide us correctly
to the contemplation of God, and a description of holy deeds that endure forever.

Clement *Instructor* 1.7[1]

Alexandria attracted and repelled people from the day its namesake and his
architects drew up its ground plan. Emperors and others went to the port on
the Nile Delta to worship, study, make money, and simply see its wonders.
Dio Chrysostom wrote that it was "situated at the crossroads of the world . . .
even the most remote nations [may be seen there] as [if Alexandria] were a
market serving a single city, displaying them to one another and, as far as
possible, making them into a kindred people," but he criticized its people for
their sexy gait, luxurious parties, and outright rudeness, advising them to pay
attention to *paideia* and logos. Another satirist quipped that Alexandrians were
"a folk to whom you need only throw plenty of bread and a ticket to the
[racetrack] since they have no interest in anything else." An earlier poet,
Herodas (ca. 200 B.C.E.), described it as "the house of Aphrodite, and everything is to be found there—wealth, playgrounds, a large army, a serene sky,
public displays, philosophers, precious metals, fine young men, a good royal
house, an academy of science, exquisite wine and beautiful women."[2] Also
found there were scores of African and Asian cults, numerous philosophical
schools, an odd assortment of Christian communities, and an odder variety
of teachers—including Clement.

CLEMENT THE PERSON

Like Alexandria, Clement attracts and repels. Because he intended to puzzle people, responses to him are mixed. Some denounce him as a closet Valentinian, diluter of Christian truth, and plagiarizer. Advocates claim that he is the earliest known self-conscious Christian theologian, ethicist, and mystic. His historical identity and theological intentions have been obscured by unreliable and probably fictionalized versions of his career.[3] Clement, fortunately, slipped some personal reflections into his writings and these, with other clues in his works, aid in discerning his identity and in understanding his ideas.

Using his list of emperors as a reference point, it is likely that Clement lived from around 150 to 215. He was silent about his place of origin and entry into the church. Instead of a family tree, Clement gave a *paideia*-based pedigree, signaling that educators were more important than parents. He teased his readers about his teachers (all Christians) and what he studied with them, linking elements from autobiographical passages to his genealogies of pagan philosophical schools to prepare readers for subtle points. For example, Clement wryly denied that Greece proper had birthed any philosophical tradition; rather, philosophy began among the so-called barbarians in Egypt, Syria, and Mesopotamia. It so happened that three of Clement's teachers came from those very regions, which Clement also linked to Abraham, the first philosopher, and Moses, the greatest philosopher. Finally, a fourth teacher, perhaps the greatest, was a Palestinian Jew who became a Christian. This may have been the teacher with whom Clement settled in Egypt. Clement claimed that his biblical and philosophical understandings originated with Abraham and Moses, were retrieved from pagan philosophies by his own teachers, and were validated by the final teacher, who came from the same Holy Land as did the Truth incarnate, Jesus. It was scarcely coincidental that Clement and his greatest teacher settled in Egypt, the land where God's philosophy was first taught.[4]

Clement's educational travelogue disclosed still more. His report of his *paideia*-journey, his use of Septuagintal wisdom materials, and his interpretive methods presented his readers with a theological project. I think Clement saw himself as the Christian Sirach. He operated a school in Alexandria in which he used the forms and vocabulary of Greco-Roman *paideia*, rhetoric, and dialectic, and added heady doses of Middle Platonism, Stoicism, and Philo's thought. In his school, he offered courses in Christian rhetoric, logic, and ethics plus higher studies, that is, he had both undergraduate and graduate theological programs. He derived the project from his wisdom-based interpretation of the Scripture and the works that he considered to be the New Testament. From Clement's point of view, education was the path to salvation and educators were essential to God's plan to fulfill humanity. His writings reflected four aspects of education. One was the experience of the persons who were being guided and instructed, that is, their responses and development. Another took the standpoint of the educational leader who employed outlines, built the curriculum, and set goals for the students. The third aspect of education involved the strategies used and the stages through which students and teachers progressed. The last aspect was the actual content of the educational program, that is, doctrinal and ethical instruction. Christian education, thought Clement, embraced all these aspects. It was God's way of imparting the truth that would guide students and teachers to contemplate God aright and to live righteously. Through education in its various senses, each person would know God at the level of the person's ability.

Clement expressed his project in three treatises that he used in his school and that others used after he passed from the scene. The works correlated to the philosophical stages of logic and ethics and prepared for the final stage of higher studies in cosmology and theology. His *Exhortation* (*Protreptikos*) invited potential students to move from inappropriate pagan to appropriate Christian actions. At that level, they learned basic points about society, God, the Logos, and themselves. Those who completed the first stage progressed to ethics. Clement's *Instructor* (*Paidagogos*) and *Miscellanies* (*Stromateis*) dealt with specific ethical duties and exoteric general principles through which students mastered their habits, actions, and passions. At that point, persons with incentive and ability were initiated into the stage of cosmology-theology, learning the esoteric *gnōsis* that Jesus supposedly taught his inner circle. True Gnostics were the sages who interpreted the Scripture and guided Christians to salvation through schools such as Clement's. Clement necessarily adopted a looping process through which he planted seeds of *gnōsis* and covered them with ornate rhetoric to hide them from those not yet able to discern the full meaning of God's truth. He went on to other subjects that seemed irrelevant, such as the alleged bisexuality of hyenas, only to return and tend the delicate plants, that is, the deeds and characters that had germinated from the seeds as the students improved their souls. Readers, then, were bewildered yet attracted and then drawn in by his personal teaching and literary style.[5]

Inadvertently, Clement disclosed still more about himself, his students, and Christians whom he knew. The tone and extent of his advice to Christians who were wealthy, accustomed to luxury, and owned slaves indicate that he moved often and comfortably among successful merchants and aristocrats. They and their dependents, perhaps including women, were enrolled in his school and depended upon him as their spiritual guide. Picking up Dio Chrysostom's challenge, he focused on the *paideia* and logos of God.

CLEMENT ON THE CREATOR AND CREATION

Clement relied on Gen. 1, as refracted through the wisdom literature and Philo's writings, in combination with Platonic and Stoic ideas. Some aspects of Clement's theology are clarified by visualizing the cosmos as a cone with its vertex towering above its base. The image describes God's actions as Creator in spatial terms. The Most High, who dwelled above the vertex, that is, beyond the possibilities of change and disunity, generated the Logos to shape the cosmos-cone according to God's plan. Logos spiraled downward, creating many heavenly places and angelic beings. Having reached what God willed to be the base of the cone, Logos swung about in a circle to make the physical world. Completing the initial creative task, Logos returned to the vertex and God. On the return journey from the earth through the heavens, the Logos tuned and harmonized the cone to be a choir praising and serving God.[6]

Clement insisted, as did Philo and Justin, that God and the Logos were the Creator and the creative agent who had planned and made the cosmos. Clement rejected without exception any Marcionite and Valentinian interpretation of Scripture or experience that removed the Deity and the Logos from the intentional making of all that exists. Next, Clement's theology of the Creator and creation led him to affirm almost rapturously that God never made anything that God hated or would destroy. No place in the cosmos could ever be called God-forsaken, because the Logos had been everywhere. In the first coming as the agent of creation, the Logos not only planted the seeds of *gnōsis* in the world but made the world a place that God cherished and loved. Third, Clement's view of the origin and role of evil differed from the views of other known first- and second-century Christians. Although he acknowledged the account of the fall of the angels (Gen. 6:1-4 and *Enoch*), he chose not to use it against women, heretics, and Jews, citing it halfheartedly when he criticized pagan poets and philosophers. Instead, he was convinced that evil and ignorance could be overcome by the Logos and *paideia*. Clement's conviction that the loving and good Creator would never condemn any creature eternally, perhaps even fallen angels, left no room for hell in his cosmology or theology. In biblical passages referring to damnation, torment, and worldwide judgment, the Logos was scolding and disciplining God's beloved creatures to motivate them to resume their education to salvation.[7]

CLEMENT ON HUMAN NATURE AND DESTINY

When the Logos swung along the base of the cosmos-cone to create the physical world, the Logos created human beings. Unlike crickets, which make melody with their legs, women and men are designed to be intelligent singers in the cosmic choir. More particularly, the Alexandrian teacher turned to the statement about people. Clement held that all humans were made in the image and likeness of the Logos, and that the Logos was in the image and likeness of the supreme God. Male and female humans were in the image of the Logos through the use of their souls' reason (logos), and they had the inner incentive as well as ability to develop into the likeness of the Logos. There was, then, a hierarchy that reached from the unseeable God to the Logos, who was the image and likeness of God, to humans, who were growing into the image and likeness of Logos.[8]

Clement had three fundamental theses on human nature. First, human beings had free will. They were categorically different from all other terrestrial creatures because humans alone had the gift of reason and free will. As God would never make anything that God did not love, so, too, God would neither coerce a person nor demand that a person do what that person was not able to do. The second point followed from the first: humans were educable. Through the Logos and those whom the Logos raised up, humans were enabled to improve their souls and develop into what God had given them the capacity to be, heavenly beings. Third, while individuals were responsible for their own educational progress to salvation, God provided them with teachers and schools. Clement continued that women engaged in the process equally with men and that knowing God entailed loving humans.

Humans were destined for what they never dreamed possible: they would become gods, that is, angels of the highest rank. In discussing human nature and destiny, Clement turned to Gen. 2, the account of Adam and Eve in the garden. Clement insisted that the primal couple were immature children who did not know how to use their reason properly. God intended Eden to be just one classroom in their educational journey. Through effort and obedience to the Logos they were to govern their souls and grow to angelhood. Instead of growing morally and spiritually, humanity had become beastly because of willful, ignorant disobedience. Nevertheless, God did not reject humans but gave them the opportunity to become educable children again. Clement assumed that a child was both male and female; gender differentiation occurred through misdirected actions, habits, and passions. Clement concluded that when Jesus told his followers that they had to become children to enter the kingdom, and when Paul promised believers that there was neither male nor female in Christ, and when the author of Hebrews counseled believers to become mature in Christ, they were teaching persons to fulfill their destinies by being images and likenesses of the Logos. In Clement's educational program, Logos-initiated teachers such as himself used all the techniques of *paideia* to lead persons to that destiny by teaching them to control their habits, actions, and passions. The gifted few were initiated into the ranks of the true Gnostics.[9]

Clement's language, which grew daring and probably too dangerous for later church authorities, has a buoyant quality in spite of his ornate rhetoric. As he engaged his readers' imagination, he set them up for each succeeding stage in the educational program to salvation. His advice about daily life seemed practical, but his attention was directed heavenward. Did he really take life in this world seriously? By regarding the current sphere of existence as a preliminary classroom and by his consistent educational understanding of life, he lost the historical, earthly specificity of both creation and humanity. He mentioned imperial despots but passed over their deeds. Did tyranny and terror wreck his progressive understanding of salvation? The grittiness of what Christians called sin and its often tragic results were glossed over. God's wrath toward sinners and demands for justice faded in allegories and pedagogical methods. Questions about his views of creation and humanity deepened when he turned to Jesus.

CLEMENT ON THE IDENTITIES OF JESUS

Clement blended themes so artfully that to consider one feature engages readers in his whole theological project. This is particularly evident in his presentation of Jesus. I think his exoteric instruction tilted toward understanding Jesus as the highest of the gods, but his esoteric teaching perhaps tended to see Jesus as a manifestation of the supreme Deity. In any event, Clement employed many titles and images as he carefully built an identity for Jesus. He regarded Jesus as the Logos (Clement's favorite designation), Wisdom, Mind, Son, and Image and Likeness of God. Jesus was also the Shepherd, Light, Guide, and Teacher of humanity. By means of allegory and typology, Logos-Jesus was identified as the spiritual Isaac, Jacob, and Moses. Naming Jesus "the breasts of God" does stretch the imagination. Eventually, his expressions formed a coherent, sometimes disturbing, set of identities for God, Jesus, and humankind.

The identity of Jesus began within the supreme God and proceeded down the cosmic cone. The cone may now be understood in terms of change instead of space. The Logos, sent on the spiraling journey to create the cosmos, built in the capacity for beings to change by drawing closer to God or moving away. Beings that moved toward God changed by becoming more fully what God planned for them to become. The Logos made the visible earth and planted seeds of gnostic truth in all cultures and teachings but (as Wisdom) imparted the true philosophy to Abraham, Moses, and the other scriptural heroes. They, in turn, taught it to others. Traversing the circuit, Logos acted in human history, especially the history of Israel, to exhort, instruct, and—for those able to bear it—teach God's holy principles. When, therefore, the biblical writers indicated that "God" spoke and acted, they meant the Logos. In that the Logos was the agent of creation who made men and women in the image and likeness of the Logos, the Logos was properly called the father of humankind.

People needed to experience God more directly in their *paideia* to salvation, so Logos became visible. Considering the initial space-change action as the first coming of the Logos, Clement termed the visible appearance of the Logos as Jesus the parousia. At this point the Alexandrian introduced a startling idea:

> Behold the mysteries of love (*agapē*), and then you will have a vision of the bosom of the Father, whom the only-begotten God alone declared. God in his very self is love, and for love's sake he became visible to us. And while the unspeakable part of him is Father, the part that has sympathy with us is Mother. By his loving, the Father became female (*ethēlynthē*), a great sign of which is he whom he begat from himself; and the fruit that is born of love is love. This is why the Son himself came to earth, this is why he willingly endured humanity's lot, that having been measured to the weakness of us whom he loved, he might in return measure us to his own power.[10]

The Unbegotten became female as well as male. God as ineffable Father and knowable Mother parented the Logos as Jesus. The female dimension within God transmitted divine love for humanity and was the bond of compassionate participation between the life of God and the life of humanity. Clement continued: "This is our nourishment, the milk flowing from the Father by which alone we little ones are fed. I mean that he, the well-beloved, Logos, our provider, has saved humanity by shedding his blood for us. There-fore we fly trustfully to the 'care-banishing' breast of God the Father; the breast that is the Logos, who is the only one who can truly bestow on us the milk of love."[11] The mystery of love began with God's love and progressed to the revelation that God was Father and Mother for the sake of humanity. The genders attributed to God were ways in which God related to and was revealed in the cosmos and to humanity. Through the feminine nature, the milk of love and truth nourished women and men, a daring image and a deft reversal of the Valentinian Sophia.

Clement's daring characterizations of Jesus in the esoteric writings were directed toward describing the Logos's functional relationships to humanity and also may have pointed toward more speculative ideas in the esoteric teachings. Before, during, and after the parousia, the Logos educated persons to control their habits, actions, and passions. *Paideia* began with habits. Bad habits were broken and good habits developed through exhortation (*protreptikos*) to proper conduct. In the beginning phase, the Logos was the exhorter who invited persons into the school of truth, critiqued pagan *paideia*, and gave them basic lessons in Christian logic. Clement wrote his *Exhortation* for the initial educational stage. Actions and passions were dealt with in the second division of philosophy (namely, ethics) through preceptive and persuasive discourses. In ethics, the progressing learner experienced the Logos as the Instructor in specific duties and exoteric general principles. Clement's *Instructor* and *Miscellanies* were ethical course materials. The few students who persevered or lived long enough to master their habits, actions, and passions so that they did God's will spontaneously were initiated by Logos-Teacher into the teachings of the esoteric *gnōsis* of God. Because the lore in the third division of philosophy (cosmology or theology) was secret and unwritten, it was preserved through oral tradition among initiated teachers such as Clement.

The soul's earthly career was not long enough to complete the educational plan to salvation, but neither change nor space was limited to existence at the base of the cone. The Logos had prepared still more places for learning. Death on earth simply transferred the soul from one classroom to another, from which it continued to be promoted until it reached its consummation among the ranks of the gods. The grades a soul entered on its ascent depended on the improvement it had made at the previous level. In the end, the soul would reach the mansion that the Logos had readied for it. The mansions differed from one another because each soul had a different capacity to love and contemplate God. Each soul, however, would achieve consummation and be as completely as it could be in the image and likeness of the Logos. In other words, the soul was cleansed and informed until it reached divine status.[12]

Clement's identities for Jesus depended largely on Logos, Wisdom literature, the Fourth Gospel, Philo, and Middle Stoicism-Platonism. His disposition and probably his training, as well as his scriptural and philosophical sources, moved Clement to shun a parousia involving the physical resurrection of the dead, last judgment, hell, and life on the re-created earth. Clement insisted on the ongoing movement of the soul to a heavenly realm because he understood God and the Logos as creators-educators and humans as destined to be gods. In brief, Clement was consistent in moving Logos's action from heaven to earth and back to heaven again. Clement's aversion to the physicality of creation carried into his Christology. Although he appeared to affirm the incarnation of the Logos in Jesus, Clement held that the Jesus-Logos was in the image and likeness of the noncorporeal God, so Jesus' earthly body differed from human bodies. References to Jesus' fatigue, emotions (except for mercy and love), and pain were accommodations Jesus made to humans because he did not want his followers to be distracted from their lessons. He ate and drank, but his perfect system produced no waste; he neither urinated, nor moved his bowels, nor perspired. Frankly, Clement verged into a docetic Christology. Further, since women and men were growing into the image and likeness of the Logos, humans could use Jesus as the paradigm for fulfilled humanity, a paradigm of the loving, self-controlled, knowing ascetics—persons who resembled remarkably the monks of later generations. Clement's images, specificity, and heavenward orientation continued as he turned his attention to the church.

CLEMENT ON THE CHURCH

Alexandrian Christianity is as puzzling as Clement. The wealth of available information defies categories and precedents applicable to the church in other parts of the Empire. The city was a marketplace for religious movements and practices as much as it was for trade and tourism. Versions of Christianity competed with one another and other sects. Each may have had its own community of adherents who met together for worship and mutual assistance. Either affiliated or independent schools may have served as educational resources for such communities. Generally, Jews, pagans, and Christians in Alexandria tended to spiritualize the specific, physical, and literal into abstract, heavenly, and allegorical understandings. Under such circumstances, esoteric teachings and ceremonies flourished, whether among persons dedicated to Isis, Moses, Plato, or Jesus. Gnosticisms of different hues flourished in schools and fellowships, debating one another and seeking new members. Among the "Christians" were groups known as Valentinians, Basilideans, Carpocratians, Ophites, Naasenes, and Sethians. Alongside them were Marcionites, Montanists, and communities more or less recognizable as "orthodox." Just where Clement, his school, and the "church" to which he belonged fit in is still a puzzle; his reflections on the church sound familiar but have an odd ring.[13]

One set of comments described the church as a place. His are the earliest extant references to people "going" to church. Other comments about the church reflected Septuagintal and New Testament themes. These themes often escalated to allegorical representations of the church. The church, he wrote, was the heavenly pattern, holy mountain, shrine, altar, home for God's elect, and, of course, temple and body of Christ.[14] Clement then pressed the Scripture and his gnostic traditions to make the church *Ekklēsia*, a heavenly female who was one of a threesome that originated in God's mind. God's will became Cosmos, God's Wisdom was Logos, and God's Purpose (*Boulēma*) appeared as *Ekklēsia*. In a manner probably clarified in Clement's esoteric teaching, *Ekklēsia* was related to the female-mother dimension of God and the female side of humanity's image and likeness in Gen. 1. She and Logos were partners, perhaps modeled after God and Wisdom in Prov. 8, whose aim was to educate and save humanity, that is, to bring souls to their place among the gods. Clement knew and accepted traditions in which *Ekklēsia* and Logos were spouses. He was Isaac and she Rebekah, and God-Abimelek watched their chaste love approvingly. Again, Logos is her virgin-groom, God's breasts, and humanity's father while she is his virgin-bride, perhaps God's *gnōsis*, and the milkless mother of humans. Together they drew souls to their holy mansions on the cosmic cone of God's will.

A third group of comments related to the church concerned ethical issues. For Clement, the earthly was not only a worshiping and believing fellowship, but also a community of persons whose actions derived from and witnessed to its faith, hope, and love of God. Here the distinctions between Clement's school and the church were unclear, probably because he and his students were members of the same Christian community. Clement maintained that his teachings about proper conduct were derived from the Scriptures and were in agreement with the principles of what he called "the catholic church."[15] Actually, the vocabulary and much of the program that Clement proposed for Christians were used by schools with a Stoic bent. The Alexandrian specified twelve negative tones in the voice of the Logos ranging from mild admonition to harsh indignation and a complementary series of encouragements. No human activity, mental or physical, seemed to escape Clement's attention. He commented on walking, bathing, mattresses, beards, money, slaves, and sexual intercourse along with anger, greed, and envy. He discoursed at length on Christian conduct at parties and feasts, advising women and men on the etiquette of eating, drinking, laughing, and belching. Marriage, he felt, was good practice for life as a god; and he counseled believers to follow a vegetarian diet, eliminate gradually the use of cosmetics and jewelry, and allow older persons to use wine.[16] All this was part of God's project to lead people to salvation.

Clement included the Scripture interpretation throughout his theology and particularly in his ethics and ecclesiology. He is the earliest writer known to distinguish between written Old and New Testaments. He reflected knowledge of biblical texts in Hebrew, yet he used the Septuagint, included *Enoch* in the Old Testament, and was favorably disposed to a widely circulated Jewish document called the *Sibylline Oracles*. He quoted from nearly every work in the New Testament, treated *1 Clement, Epistle of Barnabas,* and *Shepherd of Hermas* as Scripture, and used the popular *Preaching of Peter.*[17] Since the Logos gave the Scriptures to humanity, they contained the open and hidden teachings of God that led persons to their fulfillment. The Scriptures had hidden senses because the children of the Logos were encouraged to inquire about and be eager to discover the words of salvation, and because the student-children needed preparation to understand the truth embedded in the Scripture. They had to grow ethically and spiritually in interpretive discernment; otherwise they risked being harmed or confused if they were not ready to fathom the truths present in the texts.[18] Clement said that the apostolic teaching tradition preserved by Christian teachers and transmitted to succeeding generations in schools such as his teachers' and his own was essential to the ongoing disclosure of God's truth contained in the sacred writings. The church, too, was essential, for it was the community in which the interpretation took shape in the lives of believers and in the fellowship of worship.

Clement regarded Scripture as a giant parable or divine enigma about God's plan to salvation through the Logos. He described three exoteric levels of interpretation for passages, words, names, and numbers. The literal level met the needs of beginners for rudimentary knowledge, and the ethical level assisted those studying specific duties. The figurative level used allegorical and philosophical techniques to open students in the higher ethical courses to the more profound, but still public, meanings. Beyond the interpretations that could be discussed publicly and committed to writing, Clement knew secret oral traditions that his teachers claimed derived from Jesus. These mystic wonders appear to have dealt with matters in the mind of God, heavenly hierarchies, the ascent of souls to the mansions, maleness and femaleness in God and the cosmos, and the consummation of all things in Logos. Students who were ready morally, intellectually, and spiritually proceeded into cosmology and theology through initiation into the ranks of the true Gnostics by their teachers.[19]

In an obscure passage, Clement wrote that Gnostics provided a model for ministry in the earthly church because they reflected patterns in the heavenly temple. The perfect Gnostic was like an apostle who had learned directly from Jesus the Logos and functioned as one of the twenty-four heavenly presbyters seated before the Lamb's throne (Rev. 4). In their apostolic-presbyterial roles, Gnostics transmitted the true doctrine of God and, like Moses' elders, judged the people. The Gnostics also functioned as deacons of God's will, serving humanity in love. Clement hinted that the Gnostics had unspecified bishop-like responsibilities connected to angelic glory.[20] If Clement's comments reflect any church polity, they point not to a bishop-centered community but to a presbyter-teacher.

Clement's startling images for the church are consistent with his theological outlook, and his ecclesiology in general reflects his careful observations of human behavior. He spoke warmly and pastorally about human foibles and problems, yet the tilt was upward and away from earthly specificity. The church, like Jesus, seemed to have a docetic character. While he encouraged inquiry and speculation, he made it clear that the Gnostics had interpretive authority to establish rules of doctrine and conduct. In his discussions of the perfect Gnostic and of the three ministerial offices, Clement moved, perhaps inadvertently, toward identifying the Gnostics with the clergy. As custodians of the apostolic tradition, interpreters of the Scriptures, and discipliners in their schools, they could be incorporated into the church hierarchy to formulate defenses against heretics, explicate doctrine for the faithful, and organize what would become schools subject to the bishops. In Clement's works and in subsequent developments, the average Christian believer was an immature child who needed to be guided and disciplined by spiritual and ecclesiastical superiors. The layers of biblical interpretation and docetic understandings of Jesus and the church may have been intellectually satisfying for some, but other Christians were bound to protest the increasingly abstract responses that leaders such as Clement offered to the challenges which faced believers.

CLEMENT ON CHRISTIANS AND SOCIETY

Clement described the relationship between Christians and society in paradoxical terms. He criticized virtually everything in Greco-Roman society from art to Zeus, making it clear that, ideally at least, Christians rejected cherished social traditions and refused to join in many important pagan activities. Yet he also affirmed the same society and many of the cultural expressions he criticized, including literature, rhetoric, and philosophy. The cause of his endorsement was theological: the Logos had sown the seeds of *gnōsis* throughout the cosmos. As a result, Clement both jabbed at and embraced Greco-Roman traditions, writings, and culture.

He mastered the rhetorical and dialectical disciplines, using their finer tactical and stylistic points in his theological project. Employing satire and logic, the Alexandrian attempted to persuade and argue his various audiences into joining the educational plan to salvation. Clement's surviving works do not include an apology, probably because the forensic mode was not his preferred style. Instead of closely argued or slashing defenses, he offered demonstrative and deliberative treatises and sermons in an attempt to persuade pagans to begin and Christians to press onward to their souls' consummation. Clement responded indirectly to accusations that Christians were atheists, traitors, cannibals, and immoral. He showed that pagans were atheists (in that they worshiped false deities) who engaged in illicit sex acts and honored heroes who had allegedly eaten their own children. He was unconcerned with matters of secular government and listed emperors only as passing reference points in God's plan. Persecution was interpreted as discipline to promote the soul's perfection. To put human rulers in their place, he reminded readers that God was the true Lawgiver.[21] When he enlisted Greco-Roman *paideia* in the service of Christian ethics, Clement not only used Stoic terms for different voices of the Logos but also presented an array of medical terms and practices.[22] References to surgery, amputation, cauterization, poultices, and the like were common in ethical discourses. Often the student was regarded as a patient under treatment. Clement's medical-ethical vocabulary may also have been a cut against pagan soul-doctors such as Asclepius, for in Clement's theology the Logos was the great physician of the soul whose medicines and prescriptions were superior to Greco-Roman therapies and therapists. His teachings of specific and general ethical duties and his description of the perfect Gnostic expressed the concern that Christians prove the validity of *paideia* of the Logos by modeling attitudes and actions superior to those of their pagan associates.

Charges of ignorance stung Clement and evoked from him lengthy and innovative responses. An obvious round of responses entailed his filling literally dozens of pages with quotations of and allusions to pagan philosophers and poets and references to pagan practices. He may have had a thorough knowledge of them or used handbooks of selected sayings, but he pulled from the obscure as well as the famous in order to show that Christians were erudite and knew the intellectual authorities of society. He added some twists of his own. One was to override the pagan writers with references to Philo, Josephus, and especially the ancient Scriptures of Abraham's and Moses' people. He also mentioned Indian philosophers whom he probably met in Alexandria or on his travels.[23] By citing the Jewish and East Asian traditions, Clement notified his Greco-Roman critics that Christians had access to philosophical truth that antedated the Greeks by centuries. Furthermore, his own complex sentences and ornate rhetoric demonstrated that Christians were eloquent, and eloquence was a mark of culture. If Isocrates meant that *paideia* made persons civilized, then Christians had perhaps even stronger claims than native-born Greeks to *aretē*. Indeed, the pagans were the real ignoramuses, because they did not interpret their own materials and traditions correctly and did not know either Israel's holy books or philosophers.

He turned the charge of barbarism to his advantage when addressing both pagan and Christian critics. He labored through chronologies to show that Abraham and Moses predated any of the Greek philosophers, and he went to great lengths to show that what was decent and true among the Greeks was actually derived from the barbarians, that is, foreigners such as the Israelites. Barbarians, not vain Greeks, were the human transmitters and custodians of truth and goodness. Philosophy in particular was the province of the descendants of the patriarchs and Moses, and Christians were the students whom the Logos instructed in divine truth. Clement now took on two audiences, critics within the church and pagans.

Apparently he and other Christian philosophers encountered Christians who argued that philosophy was not only foreign to the gospel but demonic.[24] These despisers of pagan culture and intellect apparently held that philosophy came from the corrupted heavenly secrets that the Watchers had used to corrupt humanity. Philosophy, like jewelry and cosmetics, was part of the demonic plan to destroy humanity through lies and clever arguments. Rhetoric and dialectic were instruments of mental deception to confuse the faithful, so, according to the critics, Christians ought to have nothing to do with those disciplines or with those who enticed Christians to study them. Christians who disdained philosophy would have welcomed the pagan charge of barbarism because the alternative, being a "cultured" person, entailed worshiping and being ruled by demons, joining in damnable immorality, and undermining that wisdom of God which seemed like foolishness to humans. Passages in the Pastoral Epistles as well as other materials connected to Paul, John, Peter, and Jude certainly supported negative views about philosophy and pagan culture generally. Since Alexandrian Christians honored these writings as God's New Testament with humanity, Clement nuanced his responses carefully. Philosophy, he argued, was indeed derived from heaven, and it was God's gift to humanity. Clement refused to allow the Watchers title to own God's truth. Indeed, he argued somewhat lamely, the Watchers did in fact steal the divine teaching and distort it to suit their evil purposes. Distortion, however, did not ruin the truth. Relying on the distinction between use and abuse (not throwing out the baby with the bathwater), Clement insisted that God's truth was always God's truth, even when it was in the hands of thieves and swindlers. The issue was not whether to use philosophy but how to restore it to its proper place in God's plan for salvation. For Christians to reject philosophy, then, was to give the Watchers a victory over God. Moreover, philosophy, flawed as it was, had its positive uses. First, the dialectical method sharpened Christian wits so that the believers would not be misled by cunning arguments. Philosophy remained a method to test the spirits and arguments that confronted Christians inside and outside the church. Second, philosophy still belonged to the Logos, who used it to lead gnostically gifted Christians into further understandings of the mysteries of the faith. Christians had to be careful about employing the words and ideas of pagan thinkers, yet the Logos has planted *gnōsis* throughout the world. Philosophy is an important tool that helps skillful Christians discover that saving knowledge and use it to improve their souls. Obviously, Clement's defenses reflected concern over his identity, his school, and his Logos-based theological program. Whether or not Clement persuaded Alexandrian Christians about the usefulness and legitimacy of philosophy, his affirmation and adaptation of it as a disciplined way of thinking and of making available to Christianity the cultural riches of many societies encouraged Clement to incorporate philosophy in the theological project for the salvation of all.

Philosophy, he told Greco-Romans, was a means used by the Logos to draw them to the mansions prepared for them. As God through the Logos had made a covenant with the Jewish people and sealed it by means of the Law, in like manner God had made a covenant with the Greco-Romans and made philosophy the sign of that covenant. Up to the time of the parousia of the Logos, Gentiles had learned the divine and saving truth through philosophy. The traditional philosophers had made mistakes and sometimes knowingly distorted God's truth, but the Logos always kept the kernel of truth uncorrupted within the shell of bumbling philosophical systems. The similarities between the school philosophies and the Christian teachings were due to the fact that each shared the same core of divine truth. Philosophy and philosophers struggled to find the truth that was more plainly present within the Scripture, the history of Israel, and the present teachings of the church. Many streams flowed into the broad river that led to the consummation or salvation of souls. Philosophy was a stream by means of which Greeks and barbarians might be saved. After the parousia, the Logos enabled women and men to philosophize in faith, gain self-control, and grow in love. Christians, therefore, were far from being barbarians in the sense of being uncultured. They were the most cultured and philosophical of all people. Philosophy as a form of *paideia*, an ethical discipline, and an intellectual means to understand *gnōsis* was a divine gift that aided the soul's passage to heaven and the church's fuller understanding of its role now and through the ascent to consummation.

Clement's paradoxical understanding of the relationship between Christians and society reflected his Logos theology and his conviction that this earth was but one of many classrooms through which souls passed in their education to fulfillment. The present existence was temporary, and in it evil forces sought to distract humans from their ascent to godhood. Still, Clement was ever the hopeful teacher who saw lessons—divine lessons—throughout the cosmos. Society and its cultural expressions were connected somehow to the Logos and thus to the church and Christians. And the reverse was just as accurate: Christians and the church were connected to society and its cultural expressions by the Logos.

Clement repelled and attracted contemporaries and subsequent generations. His responses to the challenges that Christians faced were scarcely conventional by later standards. He realized that Christianity's enthusiasm could be—had to be—expressed in intellectually understandable and respectable terms if the Christian community was to be understandable and respectable to itself and to prospective converts. He had the audacity to use provocative images and to offer a theological program that drew from the pagan culture as well as from the biblical tradition. Nevertheless, he was dangerous. His true Gnostics might become a self-perpetuating intellectual and ecclesiastical elite. They might exert doctrinal and jurisdictional authority over other believers on the grounds of their claim to superior insight and their having been authorized by their predecessors (with little or no discernible sanction by the community of believers) to teach and govern. Clement's spiritualizing and allegorizing of the Scripture, the kingdom, and the parousia was matched by his essentially docetic Christology and anthropology. In the long run, his responses in the second century were not discarded but became part of a restless undercurrent within Christian piety and tradition, surfacing among Christian mystics, intellectuals, and venturers who dare to seek creative answers to the challenges of their own times. And that would probably please the Christian Sirach.

> Accordingly all our life is a festival: being persuaded that God is everywhere present on all sides, we praise him as we till the ground, we sing hymns as we sail the sea, we feel his inspiration in all that we do. And the gnostic enjoys a still closer intimacy with God, being at once serious and cheerful in everything, serious owing to his thoughts being turned towards heaven, and cheerful, as he reckons up the blessings with which God has enriched our human life.
>
> *Stromateis* 7.7.35

13

Tertullian

What has Jerusalem to do with Athens, the Church with the Academy, the Christian with the heretic? Our principles come from the Porch of Solomon, who himself taught that the Lord is to be sought in simplicity of heart. I have no use for a Stoic or Platonic or dialectical Christianity. After Jesus Christ we have no need of speculation, after the Gospel no need of research. When we come to believe, we have no desire to believe anything else; for we begin by believing that there is nothing else which we have to believe.

Tertullian *Prescription Against Heretics* 7[1]

Virgil's version of the character of Queen Dido of Carthage and her relationship with Aeneas is a paradigm for the character of North Africans and their relationship with Rome. She was brave and prized loyalty, yet she was prone to implacable anger. Without knowing her strengths or flaws, Aeneas first loved, then exploited, and finally deserted her. Before he left, Dido denounced his faithlessness. Three wars later, the descendants of Aeneas conquered and ruled what came to be called "Roman Africa."[2]

"Roman Africa" is a geographically elastic and ethnically inaccurate term. Rome established four provinces along the coastal strip ranging from present-day Morocco to Libya. Even then, imperial authority was limited to the major cities and towns and scattered military outposts in the hinterland. African aristocrats adopted Greco-Roman manners and language, often intermarrying with Latins who settled in Africa. The authorities encouraged the establishment of philosophical schools and the blending of indigenous cults with Greco-Roman religions. People in the lower socioeconomic classes, however, retained their character and their animosity toward Rome. European settlers and latinized Africans respected the indigenous people's courage but resented their stubbornness. Intelligence and toughness characterized Dido and her descendants, and so did fierce anger, biting rhetoric, and demands for loyalty. Tertullian was a son of Africa by birth and a child of Dido by temperament.

TERTULLIAN THE PERSON

Tertullian embarrasses Christians. Many of his responses to the challenges faced by the church were essential to what became normative or orthodox Christianity. He also had attitudes and used language that suppressed dissent, scholarship, and women. Moreover, his Dido-like denunciations of Rome's bishops and his adherence to Montanism flustered later Christians; how could the church use a schismatic and possible heretic as a source for truth and order? His answers to Christian questions and pagan criticisms proved so valuable that either he is not cited as their author or else the use of them is justified by means of adroit chronologies of his career and writings. Careful analysis, however, has shown that the usual biography and the traditional dating of his works are based on misinterpretations and guesswork.[3] Tertullian's references to himself, our knowledge from other sources concerning events in which he was involved, and modest inferences drawn from his writings allow some generalizations about his life and personality.

Tertullian was active in Carthage (near modern Tunis) approximately from 170 to 220. He was a husband and probably a father. Able to write in Greek as well as Latin, he was versed in the works of Juvenal and Cicero, knew the major philosophical schools, and was familiar with historians such as Tacitus. His handling of rhetorical forms indicates that he might have taught in one of the schools at Carthage. Although there is no evidence that Tertullian was either a presbyter or deacon, other Christians consulted him about doctrinal and ethical matters. He promoted the New Prophecy and broke with the bishops of the church at Rome over their attitudes toward new revelations, sin, and marriage. Impatient with people who were indecisive and merciless toward those whom he thought disloyal to God, he occasionally recognized his own failings and need for God's help. His invectives and condemnations were rhetorical devices but were also meant seriously. Minus polemics and posturing, Tertullian's theology emerged as a coherent response to the challenges that faced the church. Vincent of Lerins (ca. 435) offered a balanced if pungent summary of Tertullian:

> For who was more learned than he, who more versed in knowledge whether divine or human? With a marvellous capacity of mind he comprehended all philosophy. . . . Was not his genius of such unrivalled strength and vehemence

that there was scarcely any obstacle which he proposed to himself to overcome, that he did not penetrate by acuteness or crush by weight. . . . [Yet] he deservedly made both himself and his writings obnoxious.[4]

TERTULLIAN ON THE CREATOR AND CREATION

Tertullian repeated a creedlike "Rule of Faith" that probably was used in the Christian communities he knew. It began with the affirmation "that there is one only God, and that He is none other than the Creator of the world, who produced all things out of nothing through His own Word, first of all sent forth. . . ."[5] While his designation of God and the Word as responsible for creating everything agreed with several Scptuagintal and New Testament traditions as well as other second-century Christians, Tertullian's description of the Creator was distinctive and resounded through his theology. His basic principle was that God was the one, great, unique Supreme Being.[6] Obviously the rule and Tertullian's understanding of God as "the Supreme" entailed a vigorous rejection of the pagan pantheon, any gnostic Pleroma, and Marcionism. Tertullian went further.

First, he agreed with the Platonic and biblical authors that the Supreme transcended time, space, and change. God was the One; all else was relegated to the many. He swept aside angelic cosmologies and restricted the use of "God" to the One. In his argument, Tertullian introduced the word "substance," a key philosophical and legal term meaning underlying property or essence. The substance that was one, great, unique, and supreme was God, and the name "God" was implicit within those qualities. Anything that lacked the fullness and unique union of those attributes could not be and must not be referred to as God. The Creator was the sole being who had the substance—and that included ultimate authority and power—to be considered God. To claim that there was more than one such supreme, unique substance was foolish and perverse.

Second, among the few human comparisons Tertullian allowed to God was that of emperor. Tertullian's version had little to do with the historical office or emperors in his own time, for God neither ruled with a senate nor as a Commodus-like tyrant. God laid down the laws, battled enemies, punished evildoers, and rewarded the obedient. The emperor of the cosmos deserved unquestioning loyalty and self-sacrifice from all beings. Tertullian emphasized that God was the One, the Ruler, and the Judge.

Third, God created the cosmos "out of nothing." The immediate question was whether or not matter existed before God created the world. In terms of a modern theory, such "stuff" would be the particles and gases that exploded in the "big bang" from which the universe resulted. Greco-Roman philosophers assumed that matter had always existed along with some sort of divinity. Usually the matter was considered to be formless or chaotic. The Divinity, directly or through intermediary powers, shaped the matter into the cosmos. Creation, then, was a process through which God or the gods made a beautiful whole out of the primal chaos. The authors of the biblical creation accounts either assumed the presence of such matter or were unconcerned about the issue. By the second century, however, pre-creation matter was an issue in the church. One cause for its importance was its role in pagan philosophy. Another cause was the Marcionite and Valentinian denigration of the material world and its maker—a position that cited Scripture for support. Both causes questioned the oneness and sovereignty of God. If matter always existed with God before creation, then matter was eternal and could be regarded as a second, even a rival deity. Tertullian rejected the eternity of matter out of hand. Instead, he posited that God transcended the limits of human reason and exercised supreme authority and power in creating matter out of nothing. He blended Genesis 1, Proverbs 8, and John 1 by having the Word-Wisdom of God shape the matter that had been summoned into existence. Tertullian insisted that creation began at a particular time and that at God's command matter would cease to exist and the whole creation would die. The death of creation set the stage for God's summoning beings endowed with free will to be judged worthy of everlasting blessedness or torment.

Finally, Tertullian's understanding of the Creator and creation made clear that the structure of all things and beings testified to God's existence and will. Nature disclosed the will of the divine ruler, and history confirmed that faithfulness to the righteous God was required of all. Humans did not have to wait until Moses' time to know the Law, for Adam knew it from his first breath. Through Moses, God made the Law clear not only to Israel but to all nations. No one, then, could use ignorance of the Law as an excuse for disobedience to God. Themes familiar from Logos theology, such as the universality of reason and a divine loving presence, were turned toward human accountability in prospect of the Supreme's coming to judge the cosmos.

TERTULLIAN ON HUMAN NATURE AND DESTINY

The arguments against the eternity of matter and for human accountability carried over into Tertullian's views of human nature and destiny. He stressed both the relatedness of and the distinctions between body and soul. Since the body was composed of matter, it was subject to change and death. But what was the soul and how did it relate to the body and God's will? He dismissed those who taught that the soul had always existed and those who theorized that somehow the soul entered the body at birth; then he offered his own anthropology.[7]

First the soul's source. According to Genesis 2, God made the body of Adam from matter, but only when the Lord breathed into the form did the first human become a living soul. The soul was the life force that came from God and, while separable from the body, ruled the body. The soul is immortal in the sense that God wills it to continue forever, but it is not immortal in the sense that it always existed. Eve, taken from Adam, shared her husband's matter and soul. Neither she nor he ever were children; they always were responsible adults endowed with free will. If Adam had the original soul and Eve received hers from him, how is it that each human is said to have her or his own soul? Tertullian wrote that semen transmitted the substances of body and soul. God willed humans to be fruitful and to multiply; sexuality in itself was not evil. The soul desired to fulfill God's command, and the body was the means of carrying out the soul's rational desire. The liquidity of semen transmitted the body's substance, and the warmth of semen the soul's substance. Each human born from Adam's seed received his or her substances from Adam and could be regarded as being "in Adam." Yet each person was accountable for what his or her soul did in life.

But there was a second factor: free will and sin. The human calamity began with Eve. Bone of Adam's bone and with a soul drawn from his, she allowed herself to be deceived by the devilish serpent. Her disobedience amounted to treason against the cosmic emperor, and then she deceived her husband into joining her. Sin did not obliterate Adam's free will but severely damaged his soul. That damage was passed on to Adam's descendants conceived through sexual intercourse. The original soul was distorted by what later theologians, influenced by Tertullian, called "original sin." Adam's children and all others fathered through him were conceived not in God-willed reason but in deception and lust, and their souls were twisted toward continuing deception and lust. Tertullian rushed headlong into blaming womankind for the now-fallen creation's terrors and human damnation. He merged *Enoch*'s version of Gen. 6 into the original female deception, adding a twist from the *Testament of the Twelve Patriarchs*—the women seduced the Watchers.[8] Women were the devil's gateway through which evil entered to destroy God's image—man. As Eve's daughters, they should repent constantly for their mother's sin. The whorish activities of the women who seduced the angels continued among women who used cosmetics, jewelry, and lavish clothing. Actually, such women merely primped for their own funerals. No Christian woman ought be allowed the use of these demonic devices; instead, they were to obey their husbands. In a calculated comment, he noted that women were responsible for Jesus' sufferings and death because Christ died to wipe out the results of the female-abetted rebellion against God. Because sexuality had been polluted by women, virginity for men and women (or celibacy for the nonvirgin) assured salvation. Female virgins must be veiled so that neither hair nor face was visible, and every woman was to wear drab, baggy clothing. Women who dressed otherwise heated male passions and invited rape mentally and physically. After Adam and Eve, marriage was permitted, not advocated, by God. Tertullian bordered on calling marriage legalized lust, and he denounced all remarriages as bigamy.

A third point referred to souls. Souls had a shape and even a tinted transparent color. Citing the testimony of a woman who participated in the New Prophecy movement, he said that a person's soul resembled the person's physical appearance. At death, the never-dying soul departed from the body and went to Hades, a cavernous place beneath the earth. The souls of the dead remained there until the day of resurrection, at which time the souls would be united with their bodies. Logically, since both souls and bodies were capable of sense perception, souls had feelings in the intermediate state, and when they were reunited with their bodies both would have heightened perceptions and feelings. Persons who were condemned for their treason against God would be plunged into the abyss of torment below Hades, while those who had earned salvation through fear and good works would reside in the new heavenly Jerusalem where their substance would be like that of matchless angels.[9] Tertullian remarked that in Hades souls had a foretaste of their eternal futures. One section of Hades contained the souls of those who would be damned, and those souls suffered accordingly. Their suffering would be multiplied when they were raised with their bodies. The other section held those who would be saved. If such souls still needed to pay penalties for sins incurred in life, they were disciplined and purged while in Hades so that they would be raised pure at the judgment.

One more point about human nature and destiny. In a rhetorical flourish, Tertullian subpoenaed a hapless soul for questioning.[10] He wrung from it the admission that it was Christian by nature. Instead of maturing toward its true being, the soul was willfully corrupted by pagan education, philosophy, and culture. Still, the soul retained remnants of its origin because it acknowledged one God, feared God's judgment, dreaded death, and expected continued consciousness after death. A soul uncommitted to Christ and unenlightened by God was guilty of treason against God. It was not immaturity or ignorance or compulsion that made the soul a criminal but rebellious disloyalty. Instead of looking toward pagan culture and philosophy, the soul that longed for life and peace would turn to Christ and the church.

TERTULLIAN ON THE IDENTITIES OF JESUS

The rest of the rule of faith read:

> This Word is called His Son, and, under the name of God, was seen in "diverse manners" by the patriarchs, heard at all times in the prophets, at last brought down by the Spirit and Power of the Father into the Virgin Mary, was made flesh in her womb, and, being born of her, went forth as Jesus Christ; thenceforth He preached the new law and the new promise of the kingdom of heaven, worked miracles; having been crucified, He rose again the third day; [then] having ascended into the heavens, He sat at the right hand of the Father; sent instead of Himself the Power of the Holy Ghost to lead such as believe; will come with glory to take the saints to the enjoyment of everlasting life and of the heavenly promises, and to condemn the wicked to everlasting fire, after the resurrection of both of these classes shall have happened, together with the restoration of their flesh.

The rule clearly banned any form of adoptionism and docetism as well as any rejection of the Old Testament. It pointed toward two affirmations: the divinity of Jesus and the humanity of the Word.

First, Jesus' divinity. A number of Christians, including Tertullian, held a "fully God" Christology, but not all explained it in the same manner.[11] Tertullian laid out what became the foundation of the western understanding of the Trinity.[12] He apparently assumed that his readers knew the concepts behind and the meanings of the terms he used when he held that Christians believe in one God who is of one substance expressed in three persons. God's substance was clearly the property of being one, only, unique, and supreme. "Person" became a crucial term, but did not mean "individual" in the modern sense. The Latin *persona* and its Greek equivalent, *prosōpon*, meant face or appearance. In legal usage, a "person" was any entity that had substance, and only "persons" had standing (*status*) to bring a case to court. A slave, for example, was someone else's property and not a "person"; and a corporation is still treated as a person in the law even though it is not a human. In the theater, "person" referred to the mask that an actor wore while portraying a character on stage. Given those understandings, Tertullian's trinitarian formula means that Christians believe in one God who is uniquely and supremely divine, and that God reveals that unchanging substance in three masks or faces: Creator-Father, Logos-Son, and Spirit-Power. Tertullian insisted that the revelatory action is undertaken simultaneously, that is, God is always revealing Godself as Creator, Word, and Spirit. Jesus, then, is "Spirit of Spirit, and God of God, as light is kindled," a person distinct in function but not divided in substance from the Father and the Holy Spirit.[13]

Second, the Word's humanity. The Word became flesh and Tertullian asserted: "It is [Christ's] flesh that is in question. . . . If we succeed in demonstrating it, we shall lay down a law for our own resurrection."[14] Tertullian
denounced docetism whether offered by heretics or taught by those considered
Christian. Three major factors supported his claim that God became fully
human in Jesus.

One came from his principle that God was the Supreme who created the
world out of nothing. God's incarnational action in Jesus had no human
analogue and transcended human reason. Since, as Paul wrote, the wisdom
of God seemed as foolishness to people and all things are possible for God,
God could and did become a man. In fact, God could be changed into and
share all conditions without changing God's substance or character because
the God who created the world out of nothing was able to act in ways that
defied human understanding. Tertullian considered how Jesus' body (or flesh)
and soul related to Adam and Eve. Since Jesus was a woman's, not a man's
son, his body and soul did not contain the defiled Adamic substances. Jesus
was the second Adam, the new start for humanity. As the first Adam came
from the virgin earth, and as the first woman came from the still virgin and
obedient Adam, so Jesus was born of an obedient virgin. The seed that generated Jesus in Mary's womb came from the Supreme, so Jesus had a fully
human body and soul as well as a fully divine substance. But did Mary, as a
daughter of Adam and Eve, pass on Adamic corruption to her baby? Tertullian
said that God gave Mary a special dispensation in light of her being the bearer
of the Word, thereby supporting the tradition that Mary was conceived im-
maculately, that is, without the taint of Adam's sin.[15] In any event, Jesus did
not assume "sinful flesh" but the new Adam's flesh in which he abolished
sin through obedience to God's Law. Jesus' resurrection transformed the mortal
flesh into the incorruptible body, and, as the firstfruits from the dead, forecast
the resurrection of humanity.[16]

Second, the mission of God incarnate. The Word-Person became human
in order to die for the disobedient human race. To die the Word had to be
born, so Jesus had a genuine human body and soul that experienced sensations
and temptations just as other people did. But the humanized Word was different in that Jesus was born with a free and uncorrupted will, and that
throughout his earthly career, Jesus remained obedient and loyal to God.
Jesus' birth, then, inaugurated the possibility of a new birth for men and
women: if they followed Jesus' pattern, they could be reborn in the new
Adam. Put another way, humans are born, but Christians are made through
rebirth through the power of the Spirit. The fullness of that rebirth might not
be realized until the day of resurrection, but now Jesus could be identified
and followed by believers as the good brother, master of grace, enlightener,

and discipliner of humans. The Word came first as Jesus the suffering Servant, but Jesus was to return as Lord of all. Tertullian took the parousia literally. As the exalted Son of God, Jesus would be the unrelenting judge of those who deserted the cosmic emperor to join the devil. While God's grace in Christ was necessary for anyone to escape from God's impending wrath, humans were also to be judged by the goodness of their thoughts and works.

Third, God prepared for the incarnation and the parousia through prophecies about the Word's coming first in flesh, then in glory. Since Tertullian took the fall of Adam and Eve and the fall of the Watchers literally, he understood God and the demonic to be in dreadful combat for the bodies and souls of women and men. In that struggle, God employed prophetic agents, inspired by the Spirit, to present the divine will. While the Scripture was the surest repository of those oracles, the biblical passages and words needed to be interpreted by the Spirit. Tertullian used typology and, occasionally, allegory to "prove" the truth of Christianity, and he regarded those who rejected his interpretations as being in league with the devil. His venomous attacks on Marcion and others branded as heretics were most often related to interpretations of the text. Jews, however, presented him with explicit and implicit problems.

Tertullian heard the familiar Jewish criticisms of Christianity: the biblical witness that God made a covenant with the Jews and not the Gentiles, the discrepancies between the biblical expectations of the Messiah and Jesus' death and failure to return to begin the kingdom, and Christian noncompliance with the Mosaic Law. Tertullian ploughed through the expected answers: Christians replaced the Jews as the chosen people and Jesus came initially in the form of the suffering Servant and would return as the glorified Messiah; the moral law was always valid, and the ceremonial law was binding on God's people only through Jesus' first coming." To be sure, Tertullian was furious with the Jews for not becoming Christians, a failure that aligned them with pagans, heretics, and demons. Buried in his lengthy work against Marcion are accusations that Jews were the tormenters and killers of Jesus, who was God incarnate. Nevertheless, he handled Jews with grudging respect. Both Jews and Christians worshiped the same God, shared some Scripture, abhorred idolatry and immorality, and looked for a Messiah on the day of resurrection. Jewish communities in North Africa also suffered at the hands of the populace and government but remained loyal to God. Their ancient pedigree gave them a connection to the primeval truth that Christians needed in order to authenticate the Christian understanding of and role in God's revelation. In reality, Tertullian argued that Christianity's validity was to be proven by the deeds Christians did. The somber obverse of that position is that if the church compromises with evil, it will betray God and make a mockery of God's truth.

TERTULLIAN ON THE CHURCH

The rule of faith did not mention the church, but the church was the rule's interpreter and defender. The ascended Jesus, according to Tertullian, sent the Spirit of God to lead believers to truth and salvation. At points the Spirit seems to be the post-ascension presence of the Word on earth.[18] Tertullian's ecclesiology included three major Spirit-related aspects.

First, the Spirit is at work within the church and individual believers as the guide to salvation. The Spirit hovered over the waters at creation, overshadowed Mary at Jesus' conception, and regenerated humans into Christians through baptism.[19] Persons seeking baptism were accepted into a probationary or candidate status and assigned sponsors who monitored their progress. Candidates were instructed in the rule (probably by the congregation's presbyters and the bishop), professed acceptance of it, and were to show evidence of living according to God's Law. As the day of baptism approached, candidates publicly confessed their sins and "satisfied" God's injunction that all sins required the payment of penalties. The payments, referred to vaguely by Tertullian, included mortification (self-inflicted punishments or disciplines?) of one's body and soul. On the day before the big event, candidates fasted, prayed, and maintained a vigil. Baptism itself washed away all the sins committed up to that point in a person's life. Once baptized, the newly born Christians were under the church's authority; the church, in turn, was under the authority of the Spirit. Christians who sinned after baptism were responsible for satisfying God's justice. Just as a shipwrecked sailor would grab a plank, sinners grasped the rituals of repentance provided in the church by the Spirit.[20] The rituals seem to have involved public confession and humiliation before the penitent resumed participation in the congregation's life. Tertullian distinguished between degrees of sin, such as minor offenses and capital crimes. Only one repentance was permitted for the worst sins, such as adultery and relapses into idolatry. Habitual minor offenders were not truly repentant and should be lumped together with unrepentant sinners, excluded from the congregation's fellowship, and consigned to God's judgment.

Tertullian often likened the Christian life to that of a soldier in the emperor's army and to an athlete in training. Just as recruits took an oath (in Latin, *sacramentum*) to be loyal to the emperor, so also believers made oaths to God through baptism, worship, and their adherence to the rule. As God's frontline troops against evil forces, and as God's competitors in the arena against demons, Christians were to be vigilant, disciplined, ready to endure hardship, and even eager to die for their Lord. They were always on duty, always in training. Any participation in anything that smacked of idolatry, the fallen Watchers' chief weapon, was strictly forbidden to Christians. As a result,

Christians could not be jewelers or craftspersons involved in making images, teachers of traditional literature or philosophy, actors or workers in theatrical productions, or soldiers who might be called on to venerate the gods. Having taken care of the dress of women, Tertullian forbade men the wearing of pagan wreaths that were given champions in the names of the gods. Clearly, Christians were not to attend theaters, public games, or gladiatorial combats. Since most of the proscribed occupations and activities reflected latinized urban life, Tertullian's views had ready adherents among the indigenous populace.[21]

Second, the Spirit is at work in the church as the guide to and revealer of truth. The church in North Africa as elsewhere was faced with a wide and even wild spectrum of teachings that claimed to be the true Christian message. Tertullian attempted to cut through the maze of Gnosticisms by asserting that revelation from God through the Spirit, not *gnōsis* derived from fanciful interpretations of Scripture or angelic sources, was the sure route to salvation. The rule of faith summarized the message in clear terms accessible to all. Heretics, he argued, were not interested in truth because they were in league with the demons to deceive believers. Discussion with the likes of Marcion and Valentinus was an exercise in futility. Worse, discussion implied that the partners in dialogue sought common understandings. Heretics, however, were enemies of Christ, Judas-like betrayers and deserters, potential soul-murderers. They claimed to seek the truth, but they intended to unsettle the faithful and ambush the unwary. Heresy, moreover, was one of the fruits of "worldly wisdom." Specifically, the corrupters of Christian doctrine asked the same unanswerable questions as the philosophers and used the same method of disputation. The devil designed philosophy and heresy to make ears itch and minds churn. To aid leaders, Tertullian wrote a *Prescription Against Heresies*.

Philosophers used a "proscription" (*praescriptio*) to register an objection before starting a formal disputation. Lawyers employed it prior to a court hearing to limit issues in a suit. More generally, the term covers precepts, orders, or rules that serve as the basis for considering questions or positions. The prescription itself is not debatable but instructs participants about which fundamental points are established beyond question. Tertullian's *Prescription* offered orthodox leaders a set of principles to be imposed on discussions whether or not the heretics assented to them.

The *Praescriptio*'s first principle choked all further debate: "Christ laid down one definite system of truth which the world must believe without qualification, and which we must seek precisely in order to believe it when we find it."[22] The "system of truth" summarized in the rule did not rely on human reason or investigation and must be accepted without question. Devout persons sought what Christ taught only as long as they did not know it, and searched within the church, not in philosophical schools. To know the rule was to know all, so the rule was the hermeneutical principle by which the Bible was to be read.[23] Since heretics did not accept the whole rule, they were not to discuss the Bible with Christians, for the Scripture belongs to the church, not to humanity in general; only the church is the proper guardian and interpreter of the Bible. Easily misled or simple Christians did not need to read the Bible for themselves; they were to depend on church leaders for proper meanings. Tertullian reminded readers that salvation is by faith, not by Bible reading. The church was not the place for free speech about matters dealing with heaven and hell. Error led to damnation, so error had no place and no rights in the church. Tertullian bolstered his attack on heresy by insisting that truth was older than error, and the heretics were newcomers when compared to the orthodox. If theological discussion supported the rule, however, then it was permissible.

The *Prescription's* second principle centered on the church's authority. Jesus gave full and adequate instruction to the apostles, and at Pentecost the Spirit led them into the needed understanding of the truth. Since the apostles were sent to preach God's doctrine, the church should receive only Christ's appointees and their legitimate successors. Tertullian denied that the apostles had received any secret teachings from Jesus or the Spirit; there were no esoteric or gnostic traditions. The other apostles approved Paul's doctrine as in full harmony with the teachings Christ gave them. When the apostles established congregations, they imparted to them the same Christ-given teachings. Congregations founded by the apostles, then, agreed in every respect with one another. He listed Corinth, Philippi, Thessalonica, and Rome as apostolic churches, noting that Peter and Paul were martyred at Rome, and he held that African churches were in harmony with the church at Rome.[24] Answers to questions about the rule could be gained from the nearest apostolic church. Rome, he noted, was the church of reference for African Christians. In his own way, Tertullian held an apostolic succession of doctrine. When he argued that the heretics could not produce lists of bishops that included an apostle, he construed apostolic authority also through bishops.

Tertullian presupposed that no single apostolic church or all of them together would ever disagree about the rule. Heretics, he observed wryly, could not claim support from even one of those respected churches, so heretics were isolated from other Christians, a sign of their desertion from Christ's cause and their disloyalty to God. Apparently some heretical groups united among themselves. Tertullian mocked the result as a network of lies and distortions that lacked coherence, fear of God, and decency. Discipline, he urged, was the index to truth, and the fear of the Lord was the sure sign of Spirit. Strict discipline among Christian congregations proved that the church, not the heretics, possessed God's truth.

Third, the Spirit who guarded the rule continued to reveal truth in the church and strengthened true believers even when their fellow Christians proved false. Perhaps his African heritage made him receptive to the New Prophecy. His expectation of the parousia led him to use *Enoch* and Revelation, while his attempts to understand the Scripture under the guidance of Wisdom-Spirit turned him to the Gospel of John. He shared with Montanists the themes of apocalyptic and Spirit-guided disclosures together with an emphasis on conduct as a measure of loyalty to doctrine. Rome's initial receptivity to the New Prophecy would only have served to draw him closer to the movement when it became known in Africa. His understanding of Christian morality led him to make later and painful revisions of his early views about the church at Rome.

Discipline was the issue that caused Tertullian and many other African Christians to break with the bishops of Rome and others. Tertullian regarded Christianity as the new law of life, Jesus as the new judge, and salvation as based on fear and good works. When the church in Africa was assaulted by waves of persecution in the closing years of the second century, he and others insisted that the church had to be highly disciplined and assertive. It could allow neither compromise with society nor moral flabbiness within its ranks. The complex historical situation involved a weak-willed bishop of Rome who was succeeded by a man of dubious credentials.[25] Tertullian accused the latter, Callistus (ca. 217–222), of advancing heresy, exercising tyrannical authority, and allowing breaches of discipline. Callistus authorized the ordination to the diaconate and the priesthood of men who had been married several times, violating the Pastoral Epistles' principle that congregational leaders be married only once and the widely held Christian view which considered second marriage as little more than licit. Further, claiming that bishops had the authority to absolve persons from all sins, Callistus pardoned then restored to full membership persons who denied they were Christians in a local persecution. Some of the lapsed were clergy, and Callistus authorized them to return to their positions in the church. Heb. 6 explicitly denied repentance to apostates, and many North Africans who suffered for the faith were irate at Callistus's sweeping forgiveness. The Roman bishop seemed to champion heresy, immorality, and faithlessness. Feeling betrayed, Tertullian broke with Rome and turned to an alternate ecclesiology: the Spirit-empowered community inspired by the New Prophecy. Callistus and the churches in communion with him were rejected as treasonous and corrupt. No longer spiritual, but psychic (in need of faith and good works), they had turned from God's revealed truth by spurning the Spirit's discipline.[26] Peter had given the Roman church the apostolic teaching, but in practice its bishop denied the doctrine the congregation received. Tertullian asked who could forgive on behalf of God. He answered that only the genuinely spiritual, that is, apostles and prophets, were authorized to forgive persons, understand the wisdom of the Spirit, and bestow the Spirit's divine gifts. His response showed the resurgence of a congregationally based sense of authority in opposition to the episcopal model. The Father, Son, and Spirit abided with the community that did not grieve and drive out the Spirit through crass, worldly disloyalty. For Tertullian, the "corruption" of the Roman church was a clear sign that the end of the age was at hand.[27] God's loyal servants would remain staunch and patient in the last struggles, enduring persecution by the government and condemnation by the demons who had infiltrated the church.

The New Prophecy met Tertullian's new need. It was not so much doctrine as moral discipline, the call to martyrdom, the insistence on self-control, the demand for monogamy, and the sharing of spiritual gifts among believers that attracted persons to the movement.[28] Montanists claimed that God could fill any person with God's revelatory presence. The movement provided Tertullian with a powerful core that held his theology in place and gave him the opportunity to confront both the church and the society around him.

TERTULLIAN ON CHRISTIANS AND SOCIETY

Tertullian's anger against Jews, women, heretics, and unspiritual Christians was a prelude to his fury against society. He, like other Christians, claimed that the church was the legitimate heir of divine wisdom and Scripture from Moses to the present. Making modest use of Logos theology, he held that Reason arranged the cosmos out of opposites or rival substances such as void and solid, under the rule of divine unity. The driving theological principle of his attitude toward the world around him, however, was contained in the closing portion of the rule of faith: judgment was near. Following the eschatology of the book of Revelation, Tertullian believed that there would be a thousand-year period in which all persons would die, the forces of evil would be imprisoned in an *Enoch*-like waterless pit, and the martyrs would be resurrected to reign with Christ. Following the millennium, the demonic hosts would be unleashed, the last battles between the armies of God and evil would be fought, evil defeated, the dead raised for judgment, and eternal rewards meted out.[29] Tertullian was convinced that the struggles to bind evil were already taking place and that the millennium was near. Men and women still had time to repent and to turn to God before Jesus returned to judge them. Given that perspective, he responded to society's challenges with the defiant apologies of those who addressed judges before being sentenced. His tone was strident, even menacing, because he was convinced that the accusers would burn in eternal flames.

His refutations of the accusations of atheism, incest, and cannibalism reflected familiarity with Justin's apologies and used what was by then the standard suite of Christian countercharges, with some additional tidbits of Christian lore.[30] Charges of treason, in the hostile political climate, provoked strong responses by the government and writers such as Tertullian. Christianity was a marginal movement in western North Africa before and for decades after Tertullian's death. The first references to the faith in Roman Africa reflect the apparently severe persecutions that began in the 180s because Rome connected the church there to subversive movements. Consistently defiant and refusing to concede any ground, Tertullian insisted that no Christian ever had acted or ever would act to overthrow the government, because God instituted government among humans until the end of the present age.

Even though he made all the points about fair hearings and legal niceties, he knew that the time for toleration had passed, so he attacked: "Your cruelty is our glory."[31] He warned that persecutors died miserable deaths and advised rulers to have mercy on themselves and Africa by stopping the assault against God before the Lord destroyed them. In fact, "Our religion . . . growing stronger at the very moment when it seems to be cut down, will never perish. For whoever beholds such noble endurance will first, as though struck by some kind of uneasiness, be driven to inquire what is the matter in question, and, then, when he knows the truth, immediately follow the same way."[32] Perhaps emboldened by recent attempts to reform and codify imperial laws, Tertullian insisted that magistrates and governors were accountable to the God who would judge everyone. He lectured officials on the nature of justice and law, arguing against any government involvement in matters of religion, and pointed toward religious toleration. Ironically, the toleration that Tertullian sought was for groups outside, not inside, the church.

Tertullian held that there were eschatological prices to be paid for persecution. One price was God's postponing the end of the age until more persons took the opportunity to become Christians. Christians, then, were leaven for moral order in the imperial domain. Tertullian threatened that Christians were everywhere—in cities, islands, fortresses, towers, towns, marketplaces, military camps, tribes, town councils, the palace, the senate, the forum. They had left nothing to the pagans but their temples.[33] He predicted that the ultimate eschatological price would be the damnation of those who harmed Christians. Continued persecution would amount to war against God, and God's soldiers were guaranteed both victory and its rewards in eternal life. Evoking heroic examples of faithfulness and valor from pagan history and literature, Tertullian challenged Roman officials who submitted to mobs which clamored for Christian blood. Believers battled for truth, the wheels on which their bodies were broken were triumphal chariots, the flames that enveloped their bodies were victory robes. Tertullian stood figuratively before the dais on which the judges sat and addressed them with an intensity reminiscent of the letters of Ignatius:

> Good presidents, you will stand higher with the people if you sacrifice the Christians at their wish, kill us, torture us, condemn us, grind us to dust; your injustice is the proof that we are innocent. . . . Nor does your cruelty, however exquisite, avail you; it is rather a temptation to us. The oftener we are mown down by you, the more in number we grow; the blood of Christians is seed.[34]

The obverse of Tertullian's response to the charge of treason was his consequent insistence that believers were to live according to the Christian discipline and, when called upon, submit to martyrdom.[35] As Christ's soldiers and the Spirit's athletes, much was required of them, especially when evil forces attempted to seduce them morally and persecute them for their allegiance to the Supreme. Through the Spirit, Christians were God's colony of light in an otherwise dark and brutal world peopled by criminals, that is, sinners. Tertullian told several imprisoned believers that the outside world was also a prison and, worse, a desert where the tempter prowled continually. At least those in jail were spared the sights and sounds of society's lusts and corruptions. Echoing the Pastoral and Pauline letters, Tertullian depicted the Christian first as a warrior who has taken the oath (*sacramentum*) of allegiance to God, then as a contestant. He wrote future martyrs:

> The sweat of the brow is on everything, that bodies and minds may not shrink at having to pass from shade to sunshine, from sunshine to icy cold, from the robe of peace to the coat of mail, from silence to clamour, from quiet to tumult. . . . O blessed ones, count whatever is hard in this lot of yours as a discipline of your powers of mind and body. You are about to pass through a noble struggle, in which the living God acts the part of the superintendent, in which the Holy Ghost is your trainer, in which the prize is an eternal crown of angelic essence, citizenship in the heavens, glory everlasting.[36]

To avoid martyrdom was desertion and apostasy was treason. The punishment for both was death. Martyrs, however, were guaranteed eternal life. As expected, Tertullian condemned those who fled persecution.[37] The fact that some believers would think about escaping from the time of testing and would justify doing so on the basis of Scripture angered Tertullian; for him such conduct indicated waning devotion to the Lord.[38] Tertullian's invectives against the government and the church in Rome are understandable in light of the ferocity of the persecution in North Africa, the temptation that believers would apostasize or seek to avoid confrontations with the government, and the New Prophecy's glorification of martyrdom.[39]

The criticisms of ignorance and barbarism ignited Tertullian's ire even further. He went through the expected proofs from antiquity, attempting to show that Christianity was the oldest and best of wisdom. His vibrant belief in the fall of the Watchers led him into articulate and passionate denunciations of Greco-Roman art, literature, and philosophy. He admitted that sometimes a pagan might have said something that agreed with Christian doctrine and ethics, but those exceptions could be accounted for by the work of the Logos in creating the world. In any event, areas of agreement were minor and of little consequence. Philosophical method and rhetorical devices were of limited value for Christians, and the content of the schools' curriculum was dangerous because it had been corrupted by demons. His major worries related not so much to pagan criticisms of Christian teachings as to Christian uses of pagan philosophies. It is possible that he had heard about Christian philosophical schools in Alexandria and elsewhere that had a milder view of the Watchers and the uses of philosophy among believers. Tertullian regarded philosophy as a demonic ploy to raise doubts among simple believers and to lead Christian intellectuals into heresy. He blamed all heresies on philosophy. Using Paul and the Pastorals, he warned that the wisdom of the world was foolishness, and philosophy was worldly wisdom. He was proud to proclaim that Christian faith was out of step with philosophical reason. Philosophy was for those who had itching ears, lustful desires, and rebellious intentions. Jesus' advice to search and knock was meant for the Jews and Gentiles who were still longing for the Supreme. Once they came to Christ and learned and accepted the rule of faith, there was nothing else for them to speculate about. Indeed, if they still searched, they were disloyal to God and prone to immorality, heresy, and apostasy.

Tertullian did not consider it any more worthwhile to debate with pagans than to dialogue with heretics. Christians had the truth; if the others wanted to know what God's will for salvation was before it was too late, they could seek out Christ's soldiers. In the meantime, believers had enough to do to maintain discipline, prepare for the coming kingdom, and honor the Supreme.

Born a North African and reborn a Christian, Tertullian responded to the challenges facing Christian with an energy that has embarrassed and invigorated Christians. Later leaders, living in times when the interests of authorities in the church, in government, and in society coincided, used his ideas and formulations. They also used his attempts to defend and renew the church, explain and develop basic Christian teachings, and subordinate members of the church and society because of their gender and their conscience. His responses shaped Western Christianity directly and through those whom he influenced. He pushed and jolted Christians to formulate their teachings and practices more precisely, and he summoned them to maintain their identity when compromise might have led to their absorption. Once he addressed candidates for baptism with surprising tenderness and humility:

> Therefore, blessed ones, whom the grace of God awaits, when you ascend from that most sacred font of your new birth, and spread your hands [in prayer] for the first time in the house of your mother [the church], together with your brethren, ask from the Father, ask from the Lord, that his own specialties of grace and distributions of gifts may be supplied you. "Ask," saith He, "and ye shall receive." Well, you *have* asked, and have received; you *have* knocked, and it has been opened to you. Only, I pray that, when you are asking, you be mindful likewise of Tertullian the sinner.
>
> *On Baptism* 20

14

Irenaeus of Lyons

For the road of all those who see is a single upward path, lit by heavenly light; but the ways of those who see not are many and dark and divergent. The former road leads to the kingdom of heaven by uniting man with God, but the others bring down to death by severing man from God. Therefore must both you, and all those who look after the salvation of souls, make your way by faith, without deviation, with courage and determination, lest through lack of tenacity or perseverance you remain at a standstill in material passions, or even be led astray and turn aside from the straight path.

Irenaeus *Proof of the Apostolic Preaching* 1[1]

The crowd in Lyons howled when the Christians entered the arena. Attention focused on a frail slave, Blandina.[1] Her devotion to Christ inspired her fellow believers and made her torturers furious. Mangled and hoisted on a stake, she appeared as the crucified one himself to those who were being roasted, bludgeoned, and bitten to death. Finally, like the mother in 2 Maccabees, who sent her sons on before her, she departed "glad and rejoicing . . . as if called to a marriage supper." A report of those martyrdoms in Gaul (ca. 177) was sent to Christian congregations in Asia and Phrygia. Why? Why was the persecution in Lyons so ferocious? Why was the account sent eastward? The answers are linked.

Gallia Lugdunensis was one of several provinces into which Gaul was divided. Its mostly Celtic population welcomed Roman protection from invaders (ca. 58–50 B.C.E.). Apart from rare revolts, the people adapted to Roman rule and adjusted Roman ways to their traditions. In the late 40s B.C.E., the Romans established Lugdunum, a town named after the Celtic deity Lud, at the juncture of the Rhone and Saone rivers. In 40 B.C.E. Octarian's future son-in-law became the chief Roman official, and during the reign of Caesar Augustus, it became the administrative capital of all the Gauls.[3] Highways originating in Lyons, as Lugdunum is now called, linked the other Gauls to the capital and connected Lyons to centers such as Marseilles, Geneva, Trier, and Limoges. After Octavian was designated Augustus by the Senate, Agrippa erected an altar where representatives of the Gallic tribes assembled annually in Lyons, elected a high priest, and sacrificed to Lud, Rome, and Augustus. By the second century, Lyons and nearby Vienne were flourishing commercial centers. In the 170s German invaders crossed the northern borders, prompting Marcus Aurelius to call for sacrifices, unity, and a ban on secret societies. Persecution in Lyons was fueled in part by the traditional piety and anxiety over the German invasion.

It also was sharpened by concerns that account for the transmittal eastward of a report of the martyrdoms. Roman authorities settled foreigners, including Asians and Phrygians, in Gaul. In addition, Lyons and Vienne attracted merchants and craftspersons from the east who brought their cults with them. Usually tensions and curiosity between indigenous people and newcomers are bearable when times are good and communities secure. In the decade when Gaul was attacked, security crumbled and the economy faltered. Foreigners who rejected Gallic and Roman gods, defied the emperor's decrees, and made converts were regarded as enemies. Soon allegations spread about Christian incest and cannibalism. For society's sake, persistent offenders had to be eliminated. The report, then, went eastward because many of the victims had relatives and friends in Phrygia and Asia. Furthermore, Gallic and Eastern churches were embroiled in schisms and heresies; the report was slanted to oppose the New Prophecy and to promote unity under the church's authorities.[4] Blandina countered Priscilla, and the martyrdom of Bishop Pothinus of Lyons duplicated that of Polycarp of Smyrna. Inside and outside of the church, Christians struggled with the Empire and with each other. In the course of that struggle, Irenaeus proposed a way to salvation that involved the church's structures.

IRENAEUS THE PERSON

Irenaeus admitted that he was not eloquent, but he considered his presentations of Christianity to be persuasive and free of distortions. He reflected that as a boy he knew Polycarp and memorized his sayings; he recalled his mannerisms nearly a half century later. Yet Irenaeus omitted that Ignatius had chided Polycarp and even wrote him a letter of admonition. Since Polycarp was over eighty years old when martyred (ca. 155), it is likely that Irenaeus was born around 140. The evidence indicates that Irenaeus was born in Asia to a Christian family or one that converted while he was young, had little training in pagan rhetoric, and considered Polycarp and the presbyters of Smyrna to be his teachers of ethics and theology.[5] At some point—perhaps when he was already a presbyter—he went or was sent to Lyons, perhaps to minister to expatriate Asian Christians. Sometime later Pothinus and the congregation dispatched him to Rome to advise Bishop Eleutherus about Montanism.[6] While he was in Rome, Blandina and Pothinus and nearly fifty other Christians were martyred in Lyons and Vienne. The rage of the Gallic pagans had abated by the time Irenaeus returned, and he was elected bishop.

He took over a community ravaged by persecution and torn by internal strife. Asian believers emerged from the persecution weakened, Gallic converts may have claimed leadership positions, and believers generally were open to negative views of the Creator and humanity. Like any new chief executive officer, Irenaeus needed to establish his authority. Marcionite and Valentinian teachers had schools in Gaul and supporters in the congregations of Lyons and Vienne. Perhaps gnostic sympathizers among the presbyters were undermining Irenaeus's position because they considered the pedantic bishop unworthy to exercise authority over them. Finally, some Christians engaged in sexual activities that prompted pagan charges of incest. Obviously, the church was in a crisis. Irenaeus tried to control the situation, but his success was by no means assured.[7] The bishop responded in several treatises, two of which have survived. Rhetorically, the extant works try to persuade by means of demonstration rather than forensic argument, deliberative debate, or dialectical reasoning. The author designed *Against Heresies* to enable bishops and presbyters to refute heretics and to expound with confidence "the things of God" to those who wanted to learn the truth; his *Proof of the Apostolic Preaching* bolstered orthodoxy with biblical citations.[8] He insisted that the church had a rule of faith that summed up the tradition of Christian belief throughout the world which believers had to follow without deviation.[9] Shaped by Asian teachers, Irenaeus put before Westerners the shining path to fulfillment. Where his own journey led him is uncertain; the Gallic church claimed that he and nearly fifty others were martyred around 202.[10]

Usually a tedious writer, Irenaeus became creative when he wrote about "recapitulation." The term had four rhetorical senses. The most common was a summary in which the speaker united various points under one head or chapter. It could also mean the restoration of a position or situation to its original condition, a new start, or the development of an argument to its climax or high point. The word did not appear in the Septuagint and was rare in first-century Christian writings. Once Paul wrote that the precept to love one's neighbor as oneself recapitulated the Mosaic commandments that dealt with human relations (Lev. 19:18, quoted at Rom. 13:6), and Eph. 1:10

described God's plan to recapitulate all heavenly and earthly things in Christ. Irenaeus, relying on a reference in one of Justin's lost works, used these passages, interpreted others under the motif of recapitulation to oppose the Creator's critics, and offered a positive interpretation of God's truth.[11] He employed recapitulation as summation, restoration, new start, and climax to keep the church and its members on the road to salvation.[12]

IRENAEUS ON THE CREATOR AND CREATION

Doubts about the Creator and the creation dogged Irenaeus and his supporters. Ordinary members of the church questioned the goodness and supremacy of the world's maker. Marcionite and gnostic teachers thus had a ready-made audience, and they forced the bishop to defend his rule's key premise that the church always and everywhere believed "in one God, the Father Almighty, Maker of heaven, and earth, and the sea, and all things that are in them."[13] His arguments, taken from Justin and shared with Tertullian, were accompanied by a hierarchical cosmology. According to Irenaeus, the cosmos was a series of spheres within spheres. At the hub was this world, and above the whole of the cosmos in transcendent glory dwelled the Supreme God and Creator of all.[14] Each of the seven heavenly spheres surrounding the earth was the domain of various celestial beings, and each had designated spiritual gifts which followed the pattern in Isa. 11:2-5. From the sphere closest to God to that nearest the earth, the heavens were wisdom, understanding, counsel, fortitude, knowledge, godliness, and the fear of the Lord. All angels were included and assigned proper duties. Irenaeus left no room for a Pleroma, *Sophia*, or Demiurge. The cosmos, created good and structured to be an instrument of the perfect God's will, was destined to be recapitulated at least in the senses of being brought to a climax and given a new start. Parts of Irenaeus's version of the end of the world have been lost, but his extant comments and his reliance on Revelation permit some reconstruction. The bishop went back to the beginning. God, through the Logos, created the world in six days. The end of the present world would reflect its beginning, and since Scripture holds that a day with God is like a thousand human years, Irenaeus concluded that the present creation would die after six thousand years.[15] Although he did not clearly say so, he probably considered the seventh day of rest in Gen. 1 to be fulfilled in Revelation's millennium, that is, the thousand-year reign of Christ and the saints after the binding of evil forces and the death of all living things.[16] The first world was only a prelude of what was to come. Instead of detailing the spheres of the new cosmos, Irenaeus mentioned a new earth, a celestial paradise, new heavens—and a terrible place of eternal punishment for those who turned away from God.

His seven-orbed cosmos and the recapitulation of the creation of the world answered those who taught that the present order was the flawed product and domain of an ignorant and cruel Demiurge. He insisted that such teachings derived neither from Scripture nor from those who learned from Jesus but from pagan philosophy. The bishop insisted that his version was the same which Jesus' disciples and successors had passed on in the church and which all true Christians affirmed. The likelihood that Peter, John, and their associates heard this cosmology from Jesus is slim. It is more probable that Irenaeus reflected an Asian Christian cosmological tradition based on the *Timaeus* but cast in terms of Genesis and Revelation. The present world, then, was created to be a good, harmonious hierarchy glorifying its Creator for six thousand years, after which it would be recapitulated in a fulfilled order that will stand forever.

IRENAEUS ON HUMAN NATURE AND DESTINY

Irenaeus's anthropology followed from his cosmology. He blended the Genesis account of the creation of humans in the divine image and likeness with the account of a primal couple in paradise. Although he countered Marcion's contentions that a harsh sub-deity made the world and owned humanity, he was more concerned to overthrow Valentinian anthropologies. He rejected attempts to put humans under angelic control, categorize humans as flesh or soul or spirit, and allow any teachings not held by the bishops. When Irenaeus's substantive statements on human nature and destiny are freed from distracting polemics, four positive points emerge.

First, the cosmic setting in which humans live. Since God alone created and arranged the cosmos, everything was connected to God's purposes for the world and its creatures. The entire seven-sphered arrangement had one goal: the salvation of human beings.[17] For Irenaeus, salvation engaged the cosmos and history in a divinely planned movement toward the wholeness of humans who obeyed their Creator. From the highest angels to the least particle, the world and history aimed at fulfilling God's will for human destiny. As good as the cosmos was, it was infantile, that is, immature. It might reflect God's will and even instruct its inhabitants through the moral law that God built into it, but it needed care and guidance in order to be a fruitful and fit setting for humanity.[18] Angels were to convey God's guidance and advice on the way to fulfillment. Naturally, they were expected to obey God.

The second point dealt specifically with human nature. From one perspective, Irenaeus's rejection of the Valentinian split of humans into spirit and soul and flesh also corrected Christians who exalted the soul at the expense of the body. He held that every person was a unity of body, soul, and spirit; each part needed the others to constitute a whole human. The soul was like the artist's mind, which conceives of an action, but the mind or soul needs the body to enact its intention, while the spirit is that aspect in humans which responds to God's promptings to move persons to perfection. Soul, flesh, and spirit were capable of incorruptibility—immortal and changeless completeness—as well as corruption and mortality. In terms of the creation account, the first Adam's body came from the virgin earth, his soul from God's will, and his spirit from God's own Spirit-Wisdom. Humans, like creation, were not yet complete; they needed guidance and discipline as they traveled toward their goals.[19] From another perspective, Irenaeus related human nature to God's Logos and Spirit. Relying on the Fourth Gospel, Christian interpretations of Scripture, and Middle Platonism and Stoicism, he agreed that the Logos was God's agent who made humanity and even called the Logos humanity's father. In the same context, he held that humanity was made in the image and likeness of the Logos. He held that the Logos was concerned particularly with body and soul, while God's Spirit worked with the human spirit. Irenaeus's insistence on the unity of body, soul, and spirit and his distinction between God's Spirit and Logos help explain two movements in his theology. One moved from the top downwards: God sent the Logos to make the world and humans, and when that work was finished the Logos sent the Spirit to guide all things to their fulfillment. The other movement proceeded from the bottom upwards: God's Spirit motivated humans to seek their fulfillment as the image and likeness of the Logos. The Logos disciplined the sluggish body and soul, while God's Spirit engaged the human spirit.

His treatment of human nature led to the third point, human destiny. God, according to Irenaeus, willed humans to be the masters of the cosmos. This purpose seems not to have been disclosed to the angels, yet they were to guide humans to reach the goal for which they were created. Adam, like the rest of the world, was immature when placed in the garden. He and Eve, who was drawn from his substance, enjoyed twilight conversations with the Logos in Eden. As long as the couple exercised their free will in obedience to God, they advanced toward salvation and consummation. Their destiny can be summarized as living forever, developing fully into the image and likeness of Logos, and seeing God. A human being—that unity of body, soul, and spirit—was destined for immortality through obedience to the Spirit's promptings and the discipline of the Logos. Such a person would become accustomed to the divine presence, grow in the ability to see the Logos, and by means of the Logos increasingly know the invisible God. In the process of becoming mature, the person would achieve harmony with and be nourished by angels placed by God in the world to help humans be images and likenesses of Logos.

Irenaeus expected God to re-create a new earthly and heavenly order after the death of the old cosmos. In the new world, people would live in different yet connected realms. Which realm they lived in would be determined by the capacity of each to know and enjoy God. The obedient righteous would live on earth, rejoicing in the splendors of the new Jerusalem; those of greater ability and obedience would dwell in a luxurious celestial Eden; and the most capable would enter heavenly mansions closer yet to God. Everyone would see as much of the Logos as he or she could bear, and in that glorious vision all would know God to the height of their understanding. Humans, then, were to ascend to and surpass all angelic ranks.[20]

Obviously, God's highway to salvation was subject to detours. The fourth point of Irenaeus's anthropology was humanity's need to be engaged in re-capitulation. Progress to cosmic and human fulfillment depended on human obedience to God. Satan, God's archangel-administrator of the earth, resented humanity's future authority. He turned from God and life toward disorder and death. Satan realized that Eve was stronger than Adam, so he entered a serpent to deceive her. At first she resisted, but she was overcome because she thought the serpent was guiding her and Adam to perfection. Adam, on the other hand, fell without a murmur. In fact, his fall was worse because he himself had heard God forbid eating from the tree while Eve heard a less authoritative version of the prohibition from Adam.[21] The result was catastrophic. God expelled Adam and Eve from the garden, cursed the serpent, and hardened the once fertile earth. Cast out of from Eden, Satan lurks now beside the path to life, eager to bite humans with the lethal poison of immorality and heresy. Somberly, Irenaeus described humanity's descent from innocence to degradation, from life with God to death with Satan, and from freedom to bondage, all because of disobedience to divine authority.[22] God might have allowed the primal couple to die in misery and shame, but for God to abandon the creatures for whom the world was made would give Satan the victory. God's care for women and men led to the incarnation of the Logos and the salvific recapitulation of human history.

IRENAEUS ON IDENTITIES FOR JESUS

Some elements of Irenaeus's Christology are as expected, a few unusual, and all tied to history. As expected, he described the Logos as involved in the world's creation, revealing God's will to Old Testament figures, and becoming incarnate in Jesus. These positions became more significant when Irenaeus made clear that the Logos was fully God, signaling thereby that the highest degree of divine intervention had to be used to save humanity. While his surviving works do not detail his understanding of God, he wrote that when Christians say that God is uncreated, transcendent, and invisible, they call God the Maker, Father, and Lord of all. When they describe God as knowledge, maker of humans in the image and likeness of God, recapitulator of all things, presenter of humanity to the Father, and the one who became incarnate in Jesus, they call God Logos, Son of God, father of humanity, and Lord. With less clarity, Irenaeus wrote that when God is considered as Wisdom and Power, bestower of divine gifts and the Law, inspirer of prophets, guardian of truth in the church, and head and sanctifier of humanity, God is called Spirit. Irenaeus suggested that the Logos and the Spirit were God's two hands at work in the world.[23]

His commitment to a fully God incarnational theology was carefully balanced. The problem with the human situation was not due to the Creator or the matter that composed human beings but free will. Salvation, then, lay not with an alien God or pleromatic beings or divine seeds planted in a handful of souls. The fully God Christology maintained the holiness of God and the dignity of human nature yet recognized the reality of evil and death. If the human will after Adam and Eve's disobedience was still intact, so that humans could do God's will, there was little need for God the Logos to become a human and no need for Jesus to die or Christians to be martyred. If, however, human free will was totally ruined by the original disobedience, persons would be unable to respond to God's saving action; God would force grace on some and leave others to be damned. The solution: men and women could be returned to the upward path of salvation not by nature or compulsion but by a renewal of their will. Irenaeus folded ideas about human nature and will into a theology that expressed God's plan to recapitulate humanity through the incarnate Logos. Perhaps Irenaeus turned to history because he perceived time and change to be weaknesses in the gnostic cosmologies. He also realized that the Old Testament set creation and Israel within history and that some biblical authors described God as working in and through human events to fulfill Israel's and the world's destiny. In the same vein, Christian documents that he considered authoritative claimed that God had a plan to save humanity and re-create the cosmos through the Logos. Irenaeus combined terms such as "covenant" and "plan," speculation about periods or dispensations in which God employed particular tactics, and views about cosmic and human growth to maturity with his version of Paul's idea about a new Adam and Revelation's vision of a new creation. All these came together in his identifying Jesus as the incarnate Logos and the new Adam.

One step entailed understanding God's plan for history being revealed through a series of four covenantal dispensations that stretched from the first humans' expulsion form Eden to Jesus. According to Irenaeus, God engaged in this unfolding program in order to accustom humankind to the divine presence in their affairs so as to educate them to willingly obey God on the road to fulfillment. The first dispensation opened in Eden and stretched to the days of Noah. Adam and Eve became parents under the shadow of their disobedience to God and their bondage to sin. Cain, the murderer of the brother whose sacrifices were acceptable to God, became the first killer and prototype of those who would persecute Christians. Compared to other authors, Irenaeus minimized the fall of the Watchers.[24]

The second dispensation was opened with God's covenant with Noah and closed with the covenant made with Abraham and his children. Irenaeus depicted two of Noah's sons (Shem and Japheth) as blessed and one (Ham) as cursed by God. The bishop of Lyons identified Shem as the forerunner of the Jews, Japheth of Gentiles who obeyed the Logos, and Ham of the ungodly and heretical. Abraham, unsuccessful in his attempts to find God by himself, was found by the Logos. The Logos revealed God's promises, and the old patriarch believed them with justifying faith.

The Logos began the third dispensation with Moses, coming still closer to humankind and revealing more specifically the Creator's will. From Moses through the history of Israel until the birth of Jesus, the Logos spoke through leaders and prophets who were obedient to God, making the divine presence ever more part of human events. Finally, in the fourth dispensation, that presence took incarnate form as the Logos became flesh in Jesus.[25] The gifts of the Spirit, mentioned in Isaiah 11 and made increasingly available to obedient humans in the course of history, were bestowed upon Jesus' loyal apostles. In turn, these apostles guided the church and spread God's truth throughout the world.

The fourth dispensation began with the incarnation and will culminate in the splendors of the recapitulated world. Irenaeus speculated that six thousand years would elapse from the beginning of creation's history until the end of this world. Each dispensation-age rolled into another until the great day when an everlasting age opened. In that age, all those who obeyed God in previous centuries would be united, restored, and fulfilled through seeing the Logos and knowing God.

Irenaeus did not rest with a theological rendition of history. He discussed humanity's recapitulation through the Logos-Christ as the new Adam. Irenaeus set up a rough rather than a neat pattern between Adam and the incarnate Logos. The bishop's purpose was to describe the way in which the damage done by human disobedience was undone or repaired through human obedience rendered by Jesus.[26] In the process, Irenaeus sought to refute various heretical groups, especially the Valentinians. His pattern had four parts.

One dealt with Christ the recapitulator who restored the cosmos and humankind in their movement toward God's intended goal of maturity and fulfillment. Irenaeus focused on the opening chapters of Genesis and the Spirit who hovered over the face of the waters and the making of humans in the image and likeness of God. The Logos used clay from the virgin earth to shape Adam, and the Spirit (from Genesis 1) breathed life into the first human. Similarly, when the Logos became incarnate, God used a virgin who was overshadowed by the Spirit. The new Adam's father was God, not an ignorant demiurge, and was not in bondage to Satan but filled with the gifts of the Spirit. According to Irenaeus, when the new Adam walked on the earth, the soil hardened by the expulsion of the first couple from Eden began to be renewed because now God's presence was once more among women and men. Irenaeus continued that God's intention for Adam to rule the cosmos was being fulfilled through the new Adam, the one who would be revealed on the day of judgment to be the true ruler of heaven and earth.

An important and necessary part of Irenaeus's pattern was the uneven symmetry between Eve and Mary. Mary was the new, recapitulated Eve. She canceled the first virgin's disobedience. Mary's trust in God and obedience to the divine invitation announced by an angel untied the knot of human bondage tied by Eve when she was deceived by the evil angel. Possibly to offset gnostic docetic Christologies and perhaps to deflect claims by some Christians that womanhood was disgraced by Eve, Irenaeus insisted that the Logos took real flesh from Mary and that Mary was Eve's advocate. Later generations would elaborate on these suggestions about Mary's role in human salvation.[27]

Another part of Irenaus's view was the incarnate Logos's role in summarizing all humanity under one head. Because all persons were created in the image and likeness of the Logos, the incarnation of the Logos gave every person alive in the present the opportunity to unite with Christians now under the headship of Christ. Moreover, the Logos descended into the place of the dead after the crucifixion to proclaim liberty to Satan's captives, summoning Gentiles and Jews who lived at any time and in any place to join with the living on the road to salvation.

The third part led Irenaeus to make some curious claims about how the Logos recapitulated the whole human life cycle. To restart and sanctify humanity, according to the apostolic tradition Irenaeus said he had learned, the Logos participated in every stage from infancy to old age. As a baby, child, and young man, Christ was obedient to the transcendent Father and the Spirit rested upon him. But what of old age? On the basis of John 8:57, where Jesus' critics comment that he was not yet fifty years old, Irenaeus reasoned that Jesus was in his late forties.[28] The bishop then "remembered" the apostolic tradition that Jesus' ministry was at least ten years in length, hence Jesus became elderly and recapitulated old age.

A fourth part in the pattern of the Logos as recapitulator of humankind featured the ultimate goal of the incarnation: humanity's liberation from Satan and escape from eternal punishment for sin. While the liberation motif is present in the other parts, Irenaeus developed it more fully when discoursing on the Logos as the divine champion against the fallen powers that sought to detour humanity from God's way to salvation and onto Satan's road to condemnation. Evil forces have always attempted to thwart God through attacking humans, and now the assault was aimed at the incarnate Logos. Jesus was tested by the original rebel against God throughout his earthly career, but Jesus defeated Satan through obedience to God. Although the struggle climaxed in Jesus' death, resurrection, descent into Hades, and ascent into the heavens, the devil has turned his attention to Christ's people. Through persecutors and heretics, the evil one carries on his war against God, but God's victory was assured. Recapitulation had started already, and, in Christ, humans mounted the upward road to fulfillment by following their true image and likeness, the Logos. The path over which they had to travel involved following the ways of the church and its leaders.

IRENAEUS ON THE CHURCH'S ROLES

The church in the Mediterranean basin suffered from external political pressures and internal tensions. Irenaeus grew up in the church and dedicated his life to its integrity and order. In Lyons and elsewhere bishops were under attack. He cited twenty-one heresies by name, lumping their followers together with unbelievers, schismatics, and hypocrites, but realized that they and their allies were in the church. His Valentinian foes debated representatives of schools that he supported, and Valentinian sympathizers within the congregation peppered him with questions and criticisms through which they attracted interested listeners. The opposition accused the bishop of being a stubborn, vulgar psychic who refused to search for God's truth with them. His attempts to refute them in the presence of average believers failed, and he told believers to turn to the rule of faith, for "It is better and more profitable to belong to the simple and unlettered class, and by means of love to attain nearness to God than by imagining ourselves learned and skillful, to be found [among the] blasphemers," for knowledge puffs up while love builds up. In effect, average members should not worry about the questions but leave the answers to God.[29] Presbyters critical of Irenaeus gathered adherents for unauthorized worship and the study of Valentinian commentaries and treatises. His attempts to overthrow the heresies and demonstrate the truth of his version of Christianity aimed at steadying the wavering and encouraging the convinced believers through an ecclesiology based on obedience expressed in cosmic, historical, and geographical order.[30]

The cosmos, arranged in concentric spheres corresponding to the seven gifts of the Spirit, centered on the earth and was aimed to guide humans to salvation. Freely rendered obedience was required to achieve that goal, and such obedience was possible because God had built the Law into the world's structures. The sphere and gift of the Spirit closest to the earth, fear of the Lord, entailed obeying God as the starting point on the upward journey to fulfillment. The Spirit's gifts were symbolized in Aaron's seven-branched candelabra, which was placed in Israel's tabernacle.[31] Irenaeus saw the church as the temple of God and the place where the reality prefigured by the candelabra was fulfilled. In other words, the church was a preliminary recapitulation of the obedient cosmos. The church, properly ordered to forestall a premature rush to the higher spheres of *gnōsis* and wisdom, united the scattered elements of creation and restored the original obedience required of the cosmos by beginning anew the process of salvation. It was the place where the high point of life-fulfilling wholeness was experienced before the end of the age— as long as it was obedient to and ordered by God through the Spirit and the Logos. Persons who claimed to prophesy in the Spirit, interpret in the Spirit, worship through the Spirit, and act for the Spirit did so when they obeyed the Spirit-led bishops who traced their authenticity to the apostles empowered by the Spirit at Pentecost. After all, "where the church is, there is the Spirit, and where the Spirit and church are, there is truth and grace."[32] Yet with so many groups competing with one another, how might anyone know which community is legitimate?

History, as interpreted by Irenaeus, identified the true church with the communities headed by bishops like himself who honored the one God revealed as Creator, Logos, and Spirit. He based his position on the principle that God's truth was received, preserved, and transmitted by persons who were obedient to God and inspired by the Spirit. The process began when the Logos and the Spirit authored the truth and employed Moses and the prophets to write it in the Scriptures. God spoke through Israel's holy books (i.e., the books translated in the Septuagint), although the voices were those of humans. The message was that the Logos, who was in intimate communion with the Creator and humankind, was God's ruling power in creation, saved those who believe in him, and would be incarnate in Jesus. Israel's Scriptures were properly interpreted as predictions of coming of the Logos as a human to recapitulate humanity. The three covenantal dispensations of world and Israelite history preceding the incarnation prepared for the appearance of the Logos in the flesh. Biblical passages, then, were allegories and types that pointed toward and were fulfilled in the birth and life of Christ. Teachers and leaders interpreted the sacred books and guided members in accordance with the single message in those writings; that is, Irenaeus and bishops and presbyters like him obeyed God and led communities to life-fulfilling obedience.

After the incarnation, Christ the Logos interpreted the Scriptures about himself, taught how to live in the present age, pointed toward life in the future age, recapitulated humanity, gathered and instructed those who would preserve and transmit God's truth anew, and established the church as the new Eden on earth. While Christ may have given some private lessons to the twelve, he did not impart any esoteric *gnōsis*; the apostles and those who heard the lessons made them public either through writing or speaking—as happened with John's comments reported by Polycarp and preserved by Irenaeus. But which writings and traditions were valid? For example, there were Gospels of Philip, Thomas, and Truth as well as Matthew, Mark, Luke, and John. Which versions of even widely accepted Gospels were to be used? Marcion had an "expurgated" rendering of Luke. And how were writings such as Paul's Letter to the Romans to be interpreted?

Irenaeus was the first to specify that there were only four orthodox Gospels, and he cited traditions about their authorship and animal symbols associated with them. While his settling on four had more to do with mystical meanings than careful analysis, he was convinced that two were written by eyewitness apostles (Matthew and John) and two by "ear-witness" elders, that is, by persons who listened to those who heard and saw Jesus or the original apostles. He had a chain of listener-reporters that extended from Jesus to the Twelve and others who heard and saw Jesus, to a second generation (e.g., Polycarp), to a third generation (e.g., himself), and to whatever generations might follow. The task of each generation was to receive and transmit God's truth in obedience to the command of the Logos (Matt. 28:16-20). Jesus' immediate followers obeyed their Lord by making disciples and establishing congregations in many nations. They entered a mission field, made converts, appointed leaders to carry on the work, and then moved to new fields. Their teaching included the interpretation of Israel's Scripture, knowledge of the structure and destiny of the cosmos, the plan for human fulfillment, the dynamics of recapitulation, and warnings about the devil. The Logos entrusted the treasure of truth to the apostles, who deposited it in the church as a rich man would put money in a bank, making God's salvation available to everyone who was willing to be disciplined by the church and the apostles' successors.[33] Irenaeus's handling of the apostolic deposit of truth became central to his struggle with heretics, his ecclesiology, and his lasting influence.

First, truth had originated with God and was transmitted over time until the Logos deposited it in the church through the apostles. The teaching of the church, then, was the most ancient, genuine, and divine way to salvation available to humans. All other methods and versions of knowing God were recent and partial at best, novel and demonic at worst. So heresy deviated from truth and was disobedience to God. Conversely, truth belonged to the church and was available only through obedience to the apostles' successors, that is, the church's leaders. Indeed, the Spirit nourished true presbyters who stood with their bishops to proclaim the one God who created the world, was incarnate in Christ, and roused humanity to fulfillment.[34]

Second, legitimate teachings and practices were present in congregations connected to an apostle. The actual physical presence of an apostle was not necessarily required: Irenaeus suggested that Lyons had an apostolic pedigree through Smyrna, Ephesus, and Rome.[35] He also contributed to a tradition that still shapes Western Christianity: the primacy of the bishop of Rome. He insisted that Peter and Paul had established the congregation in Rome. Peter was the chief of the original disciples and became the leading apostle to proclaim the Christian message to the Jews. Paul, the leading apostle to the Gentiles, had visionary-revelatory encounters with the risen Logos and even went to the third heaven, Paradise (2 Cor. 12:1-4). Certainly, the reasoning ran, Rome must have the full amount of the apostolic deposit. Anyone who doubted a bishop's interpretation ought submit the question to the nearest apostolically connected congregation and its bishop. In the West, according to Irenaeus, that meant Rome and its bishop. Irenaeus jabbed that no heretical or schismatic group ever counted an apostle among its founders, and he derided the notion that the apostles had failed to understand Jesus. A confusing and perhaps emended passage seems to say that Irenaeus held that every congregation had to agree with the teachings of the congregation at Rome (*Against Heresies* 3.2). In any event, Irenaeus argued for an apostolic succession of truth in congregations through their bishops and presbyters. Knowledge of God's ways came not through inner illumination or esoteric doctrines restricted to initiates but through church tradition passed on under the Spirit's guidance to the church's public leaders. It followed, then, that obedience to the bishops was essential for salvation. Furthermore, why should disputes be referred to relatively minor apostolic congregations if Rome had Peter and Paul?

The historical dimension of the church led Irenaeus to consider the Jews. His comments seem detached and lead me to think that either he knew few Jews or that the Jews he knew were not criticizing Christianity. Given his understanding of Israel's Scriptures, he took injunctions about circumcision, diet, and Sabbath as types which were fulfilled in the incarnation of the Logos and recapitulation of humanity. He wrote that Jews in Jesus' time and later were stuck in the old law because they wanted what Irenaeus thought impossible: a relationship with God without obedience to the Logos. God's covenantal relationship with Israel was only a temporary means God used to complete the plan of salvation for all humankind; it was not the exclusive property of one people. Since the Jews refused to make the transition to the fourth and new covenant, Christians and the church replaced Israel and the synagogue as the people and place which had divine truth. Even the special relationship to God's Law, Irenaeus continued, was not exclusive. The Logos and the Spirit had implanted the Ten Commandments in the hearts of all persons; everyone could and must obey the Decalogue in order to complete the journey to wholeness. The other rules and regulations imposed on the Jews were given not because the Jews were a holy people but because they were disobedient.[36]

Irenaeus's ecclesiology had one more component: geography and the universality of the church's truth. Convinced by Scripture, his own experience, and his knowledge and revisions of Polycarp, Justin, and other Christian heroes, he held that the church's teachings were spread in many nations and languages but were one in content.[37] Everywhere and always, genuine Christians confessed the same faith in God as Creator, Logos, and Spirit; the goodness of the created world; the nature and destiny of humankind; the identity of Jesus as the enfleshed Logos; and the church as the community in which the Spirit's gifts were at work among individuals and their congregations. True Christian unity was inseparable from a bundle of obediences: to God, to the saving doctrines of the Logos to the Spirit's guidance, and to the discipline and teaching authorized by bishops. Irenaeus never tired of comparing the unity of Christian congregations with the seeming fragmentation among heretics and schismatics. He unmasked one heretical disagreement after another in order to contrast their "many" to orthodoxy's "one." Diversity within Valentinian schools, he observed gleefully, proved they were false and perverse heretics. The Logos and the Spirit permeated the world at creation and were omnipresent before the Logos became incarnate. Heretics, however, took their rise from Simon, the Samaritan magician who had tried to buy the Spirit's gifts. Heretics were like their father. mean-spirited, localized, and fraudulent. The true church was known by its geographical universality, unity, cohesion, and obedience to God.

Irenaeus understood the church to be part of God's cosmic, historical, and geographical plan to recapitulate humanity and the world. The universe's concentric spheres and heavenly patterns, the history of dispensations and deposits of truth, and the extension of one faith throughout the world focused attention on the church as the illuminated, sure road to salvation. To keep to that road, travelers had to obey the bishops and presbyters who were the successors and guardians of the deposit of truth given by God through the incarnate Logos.

IRENAEUS ON CHRISTIANS AND SOCIETY

The bishop said little about Christians and the wider society. Perhaps it was impolitic for the leader of the recently bloodied sect to critique the worship of Lud and Augustus or to formulate forensic arguments about just treatment in the courts. His highest and persistent priority was to establish his own authority in a dissension-riven congregation, and he realized that his situation in Gaul was symptomatic of a churchwide wave of social and spiritual dissatisfaction with authority and organization. Possibly his expectation of the end time, the rise of an antichrist in the church, and the recapitulation of all things in Christ made him take a patient and even positive view of pagan society. To be sure, he went through the motions of blaming philosophy for providing the seeds for heresy, but his criticisms of Greco-Roman culture were few and halfhearted. He quoted pagan authors rarely, but he once commented that Plato was a better Christian than the heretics—a pale echo of Justin.[38]

It seems odd that he expended such energy bolstering his authority against heretics only to leave members to fend for themselves as they related to pagan neighbors, officials, and institutions. I think that he was too faithful a bishop and too tenacious a Christian to risk leaving congregants to flounder in ethical dilemmas that would have made them prey for other forms of Satan's venom. His apparent blandness about society and government was perhaps motivated by his desire to rebuild the congregation and position it for missionary outreach. The economic calamities of the 170s and the persecution of 177 fell hardest on the Asian members of the congregations in Vienne and Lyons. If Christians were to flourish, they had to attract the indigenous people of Gaul. The ways in which Irenaeus wrote about the Creator, Logos, and Spirit may have provided a bridge to believers in the three-formed god, Lud. Gallican pagans and Gallican Christians shared some perceptions that the Christians would be eager to explain in terms of the Logos. Comments similar to those of Justin or Tertullian on Greco-Roman philosophy, literature, and traditions certainly would have alienated sophisticated pagans in the cities. Since Gaul furnished some of Rome's finest soldiers and needed Roman protection, Christian denunciations of the emperor and the Empire would scarcely attract sympathetic listeners, let alone converts. The heretics, on the other hand, may have appealed mostly to Asian residents and those of a more intellectual bent. The founders of the schools rejected by Irenaeus were associated with Asia, Pontus, and Egypt, not Aquitaine or Narbonne. Two factors culled from his writings may indicate his attempt to reconcile church and society and to gain new members.

First, Irenaeus commented positively on human nature in general and emphasized that the Logos had planted the moral law in all persons. Themes from popular Stoicism, criticism of any Jewish claims to special election, and denial of gnostic determinism appealed to persons who were anxious about their social and spiritual situation. Openness to Gentiles in the covenants with Noah and Abraham prepared biblical precedents for the inclusion of pagans in the divine promises of salvation. He hinted that persons who were not yet believers as well as uncultured Christians have "salvation written in their hearts by the Spirit, without paper and ink," when they believe in God as the Creator.[39] The "unwritten Scripture" was activated by the Spirit through the church's witness to the truth deposited in it by the incarnate Logos. And the theology of recapitulation, presented in a missionary context, promised to be a powerful message that would call persons to turn their wills and ways to the road of salvation. All life—and culture—could contribute to recapitulating human existence.

Second, pagans may have been attracted by Irenaeus's attitude toward the Empire. The man who may have instructed Blandina and who succeeded Pothinus praised Rome. He wrote that through the Romans "the world is at peace, and we walk on the highways without fear, and sail where we will."[40] His references to Rom. 13, a passage that informed Christians that all governing authority was from God and exhorted them to obey rulers, occasioned a mini-sermon on the omnipresence of the Logos, God's love for all persons, and the salvation of Gentiles. Denying that the "governing authorities" were angels, as the Valentinians claimed, Irenaeus stated that human rulers were God's ministers whom Christians were to obey. Rulers who were unjust would be judged by God.[41] Irenaeus clearly distanced himself and the church from those who claimed to be Christians but who demonized the state. Moreover, he opened the doors of the church to Gentiles, including government officials. The man whose name means "peace-ful" was making gestures of peace and welcome to the church's recent enemies. Ironically, Irenaeus may have been tortured and killed by the very persons he invited to join him on the safe highway to salvation.

The metaphors of journey, road, and pilgrimage not only express Irenaeus's responses to the challenges Christians faced but also describe his life. The Asian who went westward contributed substantially to the elevation of Rome as the center for ecclesiastical authority in the West and to later tensions between Eastern and Western Christianity. The presbyter who read Justin's clear statements about the Logos being an angel developed a "fully God" Christology. Running through his writings are struggles between order and freedom, diversity and unity, hostility and reconciliation. The bishop's vision of recapitulation addressed human needs, but the undercurrent of obedience was unmistakable. Obedience, the antidote to the serpent's poison, may have been a means Irenaeus used to maintain order among Christians in Lyons; it certainly became such for later ecclesiastical authorities. According to Irenaeus, the cosmos, history, and humanity were traveling to fulfillment under God's guidance. Whether or not Irenaeus joined Blandina, Pothinus, Polycarp, Justin, and Ignatius in the way of martyrdom, he undertook his journey confident that it was the way of the Logos to truth and life.

This, beloved, is the preaching of the truth, and this is the manner of our salvation, and this is the way of life, announced by the prophets and ratified by Christ and handed over by the apostles and handed down by the church in the whole world to her children. This must be kept in all security, with good will, and by being well-pleasing to God through good works and sound moral character.

Proof 98

15

Assessments

Make a real effort, then, to stand firmly by the orders of the Lord and the apostles, so that "whatever you do, you may succeed" in body and soul, in faith and love, in Son, Father, and Spirit, from first to last, along with your most distinguished bishop, your presbytery (that neatly plaited spiritual wreath!), and your godly deacons. Defer to the bishop and to one another as Jesus Christ did to the Father in the days of his flesh, and as the apostles did to Christ, to the Father, and to the Spirit. In that way we shall achieve complete unity.

Ignatius *Magnesians* 13:1-2

It was a messy, confrontational century. Social and political trends and structures in the Empire set the stage for religious and philosophical groups to organize, express tenets, and gain adherents. They jostled one another, disputing with rivals inside and outside their own camps over the truth of their respective positions. Different schools and communities struggled with fundamental questions about the world, human nature, divine presence, the community's roles, and its relationships with the broader society. How questions were asked and the assumptions of those who answered varied from group to group and from place to place. Searches for unity and truth put pagans, Jews, and Christians on courses that led to convergences and collisions between and within communities. Whether longing for the coming of God's kingdom or the return of the Golden Age, women and men wanted to hear good news about their present lives and their futures. Messages about Jesus were heard with mounting uneasiness by those attempting to retain the traditions of their pagan and Jewish ancestors, while increasing numbers throughout the Empire responded to the promises and demands, the hopes, and even the criticisms offered by Christian communities. Christians, seeking common ground in doctrine and communal organization, had to fashion some cohesive teachings, practices, and structures if their movement was to fulfill the mission to which they believed God had called them. They also had to work out patterns for living in a world that had no intention of passing away while preparing themselves for a parousia that did not come. Put positively, Christians began to develop their own *paideia* to maintain their identity and still be part of the societies in which they lived.

Our examination of five challenges and the responses of five leaders indicates the depth of the issues for Christians and the breadth of reactions to those issues. Clearly, there was no single resolution to any of the challenges, and no one person dominated the church's attempts to make sense of its teachings and practices. Still, emerging trends and directions can be discerned—and so can countercurrents.

This chapter is more than a concluding review of what we have examined; it puts the leaders into conversation with one another on the challenges the church faced. It brings the leaders together and asks, "What would they say to one another if they met at the turn of their century?"

The persistence of the issues points to the opportunity for people in later times to reexamine the challenges and the responses in new settings. The opportunity to reexamine the earlier reactions engages us with those who had the courage and ability to express themselves, along with their responses.

We are desirous of an eternal and good life; we strive for the abode of God, the Father and Creator of all; we make haste to profess our faith; we believe with firm conviction that they can attain these things who have shown God by their works that they follow him and love to make their home with him where there is no sin to cause disorder. In brief, this is what we look for and what we have learned from Christ and in turn teach others.

Justin Martyr *First Apology* 8

It is time then for us to affirm that only the God-fearing man is rich and of sound mind and well-born, and therefore the image, together with the likeness of God; and to say and believe that when he has been made by Christ Jesus "just and holy with understanding," he also becomes in the same degree already like to God.

Clement of Alexandria *Protreptikos* 12[1]

Although their faith was of recent origin, Christians had traditions derived from Judaism and perspectives about Jesus that they considered essential to daily life and salvation. Stating those traditions and perspectives to outsiders was daunting, but they were pressed even harder to find common ground among themselves and to develop structures through which they could worship God, explore God's will more fully, and prepare themselves for life in the kingdom. While the second century was a time for unhinging old assumptions and expectations, it was also a time for Christians to focus and expand their religious experiences and hopes. If new combinations were taking shape, then convergences as well as collisions could be expected. Where did the leaders concur and clash among themselves and with their fellow believers?

ON THE CREATOR AND THE CREATION

"God" and "good" are the answers the five gave to the questions about the identity of the Creator and the nature of the creation. On no other issue were they more united than in declaring that the Supreme Deity originated the cosmos, wills it to be good, and plans for its fulfillment. Their commitment to "God and good" rejected any contrary answers. The persistence of those alternatives indicates that many persons turned to messages that offered fellowship with life-enhancing divine powers and escape from this world. The Christian gospel proclaimed release from the present and hope for the future, but did that release entail repudiation of the creation and its Maker? Questions about the Creator and the cosmos exposed a fundamental collision between Christians that resulted in wary convergences in understanding God, the world, human nature, and society. In spite of differing cosmologies, each of the five respondents included two factors when maintaining that God was the Creator and creation was good.

First, they turned to the Scriptures as the ultimate authority for stating what the church considered to be the truth. They insisted that Israel's holy books, now translated into Greek, were inspired and transmitted by the Supreme God. All other literary or human claimants to divine truth were of lesser authority, and their validity was determined by their agreement with the Scriptures. In affirming the Septuagint, the leaders went to the creation accounts in Genesis and, when it suited their purposes, to relevant passages in the Psalms, Proverbs, Wisdom, and other Septuagintal works. Reliance on the Septuagint raised the issues of hermeneutical method and Christian relations to Judaism. No matter how far several of them took allegorical and typological interpretations, each held that Genesis stated that the Supreme God was directly responsible for making and giving a goal to the cosmos. The existence of the cosmos was due neither to an accident nor ill will. Use of Israel's Scripture also raised the issue of Christianity's relationship to Judaism. Here all five performed similar hermeneutical and historical gymnastics to prove to themselves and their audiences that God gave Jesus' followers the right ways to interpret the oracles of God, that those writings testified to the fulfillment of God's plan for creation through Jesus, and that the Scripture belonged to God's *ekklēsia*, the church. They added that the inspired writings included some Christian works that confirmed Christian teachings that had been fulfilled in Jesus or would be consummated at his parousia.

Second, "God and good" made the leaders face the question, How can the Supreme God be responsible for this often miserable world? Their position on the Creator, creation, and the Bible set them against those who denied that the Supreme God created the cosmos and that the cosmos was good. Given the time and effort the writers expended in countering those teachings and movements, it is clear that persons such as Marcion and Valentinus had ready audiences within the Christian community. On the basis of his analysis of the world and the human condition, Marcion split the creator from the redeemer, renounced the visible world, rejected Israel's Scriptures, and denounced the Jews. To prove his points, the merchant-scholar engaged in careful hermeneutical work that embarrassed opponents because of his attention to the problematic meanings of passages and flustered them by his use of a core of Christian documents. Numerous gnostic groups also denied the answers "God and good" on grounds different from but with results similar to Marcion's. They usually claimed that the world was due to a flaw in the heavenly Pleroma, and the creator was a jealous ignoramus. Such Gnostics retained Israel and Israel's Scriptures but subjected both to interpretations disclosed by a redeemer-revealer to an initiated elite. Together with Marcionites, Gnostics generally disparaged the physical world, dismissed the idea of a divinely approved moral law in nature, and taught the necessity of escape from the wretchedness of the present. The five writers' responses included four principles: order, reason, Logos, and authority.

Their initial principle, order, emphasized that the world was designed to be a cosmos, not a chaos. Harmony, hierarchy, and balance were signs of the goodness and purposefulness that the Creator structured into the creation. Instead of a jumble ("the many"), God's plan provided an undergirding oneness for all that existed. The Maker's glory, power, and will were evidenced in the hills and the heavens as well as in the connections between living things. Disorder, then, was not due to God or, if attributed to the Creator, it was punishment for those who broke with God-ordained order. While Scripture was cited as the divinely inspired written evidence for God's ordering of creation, the five—including Tertullian—also relied on a Stoicized Platonic atmosphere that presupposed a divine presence, harmony, and purposefulness throughout existence.

Another principle, reason or logos, more readily discerned in that philosophical atmosphere than in the Bible, underscored system rather than anarchy, plan rather than caprice, virtue rather than vice. In a syncretism of

Middle Stoic and Platonic themes with biblical interpretations reflected in Jewish authors such as Philo, logos was described as having a divine origin and as permeating existence. Nature, law, reason, and divinity were wrapped together in logos, so that reason filled the whole cosmos, connecting divine spheres to the physical realm. All parts of and persons in the cosmos, then, were linked to one another not only by the fact of their existence but by the inner presence and drive of God's logos. God's will and wisdom were both present and knowable in the structures of nature and the events of history. Although transcendent and unapproachable in essence, the One was not an alien, and the cosmos was neither an abortion nor a prison. Evil was perverse ignorance of and rebellion against the divine logos. The five leaders used logos to appeal for justice from the government, criticize and affirm aspects of pagan society, use or reject elements from Greco-Roman *paideia*, make ethical exhortations to Christians, and invite those outside the church to come inside.

The next principle took logos one step further: God made the cosmos through the Logos, that is, through a divine creative agent. In employing a Logos-oriented view of creation the leaders distanced the transcendent God from the acts of speaking into the darkness and shaping Adam. All angels and earthly beings were subject to the Logos since the Word was considered to be either the first of all creatures or a manifestation of the One. By making the Logos the active creator of the cosmos, these Christians put their Logos in the place of Plato's Demiurge, Stoicism's logos, Philo's Logos, and Judaism's Wisdom. And, obviously, they would weave the Logos into their anthropologies and Christologies.

Authority, the fourth principle, grew in importance during the century. The authority of Scripture and the authority of the church were inseparable. Greco-Roman criticisms to the effect that Christianity was a new and barbaric religion certainly moved church leaders to claim that through the Bible they had a more ancient and cultured tradition than any other people or philosophy. The five respondents concurred in speaking of the Logos in ways that enveloped all human goodness and truth, no matter how people and demons might damage that truth. Through Scripture, interpreted by means of the Logos and the Spirit in the church, Christians attempted to understand the Creator's revelations in the cosmos and history. Marcionite critiques pushed persons such as the five leaders toward allegorical and typological views of the Old Testament, while Gnostics thrust the leaders and the church back toward more text-centered interpretations. The *ekklēsia* countered by asserting that it was God's chosen community in which truth abided, and that its leaders determined which works were sacred and what they meant. Each of the five, in his own way, contributed to the expulsion from the Christian fellowship of those who rejected the Creator and the creation. In the process, each also promoted increased authority for the church's officers or for teachers who eventually were drawn into the orbit of those officers.

Yet did they answer the criticisms and rejections of "God and good?" They offered and discussed the issues of creation at length. In the course of their writings they presented insights and themes that later Christians developed, e.g., the goodness and harmony of the world, the makeup and use of the Bible, relationships with Judaism, and the authority of the church. They attempted to demonstrate from Scripture, culture, and experience that the Creator is the transcendent yet loving God who designed the cosmos to be orderly, rational, and shaped by Logos. Instead of blaming God or matter for evil and disorder, they shifted the challenge from God to creatures.

ON HUMAN NATURE AND DESTINY

One set of inquiries raises others. Questions about the Creator and creation lead to human nature and destiny. Because the quintet agreed so readily on the Creator's identity and the world's original goodness, we expect and find significant convergences on the anthropological challenge. Their differences sometimes are compatible variations on similar themes, but at critical junctures one or more authors contradicted the others, setting up conflicts that still endure. Both convergences and conflicts cluster around the questions, What has happened, is happening, and will happen to humans?

What has happened to women and men involves what has happened to God's good, orderly creation. The cluster of responses starts from two positions derived from the answers "God and good." First, humans have been created by the will and action of the same God who made the world. No person, then, is by nature formed from evil or illusory matter or for wicked purposes. Moreover, people are not simply units of mobile matter; everyone is a composite of physical substance and a "divine dimension." The divine dimension may be called by various authors (and even the same author) soul, spirit, mind, reason, image and likeness of God, or logos. The point is that humans are distinct from both animals and angels, yet they are joined in some God-designed way to the physical world and to the celestial realm, even to God. Second, the first humans were gifted with free will and with the promise of immortal life in fellowship with God. Their descendants have at least some residue of that free will, so they are able to respond to or reject heavenly promptings to turn toward God, keep or break the moral law that the Creator structured into the cosmos, and seek or pervert the divine truth that leads to life eternal. Each of the leaders relied on the high view of human nature, free will, and destiny in Genesis 1–2.

   The most striking difference among them was the manner in which Clement and Irenaeus, on the one hand, and Tertullian and probably Justin, on the other, understood the maturity of the world and of Adam and Eve.[2] From their quite different intellectual perspectives, Irenaeus and Clement developed the claim that the couple was immature or childlike. By giving some leeway to the advancement of human nature, both theologians permitted flexibility in dealing with human responsibility, ethical integrity, and attitudes toward the surrounding culture. Tertullian and, I think, Justin regarded Adam and Eve as mature and immediately accountable for their actions; and both believed that their descendants shared in the results of what the primal parents did. The North African and the Samaritan took a hard line against the wider society when it opposed Christian teachings and the church, and were even harsher when dealing with those whom they considered heretics, but were more open to potential converts from paganism and Judaism. Justin and Tertullian quickly consigned those who remained outside the church to eternal punishment. Clement's Logos Christology can be likened to the others, particularly to Justin, and his anthropology opposes Valentinian determinism in regard to human will; but he indicates that a few human beings are of divine origin because the Logos made them the "elect of the elect." Possibly a reflection more of Philo than of Valentinus, Clement's gradations of human beings are determined by God, not by each person's disciplined free will and intellect.[3] Yet his handling of the origins of human nature sounds suspiciously like a revised Valentinism.
   But what happened to God's orderly cosmos and marvelous humans? Genesis provided the basis for the anthropological agreements and contrasts. Our writers emphasized the fall of the angels (Gen. 6) and events in the garden (Gen. 2–3). While all five used Genesis 6, they did so in different ways and to different degrees. Ignatius did not have either the need or the opportunity to amplify his version, but he held that spiritual disobedience and rebellion resulted in disorders from which came all evil, corruption, sin, and idolatry in the cosmos plus schism and heresy in the church. Humans might still have free will to join or resist the forces of perversion, but people and the world needed God to intervene to set the world back into order again. Justin and Tertullian concurred heartily, made significant use of *Enoch* and Revelation, and blamed much of humankind's misery on jealous and deceitful angels. Justin condemned them for pagan religion, corruptions of philosophy, and societal immortality, adding that the demons inspired arch-heretics such as Simon and Marcion. Tertullian used Justin and attacked women as well. Of course, Jews were counted among those who gave themselves to the ways of the evil ones. In his explanation of the plight of humanity and the world, Tertullian stressed Adam and Eve more than Ignatius and Justin did. The charges against humanity—especially females—mounted. Tertullian's view

that corruption stems from Adam through his children echoes Pauline themes but also sounds the despair of 2 Esdras, while Justin's view of human free will resembles that of *2 Baruch*. Justin and Tertullian built on themes from intertestamental demonology, but both maintained that evil was a matter of will—angelic will compounded by human duplicity.

Clement and Irenaeus were more restrained in explaining the misery of the cosmos by any angelic lapse. Clement avoided the emphasis on angelic corruption for at least two reasons. First, he faced Christians in Alexandria who were eager to use such an account to reject pagan culture, especially philosophy. Because he considered philosophy to be useful for Christian purposes, he insisted that it could be rehabilitated to assist the Logos in educating humans to salvation and deeper understanding of God's truth. Second, he perceived that such an account could lead to a denial of free will and play into the hands of the Valentinian Gnostics. While he used Revelation and knew of Justin's works, Irenaeus was cautious in handling the fall of the angels. Irenaeus and Clement agreed that humans were immature and needed education and discipline to develop into angelic images and likenesses of the Logos. It would have been theologically distracting and even contradictory for them to concentrate on Genesis 6. They were concerned chiefly about moving from the present disheveled, unfulfilled condition of the world and humans to the destiny God planned for the cosmos. Neither Irenaeus's vision of recapitulation nor Clement's version of the journey of the Logos to create the cosmos allows much room for the world to be as permeated by evil powers as Tertullian described.

(?) The second cluster of issues—what is happening to humans now?—involves the leaders' convergences and clashes on creation and human nature. After agreeing that the incarnation of the Logos in Jesus was the decisive step in offering humans the opportunity to be restored to God's saving order, the authors part company. Ignatius held that God's actions in Jesus to restore and fulfill the cosmic order led to a new structure in the world—the church—and a new type of humanity—Christians. If God broke the divine silence to address the chaotic, demonically destabilized world, then women and men were re-created by the Logos. The catholic church, the community of those who were faithful to God through being obediently united with the bishops, replaced the original Eden. The present, then, was the time of struggle in which the powers of darkness and disorder were fighting a losing battle against God's mighty enfleshed Logos. Humans were caught in the conflict. Christians, Ignatius admonished, needed to guard against Satan's subversive tactics to corrupt the church through schism and heresy, that is, divisions among and rebellions against the church's officials. Weakened by sin and prone to disorder, humans nevertheless were responsible for standing with or against God and for expressing their loyalty through their unity with bishops, elders, and deacons.

Justin's themes of struggle, demonic presence, and human responsibility moved in two directions. One deepened concern over the powers of evil. Expressed in terms of the demonic angels, these evil powers dominated pagan culture, inspired imperial persecutions, hardened Jews, spurred heretics and schismatics, and attempted to trick faithful believers. His arguments, however, emphasized the role of the Scriptures and made people responsible for their own beliefs and actions without reference to apostolic or church authorities. The other direction began with the Logos as God's agent in creation. Reason as the spermatic word and the Logos as divine Wisdom led Justin to affirm human beings as God's creatures, who could be persuaded by reasoned experience to understand and adhere to God's truth. Rhetoric and dialectic plus the example of the martyrs prepared nonbelievers for enlightenment about God's ways. *Paideia* was possible because humans were educable, persuadable, and reasonable.

Justin's development of logos ideas appears to have had some influence on Tertullian, but the Carthaginian took more than a full measure from Justin's demonology, the intertestamental literature, and even Marcion's negative view of life after Eden and the giants. Tertullian's version of the present human condition stressed the pervasiveness of evil in the world and the power of sin and guilt in the soul, in culture, and even in the church. Discipline, vigilance, asceticism, and loyalty, all under the Spirit's revelatory direction, marked his response to the confusion and dangers of the present age. Military, athletic, and legal images give Tertullian's perspective a harsh, adversarial cast. Demons stalk those who are loyal to God, seeking to entrap them through the lures of sexuality, adornment, idolatry, literature, and philosophy. Nothing—not even Bible study or the office of the bishop of Rome—is so sacred that the devil cannot attempt to corrupt it. Believers, then, must be on guard not only against obvious foes but even against one another and their own impulses. As the world worsens in the days before Jesus returns in judgment, Christians are to prepare for battle, especially for martyrdom.

Irenaeus had a more ambiguous approach to the present situation of humanity. When he felt that the church was menaced by heretics and schismatics, he sounded the alarm against the devil and resorted to Revelation. Yet his theology moved toward a developmental understanding of God's action as moving humans to maturity through history. The incarnation of God in Jesus was so not much the signal that the wrath of the divine Judge would be unleashed on treasonous angels and humans as it was the central act in the drama of the recapitulation of all things in the human-divine Lord. Irenaeus did not minimize the effect of Adam and Eve's ignorant disobedience, and he

insisted on the endurance of the damaged human will's freedom and responsibility, but he presented the human plight without falling into the military
and legal language of his Latin North African counterpart. Irenaeus envisioned
women and men as making progress in God's plan for fulfillment through the
church and adherence to right teaching. He steered away from the logic of
Gen. 6, favoring instead the symmetry of recapitulation of humanity in a new
Adam and the obedience of the new Eve.

At first hearing, Clement and Irenaeus appear to agree about the present
state of human affairs. Both consider men and women to be in the image and
likeness of Logos, educable, and progressing to maturity. They resist Valentinian and Marcionite determinism and insist on the reality of human free
will. Gen. 1 and 2 rather than Gen. 6 shape their cosmologies and anthropologies, and each uses typology and allegory. Clement's agreement with
Irenaeus, however, is more apparent than real. The differences between Clement and Irenaeus may be due to the works that survived both authors. Clement's
extant writings are far more detailed than the bishop's on human nature and
the Logos's ways to improving the soul. Clement's insistence on the roles of
gnōsis and *paideia*, however, mark him as distinctly different from the rest.
The Alexandrian's theology made the ascent through beginner, progressor,
and *sophos* into esoteric knowledge essential to human development in the
image and likeness of the Logos. According to Clement, secret *gnōsis* had to
be part of the present educational program, but the others would reject such
gnōsis as a dangerous, unwarranted, and wrong-headed concession to the
heretics. Clement was willing to take the risk, convinced that the Logos would
provide the right guidance now and in the future. Certainly Clement and
Tertullian would have scant areas of agreement, especially on matters related
to the demonic, philosophy, and culture. Clement's *paideia*-based understanding of God and humanity and his advice that prudent Christians could legit-
imately avoid persecution would infuriate Tertullian. Indeed, the latter's heated
references to a Christianity blotched by philosophy might indicate that he had
heard about Alexandrian teachers such as Clement.

And human destiny? Our five writers hold that humans are destined to
become angelic beings. Justin and Tertullian did not develop the theme as
fully as other points, but Irenaeus and certainly Clement devoted time and
space to the deification or apotheosis of humans. Justin, Tertullian, and
Irenaeus reflected the traditional Jewish and Christian teachings about a decisive day of judgment on which Jesus would return in glory and on which
the dead would be physically resurrected. They also depicted a literal place
of punishment for evil angels and people. Irenaeus's cosmology had angel-
humans ruling the re-created world and other celestial creatures while enjoying
the closest possible fellowship with God through the Logos. As far as Clement

was concerned, there would be no physical day of judgment, return of Jesus, or hell. He conceived of the future as a series of classrooms or individualized tutorials through which the soul advanced to its proper mansion in the heavens. As the soul, already in the image of the Logos, advanced, it was increasingly formed into the Logos's likeness. The ascent into divinity was actually the completion of the soul's creation, and on the journey the soul was admitted to greater and greater *gnōsis*.

Each writer emphasized that human beings were deeply engaged in the calamities that had befallen God's good cosmos. The disorder and evil that stalked the creation were due to angels who then gained the support of humans. For Ignatius, it appeared that humans may be somewhat hapless creatures who were both victimized and enslaved by the forces of evil. Justin, Tertullian, and, to a lesser extent, Irenaeus developed the demonic theme while they retained the culpability of persons. Justin allowed for the work of the Logos to plant reason in the creation, yet he used that action to indict rulers and heretics for following the promptings of the evil powers. Tertullian's stress on the demonic motif led him to demand disciplined allegiance by Christians in light of the coming judgment of God on the cosmos. Irenaeus leaned toward Tertullian while he opposed heretics and schismatics in defending the church and its apostolic deposit of faith, yet his theology moved him to a cosmic perspective on the dignity of humanity as future angels. Clement's cosmology and theology avoided the physical and historical while he affirmed human free will, divine initiative, the soul's ascent to heavenly mansions, and esoteric traditions, all in the consummation of human destiny to be in the image and likeness of the Logos. But who was the Logos, the divine figure each claimed to be at the heart of God's action?

ON IDENTITIES FOR JESUS

As expected, the five can converse readily about the Logos as God's agent through whom the cosmos was created and as the one who, in some manner, appeared in human form in Jesus. Although debate continues about Ignatius's knowledge of the Fourth Gospel, the Christology of each leader depends on that Gospel's Logos theology. In addition, each has been influenced to some degree by the Septuagintal wisdom literature and by Middle Platonic-Stoic views of logos. Further, while Justin admits that some Christians are adoptionists, neither he nor the others considers that christological option acceptable. General agreement, however, ceases after those points.

A critical difference surfaces in their understandings of Jesus' relationship to the Supreme God. Probably Ignatius, and certainly Justin, held that Jesus (the Logos) was the supreme angel, the highest in the divine rank called gods, a manifestation of the Most High. This was probably Clement's usual position as well. It is equally clear that Tertullian and Irenaeus taught that the Logos was a manifestation of the Supreme God. Those who held the "fully God" Christology insisted that the highest level of divine intervention was needed in order to restore to humans the gift of immortality that was lost through sin. While Ignatius and Justin took sin seriously as bondage to evil powers, they considered the Logos to be a powerful enough agent to break the devil's grip on humanity through Jesus' death and resurrection. Clement, true to his reliance on *paideia*, tends to avoid slave imagery in his descriptions of the human situation. Since the Logos is the paradigm for humanity's origin and destiny and is in the image and likeness of the Supreme Deity, Clement's exoteric instructions move toward an angel Christology, but his esoteric teachings may link the Logos to the Most High. Tertullian faced several teachers who also claimed that Jesus was fully divine but collapsed the Father into the Son, and then merged the Son into the Spirit.[4] His presentation of God as simultaneously Father, Son, and Spirit would have been totally alien to Justin, Ignatius, and Clement. Irenaeus claimed that Jesus was fully divine primarily because he was convinced that only the God who gave the first humans immortality could restore immortality to their children.

A second difference is their treatment of Jesus' physical humanness. Ignatius set the tone for insisting that Jesus had a genuine humanity from his conception forward. His reasoning was clear: if Jesus was not human, then he neither died nor was resurrected; therefore the devil was not defeated and humans were not yet saved. Ignatius's incarnational theology rejected any semblance of docetism, even at the price of avoiding scriptural (probably Septuagintal) passages that appeared to contradict a divine incarnation. The same logic, nuanced for the details of their anthropologies, led Irenaeus and Tertullian to demand that believers hold that Jesus had a genuine human body that was subject to birth and death. While Justin probably held to the incarnation of the highest-ranking angel, he did not give priority to the flesh-and-blood qualities of Jesus. The Samaritan was more interested in defending the faith and convincing doubters. Once more, Clement presented a different view: the physicality of Jesus was embarrassing. Clement attempted to have the Logos transcend the grittiness of human limitations by understanding Logos as the true man, that is, the one who is in the image and likeness of God and after whom women and men are patterned. This approach also allowed Clement to be patient with the foibles of humans in their current state; they will move onward and away from their physical entanglements.

Agreements and differences among the five continue into their ideas about the effects of Jesus on the human situation. Because they relied on the Septuagint, the writers could draw from a common stock of typological and allegorical models when they discussed Jesus' identities and actions. The works that became the New Testament and other materials also furnished them with basic images for Jesus and for what the faithful believed he did for humanity and the cosmos. Themes and pictures such as the new Adam, Noah, Moses, and David; Logos, Wisdom, and Mind; shepherd, king, and priest; and light, song, and law weave through their writings. The second-century authors, following the lead of earlier Christians and Jews, cited a wealth of terms, titles, and precedents to express their conviction that somehow God acted in a unique and decisive way through Jesus to restore humanity to its God-designed place in a reordered cosmos. Jesus is the enlightener, teacher, Savior, ransom, Servant, Christ, hope, and master of mysteries, as well as general, judge, and renewer. The scriptural and first-century reservoir of images, metaphors, and examples enabled the leaders to share titles for and ideas about Jesus, yet there were underlying tensions between them. I think those divergences are due to differences in their understandings of human nature and destiny as well as the personalities and situations they faced.

For Ignatius, Jesus was "our God" and Savior, the divine Logos who started the restoration of God's order in the cosmos. Champion over evil, Jesus broke the power of idolatrous magic and demonic influences. As head of the church, Jesus set the tone and led the chorus in the hymn that all creation sang to God. In times of trial and disunity, Jesus modeled patience, faithfulness, and true discipleship for the church's leaders and average members, even to the point of martyrdom. Ignatius's pictures of Jesus were used and adapted by Irenaeus. Irenaeus's Syrian-Asian origins and adherence to traditions that included Ignatius and Polycarp were reflected in his attacks on heretics and schismatics and in his theology of recapitulation. Irenaeus's understanding of the harmonies of history, human nature, and destiny, and the source of all life in the Supreme God, were essential to his insistence that Jesus was fully God.

Justin's insistence that Jesus was the supreme angel and savior was a powerful argument in the contexts he faced: adoptionist Christians, critical Jews, hostile pagans, and critics of the Creator. The prospect that Jesus might be one with the Most High did not occur to him or Christians he knew. His self-understanding as a biblically grounded philosopher-interpreter led him to envision the cosmos as headed by a transcendent God who related to the world through a hierarchy of angelic beings headed by Jesus. Justin was driven to depict Jesus as the divine messenger who fulfilled scriptural roles such as the Servant, the new Moses whose new law who would guide men and women safely through this life and beyond to the impending day of judgment, and the Logos through whom all was made and toward whom all life was directed.

Clement was simultaneously vaguer and more explicit than most of the others. He retained Philo's ambiguity about the relationship between the Logos and the Supreme God, and he was somewhat clearer about the intimate connection between the Logos and humans through the image and likeness of God. He was clearest when describing the Logos as the exhorter, instructor, and teacher of humanity; the *paideia*-stimulated growth of humans to angelhood; and salvation as the consummation of creation. Christians paid a price for Clement's education-to-salvation Christology: a docetic view of Jesus and of human nature. Unlike those who disparaged the physical and earthly, Clement did not consider the world evil or human nature corrupt. He elevated the dignity of humans so that they could be raised to divine rank and be united with their heavenly image and likeness.

Of the five, Tertullian especially demanded that full attention be given to Jesus' pain, shame, and suffering. Jesus was the price paid for human sin and rebellion. God's judgment and wrath, human sin and shame, demonic cunning and perversion were all wrapped up in the crucifixion and resurrection of Jesus, the work of the Spirit, and Tertullian's demands for understanding the three-in-one dimension of God. Tertullian would not relieve Jesus' pain or human guilt by giving priority to some sort of divine plan for salvation, or cosmic unity, or burst of friendliness toward people on God's part. Jesus was primarily the victim and the leader, the incarnate God who demanded loyalty of those who sought to follow the Lord. If anything, Tertullian was clear and certain about Jesus the athlete, general, Logos, and Supreme Divinity—together with the paradox of affirming Jesus' heroic humanity.

The initial convergences regarding Jesus, while based in biblical and early Christian traditions, foreshadowed collisions about Jesus that still occur among Christians. Adoptionism was not an issue; docetism was. Those who argued that Jesus was the highest and most powerful angel directed their energies against groups and individuals who made Jesus a lower type of celestial being and who argued that he and his followers were frauds. The partisans of the angel Christology had yet to face the determined opposition of those who claimed that Jesus was fully divine. There was no argument among the five that Jesus called persons to follow after and learn from him, and there was no argument that to follow Jesus entailed becoming part of the Christian community, the church.

ON ROLES FOR THE CHURCH

The leaders agreed that the church was essential in God's plan for the salvation of humans and the cosmos. Once again the biblical material provided a wealth of ideas, images, and precedents. The church could be identified as anything from a local community of believers to a cosmic assembly that united celestial and human beings in praising and serving God. Contributions from works such as the *Testament of the Twelve Patriarchs* as well as themes developed from Septuagintal writings made it possible for the five to consider worship, Temple, and church as heavenly models that were duplicated and then fulfilled on earth.

There were two important considerations regarding time. All five persons wanted to show that the Christian *ekklēsia* was in continuity with the Old Testament *ekklēsia*, and therefore the community that followed Jesus was the faithful remnant whose history stretched back through the prophets, Moses, and the patriarchs to the Logos-Creator. The historical dimension gave the church and its teachings standing in the presence of the ancient traditions of Greece and Israel, or so thought Justin and other Christians. The other consideration regarding time was emphasized particularly by Irenaeus and Tertullian: the church guarded and interpreted the truth and the traditions entrusted to it by Christ through the apostles. Whether apostolic succession was construed in terms of officials in a lineal descent from the apostles or as the approved interpretation of the tradition stored in the church by Jesus and his earliest followers, time was used to validate authority and authority figures. These two considerations regarding time were especially useful in combating heterodox movements; could those marginal and rejected movements demonstrate their positions from Scripture, tradition, and the apostles?

The dimension of space was developed especially by Ignatius, Irenaeus, and Clement with contributions from Tertullian and Justin. Again, there are two aspects. First, they said the church is a community extended horizontally throughout the world. Ignatius and Irenaeus, echoed by the others, regarded the *ekklēsia* as catholic, that is, possessing a universally accepted and recognized set of teachings or rule of faith. Their statements about content of the rule varied and even clashed, but they emphasized that Christians in different cultural settings were in harmony with one another, and that such harmony pointed to the truth of their teachings. The church, then, stretched not only backwards and forwards in time but sideways in present societies. No place on earth would remain untouched by the Logos and the people of the Logos, and no true Christian congregation could be isolated from the others. The congregations could expect to share mutual support, fellowship, and accountability in Christ and the Spirit. What happened in Lyons was communicated to Smyrna, and events in Rome concerned believers in Alexandria and Carthage. A prisoner traveling from Antioch would be aided by and feel able to exhort Christian communities on his way to Jesus. In spite of differences and outright contradictions between them, the leaders and the congregations regarded themselves as partners in salvation and service. Violations of that partnership were frequent and unsettling: heretics and schismatics were condemned, and Tertullian branded the bishop of Rome a violator the church's holiness.

Perhaps several of our writers, certainly Clement and Irenaeus, emphasized the second aspect: the church's vertical extension, its heavenly reality. Clement's allegorical approach to biblical passages encouraged him to fix on passages that clearly described a celestial temple, worship pattern, and divine plan. Ephesians and other Christian writings spurred him to identify his Septuagintal findings with the Christian *ekklēsia* now revealed and consummated in Christ the Logos. Clement associated *ekklēsia*, Spirit, Wisdom, and school with one another in a loose configuration that probably became tighter in his esoteric teachings. If he did not spend the time Ignatius and Irenaeus did on church officials and authority or describe worship in the same detail that Justin did, Clement may be described as presenting the church as the divine university in the wider cosmos. In the university-*ekklēsia* were different classes, degree programs, faculties, and student bodies. Students and teachers moved forward ethically as they advanced spiritually into the higher regions of the cosmic campus. Obviously, Clement could be taken by some as being indifferent to offices such as bishops and presbyters, and he could be read as setting the stage for identifying the superior Gnostics with the clergy.

The celestial spatial aspect meant little to the other North African. Tertullian cut through Alexandrian speculation and Syrian-Asian organizational concerns. He insisted on a Spirit-driven moral authority among leaders and general believers, disciplined life-styles, and adherence to the rule of faith. He had no patience with poetic visions and only scorn for those who used church offices to excuse sins in others and themselves. In the new Jerusalem, according to Revelation, there would be no temple—and therefore no officials to rule those who were redeemed by and were loyal to Jesus. Tertullian and the other leaders cherished the church even though they agreed and disagreed about its dimensions. They also realized that the church and its members had to come to terms not only with its internal arrangements but also with the societies in which they lived—at least until the parousia.

ON CHRISTIANS AND SOCIETY

As the century's decades went by and Jesus did not return, Christians coped with and settled into the Empire's cultural and social patterns. The process was laden with risks and opportunities. Trypho needled Justin by observing that church members were indistinguishable from pagans, but Tertullian once boasted that Christians were everywhere, even in the military and government services. Yet Jesus' followers had odd relationships with the world. If we locate those relationships along a continuum from the positive to the negative, the views that this world was God's good creation, that humans had free will and could be educated toward salvation, and that the Logos was their enlightener and teacher would be grouped together toward the positive pole; while the views that this world was under Satan's evil influence, that humans were in bondage to sin, and that the Logos effected salvation by taking on the roles of victim and liberator would be toward the negative pole. In actual practice, however, Christians combined views of both sorts with some confusing or at least mixed results.

Clement was dedicated to the positive pole. His commitments to the Logos, free will, *paideia*, and the ultimate consummation of the human soul in the heavens led him to find the seeds and shadows of God's truth throughout society. To be sure, he found much to criticize, but on balance he affirmed the creative presence of the Logos in the world. He gave advice about—but did not condemn—marriage, wealth, cosmetics, jewelry, and parties. He was more than tolerant, however; his understanding of God's goodness led him to insist that God never made anything hateful—and that included the nucleus of philosophy, literature, and cultural expressions.

Tertullian stood at the other end. His faith in the Creator did not modify his conviction that the soul and society had been corrupted by demonic powers and human rebellion. The state, education, religion, art, and literature were infected with evil. Sexuality, adornment, women, and marriage were parts of a package that could lead to damnation. Emphasizing the biblical themes of the separateness of God's true people and the fewness of the faithful remnant, Tertullian took strength from the opposition he faced outside and inside the church. Building on Paul's declarations that believers should not be conformed to this world but transformed by God's power, he defied the government and social conventions. Drawing on the same apostle's pitting of worldly wisdom against God's wisdom, the North African attempted to limit philosophical influences among Christian teachers and congregations. Relying on a wealth of athletic and military images, he described the Christian life as a contest and war against the demons. Recalling Jesus' message of the kingdom and claiming to be inspired by the Spirit, Tertullian regarded the present social order as doomed and Christians as summoned to holiness in anticipation of the coming judgment.

While Ignatius did not directly address Christians' relationship to society, his eagerness to be with the heavenly Jesus and his sense of demonic disorder point toward a wary if not separatist attitude toward pagan society. If the church was the sign of the cosmic restoration of harmony in Jesus, the current social structures were freighted with dangerous evil influences. Justin and Irenaeus seem to ricochet between Clement and Tertullian. Justin's understanding of God as the Creator and of the role of the Logos in filling the world with logos incline him to hear God's truth in philosophers' mouths. But his belief that demons influenced ruling officials, mobs, and heretics pushed him toward Tertullian's position. Irenaeus might be expected to follow Justin's movement, and he does when he deals with heretics and schismatics, but his logic yields to tact when he discusses the blessings of government and Christian loyalty.

On balance, the five contributed to the affirmations, condemnations, and hesitations that Christian individuals and congregations experience as they live in society. On the one hand, the expectation that the kingdom is coming and Jesus will return makes all human structures temporary and provides Christians with resources to oppose evil and injustice. Jesus' followers remember Paul's advice, "Do not be conformed to this world, but be transformed by the renewing of your minds, so that you may discern what is the will of God—what is good and acceptable and perfect" (Rom. 12:2). On the other hand, Christians can hear these leaders say, in mixed ways, that God made a good world, created humans in the image and likeness of the Logos, and has joined and is still with them in the world through the Logos. Believers, then, are called to realize that they have a stake in society and in meeting the physical as well as spiritual needs of other persons. Jesus' followers also recall the passage in the Gospel of John that the evangelist may have attributed to Jesus: "Indeed, God did not send the Son into the world to condemn the world, but in order that the world might be saved through him" (John 3:17).

The challenges provoked convergences and collisions from the leaders who attempted to understand Christianity's message and standing in a time of change and risk. The Christian community needed coherence and unity as it dealt with internal tensions and external pressures. Did the five provide what the church needed? Probably not, if coherence and unity are reckoned as consistent clarity and unconditional compliance. If the contexts of the challenges and the circumstances of the leaders are factored in, then coherence and unity may include a diversity in content and expression. Did they meet the needs of the church? Yes and no. Often they were vigorous, and imaginative when the church needed those qualities. Sometimes they contributed to the confusion and tensions that still engage and divide Christians. And occasionally their positions supported belligerent and oppressive practices, attitudes, and structures in the church and the wider society. The challenges are always present, and they surface when old combinations are loosened and the community is under pressure to react. In those circumstances, the responses of the second-century leaders are available and even valuable.

> Let us . . . love the patience of God, the patience of Christ; let us repay to Him the patience which He has paid down for us! Let us offer to Him the patience of the spirit, the patience of the flesh, believing as we do in the resurrection of flesh and spirit.
>
> Tertullian *On Patience* 16

Abbreviations

ACW	Ancient Christian Writers. New York: Newman, 1946–.
ANF	Ante-Nicene Fathers, ed. A. Roberts and J. Donaldson. Buffalo: Christian Literature, 1885–96; repr. Grand Rapids: Eerdmans, 1951–56.
BAGD	W. Bauer, F. W. Gingrich, and F. W. Danker. *A Greek-English Lexicon of the New Testament and Other Early Christian Literature*. 2d ed. Chicago: Univ. of Chicago Press, 1979.
FOTC	The Fathers of the Church. Various publishers.
LCL	Loeb Classical Library. Cambridge: Harvard Univ Press; London: Heinemann, 1912–.
LSJ	H. G. Liddell and R. Scott. *A Greek-English Lexicon*. 9th ed., H. S. Jones and R. McKenzie. Oxford: Clarendon, 1940.
LXX	The Septuagint. Alfred Rahlfs, ed. *Septuaginta*. Editio minor. 2 vols. in 1. Stuttgart: Deutsche Bibelgesellschaft, 1935.
MT	The Masoretic Text of the Hebrew Scriptures. K. Elliger and W. Rudolph, eds. *Biblia Hebraica Stuttgartensia*. Stuttgart: Deutsche Bibelstiftung, 1966–67.
NPNF	Nicene and Post-Nicene Fathers, ed. P. Schaff et al. 2 series of 14 vols. each. New York: Christian Literature, 1887–94; repr. Grand Rapids: Eerdmans, 1952–56.
TDNT	G. Kittel and G. Friedrich, eds. *Theological Dictionary of the New Testament*. Translated by G. W. Bromily. 10 vols. Grand Rapids: Eerdmans, 1964–76.

Notes

Notes for Chapter I

1. Mic. 4:1-5, 6:6-8; Isa. 2:1-5; and Jer. 31:27-34.

2. Zech. 14:8-9.

3. The earliest indications of a special arrangement between Jewish and Roman authorities date from the Maccabean struggles against the Syrians (1 Macc. 8). Julius Caesar continued the policy because Jews assisted him in his campaigns in Egypt. Augustus followed suit and regarded the Jews with respect because they were ancient and well-established. See W. H. C. Frend, *Martyrdom and Persecution in the Early Church* (Oxford: Blackwells, 1965)

4. Note Acts 19:1-7, John 1:6-8, and the manner in which Jesus' baptism by John is handled (Mark 1:4-11; Matt. 3:13-17; Luke 3:1-22; John 1:19-34) for indications of tensions between the followers of the Baptizer and Jesus. The ancient and still existing community of Mandaeans claims that John was the Messiah.

5. For biblical references see especially Acts, Romans, 1 and 2 Corinthians, Galatians, Philippians, and Colossians. Note also the *Didache.*

6. See Galatians and Acts for public disputes. In Philippians, Paul reported that some Christians gloated over his imprisonment, and at 2 Cor. 11:26 he wrote that he was endangered because of "false brothers." *1 Clement* hinted that envy among Christians might have been involved in the deaths of Peter and Paul.

7. See 1, 2, 3 John; Rev. 1-3; 1 and 2 Thessalonians.

8. See LSJ, 9th ed., 1343, for references to the papyri and inscriptions.

9. 2 Pet. 3:8-13, alluding to Ps. 90:4.

10. 2 Pet. 3:14-15 and *Epistle to Diognetus* 7:1–10:4.

11. See, e.g., Mark 13 and parallels in Luke and Matthew, Acts 1:1-11, and James 5:1-18.

12. See, e.g., Jude, the epistles of John, Revelation, 1 Peter, Ephesians, James, Hebrews, 1 and 2 Timothy, Titus, and the four Gospels.

13. Originally, the Gospel probably ended at 20:31.

14. See esp. John 3 and 11.

Notes for Chapter 2

1. Rom. 5:1. See, e.g., Rom. 1–4.

2. See Krister Stendahl, *Paul Among Jews and Gentiles* (Philadelphia: Fortress, 1976), 1–31.

3. See, e.g., Acts 17–19.

4. Some writings that have a shorter history are considered to be Scripture, notably the Qur'an for Muslims and the Book of Mormon for the Latter-day Saints.

5. See the visions in Dan. 7–13 and Zechariah in which the seer-scribe writes what is seen and heard. Note that Enoch is the scribe of righteousness who wrote what he saw in the heavens and heard about the future (*1 Enoch*). Among passages in the New Testament, note 1 Cor. 10:1-13, in which the wilderness punishments are said to have been meant as warnings for first-century Christians.

6. See 2 Esd. 14:37-48. According to that popular story, any work not written in Hebrew and which had a historical setting after the time of Ezra was not considered sacred by Jews. Obviously that eliminated several of the extra books of the LXX and the New Testament.

7. See Mark 8:31—9:50 (and parallels); Luke 24:21-48.

8. John 14:15-31.

9. See Karlfried Froehlich, *Biblical Interpretation in the Early Church* (Philadelphia: Fortress, 1984), 30–36. Rabbi Hillel had seven rules; Rabbi Ishmael had thirteen.

10. James Kugel, "Early Interpretation: The Common Background of Late Forms of Biblical Exegesis," in James Kugel and Rowan Greer, *Early Biblical Interpretation* (Philadelphia: Westminster, 1986), 81.

11. See Mark 4:10-20 and parallels; Matt. 13:36-43; possibly John 15:1-11; Gal. 4:21-31.

12. E.g., Melchizedek in Heb. 7:1-17.

13. See esp. John 3 and 11.

14. An incident involving Christians and reported in the New Testament (Acts 19:23-40) reflects the political importance of the *ekklēsia*. The mob (*ochlos*) is in danger of being accused of sedition because it has usurped the place where the *dēmos* meets in assembly.

15. The Hebrew *qāhāl* stands behind almost all of the LXX renderings of *ekklēsia*. *Qāhāl*, however, could also be translated by other terms such as *synagōgē* (e.g., Lev. 16:17). On occasion, *ekklēsia* was the translation for *maqhēlâh* (e.g., Ps. 67:27 LXX = 68:27 MT); *'ēdâh* (e.g., Num. 20:8).

16. In Greek, *epimiktos polys*, Exod. 12:38. There may be a cross-reference to the term in 2 Esd. 23:1-3 LXX (Neh. 13:1-3).

17. Deut. 4:10-14.

18. Deut. 4.

19. See Deut. 9; 18; 31–32. When recalling Israel's sins with the golden calf and the rebellion at Kadesh-Barnea, Moses spoke of his own angry actions to discipline the community and then of his role as an intercessor with God to obtain forgiveness

for the *ekklēsia*. Moses also looked forward to the *ekklēsia*'s worship in the promised land. He gave instructions about the duties and means of support of Levites and priests, and he laid down stern orders about the treatment of idolatrous soothsayers, necromancers, and wizards. The old leader comforted the *ekklēsia* about his impending death with assurances that God would raise up a prophet like himself who would speak Yahweh's word truly. Dire warnings about false or lying prophets were attached to the promises. He told the community to exclude from the *ekklēsia* men with crushed testicles, bastards, and, with some exceptions, non-Israelites. In the same context, he set down rules of hygiene, economics, vows, and neighborliness.

20. See LXX 2 Chron. 28:1—30:27. What his father began, Solomon capped at the dedication of the Temple. The king and "all Israel with him, a very great *ekklēsia*" engaged in a seven-day feast after which the Lord made a new covenant with Israel and Solomon because of the Temple's holiness. After Solomon's death, the *ekklēsia* of Israel gathered to admonish Rehoboam to ease the burdens his father had imposed. Leaders, then, were not immune to the *ekklēsia*'s reactions to their policies. Generations later, Jehoshaphat summoned the *ekklēsia* to the Temple, proclaimed a fast, and led a lament to God over what appeared to be an imminent defeat for Judah. An inspired Levite proclaimed in the midst of the *ekklēsia*, and in words that were virtually identical to language in Deut. 4, that God would give Judah victory without any of the covenant people's blood being shed. After its miraculous victory, the joyful *ekklēsia* reassembled at the Temple, making glad sounds with harps, lyres, and trumpets. Once he became king, Hezekiah reopened the doors his father, Ahaz, had shut, summoned the Levites and priests to cleanse the holy place, and made a new covenant with God. The chroniclers emphasized the roles of the priests and described the Temple's rededication and a magnificent Passover at the Temple. Sacrifices were offered for the *ekklēsia*'s sins, and the *ekklēsia*, summoned by Hezekiah, stayed at the Temple. See 1 Chron. 13; 28; 29.

21. 2 Chron. 7. Nehemiah summoned an *ekklēsia* that included those who opposed him. Following a forceful address by the governor, the *ekklēsia* responded with a resounding "Amen" and set about doing his will. Apparently readers are to understand that Nehemiah presided over Ezra's reading of the Law in the presence of the *ekklēsia* at the water gate and at the restoration of the Levitical festival of Booths. When Jerusalem's rebuilt wall was dedicated, there were appropriate ceremonies, readings of the Law, and enforcement of a version of Moses' prohibitions of persons from the *ekklēsia*. In that act, the called-out people separated "from Israel all those of the mixed multitude" which had been present since the days of Egypt. The *ekklēsia* was now free of foreigners.

22. In the LXX numbering, these Psalms are 21; 25; 34; 39; 67; 88; 106; 149. In the Hebrew, they are 22; 26; 35; 40; 68; 89; 107; and 149.

23. That is, *prōtotokon* (LXX = 89:28 MT).

24. In the Hebrew, Ezra and Nehemiah are separate works. 1 Esdras (LXX) is an apocryphal work and is called 3 Esdras in the Latin translation (Vulgate). In the LXX, 2 Esd. 1–10 corresponds to the Hebrew Ezra, and 2 Esd. 11–23 corresponds to Nehemiah. A largely first-century c.e. Jewish work in which Christians made some interpolations is sometimes called 2 Esdras or 4 Esdras. The NRSV titles it 2 Esdras. In this book, I refer to the Nehemiah-based work as 2 Esd. (LXX) and the later writing as 2 Esd.

25. 2 Esd. 2:64. Apparently the author did not include the accompanying 7,300 servants, 200 singers, and livestock.

26. 2 Esd. 10.

27. Where the Hebrew text reads "tent of meeting" and "tabernacle," the LXX usually reads, respectively, "tent of testimony" (*skēnē tou martyriou*) and "tent" (*skēnē*).

28. 1 Chron. 28:19 LXX; cf. Exod. 25–28.

29. Wisd. of Sol. 9:8. The idea of a heavenly Jerusalem and Temple is also in the *Testaments of the Twelve Patriarchs* (*T. Levi* 5) and *2 Apoc. Bar.* 4. The latter mentioned that God showed Moses a likeness of the heavenly tabernacle when Moses was on Sinai to receive the Law. *2 Apocalypse of Baruch* is probably from the late first century C.E. and may not have interpolations by Christian scribes. The dating and textual integrity of the *Testaments of the Twelve Patriarchs* are debated. Clearly, Christians interpolated material at points, but *T. Levi* 5 does not seem to have been affected. Conjectured dates for the *Testaments* range from 100 B.C.E. to 100 C.E.

30. W. H. C. Frend, *The Rise of Christianity* (Philadelphia: Fortress, 1984), 120–60, on the "Christian synagogue." While the discussion of the similarities between the Jewish synagogue and the early Christian gatherings is enlightening, it is appropriate to note that the Christians did not use *synagōgē* but *ekklēsia*.

31. See John 1:14; 2:13-22; and 4:7-26.

32. Christians used the language of sacrifice when speaking about dedicating themselves to God and Jesus. See, e.g., Rom. 12:1; Phil. 2:17; 4:18; Heb. 13:15; 1 Pet. 2:5; *1 Clem.* 29:3; 36:1; *Did.* 14:1.

33. See, e.g., Philippians, Colossians, 1 Corinthians, Hebrews, Revelation, and *Shepherd of Hermas*.

34. Rev. 2:9; John 8:44; *Diogn.* 3–4.

35. Note Ephesians, Colossians, 1 Corinthians, Hebrews, and Revelation.

36. "Law" does not render the Hebrew *tōrâh* accurately. In a sense, the Torah is a body of literature, the first five books of the Hebrew Bible (in Greek, the Pentateuch). A second sense focused on the precepts, commandments, and regulations in those books. Rabbinical authorities were undertaking the study and discussion that led their successors in the fourth century to number God's positive and negative injunctions at 613, the same number, according to their calculations, as the parts of the human body. There may also be portions of the Torah which are binding on all people in a general sense, e.g., the Ten Commandments. It was in the third sense that the rabbis held that the Torah of the Lord was summarized in Deut. 6:4-5 and Lev. 19:18. Jesus was reported to have told his disciples to obey the scribes and Pharisees because these interpreters sat on Moses' seat, and that no one among his followers was to relax or teach the easing of a commandment (Matt. 5:17-20 and 23:1-11).

37. See esp. Galatians, Romans, and 2 Corinthians.

38. See Acts and esp. Paul's letter to the Galatians.

39. See Heb. 8 on the true *skēnē* or tent.

40. Perhaps the Gospels' polemic against Jews is being directed in part against Judaizing Christians.

Notes for Chapter 3

1. See Hesiod *Works and Days* 91–203.
2. Virgil, *The Aeneid of Virgil*, translated by Allen Mandelbaum (New York: Bantam, 1971). The passages cited are from Book 6, 1044–50 and 1110–37.
3. Ovid, *Metamorphoses*, translated by Mary Innes (New York: Penguin, 1955), Book 1, 76–111.
4. *Metamorphoses* 1.127–51.
5. *Metamorphoses* 15.831–72.
6. Tacitus *Annals* 15.44.
7. Suetonius *The Twelve Caesars* 6. See also Miriam Griffin, *Nero: The End of a Dynasty* (New Haven: Yale Univ. Press, 1984); Michael Grant, *The Roman Emperors* (New York: Scribners, 1985); Michael Grant, *History of Rome* (New York: Scribners, 1978); and Michael Grant, *The Twelve Caesars* (New York: Scribners, 1975).
8. Tacitus *Histories* 1.4.
9. Kenneth Wellesley, *The Long Year: A.D. 69* (Boulder: Westview Press, 1976). The term "the long year" is from Tacitus *Dialogue on Oratory* 17.
10. Suetonius.
11. *The Letters of Pliny the Younger*, translated by Betty Radice (New York: Penguin, 1975). See the letters to Tacitus, Book 6, letters 16 and 20.
12. Tacitus *Histories* 5.1–12.
13. See Dio Cassius, *The Roman Histories*, Book 68.
14. He opposed a revolt by another commander in Germany against Domitian less out of faithfulness to the man who claimed to be *dominus et deus* than out of duty to the good order of government.
15. See Herbert Musurillo, *The Acts of the Christian Martyrs* (Oxford: Clarendon, 1972); and W. H. C. Frend, *Martyrdom and Persecution in the Early Church* (Oxford: Blackwells, 1965).
16. See Epistles 96 (Pliny to Trajan) and 97 (Trajan to Pliny).
17. Dio Cassius 68.32.
18. Aelius Spartianus, "Life of Hadrian," 21, *Lives of the Later Caesars*. This is a curious, controversial work. Scholars are divided over the number of authors and dates, and the accuracy. The various extant "lives" cover the emperors from Hadrian through the fourth century. The uneven quality of the writings together with the anecdotes and bits of gossip alert readers to the need to be cautious in using these materials uncritically. Yet the "Lives" provide insights of the times, attitudes, and reputations of the persons considered. For fuller discussions of the *Later Lives* see *Scriptores Historiae Augustae*, translated by David Magie, in three volumes, LCL 1921, and *Lives of the Later Caesars*, edited and translated by Anthony Birley (New York: Penguin, 1976).
19. Dio Cassius 69.12.
20. Aelius Lampridius, *Lives of the Later Caesars*.
21. Aelius Spartianus, "Life of Aelius," 5, *Lives of the Later Caesars*.
22. Julius Capitolinus, "Life of Antonius Pius," 2, *Lives of the Later Caesars*.
23. Dio Cassius 72.34 and Julius Capitolinus, "Life of Marcus Aurelius," 27.11–28.13.
24. Tacitus *Histories* 1.3.

25. Marcus Aurelius *Meditations* 4.42–45, translated by W. J. Oates in *The Stoic and Epicurean Philosophers* (New York: Modern Library, 1940), 514.

Notes for Chapter 4

1. His family had honorable Roman connections as well as Roman citizenship and was included in the equestrian class.

2. See *On Consolation*.

3. Robert Grant, *Gods and the One God* (Philadelphia: Westminster, 1986).

4. See esp. "Philosophies for Sale," "Zeus Catechized," and "The Death of Peregrinus."

5. Over fifty meanings are listed for *logos* in LSJ, 1057–59.

6. Plato *Timaeus* 23.

7. Plato *Republic* 2.369.

8. For a concise, yet clear discussion of Plato's views of the forms, see Frederick Copleston, *A History of Philosophy* (Garden City: Image, 1962), vol. 1, part 1, 188–231.

9. *Republic* Book 7.

10. *Republic* Book 10.

11. It is clear that Plato and his successors had more to say about cosmology and theology than the surviving documents disclose. See Aristotle *Metaphysics* 1.987.

12. Of the first three key figures, two were from Cyprus and one from Asia Minor. The founder, Zeno (ca. 335–263 B.C.E.) came from Citium on Cyprus's southern coast; Cleanthes (ca. 330–230) from Assos (about forty miles south of ancient Troy); and Chrysippus (ca. 280–206) from Soli on Cyprus's southern coast. Later important figures were Panaetius (ca. 185–110), from the island of Rhodes, and Posidonius (ca. 135–51) of Apamea, about sixty miles south of Syrian Antioch. The lame former slave Epictetus (ca. 50–138 C.E.) was an exception. He came from the west coast of Greece, gained his philosophical education in Rome, and settled in Nicopolos, about one hundred miles from Delphi.

13. Translated in Arrian *Discourses of Epictetus* 1.2 and 3.1., *Stoic and Epicurean Philosophers*, edited by Whitney Oates (New York: Modern Library, 1940).

14. For discussions about "Homer" and the possibilities of multiple Homers, see Oliver Taplin's study in *The Oxford History of the Classical World*, edited by John Boardman, Jasper Griffin, and Oswyn Murray (Oxford: Oxford Univ. Press, 1986), 50–77.

15. *Iliad* Book 9. In the *Odyssey* (beginning at Book 6) the poet mentions the queen mother of the Phacians, Arete, and her noble demeanor. See Werner Jaeger, *Paideia: The Ideals of Greek Culture*, 3 vols., translated by Gilbert Highet (New York: Oxford Univ. Press, 1939, 1943, 1944); H. I. Marrou, *A History of Education in Antiquity*, translated by George Lamb (New York: Sheed and Ward, 1956); and E. B. Castle, *Ancient Education and Today* (Baltimore: Penguin, 1961).

16. See his *Iphigenia at Aulis* in which Achilles is depicted as self-interested and lacking in courage, and *The Trojan Women*, in which the heroes of Troy's destruction (Odysseus and others) are shown to be cruel, greedy, and lustful while the defeated women are persons of valor and wise words.

17. In *Iphigenia among the Taurians*, shepherds and simple folk clearly are more honorable than Orestes and his sister.

18. See *The Bacchants*, in which ideas about the gods can be called "honorable falsehoods," and *Iphigenia at Aulis*, in which the chorus asks if the poets have made up the tales. Throughout his plays, Euripides questioned the traditional forms of piety.

19. See esp. Plato's *Protagoras, Theaetetus, Sophist,* and *Statesman*.

20. Aristophanes (ca. 400) criticized Socrates for sophistical tendencies and methods in *The Clouds*.

21. Isocrates *Antidosis* 285.

22. See his *Against the Sophists*, in which he distinguished his school from that of rivals.

23. Plutarch *Lives of the Orators* 838D.

24. Arrian *Discourses of Epictetus* 1.2.

25. See Dio Chrysostom's (ca. 50–120 C.E.) oration "To the People of Alexandria," in *Dio Chrysostom*, translated by J. W. Cohoon and H. Lamar Crosby, LCL (London: William Heinemann, 1940), vol. 3, 187–90.

26. See esp. Jaeger and Marrou.

27. Aristotle held that rhetoric was "observing in any given case the available means of persuasion. . . . [Its] function is not simply to succeed in persuading, but rather to discern the persuasive facts in each case" (*Rhetoric* 1.2.1355b and 1.2.1356–57.) He also noted that rhetoric combines logic and ethics, and is partly like dialectic and partly like reasoning (1.4.1359). The pseudo-Aristotelian *Rhetoric to Alexander* added, "persuasion is an exhortation to some choice, speech or action. . . . [He] who persuades must show that those things to which he exhorts are just, lawful, expedient, honorable, pleasant and easy of accomplishment" (*To Alexander* 1.1421.20.)

28. As reported by Philostratus in *Lives of the Sophists*.

29. Usually the period is called the "Second Sophistic."

30. The Greek designations for these are, respectively, *dikanikē, symbouleutikē,* and *epideiktikē*. See also *To Herennius* 1.2. and *Rhetoric* 1.3.1358b.

31. The fourfold structure of a speech with their Greek and Latin equivalents are introduction (*prooimion, exordium*), statement of the situation (*diēgēsis, narratio*), proofs of the speaker's position with rebuttals of other views (*pistis, probatio*), and appropriate conclusion (*epilogos, peroratio* or *conclusio*). As the speaker worked on a speech, five steps were considered: invention (*heuresis*), arrangement (*taxis*), style, (*lexis*), memory (*mnēmē*), and presentation (*hypokrisis*).

32. See Aristotle *Rhetoric* 1.3.

33. See the helpful general articles on rhetoric in *The Harper Dictionary of Classical Literature and Antiquities*, edited by Harry Peck (New York: American Book Co., 1896), 140, 1372–74; *Oxford Classical Dictionary*, edited by N. Hammond and H. Scullard, 2d ed. (Oxford: Clarendon, 1970), 920–21; and William Schoedel, *Ignatius of Antioch: A Commentary on the Letters of Ignatius of Antioch* (Philadelphia: Fortress, 1985), 7–8. Note also Harald Riesenfeld, "Reflections on the Style and Theology of St. Ignatius of Antioch," in *Studia Patristica* 4 (1961): 312–22.

34. *Rhetoric* 1.1–3.

35. Aristotle *Topics* 1.2.10.

36. Seneca *Epistles* 94–96.

37. Acts 17:22-23.
38. See Apuleius, *The Golden Ass,* and Lucian, *The Death of Peregrinus.*
39. See Apuleius, and also Plutarch, *On Isis and Osiris* and *The Eta at Delphi.*

Notes for Part 2

1. See esp. Matt. 5:1-7, 28; 23:1-3; 13:18-23, 51-52; 18:7-21; 24:1-51; 25:1-30; 28:8-20.
2. See LSJ, 41–42, and BAGD, 23–24. Note that at Acts 24:14 Paul is presented as saying that the Jews called the Way a heresy in the sense that it was a sect, perhaps with a negative implication.

Notes for Chapter 5

1. See Gen. 2:4b-25.
2. See James Pritchard, ed., *The Ancient Near East,* 2 vols., (Princeton: Princeton Univ. Press, 1973); D. Winton Thomas, *Documents from Old Testament Times* (New York: Harper and Row, 1961); N. K. Sandars, *Poems of Heaven and Hell from Ancient Mesopotamia* (Baltimore: Penguin, 1972); and Samuel Hook, *Near Eastern Mythology* (Baltimore: Penguin, 1963).
3. See esp. Ps. 89:10 and Isa. 51, which mention Rahab the dragon. Among the Psalms that deal with the ocean depths, often a metaphor for human death as well as God's struggle to create and maintain the world, note Ps. 71; 77; 104; 106; 107; and 130. Job (references to the ocean depths and to the sea monster, Leviathan) and Exod. 15 indicate a connection between the deeps and God's exertions of sovereignty over creation.
4. Note particularly Prov. 8. The Hebrew and Greek words, *hokmâh* and *sophia,* respectively, are feminine gender. The Hebrew for "spirit" (*rûaḥ*) also is feminine, while the Greek (*pneuma*) is neuter.
5. Wisd. of Sol. 7:23-26.
6. Deut. 4:19-24.
7. Isa. 45:7. The Hebrew and the LXX both read "peace" and "evil" (and the King James Version translates the passage as such), but the RSV and NRSV render these words "weal" and "woe."
8. In 2 Sam. 12:31 God ordered David to take the census and then punished him for carrying it out.
9. The "Salathiel" source in 4 Esdras (= 2 Esd. 3-14 in NRSV) is an exception among Jews. Adam was blamed for cultivating an evil seed or impulse within his heart. The bitter legacy of disobedience, guilt, and punishment passed on by Adam to all his descendants caused Ezra's anguished laments. Eve was not mentioned. Paul used Adam as one way to express a view of the human condition and Paul's hope. The Pastoral Epistles use Gen. 2–3 in the argument for silencing women in the church.
10. The works that used a version of the tale were *1 Enoch* (= Ethiopic Enoch), *Jubilees,* and the *Testaments of the Twelve Patriarchs.* Christian interpolations in these texts usually can be identified readily. The brief New Testament document, Jude, quoted *Enoch* and called it Scripture. Clement, Tertullian, and perhaps Justin regarded it as

part of the Old Testament. Ignatius certainly knew it. Irenaeus was acquainted with the work but did not indicate its authority in the congregations he served. The angelology-demonology described in *Enoch* was basic to the world-view Christians shared with Jews in the first and second centuries and is reflected throughout the New Testament. See R. H. Charles, *The Apocrypha and Pseudepigrapha of the Old Testament* (Oxford: Clarendon, 1913), vol. 2, and James Charlesworth, ed., *The Old Testament Pseudepigrapha* (Garden City: Doubleday, 1983–85).

11. Apart from his participation in a delegation of Jews to Emperor Gaius Caligula (ca. 38–39), Philo makes no references to any official post that he may have held in government or within the Alexandrian Jewish community. See Philo's fast-paced treatise *Embassy to Gaius* for a chilling account of the emperor's style. Note that a different perspective on the emperor is taken by Anthony Barrett, *Caligula: The Corruption of Power* (New Haven: Yale Univ. Press, 1990). In Philo's time, the Jews had an ethnarch who related to the city, provincial, and imperial authorities. The philosopher's family was prominent among Jews and pagans in a way that must have pained Philo. Tiberius Julius Alexander, his nephew, apostasized to paganism, was appointed procurator of Judea, then became prefect (a position that included police powers) of Egypt (66–69), and served as Titus's chief of staff during the destruction of Jerusalem in 70. See Robert Grant, *Augustus to Constantine* (New York: Harper and Row, 1970), 22–39.

12. Philo *On the Creation* 1.5.

13. The treatises are *On the Creation* and *Allegorical Interpretation*. Philo continued his philosophical exposition of portions of Genesis and used the *Life of Moses* as the peroration of his discussion.

14. *On the Creation* 1.3.

15. *On the Creation* 4.16.

16. *On the Creation* 5.20.

17. *On the Creation* 56.157.

18. See, e.g., 2 Esd. 6:1-59 and *2 Bar.* 21:4.

19. Rom. 4:13-25.

20. Heb. 2:10-11.

21. Col. 1:15-17.

22. John 1:1-5, 14. The passage is fraught with theological double meanings. Generally, I followed the NRSV except to indicate points which will emerge in the course of the study.

23. John 21:31; 14:30; and 16:11.

24. Note, e.g., Eph. 6; 2 Thess.; 1 Corinthians; Revelation. The Greek word *archōn*, frequently used in this context, may mean prince and power.

25. The classic study of Marcion is Adolf von Harnack, *Marcion: Das Evangelium vom fremden Gott* (Leipzig: J. C. Hinrich, 1921). This is now available in English translation: *Marcion: The Gospel of the Alien God* (Durham: Labyrinth, 1989). More recent research and proposals about Marcion may be found in *Second Century* 6, no. 3 (1987–88). All of the articles in the issue are noteworthy: Gerhard May, "Marcion in Contemporary Views: Results and Open Questions," 129–51; Han J. W. Drijvers, "Marcionism in Syria: Principles, Problems, Polemics," 153–72; and R. Joseph Hoffmann, "How Then Know This Troublesome Teacher? Further Reflections on Marcion

and His Church," 173–91. May dismantled key aspects of Harnack's views of Marcion and rejected Hoffmann's earlier *Marcion: On the Restitution of Christianity: An Essay on the Development of Radical Paulinist Theology in the Second Century* (Chico: Scholars Press, 1984).

26. Tertullian indicated that Marcion was converted to Christianity after arriving in the capital (*Five Books Against Marcion* 4.4.3), but another tradition depicted Marcion's father as the bishop of the church in Sinope. Marcion's father, according to what may be a legend, disfellowshiped his own son before Marcion left for Rome (see Pseudo-Tertullian *Against All Heresies* 6.2, and Epiphanius *Panarion Against Heresies* 42.1). Tertullian cited the credible tradition that Marcion contributed a substantial amount of money to the Roman congregation when he was received as a member, and that the congregation returned it to him when he was expelled from its ranks (*Prescription Against Heretics* 30.2 and *Against Marcion* 4.9.3).

27. For second-century reactions see Justin Martyr *First Apology* 26 and 58; Irenaeus *Against All Heresies* 1.27, 4.8, and 4.34; Tertullian *Against Marcion*; *Prescription* 30–34; and *On the Flesh of Christ* 4–5; and Clement of Alexandria *Stromateis* 3.12–25. Justin and Irenaeus may have written separate works against Marcion, but none have survived. Justin reflected that he and Marcion were in Rome at the same time. Tertullian wrote at least three major works opposing Marcion, but two were withdrawn by him before he presented his massive five-book polemic (*Against Marcion* 1.1).

28. Justin complained, "And there is Marcion . . . teaching his disciples to believe in some other god greater than the Creator. . . . to deny that God is the maker of this universe, and to assert that some other being, greater than he, has done greater works" (*First Apology* 26). Justin continued that Marcion denied "that the Christ predicted by the prophets is his son, and preaches another god besides the Creator of all, and likewise another son" (*First Apology* 58). Tertullian summarizes Marcion's teachings as "the whole aim at which he has strenuously labored . . . centers in this, that he may establish a diversity between the Old and the New Testaments, so that his own Christ may be separate from the Creator, as belonging to this rival god, and as alien from the law and the prophets" (*Against Marcion* 4.7).

29. See Hans Leisegang, *Die Gnosis* (Leipzig: Kroner, 1924), 1. It is notoriously difficult to define *gnōsis* and Gnosticism, especially after the discovery of the Nag Hammadi materials. See Hans Jonas, *The Gnostic Religion: The Message of the Alien God and the Beginnings of Christianity,* 2d ed. (Boston: Beacon, 1963), and the more recent and comprehensive work by Kurt Rudolph, *Gnosis: The Nature and History of Gnosticism* (San Francisco: Harper and Row, 1984). Rudolph cited the failed attempt of a 1966 conference of scholars held at Messina, Italy (Congress on the Origins of Gnosticism), to agree upon common definitions and uses of terms such as gnosis and Gnosticism (56).

30. Deut. 29:29; Wisd. of Sol. 7; Isa. 40; 1 Cor. 12; Mark 4:1-34 and parallels.

31. In *Against the Valentinians* 4 the North African wrote, "Valentinus had expected to become a bishop [in Rome], because he was an able man both in genius and in eloquence. Being indignant, however, that another obtained the dignity by reason of a claim which confessorship had given him, he [Valentinus] broke with the church of the true faith." Valentinus probably taught in Alexandria, among other places.

Notes for Chapter 6

1. The NRSV, reading the Hebrew text of 8:5a literally as "gods" or "divine beings." The LXX (8:6) reads "angels."

2. Samuel Hook, *Middle Eastern Mythology* (Baltimore: Penguin, 1963).

3. See "Babylonian Theodicy," in D. Winton Thomas, ed. *Documents From Old Testament Times* (New York: Harper and Row, 1961), 97–103; N. K. Sandars, *The Gilgamesh Epic* (New York: Penguin, 1964; and James B. Pritchard, ed., "The Babylonian Theodicy," in *The Ancient Near East* (Princeton: Princeton Univ. Press, 1975) 2:160–67. Another Babylonian myth dealing with the loss of immortality through the trickery of a god is "Adapa," in *Pritchard* 1:76–80.

4. See Ps. 8 and 139; Gen. 1 and 2; and Proverbs, Sirach, and Wisdom of Solomon.

5. Ps. 51.

6. Ps. 14:3.

7. See Ps. 130 and 137 as well as the book of Lamentations.

8. At other times, it seems that he intends the paradigmatic human to be other than the Logos. Note *On the Creation* 65–70.

9. *Allegorical Interpretation* 1.1–12.

10. *Allegorical Interpretation* 1.12.

11. See esp. *Preliminary Studies; Flight and Finding; De Congressu;* and *De Fuga.* Philo's allegory included "philosophical" meanings for Mesopotamia (passion), Egypt (inferior but needed instruction), and Canaan (heavenly peace). For a more detailed study of his views on *paideia,* see Walter Wagner, "Philo And Paideia," *Cithara* 10 (1971): 53–64. Philo carried on an erudite yet sharp argument against sophistry (perhaps pagan critics of Judaism) and those within the Jewish community who wanted to jettison any hint of Greco-Roman culture.

12. *On Drunkenness.*

13. See esp. *On Abraham* and *Life of Moses.*

14. The members of the first triad were immature children compared to the members of the second triad and to Moses. The pattern of beginner, progressor, and sage was implicit in each triad. Enosh (Gen. 4:26, Seth's son) was the doorkeeper of the vestibule that led to the *aretē* of encyclical *paideia;* Enoch encouraged the soul's improvement through repentance; and Noah was the best man of his time. The second triad's members were philosophy's athletes in the contest against the passions. Abraham pursued the good through discipline in the proper teaching (*didaskalia*). Logos gave him an angelic guide, Rebuke (*Elenchos*), to discipline him and as a guide for reason. *Elenchos* may have been a model for the angel of repentance who shepherded Hermas. Jacob came to know divine truth through being a shepherd and by wrestling with his passions, that is, through stringent exercise (*askēsis*). He knew Logos as the shepherd who cured passions by means of toil (*ponos*) and discipline (*paideia*). Isaac was the offspring of Sarah-*Sophia* and Logos, not Sarah and Abraham. Sarah-*Sophia* was a virgin mother, and Isaac was born on the brink of initiation by Logos into the Mystery. See *On Abraham* and *The Sacrifices of Abel and Cain.*

15. Both apocalypses were written in Palestine between 70 and 100 in Hebrew, were translated into Greek, and then were rendered into other languages. For discussions of 2 Esdras's date, manuscript traditions, authors, and theology, see G. H. Box, "4 Ezra," in *The Apocrypha and Pseudepigrapha of the Old Testament,* ed. R. H.

Charles (Oxford: Oxford Univ. Press, 1913), 542–59; and Jacob Myers, *I and II Esdras,* Anchor Bible 42 (Garden City: Doubleday, 1974). Most scholars recognize that the bulk of chapters 3–13 is a unity. The section was called the "Salathiel Source," by Richard Kabisch, *Das vierte Buch Esra auf seine Quellen untersucht,* (Göttingen: Vandenhoeck and Ruprecht, 1889). Myers (120) agrees with W. O. E Oesterley and M. R. James that the "Salathiel Source" is a "ghost book." Both 2 Esdras and *2 Baruch* are composite works. The latter's closing portion apparently circulated separately and was included in the Syriac Bible. For a discussion of the titles, manuscripts, and theology of the work, see R. H. Charles, 470–80. *2 Baruch,* less adaptable to Christian purposes than 2 Esdras, was not used directly by the church. Both works are closely related and share common concepts (e.g., *2 Apoc. Bar.* 47:40; 2 Esd. 7:45-48; *2 Apoc. Bar.* 85:10; 2 Esd. 5:51-55). They reflected questions about the end of the age and the resurrection that appear in the Gospels, the Pauline writings, 2 Peter, Jude, and Revelation.

16. 2 Esd. 3:1 implies that Jerusalem was destroyed about thirty years before "Esdras" began his questioning and visions. Interpretation of several teachings and parables attributed to Jesus may be enhanced through comparing them to 2 Esdras, e.g., Matt. 13:1-34 and 2 Esd. 3–13. It is widely accepted that Paul did not write Hebrews and the Pastoral Epistles, and it is debated whether he was the author of Ephesians, Colossians, and 2 Thessalonians.

17. Clement of Alexandria quoted 2 Esd. 5:35 at *Stromateis* 3.16.100. It is likely that 2 Esdras also influenced 2 Peter. There appear to be several echoes of 2 Esdras in the *Epistle of Barnabas* (see *Barn.* 14 and 2 Esd. 4–7, and 2 Esd. 5:4-5 and *Barn.* 12 on the wood that will drip blood). *Shepherd of Hermas* resembles 2 Esdras in that some of the issues are the same and the chief figure converses with a guiding, sometimes reproving, angel. Hermas asked Esdras-Salathiel-style questions and received Uriel-like answers.

18. See esp. 2 Esd. 7–8.

19. 2 Esd. 7:48.

20. For a fuller but not exhaustive discussion of the *yēṣer ha-ṭôb* and the *yēṣer ha-raʿ* (the good and evil impulses or spirits) in humans, see W. D. Davies, *Paul and Rabbinic Judaism,* 4th ed. (Philadelphia: Fortress, 1980), 20–35.

21. See esp. 2 Esd. 7–8.

22. 2 Esd. 8:34-36.

23. 2 Esd. 9:7-8.

24. 2 Esd. 7:88-101.

25. 2 Esd. 7:28-29. See 2 Esd. 13 for more on a figure probably identified as the Messiah who will fight with God's enemies. 2 Esdras and Revelation shared some ideas about a messianic reign prior to the final judgment.

26. See 2 Esd. 8:46-52 for more on the paradise in which the tree of life is planted, a city is built, and a rest appointed. There are clear resonances between such themes in 2 Esdras and in Hebrews and Revelation.

27. *2 Apoc. Bar.* 54:15, 19 (R. H. Charles translation).

28. *2 Apoc. Bar.* 56:7-12.

29. *2 Apoc. Bar.* 72–73; see also 29–30.

30. *2 Apoc. Bar.* 51:7-10.

31. A wide variety of Hebrew terms form a "sin vocabulary." Among the common terms which fit the positive understanding of the free will are *ḥāṭāʾ* (used 233 times, meaning often to miss the mark, undertake erroneous action, stray, be at fault); variations of *ʿāwâh* (used 244 times, meaning often to do wrong, make crooked, pervert, etc.); *ʾāwen* (used 76 times, meaning often iniquity, vanity, wickedness, etc.); *šāgâh* (used 42 times, meaning often to err, go astray, be mistaken, be ignorant, etc.). Although somewhat biased toward Christian understandings, see the articles on *harmatanō* and *harmatōlos* in *TDNT*, vol. 1, 267–333.

32. The Hebrew noun *pešaʿ* connotes pride, rebellion, pushing someone out of a rightful place, willful breach of a relationship or alliance. This noun and the verb from the same root were used 133 times in the Hebrew Bible, often interchangeably with the other words cited above.

33. Rom. 3:9 (which is followed by a quotation from Ps. 14:1-3). See Rom. 1–2 and 5:12.

34. Rom. 7:24. See Rom. 6, also 7:14-24. Paul's treatment of the human plight was complex and drew upon elements from rabbinic traditions, including the two impulses. See Davies; J. Christiaan Beker, *Paul the Apostle: The Triumph of God in Life and Thought* (Philadelphia: Fortress, 1980); Beker, *Paul's Apocalyptic Gospel: The Coming Triumph of God* (Philadelphia: Fortress, 1982); John Reumann, *The Righteousness of God* (Philadelphia: Fortress, 1982); and Victor Paul Furnish, *Theology and Ethics in Paul* (Nashville: Abingdon, 1968).

35. See esp. Phil. 1:21-30; Gal. 2:15-21; Rom. 3:21-31; 8:18-29; 1 Cor. 15.

36. Gal. 6:2; and Phil. 2:12

37. See Phil. 1:15-2:18; 3:2—4:1; the Corinthian and Thessalonian correspondence as a whole; Philemon; Rom. 8:28-39; 13:1—14:23.

38. See Stendahl, 23–52. Paul considered himself to be a paradigm of the Christian life to be imitated by fellow believers, even though he was not yet perfect. See Philippians and the Corinthian correspondence. The suggestion accorded with Greco-Roman and Jewish Wisdom understandings of the teacher sage.

39. Matt. 25:31-46; 20:16.

40. Examples of the affirmation of free will are John 1:10-13; 3:16-21. John 17, the "high priestly prayer," presents Jesus as saying that God gave him some persons to do his will, and John 1:43-51, the call of Nathanael, indicates that Jesus already knew that Nathanael was to be a disciple.

41. Prior to the discovery of the Nag Hammadi materials in Egypt, scholars were dependent on the almost always polemical and ridiculing comments made by leaders in the church such as Irenaeus and Tertullian. The Nag Hammadi "library" provides new insights that clarify, deepen, and correct the orthodox writers. It is unclear at points, however, which of the Nag Hammadi documents belong to which gnostic group and at what periods the documents were used. As might be anticipated, scholars debate the meanings and interpretations of the works. For accessible translations of the texts, see Bentley Layton, *The Gnostic Scriptures* (Garden City: Doubleday, 1987), and James Robinson, ed., *The Nag Hammadi Library*, rev. ed. (San Francisco: Harper and Row, 1988).

42. See Elaine Pagels, *The Johannine Gospel in Gnostic Exegesis: Heracleon's Commentary on John* (Nashville: Abingdon, 1973), and *The Gnostic Paul. Gnostic Exegesis of the Pauline*

Letters (Philadelphia: Fortress, 1975). Note also *The Tripartite Tractate*, parts 2–3, in Robinson, 87–103. The translators, Harold Attridge and Elaine Pagels, note that the treatise is a revision of what may have been original Valentinian theology (58–60). In the *Tractate*, the Logos, not *Sophia*, was the aeon who fell from the Pleroma.

43. See Clement of Alexandria's *Excerpta ex Theodoto*.

44. See Pagels, *Johannine Gospel* and *Gnostic Paul*.

45. See esp. Rudolph and Jonas.

46. Translated by Kirsopp Lake in *The Apostolic Fathers* LCL vol. 2.

Notes for Chapter 7

1. "I am he" in the Greek text is *egō eimi*, that is, "I am." It reflects "I am" statements attributed to Jesus and the Hebrew name for God, YHWH (Exod. 3 and 6). The last line may also be translated "Even what I have told you from the *archē*." *Archē* may mean "from the start" (the beginning), the heavenly realm (from the place which is above), or the Mind of God (from where all originates).

2. *1 Enoch* 70–81; 1 Kings 17–21; 2 Kings 1–2; Mal. 4:6.

3. 2 Esd. 8. In Jewish lore, Isaiah was sawn asunder on orders from Manasseh. For Levi, see the *Testament of Levi* in the *Testaments of the Twelve Patriarchs*. On Moses, Exod. 33; Deut. 18 and 34; and Sir. 45. On the dispute over Moses' body, Jude 9, which quotes a lost *Assumption of Moses*. For Philo's account, see *Life of Moses* 2.288.

4. The Greek infinitive *chriein* means to spread, smear, or anoint. See *TDNT*, vol. 7, 473, and George Buttrick, ed., *Interpreter's Dictionary of the Bible* (Nashville: Abingdon, 1962), vol. 1, 413–20.

5. Passages in which the elect people may be the anointed include 1 Sam. 2:10 (1 Kings LXX = 1 Samuel MT); 2 Chron. 6:42; Ps. 27:8 LXX; 83:10; LXX and Hab. 3:13. Amos 4:13 LXX has God announce the anointed to the people. Prophets are "christs" at 1 Sam. 2:35; 1 Chron. 16:22 = Psalm 104:15 LXX.

6. Lev. 4; 6; 21; Exod. 28–29; Num. 3; 1 Sam. 2:25; 12:3; and Sir. 45. Note Lam. 4; Hag. 1–2; and Zech. 3. In Zechariah, the accuser is *ha-śāṭān* (Hebrew) and *diabolos* (LXX). In a vision, Zechariah is told in the Hebrew about "the two anointed ones who stand by the Lord of the whole earth." In the LXX, the prophet is told that they are "the two sons of prosperity (*piotētos*)." The Hebrew name Joshua was transliterated into Greek as *Iēsous*, i.e., Jesus. Note *T. Lev.* 18. Beliar, a fallen angel, was the chief of deceit and evil. See *T. Reub.* 6; *T. Sim.* 6. Joshua and Zerubbabel plus the new priest and the ruler from Judah of the *Testaments of the Twelve Patriarchs* were significant to the Qumran community, in which there were anointeds of Aaron and of Israel; see the *Manual of Discipline*.

7. E.g., 2 Sam. 1. For the eternal covenant, 2 Sam. 7. For son of David, *Pss. Sol.* 17. See also the following Psalms (Hebrew numbering is in parentheses): 2; 17 (18); 19 (20); 27 (28); 83 (84); 88 (89); 104 (105); and 131 (132). At Ps. 89:26 LXX the anointed king called out, "You are my Father, my God, and the Rock of my salvation!" The Lord responded, "I will make him the firstborn, the highest of the kings of the earth." Isa. 45:1 announced Cyrus as the messiah-christ.

8. Pss. *Sol.* 17; 18; *T. Jud.* 24–25; 2 Esd. 7:25-39; and *2 Apoc. Bar.* 72–73. According to Jacob Neusner (*Messiah In Context* [Philadelphia: Fortress, 1984]), there was no single "messiah myth" (ix).

9. Exod. 12; 19; 24; Lev. 16. For Christians, Matt. 26; Mark 14; Luke 22; John 1 and 13. In John, Jesus and the lambs die at the same time. In the Synoptics, Jesus' last meal with his disciples is the first meal of Passover. At 1 Cor. 5:7 Paul called Jesus "our paschal (Passover) lamb;" see also 1 Pet. 1:19.

10. Gen. 22. At Matt. 1 and Gal. 4, Jesus is both the son of David and the son of Abraham, and Christians are identified with Isaac. Mount Moriah was where David had a vision of God and where David determined the Jerusalem Temple was to be built (2 Chron. 3). In Ps. 22, the fate of the limbs in verse 16 (verse 17 in the MT; 21:17 in the LXX) is uncertain because the Hebrew is obscure. The NRSV has "shriveled"; the RSV has "pierced." The Greek in the LXX means "pierced" or "gouged."

11. The poems appear in Isa. 42; 44; 49; and 52:13—53:12. See Walther Zimmerli and Joachim Jeremias, *The Servant of God*, rev. ed. (London: SCM, 1965).

12. Matt. 2, using Hos. 11, identified Jesus with God's child, Israel. The other example of vicarious suffering is 2 Macc. 7.

13. Wisd. of Sol. 2—13 uses the word *pais*. It may be translated as child or servant. *Pais* is the word that the Septuagintal translators used for "servant" in Isaiah.

14. Wisdom of Solomon's treatment of wisdom and of the righteous servant influenced Paul, Hebrews, the Fourth Gospel, 1 John, and 1 Peter (e.g., Luke 23; 1 John 2; Rom. 3; Acts 2; 3). Two first-century Christian works quoted Wisdom of Solomon, i.e., *1 Clement* and *Didache*. Jesus as high priest is in Heb. 4—13. He is the Lamb who sits upon the throne in Rev. 5—6. Other themes include Adam (Luke 3; 1 Cor. 15; Rom. 5); the star from Jacob (Num. 24; Matt. 2); and Immanuel, prince of peace, and child (Isaiah 7—11, compared with the infancy narratives in Matthew and Luke). While there are no post-crucifixion appearances of Jesus in the Gospel of Mark, his exaltation is assumed. See Matt. 28 for a Deuteronomic-Moses ending, and Luke 24 and Acts 1 for a literal ascension.

15. E.g., Hesiod *Theogony*; Clement of Alexandria *Protrepticus*; Athenagoras (ca. 130) *Plea Regarding Christians*. Oedipus appeared to be deified in Sophocles' *Oedipus at Colonnus*. Hercules had a divine father; survived an attempt to kill him as a baby; battled animals, mortals, and gods; freed Prometheus; slew serpents; and triumphed over the powers of Hades and death. Finally, betrayed and suffering, he had himself sacrificed on a mountain. Zeus transported his immortal essence to the stars in a chariot. See Euripides *Philoctetes*; Ovid *Metamorphoses* 9.1-123; *Iliad* 19.90; and Pseudo-Apollodorus, *The Library of Greek Mythology*, 1.159–60. Commodus frequently styled himself as Hercules. Worship of Hercules sometimes was assimilated to that of Orpheus (Joscelyn Godwin, *Mystery Religions in the Ancient World* [San Francisco: Harper and Row, 1981], 11–16 and 144–59).

16. Emma and Ludwig Edelstein, *Asclepius: A Collection and Interpretation of the Testimonies*, 2 vols. (Baltimore: Johns Hopkins Univ. Press, 1945); and Helmut Koester, *Introduction to the New Testament* (Philadelphia: Fortress, 1982), vol. 1, 173ff.

17. Hercules raised a woman from the dead, and Asclepius raised seven persons (Edelstein, vol. 1, 37–44). See Plato *Phaedo* 118; Ovid *Metamorphoses* 15.531; Lucian, "Dialogues of the Gods." For comparisons between Jesus and Asclepius, see Edelstein; Origen *Against Celsus*; and Clement of Alexandria *Stromateis*.

18. Philostratus, *Life of Apollonius*. Pythagoras had discussions with Babylonian *magoi*, Indian Brahmins, and Egyptian naked sages. Caracalla had a shrine in which

Apollonius was worshiped, Apuleius ranked him with Moses and Zoroaster, and Severus Alexander included Moses, Jesus, and Apollonius in his worship.

19. Luke 4; 9; 7; 24; John 8; 20. Appollonius probably lived in the mid-first century C.E. Philostratus (ca. 160–240) reacted against Christianity but may have woven elements from Christian writing about Jesus in describing Apollonius. Philostratus's writings reflect popular understandings about pagan religion and culture. Second-century Christians knew of the accounts that were associated with Apollonius; see *Fox*, 253–55, and 671.

20. Arrian's *History of Alexander* and Plutarch's *Lives*.

21. *TDNT*, vol. 3, 1039–98.

22. Ebionites held that Jesus was a man raised to divine rank. See Hans Joachim Schoeps, *Jewish Christianity* (Philadelphia: Fortress, 1968); Richard Longenecker, *The Christology of Early Jewish Christianity* (Grand Rapids: Baker, 1981); and Justin Martyr *Dialogue with Trypho*. Perhaps the adoptionist view attracted Judaizing Christians and priests who became Christians (Acts 6).

23. E.g., John 1; 3; 8; 17; and Gal. 4.

24. Gen. 16; 21; 22; 30; Exod. 3; 23; Num. 20:16. As avengers, Exod. 12; 2 Chron. 32; 2 Sam. 24; and 1 Chron. 21. For angels in the presence of God, Isa. 6 and 1 Kings 22. For angels who appeared in human form note Gen. 18–19; Josh. 5; Judg. 13 (Samson's annunciation); 1 Kings 19; 2 Kings 1; Zechariah; Daniel; Tobit; probably Num. 22; 2 Kings 6.

25. At Job 1:6 and 2:1 the Hebrew has "sons of God," the LXX has "angels of God," and the NRSV has "heavenly beings." All read "sons of God" at Gen. 6:2. Dan. 3:91 LXX has "an angel of God." The NRSV has "a god."

26. E.g., Ps. 8:4 (the Hebrew and LXX read "son of man"); Ezek. 2 (used eighty-eight times to refer to Ezekiel); Dan. 8:17; and possibly Dan. 7:13-22. When the NRSV takes the term as a human, it reads "mortal" or "human." See Dan. 8:15; 7:13; 10:5 as well as Zech. 1:8. Daniel 10:5-6; 7:13-14; 12:5 have spectacular figures.

27. 1. *Enoch* 37–51 (the Similitudes, ca. 105–64 B.C.E.) and 83–90 (Dream Visions, ca. 165–161 B.C.E.).

28. E.g., Matt. 25; Phil. 2; John 3; 5; 7; 8; 14.

29. Gen. 18; 32; Exod. 24; Ezek. 1.

30. John 14; 2 Cor. 4–5; Col. 1; John 20.

31. 1 John 4.

Notes for Chapter 8

1. Acts on Paul and Apollos; 1 and 2 Corinthians.

2. Eph. 6:10-17.

3. Eph. 1:3-23.

4. Gal. 1; 2 John; 3 John.

5. An apostle is one who is sent to carry out a commission given by a superior or an organization. Apostles might baptize, but their chief task was to preach. See 1 and 2 Corinthians. According to Acts 13:1-5, Paul and Barnabas were commissioned to be apostolic missionaries. Paul's own writings do not indicate that he felt he had any

continuing responsibility to the Antioch congregation. He claimed to have been authorized by Christ to exercise disciplinary authority over the congregations he helped establish. Members of some of those congregations disputed his claims.

6. I.e., *1 Clement*.

7. The Gospels of Matthew, Mark, and John usually call them *mathētai*, disciples. Luke uses the term "apostle" for the twelve and "disciple" for the wider group. Mark called the twelve "apostles" when they returned from the teaching-healing mission, Mark 6:30.

8. Gal. 2; 1 Cor. 15; Acts 15.

9. 1 Cor. 12:4-10.

10. 2 Kings 11:18; Isa. 60:17; Wisd. of Sol. 1:6; Ps. 23; 80; Ezek. 34.

11. See 1 Pet. 2:25 for Jesus as bishop. Phil. 1:1 mentions bishops (note the plural) and deacons, but not presbyters.

12. Acts 14–21; 1 Pet. 5; 1 Tim. 4–5; James 5; 2 and 3 John.

13. 1 Tim. 2.

14. Matt. 16:13-20.

15. Eph. 4:1-7.

16. Phil. 1; Titus 1; *Did.* 15; and *1 Clem.* 44.

17. See Matt. 23:2

18. *1 Clem.* 37; 40; 47:6-7.

Notes for Chapter 9

1. See Rom. 1–2; Gal. 5; 2 Tim. 3; *Did.* 1–6.

2. Apuleius *Golden Ass* 8–9.

3. See Rev. 18 and Tacitus *Annals* 15.44.

4. See the *Mart. Pol.* 12:2. When the elderly bishop of Smyrna was led into the arena for execution, the crowd (according to a Christian writer) shouted, "This one is the teacher of Asia, the destroyer of our gods, who teaches many not to sacrifice nor to worship."

5. In the third and fourth centuries questions and arguments arose about the reinstatement of such "lapsed" members to the church's communion. The matter was sharpened when former deacons, presbyters, and bishops who had apostasized applied for reinstatement both to communion and to their previous offices.

6. See Heb. 6:1-8. The *Shepherd of Hermes* likewise denied that apostates could be forgiven.

7. It is not clear if the church had a "love feast" (*agapē*) separate from the thanksgiving or eucharist meal. By the mid–second century, it seems that most congregations had one ritual fellowship meal that combined themes from the *agapē* and the eucharist.

8. See Justin *2 Apology*; *Acts of Paul*; *Acts of Thomas*; *Martyrdom of Perpetua and Felicitas*. The latter document appears to be influenced by Montanism.

9. See Mircea Eliade, *Cosmos and History: The Myth of the Eternal Return* (New York: Harper and Row, 1959).

10. This was true also for cult of Serapis. While the cult was obviously contrived and new, claims were made that the god had an appropriately ancient past in Asia. The cult became especially popular in Egypt, where it was linked to Horus.

11. See 1 Cor. 1–2.

12. See Rom. 1–3.

13. Isocrates *Panegyricus* 50, "and [Athens] has brought it about that the name Hellenes suggests no longer a race (*genos*) but an intelligence, and that the title 'Hellenes' is applied rather to those who share our *paideuseos* than to those who share a common blood."

14. *History* 5.8, 13, 3, and 5 (in the order they are quoted).

15. See James and the Pastorals.

Notes for Chapter 10

1. Unless otherwise noted, I have followed Richardson's translations of Ignatius's letters. The hagiography on Ignatius is derived chiefly from the *Martyrdom*, Origen, Eusebius, and John Chrysostom. John Mason Neale brought the traditions together and generally accepted them (*A History of the Holy Eastern Church: The Patriarchate of Antioch* [London: Rivingtons, 1873]). He agreed with the unsupported Antiochian tradition that Peter was the first bishop of Antioch. Legends about Ignatius made him the child whom Jesus set in the midst of the disciples (Mark 10:35-37) and a student of Peter, John, and Paul. He was said to have faced Domitian and was banished for several years; was condemned in Antioch by Trajan; and died when an old man in a Roman arena. The letters written from Smyrna were to the congregations in Rome, Ephesus, Magnesia, and Tralles. Those written from Troas were addressed to Polycarp of Smyrna and the congregations at Philadelphia and Smyrna. Debate over the authenticity of the letters attributed to him was resolved basically by Theodor Zahn (Ignatius von Antiochien [Gotha: Perthes, 1873]). Milton Brown (*The Authentic Writings of Ignatius* [Durham: Duke Univ. Press, 1963]) restudied the question and concluded that the seven letters noted are genuine and five others are spurious. In 1628, the patriarch of Constantinople, Cyril Lucas, gave the Codex Alexandrinus to King James I. It contained *1 Clement* and the Ignatian epistles along with biblical materials. Thereafter, numerous English Christians sought to use Ignatius to legitimize their claims about particular forms of church governance, worship, and doctrine. A tradition used by Eusebius (*Ecclesiastical History* 3.36) holds that Peter was the first bishop of Antioch, then Euodius, followed by Ignatius, who was succeeded by Heron. Cyril Richardson suggested that Lucian mocked Ignatius in *The Death of Peregrinus* (*The Christianity of Ignatius of Antioch* [New York: Columbia Univ. Press, 1935], 90). Note Edward Gibbon, *The Decline and Fall of the Roman Empire* (New York: Modern Library, n.d.), vol. 1, 474. B. H. Streeter turned to a psychological explanation in *The Primitive Church* (London: Macmillan, 1929). R. G. Tanner disagreed, "Martyrdom in St. Ignatius and the Stoic View of Suicide," *Studia Patristica* 16, part 2 (1985): 201–5. See H. Schlier, *Religionsgeschichtliche Untersuchungen zu den Ignatiusbriefen* (Giessen: Toepelmann, 1929); Christine Trevett, "Apocalypse, Ignatius, Montanism: Seeking the Seeds," *Vigiliae Christianae* 43 (1989): 313–38; and Virginia Corwin *St. Ignatius and Christianity in Antioch* (New Haven: Yale Univ. Press, 1960). See Polycarp's *Epistle to the Philippians* 9:1 and 13:1-2. *The Martyrdom* is in ANF, vol. 1, 129–31. Origen referred to Ignatius in the Prologue to his commentary on the Song of Songs and in Homily 6 on Luke. Eusebius cited Ignatius and quoted from Ignatius *Romans* at *Ecclesiastical History* 3.36.

Jerome depended on Eusebius in commenting on Ignatius (*Lives of Illustrious Men* 16). John Chrysostom gave a florid oration on the traditional anniversary of Ignatius's death. Among recent writers who appreciate Ignatius are Karin Boemmes, *Weizen Gottes* (Cologne-Bonn: Hanstein, 1976); Peter Meinhold, *Studien zu Ignatius von Antiochien* (Wiesbaden: Steiner, 1979); and Sergio Zanartu, *El concepto de zoe en Ignacio de Antioquia* (Madrid: Eapsa, 1977). Note also Harald Riesenfeld, "Reflections on the Style and Theology of St. Ignatius of Antioch," in *Studia Patristica* 4 (1961): 312–22. Both Schoedel and Riesenfeld refer appreciatively to Othmar Perler's "Das Vierte Makkabäerbuch, Ignatius von Antiochien und die Ältesten Märtyrerberichte," in *Revista di archeologia christiana* 25 (1949): 42–72. See Schoedel (*Ignatius*), Frend (*Martyrdom and Persecution*), Perler, Corwin, Boemmes, Meinhold, and Robert Grant (*The Apostolic Fathers*, vol. 4 [London: Thomas Nelson, 1966]); all mentioned his use of the work but did not carry that use through in their analyses of his rhetoric and theology. Fourth Maccabees is an expansion of 2 Macc. 6:18—7:42. Several recent critics discern a potential gnostic heretic, a forerunner of Montanism, or a defender of Christian faith and order. The scope of those findings matches that of scholars from the seventeenth through the nineteenth centuries; Roman Catholics, Episcopalians, Presbyterians, and Congregationalists alike cited him as an authority for their respective versions of church government. Finally, biblical theologians are not sure if he deviated from, adhered to, or broke new ground with regard to Pauline and Johannine understandings of Christianity. It is still a matter of discussion whether or not he knew the Johannine material. See L. W. Barnard, *Studies in the Apostolic Fathers and their Backgrounds* (Oxford: Blackwells, 1966); and Meinhold. On the positive side, he was praised. Within months of meeting him, Bishop Polycarp of Smyrna collected Ignatius's letters and commended them to the congregation in Philippi. Debate over how many letters attributed to Ignatius were actually by him and discussion over the manuscript traditions of those letters is ongoing. Generally, it is agreed that he wrote to the congregations in Ephesus, Magnesia, Tralles, Rome, Philadelphia, and Smyrna, and to Polycarp, bishop of Smyrna. See William R. Schoedel, *Ignatius of Antioch: A Commentary on the Letters of Ignatius of Antioch* (Philadelphia: Fortress, 1985), 1–10, for a discussion of the recensions and authenticity of the letters.

2. Ign. *Rom.* 4. Virginia Corwin suggested a two-week period, projecting that the journey from Antioch to Smyrna took six weeks (*St. Ignatius and Christianity in Antioch* 20).

3. According to Eusebius's chronology, Ignatius died in 108. Adolph Harnack (*Die Zeit des Ignatius* [Leipzig, 1878]) and J. B. Lightfoot (*The Apostolic Fathers*, part 2 [London: Macmillan, 1889]) prefer 100–118. Richardson (*Early Christian Fathers* [Philadelphia: Westminster, 1953]) stretches it from 98 to 118.

4. *Magn.* 14.

5. See *Phld.* 7. He made one explicit reference to his charismatic authority, and then it was to defend himself from charges by other Christians that he staged an ecstatic utterance.

6. See Ign. *Eph.* 8:1; 18:1; 21:1; *Trall.* 13:3; *Smyrn.* 10:2; *Rom.* 2:2; 4:1-2; *Pol.* 2:3; 6:1.

7. See William Schoedel, "Theological Norms and Social Perspectives in Ignatius of Antioch," in Sanders, 30–56.

8. *Smyrn.* 11; *Phld.* 10; *Pol.* 7.

9. 4 Macc. 9:28, my translation.

10. 4 Macc. 1:11; 6:28; 17:21; 18:4.

11. See 4 Macc. 17:11—18:20; Ign. *Eph.* 1:2; *Trall.* 3:3-4; and *Rom.* 4:1—6:2.

12. *Poly.* 5:2, Lake's translation. At *Rom.* 2:2, Ignatius referred to himself as "the bishop of Syria." He probably meant "from Syria," not that he was the overseer of all or some of the congregations in the province. John Chrysostom, however, referred to Ignatius as "archbishop" in "Homilies on St. Ignatius," NPNF, series 1, 135–40. *Pol.* 1:2 may be a "bishop's mirror" (Meinhold, 5).

13. E.g., *Trall.* 7:1—12:2. Whether Ignatius reacted against more than one group of opponents is not clear. I hold that he faced one set of docetic opponents.

14. Ign. *Eph.* 7:1-2. The ambiguity ("[the] God" or "a god"?) is obvious in the passage. "A god incarnate" translates *en sarki genomenos theos*. While following Richardson's translation generally, the cited portion is my rendering.

15. See *Trall.* 7:1—12:2; portion cited is 9:1-2.

16. See Ign. *Eph.* 18–19.

17. Ign. *Eph.* 19

18. *Trall.* 10–11. The word "sham" translates *dokein*.

19. *Smyrn.* 3–4.

20. See *Smyrn.* 7:2; *Phld.* 5:2; 8:2; 9:1-2.

21. See esp. Ign. *Eph.* 3.

22. *Smyrn.* 6:1.

23. For the descriptive terms and quotations, see Ign. *Eph.* 4, 9, and 15; *Pol.* 4–6; *Phld.* 9; and *Magn.* 7. At *Smyrn.* 8:2 he wrote, "Where the bishop is, there let the congregation gather, just as where Jesus Christ is, there is the *katholikē ekklēsia*." *Katholikos* means general, sometimes whole.

24. See *Phld.* 2; *Smyrn.* 8. Ignatius also held that the apostles formed an advisory council for Jesus during his earthly career.

25. Ign. *Eph.* 3:2—4:1 and *Magn.* 13:1.

26. The quotations are from *Smyrn.* 8:2 and *Pol.* 6.

27. *Smyrn.*4; 7; 8.

28. The quotations are from *Magn.* 10 and *Phld.* 6.

29. *Magn.* 5:1. The Greek for "stamp" is *charaktēr*, that is, impression, as on a coin or person.

30. He refused to disclose anything to the weak Trallians (*Trall.* 5) but hoped that he could be more forthcoming in another letter to the Ephesians (Ign. *Eph.* 20).

Notes for Chapter II

1. The translation is from Thomas B. Falls, *Writings of Saint Justin Martyr,* FOTC (New York: Christian Heritage, 1948.) I have used the literal translation "becoming perfect" (footnote, p. 160) in place of Falls's rendering "becoming a Christian." Justin's writings were translated into Latin so that he was read in the western as well as eastern portions of the Empire. The now lost treatise on heresies and the *Apologies*

became models for other authors, and Eusebius credited him with five other works: the *Discourse to the Greeks, Admonition to the Greeks, On the Divine Monarchy,* the *Psalmist,* and *On the Soul (Church History* 4.18). Several other spurious works were attributed to him by other authors; see Falls, 15. Much of *1 Apology* 68 and all of 69–71 are later additions.

2. 1 Cor. 1:20a. The triad *sophos, grammateus, syzētētēs* reflects Gentiles and Jews. *Sophos* refers to the gentile philosopher and Jewish sage. *Grammateus,* scribe or secretary, reminded readers of the interpreters of the Torah and tradition who opposed Jesus, was the term for pagan officials who registered citizens, and applied to scholars. *Syzētētēs* means co-inquirer, fellow disputant, and co-critic. Rabbis who dialogued pointedly over the meanings of texts in order to expose the truths within them and gentile critics, sophists, and legal disputants could be encompassed by the term.

3. Justin also attacked Simon's disciple Menander. See Eusebius *Church History* 2.13; Irenaeus *Against All Heresies* 1.23.4; and Tertullian *Apologia* 13 for more on Simon. The Simon to whom he referred probably was not the same mentioned in Acts 8:9-24. According to Justin, Simon claimed to be a manifestation of the "first God" and traveled with Helena, a former prostitute. His appeal was great enough for Justin to complain that "Almost every Samaritan and even a few from other regions worship him" (*1 Apology* 26). Whoever Simon was and whatever he preached, he was dangerous enough for the church in Justin's Rome to oppose him as a rival messenger of salvation and therefore an ally of the evil angels.

4. *The Martyrdom of the Holy Martyrs,* ANF 1:305–6, compared Justin with Socrates. *2 Apology* indicates that Socrates had a partial knowledge of Christ (*2 Apol.* 10). See Trypho 2 and *2 Apology* for Justin's comments about his own life.

5. *First Apology* followed the outline for an apology delivered when the authorities were hostile to the defendant.

6. Robert Grant, *Greek Apologists of the Second Century* (Philadelphia: Westminster, 1988) studied the "apologists." The *Dialogue* is too long and literary to be the record of a historical account and at points is more useful in opposing heretics than Jews.

7. "If you think our statements are in accordance with reason (logos) and truth, respect them; if they seem silly, despise them as such. But do not impose the death penalty against those who have done no wrong, as you would against your enemies" (*1 Apology* 68).

8. See *Trypho* 80. In chapter 141 Justin referred to a Marcus Pompeius as the one for whom he reported the discussion. Justin appears to know some Jewish interpretations of biblical passages, e.g., *Trypho* 50 and 77.

9. The *Dialogue* is carefully if loosely constructed. The opening matches the conclusion stylistically and theologically. The formal starting point has Justin hailed by a group of young Jewish men, engage in a conversation about philosophy, and eventually retire for a two-day discussion in the middle of a stadium. Within that introduction Justin tells of his encounter with the "old man"—a philosopher whom he met while a student of Platonism. That earlier dialogue ended inconclusively but eventuated in Justin's thorough study of the Scripture and conversion to the Christian philosophy. In a similar manner, the *Dialogue with Trypho* ends inconclusively. Yet several of Trypho's friends have questioned their traditional interpretations and there is a hint that Trypho, as had a younger Justin, has met an old man–philosopher who may have set him on

the way to salvation. The text is damaged around chapter 74. The *Dialogue* proper is presented as a dialectical exercise that examined the validity of the Christian faith as forecast in the Septuagint.

10. *2 Apology* 5.

11. *Trypho* 79–81. Others with whom he agreed were Papias and Irenaeus.

12. *Trypho* 88 and 124.

13. *1 Apology* 63; 21–24; Trypho reflected that he knew adoptionist Christians who kept the Mosaic Law at chapter 47. The ambiguous reference about the Logos is in chapter 61. The Logos is compared to a fire kindled from another fire, which shines without lessening the brilliance of the original fire.

14. *Trypho* 67 and 92.

15. Passages that reflect Justin's views are, e.g., *1 Apology* 36; 37; 38; 52; 53; 63; note also Zech. 2:6; 12:10-12. Challenged by Trypho to prove that the Scriptures intended to speak of Jesus as the Messiah, Justin embarked on extended treatments of various biblical passages. His agenda was first to lay the groundwork that the Jewish Scriptures indeed spoke of a Messiah who was to come. Eventually Justin reached that point and with it what may be the climax of the *Dialogue*. He used Ps. 22 as the critical passage (98–108), joining to it treatments of numerous other texts. See also *Trypho* 17.

16. At *Trypho* 135, Justin pointed to an allegory in which Rachel was the symbol of the church for whom Jacob-Christ labored, while weak-eyed Leah represented the weak-souled Jewish synagogue.

17. *1 Apology* 66. The congregational worship pattern described in *1 Apology* reflects the *Didache*, a Syrian-Palestinian manual, M. A. Smith, "Did Justin Know the Didache?" in *Studia Patristica*, vol. 7, 287–90.

18. *Trypho* 47.

19. *Trypho* 80. The group may have been one of the gnostic schools.

20. *1 Apology* 58.

21. *1 Apology* 58; 26. See *Trypho* 35 for the enumeration of those who ate meat sacrificed to idols.

22. *1 Apology* 60.

23. *1 Apology* 2.

24. *1 Apology* 46. Ananias, Azarias, and Misael are Shadrach, Abednego, and Meshach in Daniel.

Notes for Chapter 12

1. Translation by Simon P. Wood, *Clement of Alexandria: Christ the Educator* (New York: Fathers of the Church, 1954). Quotations from the *Instructor* are from Wood. Those from the *Exhortation to the Greeks, Who Is the Rich Man Being Saved?* and *To the Newly Baptized* (or *Exhortation to Endurance*) are from the LCL translation by G. W. Butterworth. Other translations are available in the ANF, vol. 2. For the *Stromateis*, Books 3 and 7, see *Alexandrian Christianity*, Library of Christian Classics, vol. 2. translated by Henry Chadwick (Philadelphia: Westminster, 1954). The Greek texts are from the edition by Otto Stählin, *Die griechischen christlichen Schriftsteller der ersten drei Jahrhunderten*, 3d ed. (Berlin: Akademie Verlag, 1960).

2. The quotations are from Dio Chrysostom's "To the People of Alexandria," Oration 32 in *Dio Chrysostom*, vol. 3, translated by J. W. Cohoon and Lamar Crosby, LCL, 187; Dio Chrysostom cited a commentator probably familiar to his audience but unknown to readers in later centuries for his "hippodrome criticism" (Discourse 32, paragraph 31); quoted in Will Durant, *The Life of Greece* (New York: Simon and Schuster, 1939), 593.

3. Eusebius provided the basic "biography," which no longer can be maintained; see *Ecclesiastical History*, Books 4 and 5. See Walter Wagner, "A Father's Fate: Attitudes Toward and Interpretations of Clement of Alexandria," *Journal Of Religious History* 6 (1971): 209–30, for a survey of Clement's theology and reputation.

4. Clement's major autobiographical passage is *Stromateis* 1.11. The passage may be read to mean that he had four or five teachers. He traced Moses' parents to Chaldea (hence his knowledge of astrology) and Syria through Abraham. Clement was in Palestine while Jewish scholars were collecting the interpretations and teachings of their rabbis. The Palestinian process resulted in the compilation of the Mishnah (ca. 250). See Shaye Cohen, *From the Maccabees to the Mishna* (Philadelphia: Westminster, 1987).

5. There are several theories about the relationships among the treatises. See Walter Wagner, "Another Look at the Literary Problem in Clement of Alexandria's Major Writings," *Church History* 37 (1968): 251–60.

6. The image of the cone is suggested by *Exhortation* 1 and 6.

7. See esp. *Instructor* 1.1–9.

8. See esp. *Exhortation* 1–10 and *Stromateis* 3.17.

9. See esp. *Exhortation* 1, *Instructor* 1, and *Stromateis* 3.17.

10. *Who Is the Rich Man Being Saved?* 37.

11. *Instructor* 1.43.

12. See esp. *Stromateis* 3; 6; and 7.

13. In the mid-1940s a library of gnostic writings was discovered near Nag Hammadi, Egypt. Clement knew and quoted from several works that have been found there, e.g., the *Gospel of Thomas* and the *Gospel of Philip*. See James Robinson, ed., *The Nag Hammadi Library*, rev. ed. (San Francisco: Harper and Row, 1988). Clement also took notes on a treatise by a Valentinian teacher; see Robert Casey's translation of the *Excerpta ex Theodoto of Clement of Alexandria* (London: Christophers, 1934).

14. See *Instructor* 16; *Stromateis* 3.6–8.

15. *Stromateis* 7.17. See also *Instructor* 1.6; 9.8; 2.10; 3.11; *Stromateis* 1.19; 7.16–17.

16. See esp. *Instructor* 2; 3; *Stromateis* 3; 6.

17. The exceptions are 2 and 3 John and Philemon.

18. See, e.g., *Stromateis* 1.28 and 6.15.

19. See, e.g., *Stromateis* 6. Perhaps the initiation was a nocturnal rite which included human gnostic teachers breathing the Spirit into the candidates as Jesus breathed upon his disciples in their special room after the resurrection (John 20) and in harmony with the creation of humanity (Gen. 2).

20. *Stromateis* 6.13.

21. See, e.g., *Exhortation* 4; *Stromateis* 1.21.

22. See, e.g., *Exhortation* 1.

23. *Stromateis* 5.4.

24. See, e.g., *Instructor* 3.12; *Stromateis* 1; 6; 7.

Notes for Chapter 13

1. Tertullian reflects Wisd. of Sol. 1:1.

2. *Aeneid*, Books 2 and 3. Phoenicians established colonies in present-day Tunisia. Carthage was located about ten miles from today's Tunis. In the second century C.E., there were four provinces: Mauritania Tingitana (portions of Morocco), Mauritania Caesariensis (much of western Algeria), Numidia (eastern Algeria), and Africa Proconsularis (most of Tunisia and eastward into Libya).

3. See W. H. C. Frend, *The Donatist Church* (Oxford: Clarendon, 1952; and Timothy Barnes, *Tertullian: A Historical and Literary Study* (Oxford: Clarendon, 1971). For the traditional biographies of Tertullian see Eusebius *Church History* 2.2.4; and Jerome *Lives of Illustrious Men* 53, translated by W. H. Fremantle in NPNF series 1, vol. 3.

4. Vincent of Lerins *Commonitory* 18, translated by C. A. Heurtley in NPNF series 1, vol. 11.

5. *Prescription* 13. The translation used here is that of Peter Holmes in ANF, vol. 3. Thirty-eight of Tertullian's writings survive and some fifteen are no longer extant.

6. See esp. *Against Marcion* 1.3 and *Against Hermogenes*.

7. See esp. his *Apology, Soul's Testimony*, and *On the Soul*.

8. See *Against Marcion* 5.18; *On the Apparel of Women*; *On the Veiling of Virgins*; *To His Wife*; *On Exhortation to Chastity*; *On Monogamy*; and *On Modesty*.

9. *Against Marcion* 3.25.

10. *Soul's Testimony*.

11. Praxeas, a confessor from the province of Asia, apparently took God's unity as a point, and God's rule (*monarchia*) like that of a single ruler. He impressed a bishop of Rome (Zephyrinus?) with his version of "modalistic monarchianism." According to him, God was first Creator or Father, then became Son, and now is Spirit. Attempts were made to harmonize Praxeas's views with those of Sabellius, a Libyan (ca. 220). Praxeas appears to have influenced Zephyrinus to oppose Montanism, prompting Tertullian to remark that Praxeas served Satan by driving prophecy out of Rome and importing heresy (*Against Praxeas* 1).

12. Trinitas appeared in Tertullian's earlier work *On Modesty*. Tertullian understood monarchial rule to be that exercised by officers under one ruler. God's rule, for example, involved legions of angels.

13. *Apology* 21.

14. *On the Flesh of Christ* 1. See also *The Resurrection of the Flesh* and *Against Marcion*.

15. The immaculate conception of Mary was declared a dogma of the Roman Catholic Church in 1854 by Pope Pius IX (*Ineffabilus Deus*).

16. Tertullian relied on 1 Cor. 15.

17. See his *An Answer to the Jews*. The *Answer* shows a resurgent Jewish community capable of winning converts, and Christian rhetors could not best them. He never finished the *Answer*, and he avoided Jewish criticisms.

18. See *On Prayer* 1.

19. See especially *On Baptism* and *On Repentance*.

20. See *On Repentance* 4 for the example of the plank. The example was used in the development of the medieval sacrament of penance.

21. See Frend's *Donatist Church* on African-Christian opposition to latinized authorities. Tertullian's *On the Pallium* opposed Roman ways and endorsed African styles and experiences.

22. *Prescription Against Heretics* 9, translated by Daily, Arbesmann, and Quain.

23. Tertullian observed that some heretics rejected specific books and others insisted on different manuscript readings. A number of them accepted all the sacred writings but dwelled on obscure readings and forced their own views onto the texts.

24. He omitted Jerusalem, Antioch, and Cyprus, and he did not list Alexandria, associated with Mark. He also placed John in Rome.

25. The Latin-African bishop of Rome, Victor I (ca. 189–99), prevailed on Commodus's Christian mistress to obtain the release of some Christians sentenced to the mines in Sardinia. He was succeeded by the Roman-born Zephyrinus (ca. 199–217). Callistus, a convicted embezzler and one of the prisoners released from Sardinia, influenced Zephyrinus when persecution was muted in Rome but severe in Africa. Callistus succeeded Zephyrinus, and his episcopate (ca. 217–22) was denounced by Tertullian and Hippolytus (*Refutation of All Heresies* 9.2 in ANF, vol. 5.). Callistus was martyred and declared a saint.

26. See 1 Cor. 2:10—3:3. See Tertullian's *On Fasting: Against the Psychics*.

27. Tertullian appealed to the book of Revelation, which anticipated the defection of many believers before the final battle.

28. Tertullian referred to Christ as Logos (male) and *Sophia* (female). He may mean that in the body of Christ (the church) male and female are one, and that in the Spirit the Lord may be approached as male or female. This could account for his respect for women prophets and Priscilla's saying, "Under the appearance of a woman, clothed in a shining robe, Christ came to me." See Elaine Huber, *Women and the Authority of Inspiration* (New York: University Press of America, 1985), 222.

29. See, e.g., *Apology* 37. See also *To Scapula, Apology, On the Crown,* and *To the Nations.*

30. Tertullian knew Christians who observed the dietary restrictions of Acts 15 and a tradition that Pontius Pilate became a Christian; see *Apology* 9 and 20.

31. *To Scapula* 5. Scapula governed Proconsular Africa from 211 to 213.

32. *Scapula* 5, translated by Daily, Arbesmann, and Quain.

33. *Apology* 37. In earlier comments about occupations in which Christians ought not engage, Tertullian addressed fellow believers, but in speaking to a pagan audience in the above text, he emphasized the presence of Christians throughout society.

34. *Apology* 50, ANF translation.

35. See especially *To the Martyrs.*

36. *Martyrs* 3, ANF translation.

37. *On Flight from Persecution.*

38. See Matt. 10:23.

39. A Montanist report, *The Passion of Perpetua and Felicitas,* included written accounts by those about to be martyred. Perpetua dreamed that she was a victorious male gladiator who crushed the head of God's evil foe (*Passion* 3).

Notes for Chapter 14

1. Irenaeus, *Proof of the Apostolic Preaching*, translated by Joseph Smith (New York: Newman, 1952), 47f. For English translations of Irenaeus's other works, see ANF, vol. 1, translated by Alexander Robertson and W. H. Rambaut. The *Proof* was discovered in 1904 in an Armenian version. The ANF contains *Against Heresies* (as the *Refutation and Overthrow of Knowledge Falsely So-Called* is commonly known) and fragments ascribed to Irenaeus by Eusebius and others. Irenaeus probably wrote in Greek, and some portions of his writings survive in that language. The manuscripts containing *Against Heresies* are in Latin and Armenian, while most of the fragments are in Greek.

2. See Eusebius *Church History* 5.1. Martyrs from Vienne, a town in Gaul fifteen miles from Lyons, are also mentioned in the account.

3. Lud, often depicted as a three-formed god, was readily related to Mars, Apollo, and Mercury. See Julius Caesar, *The Gallic Wars*.

4. The writer(s) named several martyrs, observing that they came from Asia and Phrygia.

5. Polycarp was his mentor and his authority regarding Jesus, the apostles, and episcopal integrity. Irenaeus reported that Polycarp referred often to "John, and the rest of those who had seen the Lord." See also *Against Heresies* 3–5 for anecdotes about the disciple John and Polycarp. Irenaeus insisted that Polycarp was instructed by apostles, talked with many who had seen Jesus, and was appointed bishop by apostles in Asia. Polycarp may have been born around 70 and could have known John and others who knew Jesus personally, but he did not refer to apostolic connections in his letter to Christians in Philippi. Ignatius reflected nothing of Irenaeus's version of John and the other apostles and elders. Irenaeus's claim that John the disciple-apostle wrote the Book of Revelation is considered untenable by most biblical scholars. The church at Smyrna was addressed by the Son of Man (Rev. 2:8-11) and that may account for Irenaeus's stress on connecting "John" to the city and Asia. Irenaeus quoted Ignatius's letter to the Romans but reflected no knowledge of other Ignatian materials. According to Irenaeus, the disciple-apostle John lived in Ephesus through the reign of Trajan (*Against Heresies* 2.24; 3.3) and Clement of Rome knew "the blessed apostles" (3.2). Irenaeus knew a story about Polycarp's journey to Rome and how he kept unity among the bishops in spite of diverse practices with respect to the date for celebrating Easter. For Irenaeus's trip to Rome and the debate about Easter, see Eusebius *Church History* 5.24.

6. See Eusebius *Church History* 5.3-4. According to Eusebius, Gallic Christians sent Irenaeus to Rome with a letter describing their understanding of Montanism. A number of believers, according to Eusebius, had already been jailed in Lyons. Eusebius also reports that Irenaeus later advised Victor I on his controversy with Eastern bishops regarding the date of Easter.

7. See *Against Heresies*, Books 1 and 2. Irenaeus addressed practices such as sexual promiscuity among believers.

8. See *Proof* 1. The full title of the work usually called *Against Heresies* is the *Refutation and Overthrown of Knowledge Falsely So-Called*. The second's title is literally "The Demonstration of the Apostolic Proclamation." See Gérard Vallée, *A Study in Anti-Gnostic Polemics: Irenaeus, Hippolytus and Epiphanius* (Waterloo: Wilfrid Laurier Univ. Press, 1981).

9. *Proof* 6 and 3.

10. See Gregory of Tours *A History of the Franks* 1.29. Gregory claimed that Polycarp sent Irenaeus to Lyons.

11. At *Against Heresies* 4.6 Irenaeus quoted Justin's lost work against Marcion.

12. See John Lawson, *The Biblical Theology of Saint Irenaeus* (London: Epworth, 1948), 140–98, and H. E. W. Turner, *The Patristic Doctrine of Redemption* (London: A. R. Mowbray, 1952). Gustav Wingren, *Man and the Incarnation: A Study in the Biblical Theology of Irenaeus* (Edinburgh: Oliver and Boyd, 1959), considered the motif to the incarnate Logos alone, and Gustaf Aulen (*Christus Victor* [New York: Macmillan, 1969]) limited Irenaeus to one view of the atonement.

13. *Against Heresies* 1.10.1 (ANF).

14. See esp. *Proof* 9. One Valentinian cosmology cited in *Against Heresies* 1.5.2 has seven heavens, above which is located the Demiurge, and beyond him the Pleroma.

15. Ps. 90:4.

16. See Rev. 20:4-14 and, e.g., *Against Heresies* 5.28.

17. *Against Heresies* 5.29.

18. See Robert Brown's "On the Necessary Imperfection Of Creation: Irenaeus' *Adversus Haereses* IV, 38," in *Scottish Journal of Theology* 28 (1975): 17–25.

19. See *Against Heresies* 4.20; 2.33; 5.6-12; and *Proof* 32.

20. See *Proof* 11–14 and *Against Heresies* 5.28-36. Irenaeus's biblical references include Genesis, Revelation, and Matt. 13.

21. *Proof* 11–16 and *Fragment* 14 from Anastasius of Sinai.

22. See, e.g., *Proof* 16–32 and *Against Heresies* 3.12-18 and 5.21-24.

23. See esp. *Proof* 6–7 and *Against Heresies* 3–4.

24. He omitted references to Gen. 6:1-4 in *Against Heresies* and gave an abbreviated version in *Proof* 18.

25. See Juan Ochagavia, *Visibile Patris Filius: A Study of Irenaeus' Teaching on Revelation and Tradition* (Rome: Pontifical Institute of Oriental Studies, 1964).

26. Irenaeus favored "Logos" and "Christ" over the name Jesus when referring to the incarnate one. While recapitulation is mentioned throughout *Against Heresies*, see especially Books 3–5. Note also *Proof* 31–32.

27. See *Proof* 33. Western Christianity's Marian devotion led to traditions about Mary's immaculate conception, perpetual virginity, and bodily assumption. She became an intercessor for sinners, the patroness of the church against heresies, co-redemptrix and co-mediatrix, etc.

28. *Against Heresies* 2.22. Irenaeus cited the disciple John as his source.

29. *Against Heresies* 2.11-28.

30. See *Against Heresies* 1, preface; 3.15; 4.26.

31. See Num. 8:15 and *Proof* 26. The lampstand's pattern had been disclosed to Moses by God. See also *Against Heresies* 5.35 for the tabernacle, Temple, and Jerusalem as heavenly patterns.

32. See Acts 2; *Proof* 9 and 26; and *Against Heresies* 3.24.

33. *Against Heresies* 3.4.

34. *Against Heresies* 4.26.

35. He claimed that John and unnamed presbyters who saw and heard Jesus were active in both Ephesus and Smyrna. It seems that he regarded Ephesus as the most

apostolically authoritative congregation in Asia because of Paul and John. Smyrna could claim John, Ignatius, and the unnamed presbyters whom Polycarp heard. Polycarp's journey to Rome linked him to Peter and Paul. Irenaeus derived his own authority from Polycarp and could add his experience in Rome. He may have suggested an ecclesial symmetry in which Lyons was analogous to Smryna, Rome to Ephesus.

36. *Against Heresies* 4.15-16.

37. The others included Papias, *1 Clement*, and Ignatius.

38. *Against Heresies* 3.25.

39. *Against Heresies* 3.4.

40. *Against Heresies* 4.30.

41. *Against Heresies* 4.37.

Notes for Chapter 15

1. The translation is by G. W. Butterworth. The quotation within the passage is from Plato *Theaetetus* 176B.

2. Ignatius's view about the maturity or immaturity of the primal couple cannot be discerned from his letters.

3. See Philo of Alexandria's *On the Giants*, in which he posits that the souls of men came down from the sphere just above the earth (*aēr*) and entered bodies to become humans. Those who avoided passions (identified as feminine) pursued divine philosophy and re-ascended to the heavens to take positions which were higher than those they left earlier.

4. See *Against Praxeas*.

Glossary

apotheosis: The elevation of a human being to divine status, making someone (e.g., an emperor or a hero) a god. Some Christians considered Jesus to be an apotheosized human.

esoteric: Secret, usually unwritten. The term often referred to teachings and revelations kept within a limited circle or school. These mysteries were disclosed orally by teachers or masters to disciples who passed through preliminary instruction and were then initiated into the inmost understandings of the school or cult.

exoteric: Public, or open. The term often referred to teachings that were made in public sessions and could be written down. Members of schools and religious groups advanced toward initiation through learning first the exoteric teachings of the group.

gnōsis: Esoteric knowledge revealed to initiated persons by God or other divine powers through teachers and in rituals. *Gnosis* purports to give the truth about the underlying realities, structures, and destinies of the cosmos, divinities, and humans.

logos: Greek term meaning word, thought, reason, discourse, and order. It was especially important in Stoic ethics. Among Jews, it connoted God's reason, power, and revelatory action.

Logos: The personification of logos, often as a divine power or being just below the Supreme God or as an emanation of God. Christians came to identify Jesus as the Logos in human flesh. Both those who considered Jesus to be the highest of the angelic beings and those who believed him to a manifestation of the Supreme God appealed to Logos Christology.

paideia: Greek word that may be translated as "education," "discipline," or "culture." It was used for the system and process of education and the externalizing of the individual's *aretē*. Some Christians used it for the Christian process and system which led to salvation.

271

parousia: Greek word that may be translated "arrival" or "presence." Christians used it to refer to (1) Jesus' anticipated return at the end of the present age to judge the resurrected dead and to begin the kingdom of God, and (2) Jesus' presence within the believer and the church.

Septuagint: Translation into Greek of the Hebrew Bible plus other religious writings considered especially important by Jews. Abbreviated LXX.

Bibliography

TRANSLATIONS OF MAJOR PRIMARY SOURCES

Collections of Early Christian Writings

Glimm, Francis, Gerald Walsh, and Joseph Marique. *The Apostolic Fathers*. FOTC. New York: 1948.

Grant, Robert, ed. *The Apostolic Fathers: A New Translation and Commentary*. New York: Nelson, 1964.

Kleist, James, trans. *The Epistles of St. Clement of Rome and St. Ignatius of Antioch*. ACW. 1946.

Lake, Kirsopp, trans. *Apostolic Fathers*. LCL. 1912–13.

Lightfoot, J. B., trans. *The Apostolic Fathers*. London: Macmillan, 1889–90.

Richardson, Cyril, ed. *Early Christian Fathers*. New York: Macmillan, 1953.

Ignatius of Antioch

Schoedel, William. *Ignatius of Antioch: A Commentary on the Letters of Ignatius of Antioch*. Philadelphia: Fortress, 1985.

Justin Martyr

Falls, Thomas, trans. *St. Justin Martyr*. FOTC. New York: Christian Heritage, 1948.

Clement of Alexandria

Butterworth, G. W., trans. *Clement of Alexandria*. LCL. 1960.

Casey, Robert, ed. *The Excerpta ex Theodoto of Clement of Alexandria*. London: Christophers, 1934.

273

Chadwick, Henry, and John Oulton, eds. *Alexandrian Christianity*. Library of Christian Classics. Philadelphia: Westminster, 1954.
Wood, Simon, trans. *Clement of Alexandria: Christ the Educator*. FOTC. New York: Fathers of the Church, 1954.

Tertullian

LeSaint, William. *Treatises on Marriage and Remarriage: To His Wife, An Exhortation to Chastity, Monogamy*. ACW. 1951.
Daily, Emily, Rudolph Arbesmann, and Edwin Quain. *Tertullian: Apologetical Works*. FOTC. New York: Fathers of the Church, 1950.

Irenaeus of Lyons

Smith, Joseph, trans. *Proof of the Apostolic Preaching*. ACW. 1952.

TRANSLATIONS OF GENERAL PRIMARY SOURCES

Aland, Kurt et al., eds. *The Greek New Testament*. 3d ed. New York: United Bible Societies, 1975.
Apollodorus. *The Library of Greek Mythology*. Translated by Keith Aldrich. Lawrence, Kans.: Coronado Press, 1975.
Apuleius. *The Golden Ass*. Translated by W. Adlington; revised by S. Gaselee. LCL. 1947.
Aristophanes. Translated by Benjamin Rogers. 3 vols. LCL. 1924–30.
Aristotle. 23 vols. LCL. 1926–36.
Arrian. *History of Alexander and Indica*. Translated by P. A. Brunt. 2 vols. LCL. 1976–.
Caesar. *The Gallic War*. Translated by Moses Hadas. New York: Modern Library, 1957.
Charles, R. H. *Apocrypha and Pseudepigrapha of the Old Testament*. 2 vols. Oxford: Oxford Univ. Press, 1913.
Charlesworth, James. *The Old Testament Pseudepigrapha*. 2 vols. Garden City: Doubleday, 1983–85.
Dio Cassius. *The Roman Histories*. Translated by E. W. Cary. 9 vols. LCL. 1925.
Dio Chrysostom. Translated by J. W. Cohoon and H. Lamar Crosby. 5 vols. LCL. 1932–51.
Diodorus Siculus. 12 vols. LCL. 1933–.
Diogenes Laertius. *Lives of Eminent Philosophers*. Translated by R. D. Hicks. 2 vols. LCL. 1925.
Dupont-Sommer, A. *The Essene Writings from Qumran*. Cleveland: World, 1962.
Edelstein, Emma, and Ludwig Edelstein. *Asclepius: A Collection and Interpretation of the Testimonies*. 2 vols. Baltimore: Johns Hopkins Univ. Press, 1945.
Euripides. Translated by Arthur Way. LCL. 1978–80.
Gregory of Tours. *The History of the Franks*. Translated by Lewis Thorpe. London: Penguin, 1977.

Hesiod. *Theogony; Works and Days*. Translated by Apostolos Athanassakis. Baltimore: Johns Hopkins Univ. Press, 1983.

Homer. *The Iliad of Homer*. Translated by Ennis Rees. New York: Oxford Univ. Press, 1991.

————. *The Odyssey of Homer*. Translated by Allan Mandelbaum. Berkeley: Univ. of California Press, 1990.

Isaeus. Translated by Edward Forster. LCL. 1927.

Isocrates. Translated by George Norlin and LaRue Van Hook. LCL. 1928–45.

Lucian. 8 vols. LCL. 1936.

Musurillo, Herbert, ed. and trans. *The Acts of the Christian Martyrs*. Oxford: Clarendon, 1972.

Oates, W. J. *The Stoic and Epicurean Philosophers*. New York: Modern Library, 1940.

Ovid. *Metamorphoses*. Translated by Mary Innes. New York: Penguin, 1955.

Philo. Translated by F. H. Colson and G. H. Whitaker. LCL. 1929–62.

Philostratus. Translated by F. C. Conybeare and Arthur Fairbanks. 2 vols. LCL. 1912, 1931.

Philostratus and Eunapius. *The Lives of the Sophists*. Translated by Wilmer Wright. LCL. 1952.

Plato. 12 vols. LCL. 1914–25.

Pliny the Younger. *The Letters of Pliny the Younger*. Translated by Betty Radice. New York: Penguin, 1975.

Plotinus. *The Enneads*. Translated by Stephen MacKenna. 4th ed. London: Faber, 1969.

Plutarch. 27 vols. LCL. 1914–36.

Quintilian. *Institutio oratoria*. Translated by H. E. Butler. 4 vols. LCL. 1920–22.

Scriptores Historiae Augustae. Translated by David Magie. 3 vols. LCL. 1922–32.

Seneca. 10 vols. LCL. 1935–61.

Sophocles. Translated by F. Storr. 2 vols. LCL. 1924–28.

Strabo. *Geography*. Translated by Horace Jones. 8 vols. LCL. 1917–33.

Suetonius. *The Twelve Caesars*. Translated by Robert Graves. New York: Penguin, 1979.

Tacitus. *Tacitus*. Cambridge: Harvard Univ. Press, 1967.

Thomas, D. Winton. *Documents from Old Testament Times*. New York: Harper and Row, 1958.

Virgil. *The Aeneid*. Translated by Allen Mandelbaum. New York: Bantam, 1971.

————. *The Poems*. Translated by James Rhoades. Chicago: Encyclopedia Britannica, 1952.

SECONDARY SOURCES

Armstrong, Arthur. *The Cambridge History of Later Greek and Early Medieval Philosophy*. Cambridge: Cambridge Univ. Press, 1967.

Aulen, Gustav. *Christus Victor*. New York: Macmillan, 1969.

Barnard, L. W. *Justin Martyr: His Life and Thought*. Cambridge: Cambridge Univ. Press, 1967.

————. "Justin Martyr's Eschatology." *Vigiliae Christianae* 19 (1965): 86–98.

————. *Studies in the Apostolic Fathers and Their Background*. Oxford: Blackwells, 1966.

Barnes, Timothy. *Tertullian: A Historical and Literary Study*. Oxford: Clarendon, 1971.

Barrett, Anthony. *Caligula: The Corruption of Power*. New Haven: Yale Univ. Press, 1990.

Bauer, Walter. *Orthodoxy and Heresy in Earliest Christianity*. Translated and edited by Robert Kraft and Gerhard Krodel. Philadelphia: Fortress, 1971.

Beker, J. Christiaan. *Paul the Apostle: The Triumph of God in His Life and Thought*. Philadelphia: Fortress, 1980.

_____. *Paul's Apocalyptic Gospel: The Coming Triumph of God*. Philadelphia: Fortress, 1982.

Bigg, Charles. *The Christian Platonists of Alexandria*. Oxford: Clarendon, 1886.

Boardman, John, Jasper Griffin, and Oswyn Murray, eds. *The Oxford History of the Classical World*. Oxford: Oxford Univ. Press, 1986.

Boemmes, Karin. *Weizen Gottes: Untersuchungen zur Theologie des Martyriums bei Ignatius von Antiochien*. Cologne-Bonn: Hanstein, 1976.

Brown, Robert. "On the Necessary Imperfection of Creation: Irenaeus's *Adversus Haereses* IV, 38." *Scottish Journal of Theology* 28 (1975): 17–25,

Buttrick, George. *Interpreter's Dictionary of the Bible*. 4 vols. Nashville: Abingdon, 1962.

Castle, E. B. *Ancient Education and Today*. Baltimore: Penguin, 1961.

Chadwick, Henry, and G. R. Evans, eds. *Atlas of the Christian Church*. New York: Facts on File, 1987.

Cornell, Tim, and John Matthews. *Atlas of the Roman World*. New York: Facts on File, 1986.

Cohen, Shaye. *From the Maccabees to the Mishna*. Philadelphia: Westminster, 1987.

Copleston, Frederick. *A History of Philosophy*. Garden City: Image, 1962.

Corwin, Virginia. *St. Ignatius and Christianity in Antioch*. New Haven: Yale Univ. Press, 1960.

Davies, W. D. *Paul and Rabbinic Judaism*. 4th ed. Philadelphia: Fortress, 1980.

De Faye, Eugene. *Clement D'Alexandrie: Etude sur les rapports du christianisme et de la philosophie grecque au IIe siècle*. 2d ed. Paris: Ernest Leroux, 1906.

Droge, Arthur. "Justin Martyr and the Restoration of Philosophy." *Church History* 56 (1987) 303–19.

_____. *Homer or Moses*, Tübingen: J. C. B. Mohr (Paul Siebeck), 1989.

Durant, Will. *The Life of Greece*. New York: Simon and Schuster, 1939.

Eliade, Mircea. *Cosmos and History: The Myth of the Eternal Return*. New York: Harper and Row, 1959.

Fox, Robin. *Pagans and Christians*. New York: Alfred A. Knopf, 1987.

Frend, W. H. C. *The Donatist Church*. Oxford: Clarendon, 1985.

_____. *Martyrdom and Persecution in the Early Church*. Oxford: Blackwells, 1965.

_____. *The Rise of Christianity*. Philadelphia: Fortress, 1984.

Froehlich, Karlfried. *Biblical Interpretation in the Early Church*. Philadelphia: Fortress, 1984.

Furnish, Victor Paul. *Theology and Ethics in Paul*. Nashville: Abingdon, 1968.

Godwin, Joscelyn. *Mystery Religions in the Ancient World*. San Francisco: Harper and Row, 1981.

Goodenough, Erwin. *The Theology of Justin Martyr*. Jena: Frommannische Buchhandlung, 1923.

Grant, Michael. *History Of Rome*. New York: Scribner's, 1978.

————. *The Roman Emperors*. New York: Scribner's, 1985.

————. *The Twelve Caesars*. New York: Scribner's, 1975.

Grant, Robert. *Augustus to Constantine*. New York: Harper and Row, 1970.

————. "A Woman of Rome: The Matron in Justin, *2 Apology* 2.1–9." *Church History* (1985): 461–72.

————. *Gods and the One God*. Philadelphia: Westminster, 1986.

————. *Greek Apologists of the Second Century*. Philadelphia: Westminster, 1988.

Griffin, Miriam. *Nero: The End of a Dynasty*. New Haven: Yale Univ. Press, 1984.

Guthrie, W. K. C. *The Sophists*. Cambridge: Cambridge Univ. Press, 1971.

Hammond, N., and H. Scullard, eds. *The Oxford Classical Dictionary*. 2d ed. Oxford: Clarendon, 1970.

Harnack, Adolf. *Marcion: Das Evangelium vom fremden Gott*. Leipzig: J. C. Hinrichs, 1921.

————. *Marcion: The Gospel of the Alien God* (Durham: Labyrinth, 1989).

————. *Zur Quellenkritik der Geschichte des Gnosticismus*. Leipzig: E. Bidder, 1873.

Herm, Gerhard. *The Celts*. New York: St. Martin's, 1975.

Hoffman, R. Joseph. "How Then Know This Troublesome Teacher? Further Reflections on Marcion and His Church." *Second Century* 6 (1987-88): 173–191.

————. *Marcion on the Restitution of Christianity: An Essay on the Development of Radical Paulinist Theology in the Second Century*. Chico: Scholars Press, 1984.

Hook, Samuel. *Middle Eastern Mythology*. Baltimore: Penguin, 1963.

Jaeger, Werner. *Paideia: The Ideals of Greek Culture*. New York: Oxford Univ. Press, 1939–44.

Jonas, Hans. *The Gnostic Religion: The Message of the Alien God and the Beginnings of Christianity*. 2d ed. Boston: Beacon, 1963.

Kabisch, Richard. *Das vierte Buch Esra auf seine Quellen untersucht*. Göttingen: Vandenhoeck and Ruprecht, 1889.

Kennedy, George. *The Art of Persuasion in Greece*. London: Routledge and Kegan Paul, 1963.

————. *The Art of Rhetoric in the Ancient World, 300 BC–AD 300*. Princeton: Princeton Univ. Press, 1972.

————. *Classical Rhetoric and Its Christian and Secular Tradition from Ancient to Modern Times*. Chapel Hill: Univ. of North Carolina Press, 1980.

Knauber, A. "Der 'Didaskalos' des Clemens von Alexandrien." *Studia Patristica* 16, part 1. (1985): 175–85.

Koester, Helmut. *Introduction to the New Testament*. 2 vols. Philadelphia: Fortress, 1982.

Kugel, James, and Rowan Greer. *Early Biblical Interpretation*. Philadelphia: Westminster, 1986.

Lawson, John. *The Biblical Theology of St. Irenaeus*. Edinburgh: Epworth, 1948.

Layton, Bentley. *The Gnostic Scriptures: A New Translation with Annotations and Introductions*. Garden City: Doubleday, 1987.

Leisegang, Hans. *Die Gnosis*. Leipzig: Kroner, 1924.

Longenecker, Richard. *The Christology of Early Jewish Christianity*. Grand Rapids: Baker, 1981.

Malherbe, Abraham. *Moral Exhortation: A Greco-Roman Source Book*. Philadelphia: Westminster, 1986.

Marrou, Henri-Iréné. *A History of Education in Antiquity*. New York: Sheed and Ward, 1956.

Maurer, Christian. *Ignatius von Antiochien und das Johannesevangelium*. Zurich: Zwingli, 1949.

Meeks, Wayne. *The Moral World of the First Christians*. Philadelphia: Westminster, 1986.

Méhat, André. *Etude sur les 'Stromateis' de Clément d'Alexandrie*. Editions du Seuil, 1966.

Meinhold, Peter. *Studien zu Ignatius von Antiochien*. Wiesbaden: Steiner, 1979.

Myers, Jacob. *I and II Esdras*. Garden City: Doubleday, 1974.

Neale, John Mason. *A History of the Holy Eastern Church: The Patriarchate of Antioch*. London: Rivingtons, 1873.

Neusner, Jacob. *Messiah in Context*. Philadelphia: Fortress, 1984.

Ochagavia, Juan. *Visibile Patris Filius: A Study of Irenaeus' Teaching on Revelation and Tradition*. Rome: Pontifical Institute of Oriental Studies, 1964.

Osborn, Eric. *Justin Martyr: Beiträge zur historischen Theologie*. Edited by Gerhard Ebeling. Tübingen: J. C. B. Mohr (Paul Siebeck), 1973.

Pagels, Elaine. *The Gnostic Gospels*. New York: Random House, 1979.

———. *The Gnostic Paul*. Philadelphia: Fortress, 1975.

———. *The Johannine Gospel in the Gnostic Exegesis of the Pauline Letters*. Philadelphia: Fortress, 1975.

Peck, Harry, ed. *The Harper Dictionary of Classical Literature and Antiquities*. New York: American Book Company, 1896.

Powell, T. G. E. *The Celts*. London: Thames and Hudson, 1985.

Reumann, John. *Righteousness of God*. Philadelphia: Fortress, 1982.

Richardson, Cyril. *The Christianity of Ignatius of Antioch*. New York: Columbia Univ. Press, 1935.

Riesenfeld, Harald. "Reflections on the Style and Theology of St. Ignatius of Antioch," *Studia Patristica* 4 (1961): 312–22.

Robinson, James. *The Nag Hammadi Library*, rev. ed. San Francisco: Harper and Row, 1988.

Rudolph, Kurt. *Gnosis: The Nature and History of Gnosticism*. San Francisco: Harper and Row, 1980.

Saldanha, Chrys. *Divine Pedagogy: A Patristic View of Non-Christian Religions*. Rome: Liberia Ateneo Salesiano, 1984.

Sanders, E. P. *Jewish and Christian Self-Definition*. Philadelphia: Fortress, 1980.

Schoeps, Hans-Joachim. *Jewish Christianity*. Philadelphia: Fortress, 1968.

Smith, M. A. "Did Justin Know the Didache?" *Studia Patristica* 7 (1976): 287–90.

Stendahl, Krister. *Paul among Jews and Gentiles*. Philadelphia: Fortress, 1976.

Timothy, H. B. *The Early Greek Apologists and Greek Philosophy*. Assen: Van Gorcum, 1973.

Turner, H. E. W. *The Patristic Doctrine of Redemption*. London: A. R. Mowbray, 1952.

Vallée, Gérard. *A Study in Anti-Gnostic Polemics: Irenaeus, Hippolytus and Epiphanius*. Waterloo: Wilfrid Laurier Univ. Press, 1981.

Wagner, Walter. "A Father's Fate: Attudes toward and Interpretations of Clement of Alexandria." *Journal of Religious History* 6 (1971): 209–30.

———. "Another Look at the Literary Problem in Clement of Alexandria's Major Writings." *Church History* 38 (1968): 251–60.

_____. "Philo and Paideia." *Cithara* 10 (1971): 53–64.

Wellesley, Kenneth. *The Long Year: A.D. 69*. Boulder: Westview, 1976.

Wingren, Gustav. *Man and the Incarnation: A Study in the Biblical Theology of Irenaeus*. Edinburgh: Oliver and Boyd, 1952.

Zahn, Theodor. *Ignatius von Antiochien*. Gotha: Perthes, 1873.

Zanartu, Sergio. *El concepto de zoe en Ignacio de Antioquia*. Madrid: Easpa, 1977.

Zimmerli, Walther, and Joachim Jeremias. *The Servant of God* rev. ed. London: SCM Press, 1965.

Index of Persons and
Places of Antiquity

Subject Index

285